The *Aeneid* and the Modern World

This collection of essays from a diverse group of scholars represents a multidisciplinary redeployment of the *Aeneid* that aims to illuminate its importance to our present moment. It provides a rigorous and multifaceted answer to the question, "Why should we still think about the *Aeneid*?"

The book contains chapters detailing previously undocumented modern literary receptions of Vergil's epic, addressing the *Aeneid*'s relevance to understanding modern political discourse, explaining how the *Aeneid* assists in making sense of the pressing current issues of trauma and damage to one's sense of identity, and even looking at how the epic can shape our future. The chapters build upon and extend beyond reception studies to provide the most current and complete answer to the question of the epic's current relevance.

The primary audiences for this collection are undergraduate students, graduate students, and professional academics from all disciplines. This collection should be of interest to readers whose academic interests include textual and cultural studies, classics, comparative literature, pedagogy, medical humanities, veterans studies, trauma studies, immigration studies, young adult fiction, world literature, communication and political discourse, citizenship studies, and ethnic studies.

J.R. O'Neill is Senior Lecturer and Honors Faculty Fellow at Barrett, the Honors College at Arizona State University, USA, where he teaches classics. He is also affiliated with Arizona State University's program in veterans studies and is the founding director of Barrett's Theatre of Difference Project. His research and teaching interests include Latin literature and Roman cultural history. He earned his PhD in classics from the University of Southern California, USA.

Adam Rigoni is Senior Lecturer and Honors Faculty Fellow at Barrett, the Honors College at Arizona State University, USA. He earned his JD and his PhD in philosophy from the University of Michigan, USA. His work has appeared in *Legal Theory*, *The Journal of Moral Philosophy*, *The Journal of Philosophical Logic*, and *Artificial Intelligence and Law*.

Routledge Monographs in Classical Studies

Recent titles include:

Ancient History from Below
Subaltern Experiences and Actions in Context
Edited by Cyril Courrier and Julio Cesar Magalhães de Oliveira

Ideal Themes in the Greek and Roman Novel
Jean Alvares

Thornton Wilder, Classical Reception, and American Literature
Stephen J. Rojcewicz, Jr.

Married Life in Greco-Roman Antiquity
Edited by Claude-Emmanuelle Centlivres Challet

Future Thinking in Roman Culture
New Approaches to History, Memory, and Cognition
Edited by Maggie L. Popkin and Diana Y. Ng

Aristotle and the Animals
The Logos of Life Itself
Claudia Zatta

The *Aeneid* and the Modern World
Interdisciplinary Perspectives on Vergil's Epic in the 20th and 21st Centuries
Edited by J.R. O'Neill and Adam Rigoni

The Province of Achaea in the 2nd Century CE
The Past Present
Edited by Anna Kouremenos

For more information on this series, visit: www.routledge.com/Routledge-Monographs-in-Classical-Studies/book-series/RMCS

The *Aeneid* and the Modern World

Interdisciplinary Perspectives on Vergil's Epic in the 20th and 21st Centuries

Edited by J.R. O'Neill and Adam Rigoni

Routledge
Taylor & Francis Group
LONDON AND NEW YORK

First published 2022
by Routledge
2 Park Square, Milton Park, Abingdon, Oxon OX14 4RN

and by Routledge
605 Third Avenue, New York, NY 10158

Routledge is an imprint of the Taylor & Francis Group, an informa business

British Library Cataloguing-in-Publication Data
A catalogue record for this book is available from the British Library

Library of Congress Cataloging-in-Publication Data
Names: O'Neill, J. R., editor. | Rigoni, Adam, editor.
Title: The Aeneid and the modern world : interdisciplinary perspectives on Vergil's epic in the 20th and 21st centuries / edited by J.R. O'Neill and Adam Rigoni.
Description: Abingdon, Oxon ; New York, NY : Routledge, 2022. | Series: Routledge monographs in classical studies | Includes bibliographical references and index.
Identifiers: LCCN 2021041290 (print) | LCCN 2021041291 (ebook) | ISBN 9781032008684 (hardback) | ISBN 9781032008707 (paperback) | ISBN 9781003176145 (ebook)
Subjects: LCSH: Virgil. Aeneis. | Civilization, Modern—Roman influences. | LCGFT: Essays. | Literary criticism.
Classification: LCC PA6825 .A3 2022 (print) | LCC PA6825 (ebook) | DDC 873/.01—dc23/eng/20211116
LC record available at https://lccn.loc.gov/2021041290
LC ebook record available at https://lccn.loc.gov/2021041291

ISBN: 978-1-032-00868-4 (hbk)
ISBN: 978-1-032-00870-7 (pbk)
ISBN: 978-1-003-17614-5 (ebk)

DOI: 10.4324/9781003176145

Typeset in Times New Roman
by Apex CoVantage, LLC

For Albert, Becky, and Haley—Adam
For Matt—J.R.

Contents

Figures

Contributors

Dani Bostick is a Latin teacher and former mental health counselor who has written about classics, trauma, and other topics in public-facing outlets including a guest editorial in the *American Journal of Philology* (June 2020). She has presented at conferences in the fields of education, classics, and mental health. Events in 2019–20 included: panel organizer and presenter at the Classical Association of the Atlantic States ("Beyond Content Warnings: Sexual Violence in the Secondary and Post-Secondary Classroom" with co-organizer David Wright) and the Society for Classical Studies annual meeting ("If Classics Is For Everybody, Why Isn't Everybody in My Classroom" with co-organizer Elizabeth Bobrick); invited lecturer at Wake Forest University, USA ("We Don't Need a Roman Hero: Erasure of Oppression as a Weapon of White Supremacy"); and keynote speaker at the *Res Difficiles* conference. She is also a TED Innovative Educator and a member of the National Humanities Center's Teacher Advisory Council, USA.

Nancy Ciccone teaches at the University of Colorado, Denver, USA, and holds a doctorate in comparative literature from UC–Berkeley, USA. Her research focuses on classical and medieval literatures. Her publications include articles on Chaucer's *Troilus and Criseyde* (2002), *Book of the Duchess* (2009), *The Pearl* (2017), and *Tristan* (2003); "Ariosto and Ovid's Abandoned Women" (1997); and Ishiguro's *Buried Giant* (2018). Her previous work on the *Aeneid*, "Look Who's Talking," tackles Vergil's '*si*-clauses' in the last six books as a means of undermining the foundations of empire (*Approaches to Teaching Vergil's* Aeneid, MLA, 2002). Forthcoming is an article, "Depression in Ricardian Dream Visions," to be included in *Faces of Depression* (2020). Along with reviewing for various journals, she has been a bibliographer for the International Courtly Literature Society (1996–2019). Her current research aims to elucidate older literatures in terms of current relevance.

Frances Foster teaches ancient education and the reception of the ancient world in educational contexts at the Faculty of Education, University of Cambridge, UK. She works on Servius and his commentary on Vergil, and her recent publications on this have appeared in *Language & History* and *The Classical Quarterly*. She is also actively researching the reception of the ancient world in

YA and children's literature. In addition, she has undertaken empirical work investigating the attitudes of young people to the ancient world, which appears in *The Language Learning Journal*.

Filomena Giannotti received her PhD in reception studies and the classical tradition from the University of Siena, Italy, in 2006. From 2002 to 2018 she worked as a teacher in high school and, at the same time, as a teaching fellow of Latin Language at the University of Siena. In 2015, she was awarded the "National Scientific Qualification" as an associate professor of Latin language and literature. She is a research fellow of Latin language and literature and a teaching fellow of Latin language at the University of Siena (Department of Philology and Criticism of Ancient and Modern Literatures). Her main areas of interest and publication are Vergil's *Aeneid*, late antiquity, and reception studies and classical tradition in contemporary literature.

John Hay is an associate professor of English at the University of Nevada, USA, where he specializes in 19th-century American literature. He is the author of *Postapocalyptic Fantasies in Antebellum American Literature* (2017) and the editor of the forthcoming *Apocalypse in American Literature and Culture*. His essays have appeared in scholarly journals such as *Early American Literature*, the *New England Quarterly*, and *ESQ: A Journal of Nineteenth-Century American Literature and Culture*.

Paul Hay is a visiting assistant professor at Case Western Reserve University in Cleveland, USA. He completed his PhD at the University of Texas at Austin, USA, with a dissertation on the *saeculum* and the Roman innovation of historical periodization. His research interests include Roman intellectual and social history and Roman literature of the late Republic and early Empire.

Christian Lehmann is a member of the Literature Department at Bard High School Early College-Cleveland, USA. He earned his PhD in classics at the University of Southern California, USA. He is currently working on a book project about Dickens and the classical world.

Giacomo Loi obtained his BA (2015) and MA in classics (2017) at the University of the Sacred Heart, Milan, Italy, and has furthered his studies at the Danish Academy in Rome, Italy, at the National Hellenic Research Institute, Athens, Greece, and at the Hebrew University of Jerusalem, Israel. Currently a PhD candidate in classics at Johns Hopkins University, USA (where he also collaborates with the Jewish Studies Program), he divides his time between the USA and Israel. His interests lie at the intersection of different cultures with the Greco-Roman world. He is particularly interested in the reception of the Greek language and poetry in the Italian Renaissance, in the reception of classical literature into Modern Hebrew literature and in the reuse of Greek myth in Roman auto-ethnography. He has published on a 16th-century Italian verse translation of Musaeus' *Hero and Leander*, on Israeli novelist A. B. Yehoshua's reception of Valerius Maximus, and on French Jewish author Nathalie Azoulai's reception of Vergil, Suetonius, and Heliodorus.

Evander Price received his PhD in American Studies from Harvard University, USA, in 2019. In August 2020, he began a postdoctoral fellowship at the Center for Religion and the Human at Indiana University, Bloomington, USA. He is especially interested in monumentality, time theory, ecocriticism, and ethics.

Babette Puetz is Senior Lecturer in Classics at Victoria University of Wellington, New Zealand. Before moving to New Zealand, she taught at universities in the UK and USA. Her research interests are in classical reception, especially in contemporary children's literature, Greek comedy, animals in ancient literature and ancient Greek drinking parties. She is the author of *The Symposium and Komos in Aristophanes* (2nd ed. 2007) and has published on classical reception in a number of works of children's literature, such as Harry Potter and books by Philip Pullman, Cornelia Funke, and New Zealand authors Margaret Mahy and Bernard Beckett.

George Saad holds an MA in classics from Dalhousie University, Canada. His thesis, "Eternity Visible," synthesized the *Aeneid* and the late romantic German philosophy of history in Nietzsche and Spengler. He also published "Refugees by Fate, Founders by Choice" in *Eidolon*. In this article, he adapted his interpretation of the epic to questions of modern nationhood, showing how Vergil saw Rome as a nation united in the experience of exile. He is a PhD candidate in philosophy at Memorial University of Newfoundland, Canada, with a focus on ancient and 19th-century German philosophy. He has an article forthcoming in the Heidegger Circle journal *Gatherings* on the Greek origins of Martin Heidegger's theory of existential truth.

Michael Stanford holds a JD from the College of Law at Arizona State University, USA, and a PhD in English from the University of Virginia, USA, where he wrote his dissertation on the political poetry of W. B. Yeats. He is currently Principal Lecturer at Barrett, the Honors College at Arizona State University, where he teaches a wide variety of law- and humanities-related courses, including classes on Victorian, modern, and post-colonial literature. His scholarship has appeared in the *Yeats Annual*, *English Literary Renaissance*, *Legal Studies Forum*, *Law and Literature*, and *Amerikastudien* (Germany), and his poetry in the *Seneca Review*, the *Greensboro Review*, and the *Beloit Poetry Journal*. He is co-editor, with David Kader, of the anthology *Poetry of the Law from Chaucer to the Present*.

Tedd A. Wimperis is Assistant Professor of Classical Studies in the Department of World Languages and Cultures at Elon University, USA; he earned his PhD at the University of North Carolina at Chapel Hill, USA. His main research interests include Latin poetry of the late Roman Republic and early Empire, political rhetoric and ideology in the ancient and modern worlds, and the reception of the classics in the Middle Ages, Italian Renaissance, and beyond. His work focuses on the ways in which literature constructs, reflects, supports, and critiques collective identities and political ideologies, explored through such themes as race and ethnicity, cultural memory, rhetoric, mythology, and citizenship. His current book project, *Cultural Memory and Constructed Ethnicity in Vergil's* Aeneid, examines how the fictive ethnic communities portrayed in the epic reflect aspects of collective identity construction and political practice in Greco-Roman antiquity; this study combines evidence from the poem with theoretical and comparative scholarship in a broad literary analysis of the text and a reevaluation of its engagement with Augustan ideology.

Introduction

The *Aeneid* and the modern world

J.R. O'Neill and Adam Rigoni

Why another volume on the *Aeneid?*

> Not the poem which we have read, but that to which we return, with the greatest pleasure, possesses the genuine power, and claims the name of essential poetry.
>
> —Samuel Taylor Coleridge[1]

Vergil's *Aeneid* has never lacked for scholarship and commentary.[2] Yet we believe it needs a particular kind of criticism in the current moment, one aimed at an audience not exclusively of specialists. As Ziolkowski put it: "Virgil is too important to be left to the classicists."[3] The *Aeneid* has recently received revived interest outside of the academy. Since 2017, Vergil's epic has featured in articles in the *Washington Post*,[4] *The Wall Street Journal*,[5] and *The New Yorker*. All three articles argue that the *Aeneid* speaks as much to modernity as it does to antiquity. Mendelsohn put it best, writing in *The New Yorker* that Aeneas is

> a survivor, a person so fractured by the horrors of the past that he can hold himself together only by an unnatural effort of will, someone who has so little of his history left that the only thing that gets him through the present is a numbed sense of duty to a barely discernible future that can justify every kind of deprivation. It would be hard to think of a more modern figure. Or, indeed, a more modern story.[6]

Nearly every review of various recent translations provides an impassioned reaffirmation of the epic's contemporary relevance.[7] However, scholarly practice has trailed behind scholarly rhetoric in this regard. For example, in demonstrating the modern relevance of Vergil's epic, a number of reviews from the mid-2000s briefly stress the similarities between Vergil and Kipling's views of empire.[8] Because they are poets singing of their respective empires, one might expect to find thorough comparisons between Kipling and Vergil in the scholarly literature. Remarkably, one might find articles devoted to the content and quality of Kipling's classical education and his devotion to Horace in his later years but very little explicitly considering the direct influence of Roman authors on his own writing.[9]

DOI: 10.4324/9781003176145-1

The gap between the general claims of the *Aeneid*'s relevance and a rigorous working out of the details is initially startling. However, upon reflection, the lacuna is unsurprising for two reasons. First, scholarship on the *Aeneid* typically comes from classicists focused on the text's language and poetics and its historical and cultural contexts. It is treated as an explicitly *Roman* cultural artifact. A natural direction to expand the work of classicists is to examine the *Aeneid*'s reception in other historical epochs. This is precisely what we see in recent work such as Philip Hardie's impressive *The Last Trojan Hero: A Cultural History of Virgil's* Aeneid, which catalogs centuries' worth of deployments of the epic, and Farrell and Putnam's discussion of modern criticism of and response to the *Aeneid* in their *Companion to Vergil's* Aeneid *and Its Tradition.*[10] Nearly 30 years ago, Ziolkowski's *Vergil and the Moderns* provided a study not only of receptions of Vergil's poetry, but also of the poet himself.[11] Still, these relatively recent studies of the *Aeneid*'s reception, as important and useful as they are, do not fully develop how we can deploy the epic to negotiate the present. That requires a thoroughly interdisciplinary approach that incorporates and builds upon methodologies deployed within classics in general and reception studies in particular. The second reason for scholarly neglect is that classicists tend to write exclusively for other classicists. The primary audience for most research about the *Aeneid* already believes that the underlying subject is important; there is no need to preach to the choir.

However, the general public and, perhaps more specifically, the undergraduate student are often under-recognized as stakeholders in much research, at least until it is too late. Fields in the humanities are in increasingly dire need of their support to survive. It seems as though every year, classicists are mobilized in (often futile) efforts to save classics departments from closure.[12] The most prominent and (as we write this) most recent is the decision at Howard University to close its classics department, which Cornel West and Jeremy Tate called a "spiritual catastrophe."[13] Academics may gloss over a disinterested student's questioning of the relevance of the material, but they ignore administrators at their peril.

This is not to say that we have compiled a collection of essays aimed primarily at or motivated by administrators and undergraduates, though we hope the collection enriches many undergraduate classrooms and gives ax-wielding deans some pause. We think the question of the *Aeneid*'s modern relevance is itself deeply significant and worthy of serious study. In considering how the *Aeneid* illuminates aspects of the present, we see the epic itself in new lights. This collection offers just as much for the converted as the skeptics: we offer a volume of essays from a diverse group of scholars that represents a multidisciplinary redeployment of the *Aeneid.* It neither examines the *Aeneid* solely as a decidedly Roman text nor as a literary artifact, the sum of learned nods to it. Rather, we present a volume that deploys the *Aeneid* anew, one that not only reflects the *Aeneid's* status as a "modern story" but one that inserts the *Aeneid* into contemporary discourse afresh.

In doing so, our collection offers not an answer but a set of answers to the question of the *Aeneid*'s modern relevance. As a work of vast scope and profound complexity, the *Aeneid* offers no single connection to the present. There are many different answers, some of them complementary and others entirely distinct. Our interdisciplinary approach is essential to capturing a sense of this diversity. While the venerable method of documenting the reception of the epic, in particular its influence on later artists, provides an important class of insights, a more complete picture requires additional techniques, especially when we consider the present and future, where the epic's influence is not yet determined. A thorough answer to why the *Aeneid* still matters must consider the role of the *Aeneid* in molding yesterday and today, as well as how it might shape tomorrow.

Methodology: genuine interdisciplinarity and thoroughgoing pragmatism

> Some of the classical people here [at the American Academy in Rome] are snobbish about this mess but it belongs to anyone who can dig it.
>
> —Ralph Ellison[14]

> It's only in England that dilettantism is considered a bad thing. In other countries it's called interdisciplinary research.
>
> —Brian Eno[15]

In thoroughly establishing the *Aeneid*'s contemporary relevance, we must focus on the present era and do so through the lenses of multiple disciplines. The former is fairly easy to accomplish: we have curated essays focused on the *Aeneid* in the 20th and 21st centuries.[16] We understand "modern" in this sense, not on the basis of a previous demarcation of Modernity. We also admit that the contemporary vernacular understanding of 'modern' might not include much (or any) of the 20th century. Our reasons for straying from a common understanding of 'modern' are pragmatic: the *Aeneid*'s relevance to the present cannot be divorced from its role in the recent past, as the following chapters that treat British and American imperialism, the Holocaust, and the evolution of contemporary political discourse demonstrate. Moreover, the *Aeneid*'s relevance to this period as a whole has not yet received thorough analysis. In short, we have stretched the term 'modern' only as much as needed to achieve our goal of establishing the *Aeneid*'s present potential.

Our approach must be interdisciplinary because we intend to reach readers outside of classics and speak to the non-specialists who make up a majority of readers of the *Aeneid*, especially in the context of the general liberal arts curriculum and the so-called Great Books courses taken by so many American undergraduate students. We agree with Ralph Ellison on the vital need for classics to reach beyond a narrow audience of specialists, for it to be accessed and analyzed by "anyone who can dig it." Yet we disagree with Brian Eno, whose capacious view of interdisciplinarity will feel all too familiar to instructors compelled to teach an increasingly broader range of material to compensate for the decreasing ranks of faculty (i.e., other specialists). In other words, we are quite concerned about dilettantism masquerading as interdisciplinary research, both because it is bad research and because it attempts to conceal the need for specialists. Precisely this pernicious kind of interdisciplinarity has been weaponized against classicists. For example, Howard professors Brandon Hogan and Jacoby Adeshei Carter argue that the shuttering of Howard's classics department is no catastrophe at all because faculty like them, "philosophy professors at Howard who have reverence for the classics," will provide adequate instruction in classics.[17] Indeed, they note that Howard will now offer a major in "interdisciplinary humanities" that will "incorporate classical studies."[18]

It goes without saying that there are many excellent instructors of classics who are not disciplinary classicists, and Professors Hogan and Carter may well be among them. However, we vigorously oppose the general idea that specialists in various fields of humanistic inquiry can simply replace the expertise of trained classicists. For one, nonspecialists must rely (in part or entirely) on translations. A translation is, of course, a product of the translator's own understanding of the content and context of a piece from another culture in a distant era. A nonspecialist teacher of Greek and Roman texts—no doubt under immense pressure to publish their own specialized research while also teaching an ever-expanding range of courses—is likely unable to engage at a deep level with the language of a classical text's composition, leaving them ill-equipped to challenge a given translator's preconceptions or misconceptions about the text and the culture that produced it. This entrenches the received knowledge of translators and scholars of decades, if not centuries, past, along with all their assumptions and prejudices. The serious study of the Latin language and Roman literature and culture is not static; translations take years to produce and are often taught for decades—they do not automatically update to reflect the latest insights on Rome's culture, politics, and the social embeddedness of literary production. Thus the received understanding of those matters at the time of translation (or worse, some idiosyncratic view of the translator), will continue to be propagated by a pedagogy built solely on translations. For example, in many ways Dryden's *Aeneid* provides more information about Dryden and 17th-century England than Vergil and 1st-century Rome, and teaching it without an active awareness of this fact risks conveying significant misunderstandings about Rome and Latin literature. Something similar could be said of a translation published in the United States in 1971 or 2021.[19]

Furthermore, to make an ancient text intelligible to a modern readership, translators make choices that might, as the language into which the translation is rendered evolves, later obscure the sense of the Latin. As a result, the heavy reliance of translations in liberal arts curricula largely forecloses fresh approaches to old material.[20] In other words, Dryden's *Aeneid*, or Ruden's *Aeneid*, is not *the Aeneid*.[21] To be sure, it would be difficult to find any teacher who fails to recognize that a translation of the *Aeneid* is not *the Aeneid*. And most nonspecialist instructors of ancient texts are perfectly capable of finding scholarship on a given text. But their ability to stay abreast of the most recent scholarship depends not only on being familiar with the idiosyncrasies within classics of how scholarship is organized and disseminated but also, and more urgently, on there being ample support at a diverse range of institutions for the production of new knowledge about Greco-Roman antiquity. Let us not lose sight of the fact that the dwindling number of tenure lines in classics poses a real threat to diversity and innovation in classical scholarship. Without the generation of new knowledge, only the old prejudices and assumptions remain. In short, reverence will not suffice to replace expertise.

Consider the now half-century-old debate in Vergilian studies between so-called Optimists and Pessimists.[22] Pedagogically productive discussions about how the *Aeneid* may treat imperialism and autocracy very well may arise in classrooms regardless of the translation used, but it is only in unpacking the Latin with the ever-evolving understanding of the political and social milieu in which that Latin was written can serious advances be made in terms of how the *Aeneid* might indeed speak to those issues and how that text might provide insight into contemporary problems. Dani Bostick's chapter (Chapter 9) on traumatic time provides another example of the opportunities for innovation that expertise provides. Bostick, a former mental-health professional and current Latin teacher, in unpacking various definitions of the word *iuvare* and challenging nearly a century's worth of translations of this word into English, shows how Aeneas' speech to his crew on resiliency in the face of traumatic events can give further insight into the long-term effects trauma and possibilities for mitigating them.[23]

Relying solely on translation and received assumptions about the Greek and Roman worlds can have dire real-world consequences. Take, for example, the issue of race and Greco-Roman antiquity. The notion, which in previous generations granted classics its unearned prestige, that Ancient Greece and Rome are the foundation of "Western civilization" supports and perpetuates white supremacy.[24] However, deep engagement with the evidence from antiquity has given the lie to that insidious claim and to any assertions that the Greeks and Romans would have identified or could be identified as White.[25] Such claims do not originate in antiquity, but are Early Modern inventions deployed specifically to articulate and justify European imperial and colonial projects, and are perpetuated (intentionally or not) by disinterested classicists unwilling to challenge the disciplinary status quo and by nonspecialists who lack the training to challenge the reception of the material they teach.

If the reception of Greece and Rome were truly indistinguishable from the cultures themselves, then it would not be difficult to conclude that it is simply necessary to abolish the study of Greco-Roman antiquity altogether.[26] But that foolhardy misadventure would depend on a tenacious misinterpretation of Greco-Roman antiquity itself as always already "Western" and "the exclusive property of white folks," and a conflation of reception and evidence, all of which the specialist is best placed to dismantle.[27] It is bitterly ironic that the diminishment of classics departments in the American academy seems to be hastening a retreat of the serious study of Greco-Roman antiquity into the safe haven of ultra-exclusive institutions where it can only be accessed by those of significant privilege, a handful of scholarships notwithstanding.[28] This retreat is leaving the production of new knowledge about antiquity more and more in the hands of a vanishingly small number of tenured professors, drawn almost exclusively from the same elite institutions. Meanwhile, it is depriving the vast majority of American students of access to the serious study of antiquity (and even staple courses, like Greek Mythology and Roman Civilization, taught by scholar-teachers with cutting-edge expertise in Greek mythology and

Roman civilization), which abandons classics to the ravages of not just white-supremacist groups but of a generally whitewashed Greece and Rome as presented in mass media.[29] Just as we doubt that persistent Anglo-American opinion that Jesus was White has changed in response to the shuttering of religious studies programs,[30] we also doubt that fallacious misrepresentations of Greco-Roman antiquity in popular culture will be better addressed by closing classics departments. Rather, these abuses will simply face even less resistance.

None of this is to suggest that interdisciplinary research is inherently unproductive. Having a specialist in one field work constructively with a specialist from another can lead to novel and invaluable insights. But it takes more than one discipline to make an endeavor *inter*-disciplinary. We are therefore mindful of the need of balancing perspectives from outside of classics with the essential expertise within. In our view, the chapter in this collection by the brothers John Hay and Paul Hay is the ideal type of interdisciplinary work. Paul is a classicist, John a professor of English with a specialty in American literature, and together they analyze the translation of the *Aeneid* by American author Christopher Pearse Cranch and its impact on American political and cultural identity into the 21st century. Such a perfect combination of specialists is not always easy to find, but we have worked diligently to provide similar interdisciplinary support for each chapter in the collection. A classicist (J.R. O'Neill) as well as a philosopher and lawyer with reverence for the classics (Adam Rigoni) have participated actively in the preparation of every chapter. Thus, chapters by non-classicists have been supplemented by expertise in classical studies, and the chapters by classicists have been augmented by an outside perspective. This, we hope, provides a genuine interdisciplinarity, one where experts from different disciplines work together to produce innovative scholarship.

Our approach to methodology is one of thoroughgoing pragmatism and hence pluralism. This is essential for a collection aiming to cross disciplinary boundaries. The chapters themselves employ methodologies specific to their respective fields, though the arguments of each chapter arise out of a close reading of the *Aeneid*, in Latin where the author's training allows, or in translation supplemented by the input of a Latinist. We have no desire to rehearse and continue theoretical debates on the "right" method for these looming questions, nor is this collection meant as a venue for that. The common purpose of each chapter is to establish the relevance of the *Aeneid* to its respective contemporary concern. They succeed to the extent that they convince readers that the *Aeneid* can help explore or understand that concern. We welcomed any methodology that succeeds in this sense.

Our strategy: the structure of this volume

> A mighty maze! But not without a plan.
>
> —Alexander Pope[31]

The volume is divided into four parts which jointly establish the *Aeneid* as an epic for our time.[32] We start with an analysis of the epic's influence on writers of the 20th and 21st centuries that provides the initial set of answers to the question of the *Aeneid*'s modern significance. We begin with Michael Stanford documenting the influence of Vergil's epic on Rudyard Kipling in such a way as to challenge perceptions of Kipling as an uncritical champion of imperialism. Next, Christian Lehmann investigates Vergilian references in Zora Neale Hurston's *Their Eyes Were Watching God*, revealing how Hurston rewrites the *Aeneid* from a feminist and Black perspective to oppose the privileging of White expertise at the expense of other forms of knowledge. In the tradition of Israeli literature, where Rome is well established as an oppressor of the Jews, Giacomo Loi elucidates Yehuda Amichai's daring creation of a Jewish Aeneas in flight from the Holocaust. Filomena Giannotti traces the impact of the *Aeneid* on diverse contemporary Italian authors such as Giorgio Caproni and Tiziano Rossi. The section closes with Babette Puetz bringing Vergil's epic into the new millennium and the burgeoning study of young adult (YA) fiction. Puetz investigates how Phillip Pullman's *His Dark Materials* plays with central topics of the *Aeneid* and employs an "Anti-Aeneas" as its protagonist. Thus, the first part establishes the volume in the tradition of reception studies and provides modern connections of the kind commonly found in that field.

The rest of the volume builds on that familiar foundation with increasingly novel approaches. The chapters of the second part include some analysis of reception but combine those insights with theories of nationalism and identity to demonstrate the value of the *Aeneid* in thinking about modern political discourse. The opening article by Paul and John Hay sets the stage for the more contemporary political applications of the epic by showing Christopher Pearse Cranch's 1872 translation to be a political document suggesting a new American origin myth with an emphasis on national unity for the impending 20th century. Consideration of origin myths leads to Tedd A. Wimperis's demonstration of the value of the *Aeneid* in analyzing modern political media that mobilize the past to serve ideological goals in the present. Wimperis links interdisciplinary work on nationalism and cultural memory with Vergilian scholarship to emphasize the epic's continuing relevance to today's political landscape. Finally, J.R. O'Neill brings Vergil's Daedalus to DC to take up the thorny problem of the personal and political meanings of public memorials, as realized in the Vietnam Veterans Memorial. O'Neill shows how the *Aeneid* can explicate both the difficulties inherent in attempts to commemorate war dead and how they can be overcome. His work establishes Vergil as foundational not only to our understanding of commemorating the dead but of monumentality itself.

In part 3, chapters focus on the *Aeneid* in the present moment. Here the authors establish the role of the *Aeneid* in understanding the relationship between trauma and one's sense of identity. Dani Bostick draws on her experience as a therapist working with patients with PTSD to consider current theories of trauma in the light of Vergil's treatment of time and narrative. Next, Nancy Ciccone explores how the *Aeneid* illuminates the suffering and needs of contemporary Syrian refugees, whose struggles to find a stable sense of identity sit at the center of one of the great humanitarian crises of our time. The closing chapter of Part 3 brings trauma and fragmented identity together with the very notion of modernity. George Saad argues that the virtue of authenticity (in Heidegger's sense) essentially characterizes modernity and that the *Aeneid* details Aeneas' quest for this modern virtue. He emphasizes that the search for authenticity is inextricably bound up with a sense of lost or diminished identity (Heidegger's "fallenness") and how the *Aeneid* presents the construction of an authentic self from this most modern condition.

In its final part, the volume considers the *Aeneid* with an eye toward the future. Here Frances Foster studies the perceptions of and reactions to the *Aeneid* among students in secondary schools. She finds that most secondary students are often offered only snippets of the epic, and her study offers a glimpse of the impact limited encounters have on students' general understanding of myth and history. In the closing chapter Evander Price contemplates a more distant future as he considers Vergil's Golden Bough and Carl Sagan's Golden Records, which were placed on the Voyager space probes. The Golden Records are the farthest man-made objects from earth, currently racing through interstellar space awaiting recovery by space-travelers in the distant future. Price explains that we can best understand the purpose of the records and the probes by understanding the purpose of Vergil's bough. He provides the Vergilian key to these cosmic objects that still, in Goethe's words, "draw us up" (*zieht uns hinan*, *Faust* II. 12111).

The pay-off

> All great art allows us this: a glimpse across the limits of our self.
>
> —Hisham Matar[33]

At the end of the volume, then, we have "answers" from a host of disciplinary vantage points establishing the *Aeneid*'s relevance to the (near) past, present, and future. Thus, we show that despite the passage of time, the *Aeneid* still deeply matters right now, and despite our diverse interests and perspectives, it matters for us all. Although we hope to have succeeded in sufficiently fleshing out the epic's still-living legacy, we urgently add that such success is necessarily incomplete. There are still so many things Vergil's poetry can elucidate, so many enduring echoes of his thought felt today, that this volume is just the beginning of the much larger project of detailing the epic's modern import. We hope it inspires others to join in that project, to see the *Aeneid* not as a relic but as a text as vital and vibrant as it ever was. It is perhaps trite, but still too easily forgotten, that great art offers a great gift: to let us grasp what we couldn't otherwise.

Notes

1 Coleridge 2004: ch. 1.
2 Harrison 1990: 1–20 provides a survey of Vergilian scholarship from antiquity through the 1980s, claiming that it really began in earnest with Heinze and Norden at the turn of the 20th century. More recent work includes Martindale and Góráin 2019, which contains a sizeable bibliography.
3 Ziolkowski 1993: ix.

4 Dirda 2017.
5 Spiegelman 2017.
6 Mendelsohn 2018.
7 See, e.g., Wills 2009; Stallings 2006; Dirda 2017.
8 Wills 2009; Stallings 2006.
9 Treggiari 2012.
10 Hardie 2014; Farrell and Putnam 2010.
11 Ziolkowski 1993.
12 Announced closures and significant reductions in 2021 include Howard University, University of Vermont, Canisius College, and Whitman College (see Goldman and Kennedy 2021). The Classical Association of the Middle West and South (CAMWS) activated its members in unsuccessful attempts to forestall closures at Luther College (Decora, Iowa), Calvin University (Grand Rapids, Michigan), and Carthage College (Kenosha, Wisconsin).
13 West and Tate 2021. See also Kennedy and Murray 2021; Inskeep 2021. See Lehmann, this volume, Chapter 2, for evidence of the importance of Howard's classics department in the development of Zora Neale Hurston as an author.
14 Quoted in Rule 1994.
15 Lawley 1991.
16 Hay and Hay (this volume) deals with the late 19th century but in such a way as to illustrate how Christopher Pearse Cranch's translation of the *Aeneid* helped shape classical studies in America and how his translation contributed to a discourse of national unity in the wake of the disastrous Civil War that lasted well into the 20th century.
17 Hogan and Carter 2021.
18 Hogan and Carter 2021.
19 See Mandelbaum 1971; Bartsch 2021.
20 See Kallendorf 2018: 23 on the interconnection between poetry, translation, and their respective contexts of creation.
21 For an analysis of the most popular English-language renderings of the *Aeneid* of the late 20th and early 21st centuries and the impact upon them of the cultural and political currents at the time of their initial publication, see Braund 2018; Scully 2018.
22 Bartsch writes that the "thriving industry of the interpretation of the *Aeneid*" is itself evidence of art's success in forever generating the possibility for "differing and ambiguous interpretations" (1998: 399). In other words, one never nails down the interpretation of a work of art's meaning. The job is never done.
23 See Bostick in this volume, Chapter 9.
24 Zuckerberg 2018: passim. See also Appiah 2016.
25 Sarah Bond 2017 has written about the connection between the whitewashing of Greek and Roman sculpture and architecture and the perpetuation of white supremacist misconceptions about the 'Whiteness' of the Greeks and Romans themselves. Her work led to vitriolic attacks (including death threats) from white supremacists and the far right (Margaret 2018; Flaherty 2017). On how translations of the Homeric epics perpetuate the lie of the 'Whiteness' of ancient Greece, see Whitmarsh 2018.
26 Poser 2021.
27 Hairston 2013: ix. Even Hogan and Carter 2021, which does not treat classics as "the exclusive property of white folks," nevertheless defines classics as "the texts required at predominantly White institutions" in contrast with "the Black stuff."
28 At the time of writing, Arizona State University's Tempe campus had a total undergraduate enrollment in the 2020–21 academic year of just under 54,000 (Arizona State University 2021), more than twice that of the total undergraduate enrollments for the same period of Brown (Brown University 2021), Cornell (Cornell University 2021), Harvard (Harvard Office of Institutional Research 2021), Princeton (Princeton University 2021), and Yale (Yale University 2021) combined. Despite the outsized role ultra-exclusive institutions play in the popular imagination and in the discourse about

the future of Greco-Roman studies among classicists themselves, the overwhelming majority of Americans with college degrees simply do not (and cannot) attend those institutions.

29 From the mass media the majority of our students seem to have "learned" that Achilles looked like Brad Pitt and that the Battle of Thermopylae was simply 300 cisgendered heterosexual White men opposing an effeminate, multiracial horde. For more on the appropriation of Greco-Roman antiquity by far-right and white-supremacist groups, see Bond 2018.

30 See The British Academy 2019.

31 Pope 2016: Epistle 1, l. 6.

32 The Latin text of the *Aeneid* used throughout this collection is that of R.A.B. Mynors (1972).

33 Matar 2017.

References

Appiah, K.A. 2016. "There Is No Such Thing as Western Civilisation." *The Guardian*, November 9. https://www.theguardian.com/world/2016/nov/09/western-civilisation-appiah-reith-lecture.

Arizona State University. 2021. *Facts and Figures*. www.asu.edu/about/facts-and-figures.

Bartsch, S. 1998. "Ars and the Man: The Politics of Art in Virgil's Aeneid." *Classical Philology* 93, 4: 322–42.

Bartsch, S. 2021. *Vergil: The* Aeneid. New York: Random House.

Bond, S. 2017. "Why We Need to Start Seeing the Classical World in Color." *Hyperallergic*, June 7. https://hyperallergic.com/383776/why-we-need-to-start-seeing-the-classical-world-in-color/.

Bond, S. 2018. "This is not Sparta." *Eidolon*, May 7. https://eidolon.pub/this-is-not-sparta-392a9ccddf26.

Braund, S. 2018. "Virgil after Vietnam." In S. Braund and Z.M. Torlone (eds.) *Virgil and His Translators*. Oxford: Oxford University Press.

The British Academy. 2019. "Theology and Religious Studies Risk Disappearing from Our Universities, Says the British Academy | The British Academy." May 23. www.thebritishacademy.ac.uk/news/theology-and-religious-studies-risk-disappearing-our-universities-says-british-academy/.

Brown University. 2021. *Brown at a Glance*. www.brown.edu/about/brown-glance.

Coleridge, S.T. 2004. "Biographia Literaria." *Project Gutenberg*. www.gutenberg.org/files/6081/6081-h/6081-h.htm.

Cornell University. 2021. *University Facts*. www.cornell.edu/about/facts.cfm.

Dirda, M. 2017. "Virgil's 'The Aeneid' Still Looks Strikingly Contemporary—The Washington Post." *The Washington Post*, September 13. www.washingtonpost.com/entertainment/books/virgils-the-aeneid-still-looks-strikingly-contemporary/2017/09/12/3915dfe4-97df-11e7-b569-3360011663b4_story.html.

Farrell, J., and Putnam, M.C.J. 2010. *A Companion to Vergil's Aeneid and Its Tradition*. Malden, MA and Oxford: Wiley-Blackwell.

Flaherty, C. 2017. "Threats for What She Didn't Say." *Inside Higher Ed*, June 19. www.insidehighered.com/news/2017/06/19/classicist-finds-herself-target-online-threats-after-article-ancient-statues.

Goldman, M.L., and Kennedy, R.F. 2021. "Why and How the Study of Classics is Changing." *Inside Higher Ed*, April 15. www.insidehighered.com/views/2021/06/15/why-and-how-study-classics-changing-opinion.

Hairston, E.A. 2013. *The Ebony Column: Classics, Civilization, and the African American Reclamation of the West*. Classicism in American Culture. Knoxville, TN: University of Tennessee Press.

Hardie, P.R. 2014. *The Last Trojan Hero: A Cultural History of Virgil's Aeneid*. London and New York: I.B. Tauris.

Harrison, S.J. 1990. "Some Views of the Aeneid in the Twentieth Century." In S.J. Harrison (ed.) *Oxford Readings in Vergil's Aeneid*. Oxford and New York: Oxford University Press. 477.

Harvard Office of Institutional Research. 2021. *Harvard Student Enrollment Data*. https://oir.harvard.edu/fact-book/enrollment.

Hogan, B., and Carter, J.A. 2021. "There's No Classics 'Catastrophe' at Howard University—The New York Times." *The New York Times*, May 2. www.nytimes.com/2021/05/02/opinion/howard-university-classics-department.html.

Inskeep, S. 2021. "Howard University's Decision to Cut Classics Department Prompts an Outcry: NPR." *NPR*, May 10. www.npr.org/2021/05/10/995389117/howard-universitys-decision-to-cut-classics-department-prompts-an-outcry.

Kallendorf, C. 2018. "Successes and Failures in Virgilian Translation." In S. Braund and Z.M. Torlone (eds.) *Virgil and His Translators*. Classical Presences. Oxford: Oxford University Press. 520.

Kennedy, R.F., and Murray, J. 2021. "Classics is a Part of Black Intellectual History—Howard Needs to Keep It." *The Undefeated*, June 4. https://theundefeated.com/features/classics-is-a-part-of-black-intellectual-history-howard-needs-to-keep-it/.

Lawley, S. 1991. "Desert Island Discs—Brian Eno—BBC Sounds." *Desert Island Discs*, January 27. www.bbc.co.uk/sounds/play/p0093zkh.

Mandelbaum, A. 1971. *The* Aeneid *of Virgil*. Berkeley: University of California Press.

Margaret, T. 2018. "The Myth of Whiteness in Classical Sculpture." *The New Yorker*, October 28. www.newyorker.com/magazine/2018/10/29/the-myth-of-whiteness-in-classical-sculpture.

Martindale, C., and Góráin, F. Mac. 2019. *The Cambridge Companion to Virgil*. 2nd ed. Cambridge: Cambridge University Press.

Matar, H. 2017. "Opinion | Books Can Take You Places Donald Trump Doesn't Want You to Go—The New York Times." *The New York Times*, March 16. www.nytimes.com/2017/03/16/opinion/sunday/books-can-take-you-places-donald-trump-doesnt-want-you-to-go.html.

Mendelsohn, D. 2018. "Is the Aeneid a Celebration of Empire—or a Critique?" *The New Yorker*, October.

Mynors, R.A.B. 1972. *P. Vergili Maronis Opera*. Oxford: Oxford University Press.

Pope, A. 2016. *An Essay on Man*. Edited by T. Jones. Princeton and Oxford: Princeton University Press.

Poser, R. 2021. "He Wants to Save Classics From Whiteness. Can the Field Survive?" *The New York Times Magazine*, February 2. www.nytimes.com/2021/02/02/magazine/classics-greece-rome-whiteness.html.

Princeton University. 2021. *Facts & Figures*. www.princeton.edu/meet-princeton/facts-figures.

Rule, S. 1994. "Ellison Recalled as an Artist of Great Range." *The New York Times*, May 27. https://archive.nytimes.com/www.nytimes.com/books/99/06/20/specials/ellison-recalled.html.

Scully, S. 2018. "Aesthetic and Political Concerns in Dryden's Aeneis." In S. Braund and Z.M. Torlone (eds.) *Virgil and His Translators*. Oxford: Oxford University Press.

Spiegelman, W. 2017. "Of Arms and the Man—WSJ." *The Wall Street Journal*, September 22. www.wsj.com/articles/of-arms-and-the-man-1506104780.

Stallings, A.E. 2006. "The Historical Present: Robert Fagle's Bold Solutions to the Problem of Virgil." *The American Scholar*, December 1. https://theamericanscholar.org/the-historical-present/.

Treggiari, S. 2012. *Kipling and the Classical World.* www.kiplingsociety.co.uk/rg_classical1.htm.

West, C., and Tate, J. 2021. "Howard University's Removal of Classics is a Spiritual Catastrophe—The Washington Post." *The Washington Post*, April 19. www.washingtonpost.com/opinions/2021/04/19/cornel-west-howard-classics/.

Whitmarsh, T. 2018. "When Homer Envisioned Achilles, Did He See a Black Man? | Aeon Essays." *Aeon*, May 9. https://aeon.co/essays/when-homer-envisioned-achilles-did-he-see-a-black-man.

Wills, G. 2009. "Closer Than Ever to Vergil." *New York Review of Books*, March 12. www.nybooks.com/articles/2009/03/12/closer-than-ever-to-vergil/.

Yale University. 2021. *Yale Facts*. www.yale.edu/about-yale/yale-facts.

Ziolkowski, T. 1993. *Virgil and the Moderns*. Princeton: Princeton University Press.

Zuckerberg, D. 2018. *Not All Dead White Men: Classics and Misogyny in the Digital Age*. Cambridge, MA: Harvard University Press.

Part I

The *Aeneid* and modern literature

We begin the collection by examining the *Aeneid*'s modern literary reception, using the familiar methodology of reception studies to provide the initial evidence for the *Aeneid*'s current significance. To start, Michael Stanford documents the influence of Vergil's epic on poet and novelist Rudyard Kipling. Stanford illuminates not only Vergilian echoes in Kipling's poetry but the shared complexity and ambivalence in their understandings of empire. Next, Christian Lehmann sheds further light on the *Aeneid's* influence on 20th-century Anglophone literature with his investigation of the Vergilian references in Zora Neale Hurston's *Their Eyes Were Watching God*, revealing how Hurston rewrites the *Aeneid* from a feminine and African American perspective in such a way as to challenge notions of White expertise and white supremacy.

In the tradition of Israeli literature, where Rome is well established as an oppressor of the Jews, Giacomo Loi elucidates Yehuda Amichai's daring presentation of a Jewish Aeneas in flight from the Holocaust. Here the abiding humanity of Vergil's work is on full display: Amichai uses the *Aeneid*, which on the one hand represents the mythical founding of an anti-Semitic tyranny, to poignantly depict Jewish suffering and resolve during the Shoah. Next, Filomena Giannotti traces the impact of the *Aeneid* on contemporary Italian authors such as Giorgio Caproni and Tiziano Rossi. We see that, two millennia after Vergil's death, his epic provides material for a powerful articulation of contemporary Italian cultural identity and national unity.

The section closes with Babette Puetz bringing Vergil's epic into the 21st century and the burgeoning study of young adult fiction. Puetz investigates how Phillip Pullman's *His Dark Materials* plays with central topics of the *Aeneid* and employs an "anti-Aeneas" as its protagonist, Lyra. Readers interested in the *Aeneid*'s reception with younger generations are encouraged to consider Puetz's literary insights in conjunction with Foster's empirical work on school-age reception in Part IV of this volume.

Thus, the first section begins our response to the fundamental question of this collection: why should we still study, scrutinize, and share the *Aeneid* in this day and age? It builds upon the rich literature on the reception of the *Aeneid*, connecting our interdisciplinary and multifarious answer with that important scholarship. Using this foundation, we will construct the remainder of our case for the *Aeneid*'s modern relevance.

DOI: 10.4324/9781003176145-2

1 Empire and exile

Kipling's Vergil

Michael Stanford

Rudyard Kipling, the first Englishman to win the Nobel Prize in literature, was the stunningly prolific and successful author of *Kim*, the *Jungle Books*, dozens of artful yet accessible poems, and a handful of masterly protomodernist short stories. But neither his historical honors nor his continuing popular fame have insulated him from the criticism that today, as Charles McGrath observes, has rendered him "politically toxic" in "many classrooms."[1] The primary focus of that criticism is his defense of the British Empire. In light of an accelerating scholarly effort to "decolonize" the canon of English-language literature, we can hardly expect to see Kipling return to unalloyed favor among teachers or students of the humanities. Nevertheless, it is the premise of this essay that the writer's views on empire—not nearly as single-minded as is often assumed—are historically significant and are better grasped through an examination of his under-considered relation to Vergil, the greater poet whose ambivalent fascination with imperial themes helped to mold Kipling's views. Implicit also in what follows is that Kipling's poetry can benefit from the kind of focused textual analysis that has hitherto been applied mainly to his fiction.[2]

Rudyard Kipling was born in 1865 in colonial Bombay, where his English father taught in an art school.[3] Like many colonial children, however, Rudyard was packed off to England early on, first to reside with a host family, then to attend, from the age of 12, the United Services College (USC) in North Devon. One of the country's less prestigious public schools, the USC functioned mainly to produce officer candidates for the armed services.[4] As much as Eton, Harrow, or the rest of its better-respected peers, however, the USC embodied "an educational system crafted to initiate a colonial society's sons into the codes of behavior designed to perpetuate its rule."[5] Those "codes" were transmitted largely through the study of classical literature because of the belief that "the classics afforded valuable lessons in morality, restraint, self-sacrifice, and honourable conduct."[6]

Kipling left the USC at the age of 16 and never went on to university, his four years at public school constituting the whole of his formal study of the classics. Yet the amount of classical, especially Latin, literature he consumed was, as Susan Treggiari notes, "impressive by modern standards."[7] Throughout his life Kipling would denigrate his knowledge of Latin, perhaps as a defensive reaction to the more extensive training of his Oxbridge-educated peers. But it is clear that his

DOI: 10.4324/9781003176145-3

classics master at the USC, William Crofts, ignited a fascination for, at least, the works of Horace. In his autobiography Kipling writes that Crofts "taught me to loathe Horace for two years, to forget him for twenty, and then to love him for the rest of my days and through many sleepless nights."[8] While, as Treggiari points out, Kipling exaggerates when he says that he ever "forgot" his Horace, it is true that he underwent a passionate resurgence of interest in the Roman poet in his late thirties, memorizing many of the *Odes* and even producing a series of poems in imitation of Horace. The influence of Horace on Kipling has been thoroughly traced by Stephen Medcalf and other scholars.[9]

Kipling's debt to Vergil has been far less studied, no doubt because it is considerably less obvious. Vergil, rather, "Virgil," appears by name only twice in Kipling's poems, both times in one of the imitation *Odes*.[10] Aeneas is mentioned only once, in a little-known poem focused on British history.[11] Yet we know that Kipling read the *Aeneid* at the United Services College, and in the same period that saw the efflorescence of his interest in Horace he quotes Vergil's epic at least three times in his letters as well as in a short story.[12] In that story, "Regulus," a classics master clearly modeled on Crofts, dictates the famous lines beginning *tu regere* (Ver. *Aen.* 6.851)—lines that were almost universally known and constantly cited by Britain's empire builders, who wanted a classical sanction for their rule.[13] It is striking and somewhat mysterious that Vergil's work should leave so apparently light an impress on the writer whom his contemporaries and later readers would come to think of as, in effect, the Vergil of the British Empire. I will argue, however, that Vergilian language and motifs do in fact find their way into Kipling's verse, if in an often elliptical way, and that a consideration of these Vergilian moments can illuminate Kipling's long, conflicted attempt to define his view of empire.

While many of Kipling's public school classmates had determined on military careers, Rudyard's poor eyesight debarred him from service, and a spotty academic record and shaky family finances conspired to place Oxbridge out of his reach. But the boy had developed a fascination with journalism, and thanks to family connections, he left the USC aged 16 and a half to return to India and work for the *Civil and Military Gazette*, a daily paper produced for British expatriates in the Raj.[14] Over the next few years, his first short stories appeared in the paper, as did a number of poems focused on the Anglo-Indian experience. Kipling had started writing poetry at the USC, and his schoolboy verses, including attentive imitations of contemporary poets like Swinburne and Tennyson, showed a precocious talent.[15]

Then in 1884, the year after his return to India, Kipling wrote a poem that demonstrated a marked advance in craftsmanship and maturity of concern. The poem, "Laocoön," bears the sub-head "Matthew Arnold," although it is not an homage in the vein of his earlier productions. Kipling apparently has in mind Arnold's poem "Epilogue to Lessing's Laocoön," in which Arnold uses Lessing's essay about the boundaries between the arts to argue for the superiority of poetry to painting.[16] That poem may have appealed to the apprentice writer as a form of affectionate boundary-setting against the influence of his artist father as well as of his uncle, the celebrated painter Edward Burne-Jones. But in the poem that Kipling himself writes, all trace of this theme has disappeared, as has any obvious sign of Arnold's formal influence. Instead, its subject is the beleaguered existence of British officials in India:

> Under the Shadow of Death,
> Under the stroke of the sword,
> Gain we our daily bread,
> Exile that hath no end,
> And the heaping up of our woes,
> As the gift of the Gods to men.[17]

The poem is unrhymed, as only a handful of the rhyme-loving Kipling's poems would ever be. Equally distinct and anomalous is the meter—primarily dactylic with some anapestic substitutions. Dactyls are rare in English poetry, and, far from aping the rhymed iambic tetrameter of Arnold's "Epilogue," Kipling seems to be trying to capture some more distant music. His dactylic trimeter line is a sort of split heroic hexameter—replacing the surge of that meter with a choppy rhythm appropriate to the anxious tone of the speakers.

Like any educated Victorian, Kipling would have been aware of the famous Hellenistic statue of the Trojan prophet and his sons struggling with the sea monsters. One of his lines, in fact, refers to "marble" snakes. But I would argue that, relatively fresh as Kipling was from his enforced reading of the *Aeneid*, the Laocoön episode (2.201–27)—one of the most dramatic and emotionally wrenching in the epic—would have been at least as present to his imagination. Kipling seems to have found in that scene a potent emotional equivalent for the anxiety occasioned in the servants of the Raj, even a quarter-century on, by the memory of the Uprising of 1857.

The Uprising—called then, and until quite recently in Britain, the Indian Mutiny because it began among native soldiers—lasted just over a year and led to some 6,000 British deaths. A vastly larger number of Indians would be killed in the bitter reprisals that followed the suppression of the rebellion—reprisals stoked above all by the killings of British women and children. As Margaret MacMillan notes,

> An image that recurs in Anglo-Indian writing is that of an India about to erupt. And the apprehension, at times the outright fear, that the British residents felt of India was most acute when women and children were threatened. . . . The one event above all others that symbolized British fears about India and their women was of course the Mutiny in 1857.[18]

"Laocoön" clearly embodies the "recurring image" of an India threatening its British rulers; that it does so by harking back to 1857 is evident in the second stanza:

> Lo! In a leagured town
> Compassed by many foes
> Weary citizens wait, . . .
> Only at times when a friend
> Falls from their side and is lost

Out of his place on the wall,
Lift they their hands aloft,
Crying aloud to the Gods,
The pitiless, far-off Gods:
"Spare us this last for a space—
Not for ourselves, indeed,
Seeing that this is our right,
But for our children and wives!"

The final four lines are repeated at the end of the third stanza, and then, with a variation, in the fourth and final stanza—becoming, in effect, the refrain of the poem.

The metaphor of the widely dispersed officials of the Raj as residents of a single "leagured" city draws its potency in part because most of the stories of horror and heroism during the Uprising focused on the siege by rebels of two cities—Lucknow (which was eventually relieved) and Cawnpore (which was not). The aftermath of the latter siege was especially enraging to the British because it involved the massacre of over 100 women and children who had been falsely promised safe passage out of the city by a local ruler, Nana Sahib.[19] The other "leagured" city in Kipling's mind was, of course, Troy, the city of Laocoön himself. Vergil's Laocoön cries uselessly to heaven as he and his sons are being strangled; Kipling's speakers cry to the "pitiless, far-off Gods" for themselves and their families to be spared a parallel fate. In the final stanza, Kipling's speakers attempt a stoic stance:

Neither joyed nor afraid
Of the snakes of circumstance,—
The marble snakes of mishap
That girdle our fleshly limbs,—
We of the East abide.

Here the stiff-upper-lippedness is belied by the image of the girdling snakes. "Marble" of course reminds us of the familiar statue, but in contrast with "flesh" it also evokes the hopelessness of Laocoön's struggle with the snakes ("He fought to rip apart the knotted forms," Verg. *Aen.* 2.220),[20] which might as well have been a contest between crushing stone and soft human flesh. The "town" of British India is "compassed with many foes"—the natives who overwhelmingly outnumber their rulers—as the snakes "girdle" the body of Laocoön and his sons. If the treacherous human snakes in this land of literal snakes—the rebellious native soldiers, Nana Sahib—should turn against their rulers again, a comparable horror might ensue.

We should be wary, though, of assuming that the attitude of the speakers here was Kipling's own. For one thing, as his biographer Harry Ricketts notes, Kipling as poet is a great ventriloquist—he hardly ever speaks in his own voice.[21] For another, the young journalist who wrote these lines, far from feeling personally threatened, delighted in wandering through the country of his birth and rediscovering the stunning diversity of its sights and of its peoples. As David Gilmour writes,

> [Kipling's] sensory receptiveness . . . , [his] capacity to watch and listen and not condemn, [his] pleasure in simply absorbing impressions from the Grand Trunk Road, that "broad smiling river of humanity," allowed him to experience much more of native India than most British people managed to do. He had the "quaintest details," a journalistic colleague recalled, about local habits, language, and ways of thought, so that Indians regarded him as different from other sahibs.[22]

Thus, there may be more than a touch of criticism in "Laocoön's" depiction of the anxieties felt by some British officials. Since 1858, after all, with the dissolution of the East India Company and the institution of direct rule by the Crown, India had seen no unrest on anything remotely resembling the scale of the Uprising. The relative timorousness of Kipling's speaker hardly comports with the image of a confident *pukka sahib*. Furthermore, the speaker conveys a striking sense of weariness and frustration with his role, as when he describes it in the first stanza as an "exile that hath no end." Here Kipling seems to be echoing—in a remarkably subversive way—one of the most famous lines of the *Aeneid*, in which Jupiter promises Venus that the progeny of her son will be granted *imperium sine fine*, "empire without end" (*Aen.* 1.279). Aeneas' own exile constituted the necessary prologue to the founding of an empire. For Kipling to substitute "exile" for "empire" was to reverse the Vergilian sequence and to recast the phrase in a way that hints at a kind of arduous hopelessness at the heart of Britain's imperial project. That the young Kipling harbored some skepticism about that project is evident as well from his first book of poems, *Departmental Ditties*—a collection of satirical verses mainly targeted at British officials. "Laocoön," however, was excluded, perhaps because of its fraught and somber tone; and the satirical stance of the *Ditties* is in fact fairly feathery. A more seriously critical voice can be heard in the remarkable novella "The Man Who Would Be King," first published in 1888. This story is such an obvious parable of imperial hubris and overreach that one biographer suggests that if Kipling's work had continued in the same direction, he might have become known as another Orwell, an insider condemning British rule in South Asia.[23]

Nevertheless, 11 years after writing "The Man Who Would be King," Kipling would publish his most notorious poem, the arch-imperial "White Man's Burden." For all his genuine love of India—most obvious in his fictional masterpiece, *Kim*—Kipling never favored its independence from Britain, and would write contemptuously of the peaceful nationalists of the fledgling Congress Party. In 1889, he left India, never to return except in his writing. On the long sea voyage home, he began to entertain a newly enthusiastic vision of the empire as a "great iron band circling the earth."[24] Back in England, he produced stories and poems that focused increasingly on what he perceived to be the positive attributes—the courage and competence—of British officials abroad. In 1891, he first took on the role of "imperial apostle," in David Gilmour's formulation, when he published the poem "The English Flag," criticizing the "poor little street-bred people" of the British Isles for refusing to take on the work of building the empire: "What should they know of England who only England know?"[25] In the same year, on a visit to South Africa, he formed a friendship with Cecil Rhodes and thrilled to his vision of an expanding empire "splashing red paint across Africa."[26] At the end of the decade, partly under Rhodes's influence, Kipling would give his undivided support to the Boer War, Britain's last full-scale imperial war.

But in his imagination of the empire, there was always a countercurrent. In 1890, Kipling wrote "The Widow at Windsor," one of a series of poems couched in the voices of Cockney soldiers:

> Walk wide o' the Widow at Windsor,
> For 'alf of Creation she owns:
> We 'ave bought her the same
> With the sword and the flame,
> An' we've salted it down with our bones.
> (Poor beggars!—
> It's blue with our bones!)[27]

As if the references to Queen Victoria were not disrespectful enough, later in the poem the speaker refers to the Union Jack as the "bloomin' old rag over'ead," and declares that all his fellow soldiers want is "a speedy return to their 'ome."

Less cheeky, but arguably even more challenging, was Kipling's poetic response to Victoria's Diamond Jubilee in 1897, which saw Britain gripped by a paroxysm of queen- and empire-worship. Here was a chance, surely, for a proper laureate of the empire to echo Vergil at his most Augustan. Kipling could surely, for example, have seized on the well-reported sight of colonial troops on parade in London:

> Dark-skinned infantry regiments, "terrible and beautiful to behold," in the words of a rhapsodic press, swung down the streets in a fantasy of variegated uniforms: the Borneo Dyak Police, the Jamaica Artillery, the Royal Nigerian Constabulary, giant Sikhs from India, Houssas from the Gold Coast, Chinese from Hong Kong, Malays from Singapore, Negroes from the West Indies, British Guiana and Sierra Leone; company after company passed before a dazzled people, awestruck at the testimony of their own might.[28]

More than a few of the classically educated Britons in attendance must have thought of the conclusion of Book 8 of the *Aeneid* (722–3): "All kinds of clothing, weapons, / And languages filed by in captive order."[29]

If this passage had occurred to Kipling, he sturdily resisted the temptation to borrow Vergil's images or, in fact, to deliver any sort of panegyric to empire. "Recessional," the poem he produced for the occasion, was something like the opposite—a biblically inflected warning against imperial hubris. In place of Vergil's "empire without end," Kipling foresees an inevitably declining world power:

> Far-called, our navies melt away;
> On dune and headland sinks the fire:

Lo, all our pomp of yesterday
Is one with Nineveh and Tyre!
Judge of the Nations, spare us yet,
Lest we forget—lest we forget![30]

The "Widow at Windsor"—around whom the whole celebration was designed to pivot—goes unmentioned.

"We make out of the quarrel with others, rhetoric," wrote Kipling's exact contemporary, W. B. Yeats, "but of the quarrel with ourselves, poetry."[31] For all its technical mastery and sheer memorability, Kipling's verse has been, not unfairly, criticized for lapsing too often into rhetoric. Yet few major writers have been so palpably divided against themselves as Kipling. In the words of Harry Rickett's snappy summary:

> At every stage of his life, a number of "Rudyard Kiplings" co-existed in varying degrees of compatibility with each other: devoted son/damaged "orphan," precocious aesthete/apprentice sahib, scholar gipsy/rule-bound conformist, would-be American/Empire Tory, innovative craftsman/fervent jingoist, doting father/bellicose tub-thumper—to mention only a few of the most obvious.[32]

On the subject of the empire, as on numerous others, Kipling had divided, sometimes antithetical feelings. But his quarrel with himself was fought out typically not within but between his stories and poems.

There is no more dramatic instance of this effect than the fact that, some days before producing "Recessional," Kipling had begun writing a very different poem to commemorate the Jubilee.[33] In its final version it would begin:

Take up the White Man's burden—
Send forth the best ye breed—
Go bind your sons in exile
To serve your captives' need;
To wait in heavy harness
On fluttered folk and wild—
Your new-caught, sullen peoples,
Half devil and half child.[34]

Whatever shift in mood or sense of appropriateness led to the composition and publication of "Recessional," Kipling would temporarily abandon work on the first poem, which would eventually be titled "The White Man's Burden." But even before the publication of "Recessional," he worried that it would be interpreted as "an excuse for lying down abjectly at all times and seasons and taking what any other country may think fit to give us. What I wanted to say was—'Don't gas but be ready to give people stuff.'—and I only covered the first half of the notion."[35] His expression of the second half would come when he finished "The White Man's

Burden" in the fall of 1898, under pressure of an event very different from the Jubilee: the debate in the United States over whether to annex the Philippine Islands, which the not-yet-ratified Treaty of Paris had ceded to the United States as one of the spoils of the Spanish-American War.[36] And it is in this notorious poem that Kipling once again wrestles with the influence of Vergil.[37]

In the 1908 story "Regulus," Kipling depicts a Latin master named King (clearly based on William Crofts of the USC) assigning "lines" to a delinquent pupil:

> "Hand me the Mantuan and I'll dictate. No matter. Any rich Virgilian measures will do. I may peradventure recall a few." He began:
>
> "Tu regere imperio populos Romane memento
> Hae tibi erunt artes pacisque imponere morem,
> Parcere subjectis and debellare superbos.
>
> There you have it, Winton. Write that out twice and once again."[38]

King presumably means "peradventure" ironically, since no lines from Vergil were more familiar to Britain's empire-builders, or those who educated them, than these:

> You, Roman, remember (these will be your arts) /
> To rule nations with your command and impose /
> The habit of peace, spare the subjected /
> And battle down the proud.[39]

The passage had become a sort of motto for the many British imperialists who saw themselves as heirs of the Romans, like Kipling's friend Cecil Rhodes, who enjoyed declaring "*civis Romanus sum*."[40] As Hagerman writes,

> Virgil's words about the imperial calling of the Romans "*tu regere imperio populos, Romane, memento, (hae tibi erunt artes)*" were quoted up and down the country, emphasizing the world-historical significance of the British Empire, its civilizing mission, and even the special imperial character of Britons.[41]

In one of the more telling instances cited by Hagerman, the jurist James Fitzjames Stephen, observing the many markers of British domination in India in the decade before Kipling's arrival as a young journalist, testified that such sights "irresistibly" recalled "lines which no familiarity can vulgarize: *tu regere* . . . ."[42]

Those familiar-yet-not-vulgar lines help shape "The White Man's Burden" in ways that may not immediately be obvious. There is, for example, the hortatory opening, directed at a group convinced of its own superiority yet needing to be reminded of its responsibilities: "Remember, Roman" and "[Americans,] take up the White Man's Burden." But the most distinct and telling Vergilian echo comes in the opening lines of the second stanza:

> Take up the White Man's burden—
> In patience to abide,

To veil the threat of terror
  And check the show of pride

The poem is so easy to dismiss as crude, or parody as ridiculous, that critics have tended to overlook the oddness and ambiguity of some of its language. For example, what is the threatened "terror" and what could it mean to "veil" it? Conceiving these lines as a reworking of Vergil's may suggest an answer.

The "threat of terror" might be one emanating from the newly colonized Filipinos. But there are two objections to this reading, one linguistic and the other historical. First, there is the curious word "veil." Why would the Philippines' new rulers want to disguise or cover up, rather than eliminate, a threat of rebellion? Second, by an extraordinary coincidence, "The White Man's Burden" first appeared in print on the pages of the *Times* of London, on February 4, 1899, the day the first shots were fired in what would become a brutal guerrilla war between Filipino and American forces.[43] The United States had supported the Filipino revolution against Spain, and hostilities only broke out between the former allies when it became clear that the Americans intended to replace the Spanish as colonizers. It is not at all clear that Kipling, in the long gestation of the poem, could or would have foreseen the Philippine–American war. The poem itself depicts the "new-caught" Filipinos as "sullen," not rebellious.

Given this premise, the reference to checking the "show of pride" would seem to make little sense except as a memory of the Vergilian passage's clinching word *superbi*. The colonized—Vergil's "subjected"—must be kept in check lest their sullenness turn to a reclaiming of pride and ultimately to rebellion. Kipling's "patience" captures the need for restraint after conquest implicit in Vergil's lines. But that restraint is founded on the knowledge that the colonizer has at his disposal the force necessary to "battle down" any resistance. There is only one form of "terror," then, that seems applicable to these lines—the terrifying power wielded by the conqueror himself. It should be kept "veiled" as a sign of forbearance but also, perhaps, to provide an element of surprise when it becomes necessary to unleash it. In its fractured reworking of Vergil, this part of the poem strikes a remarkably sinister, if arguably honest, note. Yet as I will point out below, this note seems out of tune with much of the rest of the poem.

Vergil's notion of imposing "the habit of peace" appears to surface in the opening lines of stanza three:

Take up the White Man's burden—
  The savage wars of peace—
Fill full the mouth of Famine
  And bid the sickness cease

"The savage wars of peace" might be read as a simple summary of Vergil's great subject: the savage (imperial and civil) wars that led to (the Augustan) peace. The phrase has a more riddling application to Kipling's own time. While it could not refer to a Philippine-American war that lay in the future, it might refer to the many "small wars" the British had fought over the two centuries it took them to become masters of one quarter of the globe.[44] Or it might be a way of describing colonial occupation, a peace under the constant but veiled threat of terror, as a series of "cold" wars, like those stirring up the anxiety of the officials in "Laocoön." But if so, the line seems strangely detached from what follows, where Kipling immediately shifts to a picture of colonizers feeding the colonized and curing their diseases. Because the phrase is strangely detached grammatically as well (the "wars" being meant possibly but not necessarily in apposition to the "burden"), it could be read as a thought thrown up by Kipling's psyche and then quickly suppressed in favor of a more positive notion. Alternatively, the wars could be those fought in peacetime against Famine (significantly, perhaps, personified as a sort of monster) and sickness. "Savage," then, would take on the tamer meaning of "extremely difficult." The references to the fight against hunger and disease reminds us that Kipling was writing at the high watermark of the New Imperialism, when the European nations competed fiercely in both a scramble for territory and in the devising of high-minded, humanitarian pretexts for that scramble.

Such a pretext became even more pressing in a poem that, in its final form, was pitched at leaders in the United States, a nation that, despite its embrace of Manifest Destiny, at that time remained conscious of itself as a former colony and harbored an anti-colonial tradition. American public opinion was also, of course, antimonarchical, which helps to explain one of the oddest and most troubling passages in the poem:

> Take up the White Man's burden—
> No tawdry rule of kings,
> But toil of serf and sweeper,
> The tale of common things.

Kipling is reassuring Americans that they can be simultaneously democratic and imperial. Yet it goes awfully far to imagine incipient colonizers as dutiful "serfs." Even more remarkable is Kipling's use of the term "sweepers"—another of those riddling bits of diction that stud the poem. It would seem to make no sense unless we follow Mary Hamer, who points to "sweeper" as a contemporary synonym for the "untouchables" (today generally called Dalits) at the bottom of the Hindu caste system.[45] While Kipling liked to point out, not inaccurately, that the functionaries of the empire worked hard at often thankless jobs, it takes a striking kind of moral blindness to associate the sahibs in their privileged enclaves with the native workers relegated to lives of cleaning sewers, disposing of animal carcasses, and other "unclean" tasks. This is a sort of *reductio ad absurdum* of the idealistic defense of empire—a notion that would be even more offensive were it not so ludicrous.

What I am suggesting is that, when Kipling tried to write a definitively "imperial" poem, a memory of the *tu regere* passage made its way, almost inevitably, into his thought and, to some extent, his language. But that the Vergilian stance appears here in only a fractured and unstable form shows the difficulty Kipling had in maintaining it under pressure of a particular historical event—America's acquisition of the Philippines—as well as, more broadly, the New Imperialist ideology of a humanitarian colonialism. Nothing in the Vergil passage suggests any humanitarian goal beyond the imposition of peace.

Yet the notion of peace as the ultimate goal of conquest—embodied perhaps in Kipling's ambiguous oxymoron, "the savage wars of peace"—cannot be written off simply as a hypocritical rationalization in the work of either Vergil or Kipling. This is because both authors depict the opposite of peace in a strikingly direct and unsparing fashion. Contemporary scholars of Vergil, like Sharon L. James, emphasize the extent to which he conveys "the violence and fury beneath the founding of Rome."[46] Richard Thomas notes that Vergil "often looks away" from "victor to vanquished" and focuses on the price involved, to all sides, on the drive for empire. According to K.W. Gransden, Vergil's theme is, simply, "War is madness."[47] As to Kipling, George Orwell may have been the first to note that, though Kipling had never been in battle, his vision of war is soberly realistic:

> He knows that bullets hurt, that under fire everyone is terrified, that the ordinary soldier never knows what the war is about or what is happening except in his own corner of the battlefield, and that British troops, like other troops, frequently run away.[48]

Gransden says that Aeneas "is reluctant to fight and not really interested in victory." In lines cited by Orwell, Kipling's common soldiers show even more reluctance and less interest:

> An' now the hugly bullets come peckin' through the dust,
> An' no one wants to face 'em, but every beggar must;
> So like a man in irons, which isn't glad to go,
> They moves 'em off by companies uncommon stiff and slow.[49]

Orwell contrasts this passage with one from Tennyson's "Charge of the Light Brigade" ("Forward the Light Brigade! Was there a man dismayed? No!"). An even better example might be Sir Henry Newbolt's popular slab of doggerel "Vitai Lampada," which compares a colonial battle to a cricket match: "And the voice of a schoolboy rallies the ranks / And cries, 'Play up! And play the game!'" Against utterances like these, Kipling's verse can sound as abrupt and unforgiving as the sword thrust that ends Turnus' life and Vergil's epic:

> When you're wounded and left on Afghanistan's plains
>   And the women come out to cut up the remains,
>   Just roll to your rifle and blow out your brains
> And go to your Gawd like a soldier.[50]

Certainly Kipling's depictions of colonial warfare were derived not from the *Aeneid* but from the testimony of the common soldiers whom he knew and admired and championed in poems like "Tommy" and "The Widow at Windsor." Yet the affinity between the poets on this issue, if not a matter of influence, was at least, I would argue, evidence of a form of moral continuity. Both writers, while achieving something like the status of imperial laureates, refused to conceal their mixed feelings about the imperial project or look away from its costs. Nor can we wholly discount the possibility of influence on this point. As Hagerman has argued, classical literature did not just provide a parcel of convenient rationales to be applied after the fact to the administrators and military officers of the British Empire; in many cases, it served as one of the filters through which they perceived their experience from the beginning. It seems plausible that the *Aeneid* helped first prepare and later reinforce his cold-eyed imagination of battle.

Yet Vergil's influence on Kipling shows up in its arguably most concentrated form after, in his late thirties, he settled for good in the English countryside, far from any contested part of the empire. In 1902, Kipling bought a house in rural Sussex, which would serve as his family home for the rest of his life. "England is a wonderful land," he wryly remarked in a letter to a friend. "It is the most interesting of all foreign countries that I have ever been in."[51] The next few years would be marked by Kipling's growing interest in studying English history and representing it in his work. Strikingly, these would be the same years that saw what Stephen Medcalf calls Kipling's enthusiastic "re-discovery" of the poetry of Horace and of classical literature in general.[52] The two developments fed each other, and Kipling would come to show a special fascination with the period in which Britain, ruled by Rome, had been an outlying province of a vast empire rather than its center.

In 1906 Kipling published *Puck of Pook's Hill*, a work of historical fiction pitched at children although extremely sophisticated in its narrative technique. The Puck of the title is the Shakespearean spirit of *A Midsummer Night's Dream*; he appears to two modern children, magically transporting characters from English history into the present to tell the children their stories and illuminate their times.[53] Kipling separates each vignette from the next with one or more poems reflecting related themes. The second poem in the book, "A Tree Song," takes the form of a charm or spell spoken by Puck. It evokes the age and continuity of English history in a celebration of three characteristic English trees—oak, ash, and thorn. It is also the first and last poem in which Kipling mentions Aeneas:

Oak of the Clay lived many a day
  Or ever Aeneas began.
Ash of the Loam was a lady at home,
  When Brut was an outlaw man.
Thorn of the Down saw New Troy Town
  (From which was London born);
Witness hereby the ancientry
  Of Oak, and Ash, and Thorn![54]

Here Kipling borrows from Geoffrey of Monmouth's 12th-century account of the legendary settlement of Britain by Aeneas' great-grandson Brutus, who built the city that would become London, naming it New Troy Town. This story does not, of course, appear in Vergil's poetry. Yet beneath "A Tree Song's" light and jaunty tone there lurks an interesting attempt to claim for England's demotic literature and legends something of the glamor of classical epic. The poem borrows its meter from nursery rhymes like "Old King Cole," and Brutus' identification as an "outlaw man" (he was exiled from Italy for accidentally killing his father) assimilates him to native outlaw-heroes like Robin Hood. Kipling-as-Puck patriotically (yet puckishly) brings Aeneas down a peg in order to elevate the native tradition.

Elsewhere in the volume, Roman and Vergilian themes are treated with more seriousness and more historical substance. The book's central chapters—three interlinked short stories amounting to a novella—focus on the fictional Parnesius, a Roman centurion of the 380s who is charged with defending Hadrian's Wall from the Picts and the newly threatening Saxons.[55] Medcalf notes, "It seems likely that [Kipling] went to the Roman poets he had read at school, Virgil and Horace, to prepare for Parnesius."[56] Kipling's imagined centurion clearly shares some characteristics with Aeneas. He is a more-or-less reluctant yet wholly dutiful warrior. He sacrifices faithfully to the gods, and Puck even refers to him as "Pious Parnesius."[57] (The centurion modestly deflects the epithet.) Yet Parnesius functions to some extent as a sort of anti-Aeneas. Rather than a leader driven to found an empire, he is a subordinate commander serving at the outer limits—geographic and temporal—of the same empire. Thus, one facet of Parnesius' tale is an ironic perspective, in the spirit of "Recessional," on Jupiter's promise to Venus: "For them I will not limit time or space."[58]

One of the poems linked to the novella, "A British-Roman Song," combines a Vergilian evocation of Rome's magnificence with anxiety over its decline. The poem, spoken by a conjectured Roman born in Britain (like Parnesius) opens:

> My father's father saw it not,
> And I, belike, shall never come
> To look on that so-holy spot—
> The very Rome—
>
> Crowned by all Time, all Art, all Might,
> The equal work of Gods and Man—
> City beneath whose oldest height
> The Race began!

The lines here echo such celebratory Vergilian passages as the one from the initial description of Aeneas in Book 1 ("War wracked him too, until he set his city / And gods in Latium. There his Latin race rose, / With Alban patriarchs, and Rome's high walls," 1. 5–7)[59] and another from the prophecy of Anchises in Book 6 ("renowned Rome / Will rule the world and raise her heart to heaven— /Blessed in her sons, with seven citadels / In one wall," 781–4).[60] But a note of anxiety enters when the speakers "prays" for reinforcements from Rome to beat back the barbarian tide. This feeling is akin to that of the Anglo-Indian officials in "Laocoön," but historically better founded, because the reinforcements would never come. Kipling gives the date of the speaker's plea as "A.D. 406"—four years before Rome would withdraw its legions from Britain for good.

In a remarkable passage from the novella, Kipling seems to question not just the stability but the moral underpinnings of Roman imperialism, and perhaps of later imperialisms as well. Parnesius is speaking with his commander, the usurper Western emperor Maximus, in the company of Allo, a Pictish prince who has allied himself with the Romans because of his fear of a Saxon invasion. Maximus asks Parnesius if he will be able to keep the Picts "contented" while Maximus makes war in Gaul. Parnesius replies, "The Picts have been too oppressed by us to trust anything with a Roman name for years and years."[61] Then Allo complains, "You shoot us Picts when we come to borrow a little iron from the Iron Ditch; you burn our heather, which is all our crop; then you hide behind the Wall, and scorch us with Greek fire."[62] This striking exercise in what Richard Thomas might call the Vergilian move of looking away from the victor to the vanquished is echoed in an accompanying poem, "A Pict Song," which opens,

> Rome never looks where she treads
>   Always her heavy hooves fall
> On our stomachs, our hearts or our heads;
>   And Rome never heeds when we bawl.[63]

Here the impressive anger of the first three lines of the stanza is somewhat undercut by the childish word "bawl" in the fourth. Nevertheless, if not quite as crisp or memorable as the accusation which Tacitus puts in the mouth of Calgacus (*Agr.* 30.5: "They make a desert and they call it peace"), the verses express a parallel indignation and disgust, and one which transcends the Roman setting. "Hadrian's Wall," writes David Gilmour, "may not be quite the North West Frontier. The Picts may not be quite Pathans in disguise. The centurions may not be exactly British officers in India," but the parallels are close enough.[64]

In 1903, as Kipling was settling into his rural home and beginning work on the Puck stories, he published a poem called "The Return." This dramatic monologue is spoken in the voice of a common soldier who has served in the Boer War and is returning to London in the wake of the 1902 treaty that ended the conflict:

> Peace is declared, an' I return
>   To 'Ackneystadt, but not the same;
> Things 'ave transpired which made me learn
>   The size and meanin' of the game.[65]

The speaker tells us that he "started" the war as "a average kid" but finished it "as a thinkin' man." Now his mature thoughts balance a memory of the war's horrors ("The pore dead that look so old / An' was so young an hour ago") with a reminiscence of the camaraderie it bred ("Men from both two 'emispheres / Discussin' things of every kind"). The soldier tries, somewhat shyly and abashedly, to sum up what he has gained from the experience:

An' last it come to me—not pride,
  Nor yet conceit, but on the 'ole
(If such a term may be applied),
  The makin's of a bloomin' soul.

While Kipling the "ventriloquist poet" is not explicitly identifying himself with the speaker, the poem has a notably heartfelt, even personal, tone. This feeling probably has its roots in the two months in 1899 which Kipling spent visiting British troops in the South African war zone, where he was deeply moved by his reception. When the writer left an army hospital after visiting the wounded, one soldier cried "God bless him; he's the soldier's friend."[66] But the poem's title also suggests a connection with Kipling's own recent "return" to his homeland, "the most interesting foreign country."

Kipling had strongly supported the Boer War, which, he declared in prose, was being fought in the name of "British principles" like the liberty of the individual. Yet "The Return" is notably free of political propaganda. It also seems to fall short of the purpose enunciated in the first stanza—to explain "the size and meanin' of the game," where "game" seems to refer to the whole endeavor of the British Empire. This is a subject Kipling has been wrestling with throughout his career, yet here he anticlimactically locates its meaning in the "making" of a single soldier's soul. It is true that a broader significance is suggested in the italicized refrain that appears twice, once after the first stanza and again after the last:

If England was what England seems,
  An' not the England of our dreams,
But only putty, brass, and paint,
  'Ow quick we'd drop 'er But she ain't!

On the surface, these lines sound defiantly and rousingly patriotic. Yet the curious double negative (England "ain't . . . not the England of our dreams")—which may even render the stanza confusing at first reading—strongly hints at unresolved mixed feelings. I want to propose that these lines become more complicated and telling when we recognize that they contain an elliptic allusion to one of the most famous passages in the *Aeneid.*

"There are two gates of sleep," we are told at the conclusion of Book 6 (893–6):

The one, they say,
Is horn: true shades go out there easily;
The other—shining, white, well-crafted ivory—
Lets spirits send false dreams up toward the sky[67]

The shade of Anchises, having shown Aeneas a vision of Rome's glorious future, leads him out of the underworld through the ivory gate. This "strange interlude" in the epic[68]—whose meaning is endlessly debated by Vergil scholars—does at least lay open the possibility that Anchises' prophecies will not be fulfilled, or if they are, will be fulfilled in a way that is considerably less than glorious.

When the speaker of Kipling's poem insists on the reality of the "England of our dreams," the emotion, I think, is real, and invested with some of Kipling's own new-found fascination and affection for his native country. But significantly, the tangible shape of the "dreams" remains unspecified. Thus, they constitute, by definition, a dream—a vision of something worthy but hard to conceive or express. Poised against this vision is a second one, of a nation "all putty, brass, an' paint." This vision, according to the speaker, is also a dream, although this time in the sense of an illusion. The flashy, tinselly decorations of the London music hall become for the speaker the equivalent of the polished and glittering ivory on Vergil's gate of false dreams. This allegedly false version of England is fiercely rejected by the speaker—a rejection emphasized by the de-italicization of the typeface. Yet that emphasis may be read as an *over*emphasis, an attempt to counteract the lingering doubts embedded in the double negative. The speaker cannot bring himself to say that England *is*—only that it is "not not"—the England of his dreams. He hopes and believes, but he cannot be sure, that he is seeing his country through a frame of horn and not one of ivory. We can read this doubtful hope back to the opening stanza, and say it reflects the speaker's (and Kipling's) mixed feelings about the larger imperial project—"the game."

Richard Thomas says of the ivory gate in the *Aeneid* that it opens on to "the second half of the poem with all its shadows and all its reservations."[69] It would probably be heartening for a politically progressive reader to discover that the reservations about imperialism disclosed in "The Return" (as well as other poems like "Laocoön," "Recessional," and "A Pict Song") went on to deepen into something like outright rejection. But Kipling's politics, if anything, hardened as he aged, becoming more conservative and even less open to the claims of anti-colonialists. Yet—except in his fiery defense of Ulster Protestants against a rising Irish nationalism—the empire itself was less and less a central subject of his work.[70] His outlook on world affairs was now shaped above all by his hatred and fear of Germany—a hatred not allayed by the death of his only son in the Great War. This was a Germany conceived not as a rival imperial power but, prophetically enough, as an existential threat to Britain itself and her European allies. He died in 1936, having lived long enough to see the rise of Hitler.

David Gilmour judges that Kipling's "prime as an imperial bard" lasted only until about 1905.[71] After *Puck of Pook's Hill* his use of Vergilian themes faded, too, along with his interest in analogizing the British and Roman empires. But he continued to read and memorize his favorite Roman poet, Horace, and write dozens of poems in imitation of him. It is in two of these imitations that Vergil's name will appear for the only times in Kipling's verse. The first is a slight and casual production ("Thirst is summer time's companion," 1910) in which Horace invites Vergil over to his house for a drink.[72] The second ("The Last Ode," 1926) is a well-constructed and distinctly lovely lyric in which Horace, on the day his patron Maecenas dies, remembers the death of Vergil 11 years earlier.[73] Kipling draws on the traditional Christian interpretation of *Eclogue* 4's portrait of a holy child as prefiguring the coming of Christ. The Horace of the poem relates that on his death-bed Vergil "prophesied / Change upon all the Eternal Gods had made / And on the Gods alike." He foresaw "A Star new-risen above the living and dead; / And the lost shades that were our loves restored / As lovers, and for ever." Movingly, Kipling shows Horace interpreting the Christian theme of resurrection in terms of the Roman poet's great theme of friendship. The poem concludes:

> Maecenas waits me on the Esquiline;
>   Thither tonight go I. . . .
> And shall this dawn restore us, Virgil mine,
>   To dawn? Beneath what sky?

Kipling understood that Maecenas had been buried on the Esquiline Hill and that Horace lived only a few weeks longer himself. It would be crude to extract a direct political message from this poem, with its focus on love, loss, and the comradeship of the arts, and it therefore reminds us that Kipling's work was not wholly, or even mostly, political. Nevertheless, the valedictory tone of the poem, with its sense of an old order changing, must draw some of its feeling from Kipling's own sense of his historical moment. In "Recessional" he had foreseen the sunset of empire—"On dune and headland sinks the fire"—and must have wondered sometimes what the sky would look like at dawn, if dawn ever came.

Notes

1 The Poetry Foundation.
2 Notable readings are found in, e.g., Jarrell 1980; Said 1993; Wilson 1977.
3 Ricketts 2000: 6–7.
4 Ricketts 2000: 32.
5 McDermott 2008: 369.
6 Hagerman 2013: 20.
7 Treggiari 2012: n. 11.
8 Kipling 1990: 22.
9 Medcalf 1993.
10 Untitled poem beginning "Thirst is summer time's companion" in Kipling 2013: III:2133 and "The Last Ode," in Kipling 2013: II: 1023.
11 "A Tree Song," Kipling 2013: II:675.
12 Treggiari 2012: n. 44.
13 "Regulus" in Kipling 1917: 239–70.
14 Ricketts 2000: 53, 55–8.
15 Ricketts 2000: 40–4.
16 Arnold 1867: 161–71.
17 Kipling 2013: II: 1221.
18 MacMillan 2018: 117.
19 MacMillan 2018: 122.
20 Translated in Ruden 2009: 2.220.
21 Ricketts 2011: 111–25.

22 Gilmour 2003: 56.
23 Ricketts 2000: 116. It is not surprising that in 1975, in the wake of the Vietnam debacle, the American director John Huston should have chosen to turn the story into a film.
24 Gilmour 2003: 75.
25 Gilmour 2003: 85; Kipling 2013: I: 291.
26 Gilmour 2003: 136.
27 Kipling 2013: I: 200.
28 Tuchman 1966: 61.
29 Translated in Ruden 2009: 8.722–3.
30 Kipling 2013: I: 614. I, 614. The destructions of Nineveh and Tyre are prophesied in the Hebrew Bible (Nahum 3 and Ezekiel 26). While the biblical allusions were no doubt uppermost in Kipling's mind, "Tyre" carries a suggestively Vergilian overtone as the birthplace of Dido, who is referred to in the *Aeneid* as a "Tyrian queen" and who founds the city of Carthage, which would in time be as definitively destroyed by the Romans as Troy was by the Greeks.
31 Yeats 1959: 331.
32 Ricketts 2000: xi.
33 Gilmour 2003: 119.
34 Kipling 2013: I: 528.
35 Kipling, letter to H. Rider Haggard, quoted in Gilmour 2003: 123.
36 Herring 2008: 321–3.
37 Not just "notorious" today. From the beginning the poem was lambasted and ridiculed by anti-imperialists. For example, it was parodied almost immediately in a poem called "The Brown Man's Burden" ("Pile up the brown man's burden / To gratify your greed"). Quoted in Ricketts 2011: 118. A more biting parody ran: "Pile on the brown man's burden, / And if ye rouse his hate / Meet his old-fashioned reasons / With Maxims up-to-date." Quoted in Gilmour 2003: 131.
38 Kipling 1917: 256.
39 Trans. J.R. O'Neill.
40 Hagerman 2013: 104.
41 Hagerman 2013: 189.
42 Hagerman 2013: 90.
43 Gilmour 2003: 126.
44 Max Boot entitled his history of America's own "small wars" *The Savage Wars of Peace*. Boot 2002.
45 Hamer 2009.
46 James 1995: 624.
47 Gransden 2003: 90.
48 Orwell 1954: 131.
49 Orwell 1954: 131; "The 'Eathen" in Kipling 2013: I: 452–5.
50 Kipling, "The Young British Soldier," *Poems*, vol II, 204–6.
51 Ricketts 2000: 279.
52 Medcalf 1993: 220.
53 Kipling 1911.
54 Kipling 2013: II: 675.
55 The three stories are "A Centurion of the Thirtieth," "On the Great Wall," and "The Winged Hats." The tale reflects the then-current but since rejected view that Hadrian's Wall was built to defend against "barbarian" incursions. See Beard 2015: 484–5.
56 Medcalf 1993: 220.
57 Kipling 1911: 177.
58 Translated in Ruden 2009: 1.278.
59 Translated in Ruden 2009: 1.5–7.
60 Translation in Ruden 2009: 6.781–3.
61 Kipling 1911: 186.

62 Kipling 1911: 188.
63 Kipling 2013: II: 722–3.
64 Gilmour 2003: 173.
65 Kipling 2013: I: 611.
66 Gilmour 2003: 149.
67 Translated in Ruden 2009: 6.893–6.
68 Gransden 2003: 79.
69 Thomas 2001: 198.
70 See, e.g., "Ulster," in Kipling 2013: II: 1064.
71 Gilmour 2003: 310.
72 Kipling 2013: III: 2133.
73 Kipling 2013: II: 1023.

References

Arnold, M. 1867. *New Poems*. London: Macmillan.

Beard, M. 2015. *SPQR: A History of Ancient Rome*. New York: Liveright.

Boot, M. 2002. *The Savage Wars of Peace*. New York: Basic Books.

Gilmour, D. 2003. *The Long Recessional: The Imperial Life of Rudyard Kipling*. New York: Farrar, Straus and Giroux.

Gransden, K.W. 2003. *Virgil: The Aeneid*. Cambridge: Cambridge University Press.

Hagerman, C.A. 2013. *Britain's Imperial Muse: The Classics, Imperialism, and the British Empire, 1784–1914*. Basingstoke: Palgrave Macmillan UK.

Hamer, M. 2009. "Notes to 'The White Man's Burden'." *Kipling Society Notes*. www.kiplingsociety.co.uk/rg_burden1.htm.

Herring, G.C. 2008. *From Colony to Superpower: U.S. Foreign Relations Since 1776*. New York: Oxford University Press.

James, S.L. 1995. "Establishing Rome with the Sword: *Condere* in the *Aeneid*." *American Journal of Philology* 116, 4: 623–37.

Jarrell, R. 1980. *Kipling, Auden and Co*. New York: Farrar, Straus and Giroux.

Kipling, R. 1911. *Puck of Pook's Hill*. London: Macmillan.

———. 1917. *A Diversity of Creatures*. London: Macmillan.

———. 1990. *Something of Myself*. Cambridge: Cambridge University Press.

———. 2013. *Cambridge Edition of the Poems of Rudyard Kipling*. Edited by T. Pinney. Vol. I–III. New York: Cambridge University Press.

MacMillan, M. 2018. *Women of the Raj*. London: Thames & Hudson.

McDermott, E. 2008. "Playing for His Side: Kipling's 'Regulus,' Corporal Punishment, and Classical Education." *International Journal of the Classical Tradition* 15, 3 (September).

Medcalf, S. 1993. "Horace's Kipling." In C. Martindale and D. Hopkins (eds.) *Horace Made New: Horatian Influences on British Writing from the Renaissance to the Twentieth Century*. Cambridge: Cambridge University Press. 217–39.

Orwell, G. 1954. "Rudyard Kipling." In *A Collection of Essays by George Orwell*. New York: Doubleday.

Poetry Foundation. *Rudyard Kipling*. www.poetryfoundation.org/poets/rudyard-kipling.

Ricketts, H. 2000. *Rudyard Kipling: A Life*. New York: Carrol and Graf.

———. 2011. "'Nine and Sixty Ways': Kipling, Ventriloquist Poet." In H.J. Booth (ed.) *The Cambridge Companion to Rudyard Kipling*. New York: Cambridge University Press. 111–25.

Ruden, S., tran. 2009. *The Aeneid*. New Haven: Yale University Press.

Said, E. 1993. *Culture and Imperialism*. New York: Knopf.

Thomas, R. 2001. *Virgil and the Augustan Reception*. Cambridge: Cambridge University Press.

Treggiari, S. 2012. *Kipling and the Classical World*. www.kiplingsociety.co.uk/rg_classical1.htm.

Tuchman, B. 1966. *The Proud Tower: A Portrait of the World Before the War, 1890–1914*. New York: Macmillan.

Wilson, A. 1977. *The Strange Ride of Rudyard Kipling*. London: Pimlico.

Yeats, W.B. 1959. "Per Amica Silentia Lunae." In *Mythologies*. New York: Macmillan.

2 Shining light onto Vergilian shadows in Zora Neale Hurston's *Their Eyes Were Watching God*

Christian Lehmann

In her 1942 autobiography, *Dust Tracks on a Road*, Zora Neale Hurston (1891–1960) relates the following anecdote about her time at Howard University.[1] While working as a manicurist at a barbershop in Washington, DC, to pay for her tuition, she was privy to the gossip and business of "bankers, Senators, Cabinet Members, Congressmen, and Gentlemen of the Press."[2] One day a reporter gave Hurston $25 and a quart of ice cream and requested that she ask a Southern congressman a question and report back to him. Hurston elaborates on why she decided not to betray the congressman in question:

> The man came in on his regular time, which was next day, and in his soft voice, began to tell me how important it was to be honorable at all times and to be trustworthy. How could I ask him then? Besides, he was an excellent Greek scholar and translated my entire lesson for me, which was from Xenophon's *Cyropaedeia*, and talked at length on the ancient Greeks and Persians. The news man was all right. He had to get his information the best way he could, but, for me, it would have been terrible to do that nice man like that. I told the reporter how it was and he understood and never asked me again.[3]

The anecdote highlights Hurston's characteristic wit and irony. In the middle of an anecdote about how she could not betray this gentleman because of his soft-spoken disquisition on honor and trust, she slides in the fact that she got him to do her homework for her. And this was homework not just on any book, but on a 19th-century staple in Greek classes: Xenophon's *Cyropaedeia*, "The Education of Cyrus." For a reader who knows what the text is, the irony is visible; to anyone else, the story remains an enjoyable curiosity.

This added layer of irony is key to understanding one of Hurston's techniques in referencing the ancient Greek and Roman worlds, and indeed her strategy of classical allusion as a whole.[4] Hurston undercuts the structuring force of allusions. They neither act as paradigms for behavior nor as models to challenge. Rather, Hurston uses them to imply the impossibility, especially for Black women in American society, of using them as a model for success. Hurston knows the lesson of the *Cyropaedeia*. In fact, she has absorbed it so well that she knows how to get a White man to do her work for her. In this chapter, I will begin by laying out

DOI: 10.4324/9781003176145-4

Hurston's classical education and looking at three examples of her explicit use of classical antiquity. I will then turn to her use of the *Aeneid* throughout *Their Eyes Were Watching God* to look at the way that she rewrites Dido and Aeneas through Janie and Tea Cake.

It is important to highlight at the outset, though, that for Hurston "Classics" is fundamentally White. We cannot look to Hurston for an expansive view of Blackness in the ancient world. In fact, she can be quite contemptuous of attempts to do just that. For instance, in a letter to Katherine Tracy L'Engle from 1945 about W.E.B DuBois' efforts to claim Alexander Hamilton as a "Negro," she writes,

> He has snatched numerous perfectly white people into the Negro race in the same way [as Alexander Hamilton]. I have decided that it comes of a monumental inferiority complex. That sort of thing is practiced by the Jews too. Those who do that, wish that they were white. Failing at that, they just borrow all the distinguished white people and get into the race with them by proxy, as it were. I resent his putting that Greek slut, Cleopatra, into the same race with me. Anyway, his pretense that ancient Egyptians were Negroes is just as arbitrary and false.[5]

For the purposes of this chapter, I will not be staking a claim on whether or not the *Aeneid* is "White," but will instead be thinking about how Hurston read and used it. Thus, when we see Hurston activate allusions to antiquity for her Black characters, we find her enacting a series of resistive readings whereby those classical texts are no longer limited to a White audience.

Hurston's classical education

Hurston's early life offered no indication that she would write a novel like *Their Eyes Were Watching God.* Even in college, she portrayed herself as having an unwavering loyalty to canonical British novelists and poets. Her earliest encounter with the myths of Greece and Rome comes in an anecdote from when she was in fifth grade and learning to read.

Hurston relates that it was common for White tourists to stop by her village school because "[a] Negro school was something strange to them, and while they were always sympathetic and kind, curiosity must have been present, also."[6] On the day she describes, two White women showed up without alerting anyone beforehand, and Hurston's class was invited to read aloud for them. Coincidentally, the reading was Pluto and Persephone.[7]

After the reading, the two women want to meet Hurston and asked whether she loved school. Hurston lies: she likes certain subjects, but hates the arbitrary nature of corporal punishment. However, she knows that these White visitors don't want to hear that: "I knew better than to bring that up right there, so I said yes, I *loved* school."[8] And with that *fiction,* Hurston gained access to another world. The next day the two women invite Hurston to their hotel, where they proceed to run her through a literacy test, presumably to check if her *bravura* performance in school was merely a performance: "I was then handed a copy of *Scribner's Magazine*, and asked to read a place that was pointed out to me. After a paragraph or two, I was told with smiles, that that would do."[9] The anecdote bears similarity to other tests of African American literacy in which White people demanded "proof" of ability.[10] Hurston's reward, and she clearly views it as such, is to gain access to (British and European) literature. First she receives a book of hymns, *The Swiss Family Robinson*, and a volume of fairy tales. After the women return to Minnesota, she receives another package of clothes and books. To the clothes, she is indifferent; to the books, rapturous:

> In that box were Gulliver's Travels, Grimm's Fairy Tales, Dick Whittington, Greek and Roman Myths, and best of all, Norse Tales.
>
> . . .
>
> Of the Greeks, Hercules moved me most. I followed him eagerly on his tasks. The story of the choice of Hercules as a boy when he met Pleasure and Duty, and put his hand in that of Duty and followed her steep way to the blue hills of fame and glory, which she pointed out at the end, moved me profoundly. I resolved to be like him. The tricks and turns of the other Gods and Goddesses left me cold. There were other thin books about this and that sweet and gentle little girl who gave up her heart to Christ and good works.[11]

In this unboxing of treasured literature, what stands out is the simultaneous taxonomic separation (Greek and Roman myth versus Norse, for example) and mixing of traditions. Christological narratives share a paragraph with Hercules and other gods and goddesses in the pantheon of her imagination. This mixed state will come to craft her frame of reference when writing *Their Eyes Were Watching God.*

Hurston's education was put on hold until she moved to Baltimore in 1917.[12] At first, she tried to save up money to get back to school, but, unable to save enough, she decided to start attending night school, which necessitated erasing a decade from her life, going from 26 to 16 years old, in order take advantage of "The Maryland Code" that "provided for free admission to public school for 'all colored youths between six and twenty years of age.'"[13] It was at night school in Baltimore that she fell in love with English literature, and poetry, thanks to a particularly dynamic teacher, Dwight O. W. Holmes, whose recitation of Coleridge's "Kubla Khan" had an epiphanic effect on the young woman. In describing him, Hurston turns to busts of Roman authors to capture his likeness:

> He is not a pretty man, but he has the face of a scholar, not dry and set like, but fire flashes from his deep-set eyes. His high-bridged, but sort of bent nose over his thin-lipped mouth—well the whole thing reminds you of some old Roman like Cicero, Caesar or Virgil in tan skin.[14]

Hurston's choice of three Roman authors is significant, and the inclusion of Vergil makes it clear that she is thinking of Cicero and Caesar in their literary capacity. I suggest that the shift to these authors is an additional way of Hurston telling us who her teachers are. She took her learning both from Mr. Holmes and from the Romans. Simultaneously, her reference to Holmes' "tan skin" as opposed to the old Romans emphasizes their dual whiteness: white because they are (likely) bust portraits, but also because she sees ancient authors as White.

This experience at night school strengthened her resolve to get an education and her confidence. She enrolled at Morgan College, which had a high school department called Morgan Academy, where she stayed for two years. She initially planned to stay at Morgan for the college program, but a chance encounter with Mae Miller and an offer of housing from her friend Bernice Hughes led Hurston to Howard University. While there, Dr. Lorenzo Dow Turner's teaching inspired Hurston to declare that

> I decided I must be an English teacher and lean over my desk and discourse on the 18th-Century poets, and explain the roots of the modern novel. Children just getting born were going to hear about Addison, Poe, De Quincey, Steele, Coleridge, Keats and Shelley from me, leaning nonchalantly over my desk. Defoe, Burns, Swift, Milton and Scott were going to be sympathetically, but adequately explained, with just that suspicion of a smile now and then before I returned to my notes.[15]

This list of texts, all canonically British, all White, are indicative of how far Hurston moves from this dream when she becomes a novelist and anthropologist, yet those texts are always still available to her to engage with.

In her Barnard transcript (where she transferred from Howard in 1925), we have evidence of the number of courses in Greek and Latin she took at Howard. Greek: grammar and elementary composition, Xenophon, Homer, prose composition, sight translation. Latin: second-year sight translation of prose and poetry, along with prose composition.[16]

However, her fantasy of teaching British literature to young Americans was soon replaced by a passion for anthropology after studying under Dr. Franz Boyd at Barnard. And once Charlotte Mason arranged for her to travel around the South and record the oral folklore of African Americans in 1928, she left those beloved texts behind.[17] She draws on this experience most when she experiments with her narrative voice in the early novels *Jonah's Vine* and *Their Eyes Were Watching God.*

Hurston's marked allusions

Despite her education and clear facility with classics, Hurston's engagement with it has largely gone unnoticed.[18] There are two primary ways in which Hurston alludes to the classical world.[19] She marks it by using an explicit term or point of reference, or she allows it to sit just beneath the surface. It is this latter narrative strategy that we see in *Their Eyes Were Watching God*, but to better understand the difference, I want now to discuss three times when Hurston marks her allusions to the classical world.

In many instances, Hurston's use of the ancient world is certainly not overly serious, although the ultimate effects of her engagement are profound. In one of her earliest written stories, "The Conversion of Sam," she makes a butt pun at the expense of classics professors.[20] The story opens with an image of Jim, who runs a restaurant. His wife works in the kitchen as he "lounged in one of the greasy chairs talking loudly on the solution of the race problem with two of his cronies, the Reverend Zephaniah Solomon Meggs and Professor Cicero Omega Butts."[21] The image of men talking in chairs readily recalls those figures in Hurston's chair at the manicurist shop. The names of the reverend and professor point to her interest in the Old Testament and her own classics professors at Howard. That "Butts" is meant as a joke is highlighted several pages later when Mrs. Jim's dislike for Sam manifests: "She suspected him of making her person the butt of many of his witticisms."[22]

Where Cicero's gluteal qualities make for a quick laugh in this early story, Hurston can also activate a classical allusion for a feminist reinscription of Roman history. In her 1927 story, "The Country in the Woman," Hurston investigates the marriage of the philandering Mitchell and his wife, Caroline. Mitchell does not keep his relationship with his girlfriend, Lucy, secret, and the people on the street watch Caroline's revenge unfold. After Mitchell and Lucy have walked off down the street, "the loungers were amazed to see a woman on Seventh Avenue strolling leisurely along with an axe on her shoulder."[23] The men have no idea what to do and watch wonderingly on:

> "We ought to call the police."
> "Somebody ought to overtake her and take that axe away."
> "Who for instance?"
> So it rested there. No one felt like trying to take an axe from Caroline.[24]

The men realize that there is no authority that can confront Caroline, who, at this point, reappears: "Over her shoulder like a Roman lictor, she bore the axe, and from the head of it hung the trousers of Mitchell's natty suit, and the belt buckle clacking a little in the breeze." The reference is to the Roman *fasces*, an axe head emerging from a bundle of sticks bound by a thong (here the belt, perhaps), and symbol of authority. Hurston has transferred the phallocentric symbol of masculine legal authority to a Black woman who is her own agent of authority. In the face of an American authority, "We ought to call the police," Caroline represents a far more ancient one. The pants and belt buckle dangling from the axe add to the scene elements of a symbolic castration alongside the male observer's inability and unwillingness to act. In this simple scene, Hurston challenges the power of the police and men, two groups that dominate Caroline's world.

While these two stories appear early in her career, Hurston's final project, a biography of Herod left incomplete at the time of her death, shows her lifelong interest in the ancient world, and especially in the ways in which the Old Testament blurs with Greek and Roman history and literature.[25] She summarizes the project in this (one of four) introduction to the Herod manuscript:

> If Herod's acts and motivation appear exotic to us of the West in the latter half of the Twentieth Century A.D., we must bear in mind that Herod belonged to, and was a very active participant, in that century of decision which still is influential in our lives at this moment. It was that almost incredible one hundred years which produced Julius Caesar, Cato, Cicero, Pompey, Cataline [*sic*], Brutus, Marius, Sulla, Augustus Caesar, Sirabo [Strabo?], Nicolaus of Damascus, Vergil, Horace, Cassius, Marc Antony, sculptors, dramatists and poets of note, of the death of the Roman Republic and the birth of the Roman Empire. Great men, stirring times. Herod was in the thick of it all—the intimate friend of both Marc Antony and Augustus Caesar, and of Agrippa, Commander-in-chief of the armed forces of Rome. It must never be lost sight of that the customs of that era were not the same as of our times.[26]

In this book, Hurston seems to abandon the ironic distance she took from the ancient world. Here she earnestly seeks to reconstruct it. But even as she offers a shrewd critique of Rome's influence on contemporary America, she falls into the trap she warns about. Two sentences frame her catalogue of male figures: "that century of decision which still is influential in our lives at this moment" and "the customs of that era were not the same as of our times." It is a critique that continues to go unheeded when, just a few paragraphs later, she compares Rome to America and Parthia to Russia. The comparisons of antiquity to the modern age are just too tempting for her to ignore.

Shadows of the *Aeneid*

Thus far we have seen Hurston make explicit reference to the ancient world, usually with a wink in her eye. But when it comes to her novels, she adopts a different technique.[27] Instead of direct allusion, she weaves together all of her knowledge such that a classical reference sits alongside biblical allusions and the influence of Haitian Vodoun. Until now, scholars have pointed to the influence of these other elements alongside African American oral storytelling[28] on her best-known novel, *Their Eyes Were Watching God*, while the presence of Vergil's *Aeneid* has gone unnoticed. In order to clarify how Hurston alludes to Vergil, who "held a central place within the black classical curriculum,"[29] I will first briefly discuss these other influences.

The Flying African[30]

Starting in 1927 and through the 1930s, Hurston traveled around the American South collecting folk tales from African Americans throughout the region, which she gathered in the collection *Mules and Men* (1935). One story she documents—but that she surely encountered more than once—is that of the Flying African. The broad outline of the thousands of such stories is that a Black person who has been stolen from Africa takes flight to return:

> Each mode of travel projects, in a structural way, a cultural and personal system of flight. Whether the Africans rode in a calabash, floated in a sea shell or

> on a leaf, soared on a wing, on the back of a bird or simply walked upon the water, they had to overcome the sea. The sea (or a body of water) represents the obstacle against return and is used as the symbol of deterrence.[31]

In *Their Eyes Were Watching God*, Hurston twice activates this folk tale, once for comic and once for catastrophic effect. There is an extended section in chapter 6 on "mule-talk," people standing around mocking a scrawny mule and making up stories about it. Joe purchases this mule because of an off-handed remark by Janie. After the mule dies, there is an elaborate and grotesquely humorous scene of a funeral oration where the speakers use the mule's distended belly as a rostra. During Sam Watson's portion of the lament, he "spoke of the joys of mule-heaven to which the dear brother had departed this valley of sorrow; the mule-angels flying around. . . . Up there, mule-angels would have people to ride on" (*Eyes*, 61). As John Lowe notes, this is a "parody" of the Flying African.[32]

But at the climax of the novel, we see a horrifying riff on the folk tale. In the midst of the hurricane, when Lake Okechobee has broken out of the levees (a scene I discuss at length later), Janie references the story directly (*Eyes*, 162):

> "De lake is comin'!" Tea Cake gasped.
> "De Lake!" In amazed horror from Motor Boat, "De Lake!"
> "It's comin' behind us!" Janie shuddered. "Us can't fly."

Janie may say they cannot fly, but in a moment of terrifying irony, she is made to fly. When Tea Cake has to lie down for a second to rest, Janie wants to comfort him and spots a piece of tarpaper. She greets it with joy and grabs it (*Eyes*, 165):

> Immediately the wind lifted both of them and she saw herself sailing off the fill to the right, out and out over the lashing water. She screamed terribly and released the roofing which sailed away as she plunged downward into the water.

The separation of self from experience, "she saw herself sailing," is a moment of seeing herself as a character in a story. But unlike the enslaved Africans who escape across the ocean, her flight is not one of freedom but of fright and ultimately destruction. She lands in the water, and Tea Cake comes to rescue her and confronts the dog whose rabies will lead to his death.

With these two riffs on the myth of the "Flying African," Hurston suggests that she is aware of paradigms but that their idealized form is not available to her characters, perhaps especially to the mixed-race heroine, Janie.

Haitian Vodoun

The influence of Haitian Vodoun on *Their Eyes Were Watching God* has recently been reinvigorated.[33] Hurston wrote *Their Eyes Were Watching God* while in Haiti performing anthropological research, the results of which she published a year after the novel in *Tell My Horse: Voodoo and Life in Haiti and Jamaica*. Hurston's instinct to use whatever she already knows as a frame of reference for new encounters can be seen when she writes in that book, "[i]t is unfortunate for the social sciences that an intelligent man like Dr. Dorsainville has not seen fit to do something with Haitian mysticism comparable to Frazer's *The Golden Bough*."[34] Frazer's famous work of comparative mythology takes its title from *Aeneid* 6. One example of Haitian mysticism is the role of Legba, whose role Mawuena Logan has discussed. Legba, a trickster god, is also associated with birth and death in *Their Eyes Were Watching God* at the moment of Joe's death: "The Little Emperor of the cross-roads was leaving Orange County as he had come—with the out-stretched hand of power" (*Eyes*, 88). Logan identifies the Little Emperor as Legba and suggests that "Joe's death allows the reader to understand the challenges, benefits, and social responsibilities that come with being the first black mayor of an all-black town, and above all, the necessity of balance that Legba embodies."[35] Studies such as this highlight "Hurston's integration of folklore and fiction."[36]

Hurston's *Aeneid*

Given Hurston's extensive classical education, one might expect it to penetrate her novels just as her studies in folklore, but there are few, if any, overt references in her works, and none in *Their Eyes Were Watching God.* But having established Hurston's uncanny ability to mark specific allusions and references, I want to spend the second half of this chapter exploring the ways in which she draws inspiration from Vergil's *Aeneid* in order to rewrite and challenge, to criticize and subvert, a poem that can be read as celebrating White patriarchal imperialistic values and knowledge. By looking at a few key scenes, I will argue that Hurston reimagines the love story of Dido and Aeneas in that of Janie and Tea Cake, such that the wealthy established woman is not abandoned by the charismatic visiting male. However, while she allows Janie-as-Dido sexual happiness, Tea Cake's Aeneas-like dedication to his mission (capitalism and adherence to a White ruling class) causes his destruction. Hurston thus can modify the *Aeneid*'s love story while resisting an interpretation of classical literature as being superior to any other form of knowledge.

Studies of Zora Neale Hurston's engagement with mythology tend to look at established patterns and archetypes.[37] My study aims to highlight the more specific literary precedents Hurston uses from antiquity. But I want to underscore what I am *not* doing: I am not saying that these models are more important than any other; I am not saying that we miss the point of Hurston's novel if we don't recognize them. I *am* attempting to add to—and in no way diminish—the marvelous layers of the novel. In fact, that is a fundamental takeaway from the novel, evident in the case of Tea Cake: privileging White expertise simply because it is White is dangerous, often deadly, and always incredibly stupid.

Their Eyes Were Watching God opens with a three-paragraph evocation of the horizon before establishing a frame narrative in which Janie returns home after burying Tea Cake. The majority of the book, however, consists of her *telling her own story* to the attentive listener, Pheoby, and, by means of narrative overhearing, the reader. We hear of her childhood, teenage marriage to the much older Logan Killicks, and how she runs off with the debonair and ambitious Jodie (Joe) Starks. Their life together, the rise of Eatonville, and Jodie's death form the core of the middle portion of the novel. Janie's relationship with Tea Cake (her third lover), their passion and happiness working in the Everglades on the Muck, a hurricane, and his death form the last third.

I want to begin by suggesting that Janie telling her own story sets off what will be a series of references to the epic tradition, particularly Odysseus telling his own adventures in *Odyssey* 9–12 and Aeneas telling his in *Aeneid* 2–3.[38] In a letter to Lewis Gannet in 1934, responding to his review of *Jonah's Gourd Vine*, Hurston expresses her enthusiasm at having her novel taken seriously. She talks about the importance of the oral tradition of Black Southern preachers:

> Our preachers are talented men even though many of them are barely literate . . . the truth is, the greatest poets among us are in our pulpits and the greatest poetry has come out of them. It is merely not set down. *It passes from mouth to mouth as in the days of Homer*.[39]

Here Hurston creates a lineage that extends from Homer to the preachers she knows. We see, then, the ease with which Hurston can access the ancient world and how she sees it as part of her own, while again melding together Greco-Roman and Biblical texts.

Janie tells her own story so that it can be passed from mouth to mouth. Pheoby wants her to tell the town what happened down on the Muck, but Janie replies, "Ah don't mean to bother wid 'tellin 'em nothin, Pheoby. 'Tain't worth de trouble. You can tell 'em what Ah say if you wants to. Dat's just de same as me 'cause mah tongue is in mah friend's mouf" (*Eyes*, 6). This is a philosophy of oral transmission, and one that is particularly suited to Vergil. After all, the *Aeneid* is sung (*cano*, *Aen.* 1.1). Given the odd spelling of Pheoby's name and her role at the beginning of the poem as a figure closely associated with creativity (Janie telling her story), we might see her as a Phoebus Apollo-like figure of poetry.

A basic building block of epic poetry is the proem, the call to a muse for help and the fronting of subject matter. The Muses were the daughters of memory (Mnemosyne); hence the poet calls upon their aid. Hurston also opens with memory (*Eyes*, 1):

> Ships at a distance have every man's wish on board. For some they come in with the tide. For others they sail forever on the horizon, never out of sight, never landing until the Watcher turns his eyes away in resignation, his dreams mocked to death by Time. That is the life of men.
>
> Now, women forget all those things they don't want to remember, and remember everything they don't want to forget. The dream is the truth. Then they act and do things accordingly.
>
> So the beginning of this was a woman and she had come back from burying the dead. Not the dead of sick and ailing with friends at the pillow and the

> feet. She had come back from the sodden and the bloated; the sudden dead, their eyes flung wide open in judgment.

Where the men find themselves helpless and mocked by Time, women are in control of Memory; they "remember everything." They know the truth that men do not: "The dream is the truth," which leads them to action. The first major action we see is Janie's decision to tell her own story. From the start of the novel, speech itself is an action.

Turning now to the *Aeneid*, Janie is both the Aeneas figure (in that she tells her story) and Dido (the lover). Yet Hurston has Janie modify the paradigm. Aeneas' journey is always onward, but Janie returns home. Aeneas abandoned Dido to pursue his divine mandate, but Tea Cake repeatedly emphasizes that he only ever wants Janie by his side. Ultimately, we will see how Hurston's novel is a rewriting of the *Aeneid*'s paradigm. Aeneas is always ensured a successful outcome because of divine prophecy. For Tea Cake, however, his trust in the knowledge of his White employers, simply because they are White, leads directly to his death. In this way, Hurston points to her personal philosophy of what the African American novel can accomplish, all while anticipating and rejecting the reactions of her male critics, most prominently Richard Wright, who claim that her work lacks depth.[40] Wright charges Hurston with a form of minstrelsy, missing Hurston's critique of that very thing. He writes, "Miss Hurston *voluntarily* continues in her novel the tradition which was *forced* upon the Negro in the theater, that is, the minstrel technique that makes the 'white folks' laugh."[41] In my reading, the death of Tea Cake reflects the dangers of following any tradition dictated by "white folks."

Having suggested a few touchstones with the epic tradition, I turn to my three specific references to the *Aeneid*, all of which are triggered at the moment of Joe's death. As Joe is dying, Hurston explains, "People who would not have dared to foot the place before crept in and did not come to the house. Just squatted under the trees and waited. Rumor, that wingless bird, had shadowed over the town" (*Eyes*, 84). There is no reason to call Rumor wingless unless you are already aware of the representation of Rumor as a winged monster, a representation that comes directly from Vergil in describing rumors of Dido's relationship with Aeneas (4.180–1). Hurston's negation of "wingless" seems almost to speak directly to Vergil, asserting her own authority over Vergil's. At the very least, she has a *different* Rumor. On the strongest interpretation, she has more authority over describing rumor than her predecessor.

Immediately after Joe's death, Tea Cake comes to town. Hurston gives us his real name only twice: first when he arrives in the story, and then when his story is over. This bookending highlights the importance, and rarity, of his name, which we learn in the following exchange (*Eyes*, 97):

> "Now ain't you somethin'! Mr. er—er—You never did tell me whut yo' name wuz."
>
> "Ah sho didn't. Wuzn't expectin' fuh it to be needed. De name mah mama gimme is Vergible Woods. Dey calls me Tea Cake for short."

> "Tea Cake! So you sweet as all dat?" She laughed and he gave her a little cut-eye look to get her meaning.

Janie immediately asks about the stranger's nickname, and we are off and rushing so quickly into a love story that we are liable to forget his real name. But a double echo of Vergil and "veritable" reveals part of Hurston's combinatory prowess.[42] His entrance, if one spots the reference to Vergil, also acts as an invitation to see Hurston's version of Dido and Aeneas begin. Hurston further invites the reader to look more closely at the polyvalence of this moment when we see Vergible give Janie "a little cut-eye to get her meaning." Hurston has signaled that she is working with multiple levels of interpretation, and we readers need to look cut-eye at the novel to get her meaning.

Broad narrative swathes remain the same. Both Dido and Janie are established powerful figures in their communities who escaped their origins. Dido negotiated Carthage's rise from a barren plot of land; Janie and Jody moved to Eatonville, where Jody built the town, and more importantly the general store, that Janie (as Lady Mayor Starks) inherited. A man comes into both women's worlds, and both initially attempt to resist their desires. The love these couples have fuels jealousy and tirades of impropriety from those around them. However, here Hurston makes the biggest change. For where Mercury comes to get Aeneas ultimately to abandon Dido to her death in pursuit of his duty, Tea Cake and Janie journey off to a new land together, a decision that lets Hurston begin her critique of the literary precedent.

When Dido resists the allure of Aeneas, she confides in her sister, Anna. I use Dryden's translation simply because it was the most popular throughout the early 20th century in America.[43] Visions of Aeneas "Disturb my quiet, and distract my breast" and she sees him as "A man descended from the gods" (Dryden, *Aeneid* 4.13, 16). Compare Janie's resistance to falling for Tea Cake (*Eyes*, 106):

> All next day in the house and store she thought resisting thoughts about Tea Cake. She even ridiculed him in her mind and was a little ashamed of the association. But every hour or two the battle had to be fought all over again. She couldn't make him look just like any other man to her. He looked like the love thoughts of women. He could be a bee to a blossom—a pear tree blossom in the spring. He seemed to be crushing scent out of the world with his footsteps. Crushing aromatic herbs with every step he took. Spices hung about him. He was a glance from God.

We find here several echoes. The distraction from a stranger, the attempt to resist attraction, and especially the focus on excellence. Tea Cake's divine lineage, "a glance from God," elevates him beyond just another suitor or vagabond. Hurston furthers his divine connections by turning him into some kind of god of Spring.

After this fragile connection at the future lovers' first meeting, Hurston accesses a more direct Vergilian response. In the *Aeneid*, multi-eyed and winged Rumor carries word to the neighboring king, Iarbas, that Dido is infatuated with Aeneas (4.173–197).

Hurston builds on her denial that Rumor has wings by making it explicit that it is the people who are monstrous for looking with Rumor's eyes upon Janie's life. The opening paragraph to chapter 12 combines Iarbas' anger with Dido's neglect of the city along with Aeneas' newfound interest in urban infrastructure (*Eyes*, 110):

> It was after the picnic that the town began to notice things and got mad. Tea Cake and Mrs. Mayor Starks! All the men that she could get, and fooling with somebody like Tea Cake! Another thing, Joe Starks hadn't been dead but nine months and here she goes sashaying off to a picnic in pink linen. Done quit attending church, like she used to. Gone off to Sanford in a car with Tea Cake and her all dressed in blue! It was a shame. Done took to high heel slippers and a ten dollar hat! Looking like some young girl, always in blue because Tea Cake told her to wear it. Poor Joe Starks. Bet he turns over in his grave every day. Tea Cake and Janie gone hunting. Tea Cake and Janie gone fishing. Tea Cake and Janie gone to Orlando to the movies. Tea Cake and Janie gone to a dance. Tea Cake making flower beds in Janie's yard and seeding the garden for her. Chopping down that tree she never did like by the dining room window. All those signs of possession. Tea Cake in a borrowed car teaching Janie to drive. Tea Cake and Janie playing checkers; playing coon-can; playing Florida flip on the store porch all afternoon as if nobody else was there. Day after day and week after week.

The first element in the paratactic catalogue of Tea Cake and Janie's activities is "gone hunting," which resonates with Dido and Aeneas consummating their relationship after a storm interrupted their hunt (*Aen.* 4.160–172). Further, Tea Cake's help in the garden shows a control over shaping the land that we also see in Aeneas when Mercury arrives to command him to go to Italy: "Arriving there [in Carthage], he found the Trojan prince / New ramparts raising for the town's defence" (Dryden, *Aen.* 4.382–3). Lastly, Dido's neglect of the city and its people for her newly arrived outsider lover mimics the way in which Janie neglects the store, which under Jodie had been the hub of the city.

The town's rising anger parallels Iarbas' fury: "He, when he heard a fugitive could move / The Tyrian princess, who disdain'd his love, / His breast with fury burn'd, his eyes with fire, / Mad with despair, impatient with desire" (Dryden, *Aen.* 4.294–7). The town's contempt for Tea Cake, represented by the constant repetition of his name, is matched by Iarbas' comparison of Aeneas to "this other Paris" (Dryden, *Aen.* 4.314). The town's criticism that Janie has stopped attending church and was dressing in blue and dancing and driving carries the judgmental tone heard when Rumor spreads word of Dido's actions (Dryden, *Aen.* 4.274–81):

> She fills the people's ears with Dido's name,
> Who, lost to honor and the sense of shame,
> Admits into her throne and nuptial bed
> A wand'ring guest, who from his country fled:
> Whole days with him she passes in delights,
> And wastes in luxury long winter nights,

Forgetful of her fame and royal trust,
Dissolv'd in ease, abandon'd to her lust.

Janie's throne is the Eatonville general store. Where Janie should be operating the central business hub of the city that she inherits from her dead husband, she is instead playing on the porch with a wanderer. However, where the action of the *Aeneid* is spurred by Juno's divine and Iarbas' mortal anger, Hurston celebrates Janie and Tea Cake taking on pleasant gardening tasks. Theirs is an epic of domestic love.

Unlike Dido and Aeneas, Tea Cake and Janie are allowed to love, which is a radical act of redirecting the violence of the epic imperative and is one of Hurston's strategies of liberation from the weight of an epic tradition. Janie summarizes this feeling when she tells Pheoby (inside the embedded story), "So in the beginnin' new thoughts had tuh be thought and new words said" (*Eyes*, 115). This statement articulates a separation from other literary traditions and anticipates criticism of the novel. However, in a lovely Hurstonian irony that undermines this very sentiment, she is quoting herself. Twice before Janie had the same feeling. When she ran off from her first husband with Jody: "Her old thoughts were going to come in handy now, but new words would have to be made and said to fit them" (*Eyes*, 32). But after Jody beats her and she becomes disillusioned with her erotic fantasy of marriage and they move into separate bedrooms, "the stillness was the sleep of swords. So new thoughts had to be thought and new words said" (*Eyes*, 81). By adding "So in the beginnin'" to this third repetition of the sentiment, Janie recalls the third paragraph of the opening of the novel. This new beginning, though, structurally operates similarly to the *Aeneid*'s "proem in the middle" (*Aen.* 7.37–45) where the poet appeals to the muse Erato to help him through the second half of his poem.[44] But where Erato (a muse more commonly associated with love rather than war) is unexpected before the long battle of books 7–12, Hurston's appeal to erotic regeneration sends Janie and Tea Cake off together into a new land to make their way.

The climax of *Their Eyes Were Watching God* comes when the hurricane arrives in the breathless Chapter 18, and Hurston activates an allusion to Furor bound from Book 1 of the *Aeneid*. In the midst of a massive storm summoned by Juno that has Aeneas and his men at a nadir of despair, Venus goes to Jupiter to plead for intercession. Jupiter's imperialistic response (*imperium sine fine*: "empire without end," *Aen.* 1.279) culminates with the following description (Dryden, *Aeneid* 1.402–7):

Janus himself before his fane shall wait,
And keep the dreadful issues of his gate,
With bolts and iron bars: within remains
Imprison'd Fury, bound in brazen chains;
High on a trophy rais'd, of useless arms,
He sits, and threats the world with vain alarms.

The allusion here is to the gates of the temple of Janus that were opened during war and closed in times of peace.[45] We see Fury in its chains as a grotesque monster but one whose presence and threat is constrained. Two thousand years after Vergil made Jupiter speak his prophecy, Hurston breaks the bonds. She summons forth various references to add force to her storm: "By morning Gabriel was playing the deep tones in the center of the drum. So when Janie looked out of her door she saw the drifting mists gathered in the west—that cloud field of the sky—to arm themselves with thunder and march forth against the world" (158). Biblical apocalypse (Gabriel) has joined the personified nature armed with thunder. We witness a nascent Titanomachia (*Eyes*, 159):

> It woke up old Okechobee and the monster began to roll in his bed. Began to roll and complain like a peevish world on a grumble. The folks in the quarters and the people in the big houses further around the shore heard the big lake and wondered. The people felt uncomfortable but safe because there were the seawalls to chain the senseless monster in his bed.

The personification of destruction in the form of a senseless monster chained by seawalls to his bed is a strong recollection of Vergil's Furor. We also see, though, a critique. For Rome will always be at war; its *performance* of peace with the gates of Janus is visual rhetoric. Similarly, the people's trust in both the seawalls and the behavior of local White people will lead to their death. Only a few pages later, the dikes fail (*Eyes*, 161):

> Ten feet higher and as far as they could see the muttering wall advanced before the braced-up waters like a road crusher on a cosmic scale. The monstropolous beast had left his bed. The two hundred miles an hour wind had loosed his chains. He seized hold of his dikes and ran forward until he met the quarters; uprooted them like grass and rushed on after his supposed-to-be conquerors, rolling the dikes, rolling the houses, rolling the people in the houses along with other timbers. The sea was walking the earth with a heavy heel.

Beautifully, the "rolling" anaphora accumulates across the sentence as the clauses get longer. Hurston has strikingly conflated two different scenes from *Aeneid* 1, the aforementioned Roman *furor* and opening seastorm, a conflation mimicked in calling the storm "monstropolous," which combines monster and the Modern-Greek suffix "-*opolous*," descendent of. Hurston's storm also follows the pattern of Vergil's, starting with the winds whipping across the land to hit the water. Vergil's storm also rolls (Dryden, *Aeneid* 1.122–34):

> The raging winds rush through the hollow wound,
> And dance aloft in air, and skim along the ground;
> Then, settling on the sea, the surges sweep,
> Raise liquid mountains, and disclose the deep.
> South, East, and West, with mixed confusion roar,
> And roll the foaming billows to the shore.

Hurston's tempestuous engagement with one of the most imperialistically charged passages in the *Aeneid* gains force as a critique for the imperial thrust of that poem.

Although she rewrites *Aeneid* 4 in favor of Janie and Tea Cake, they still don't make the right choices once they have moved to a new land. In particular, Tea Cake and the other Black laborers on the muck refuse to acknowledge Indigenous knowledge in the area. Before the storm arrives, the local Seminoles start leaving. In response to a query about where they are going, they simply answer: "Going to high ground. Saw-grass bloom. Hurricane coming" (*Eyes*, 154). The answer is deceptively simple. In the first sentence, they answer the question. In the second, they make an observation about nature, and in the third, they interpret that observation. Hurston subtly highlights the power of Indigenous knowledge, and she gives her characters plenty of time to listen. But they are caught in the thrall of White capitalism, as the narrator summarizes, ventriloquizing the attitude of the Black workers (*Eyes*, 155):

> The next day, more Indians moved east, unhurried but steady. Still a blue sky and fair weather. Beans running fine and prices good, so the Indians could be, *must* be, wrong. You couldn't have a hurricane when you're making seven and eight dollars a day picking beans. Indians are dumb anyhow, always were.

Next, the local Bahamans stop by to tell Tea Cake to get out. They have observed that the crows have left. But in full arrogant ignorance, Tea Cake throws them off, saying, "Dat ain't nothin'. You ain't seen de bossman go up" (156). Tea Cake's faith in the White landowners will kill him just as much as the rabid dog that bites him. This seems to be Hurston's critique of the epic tradition. Hurston can rewrite part of *Aeneid* 4 to make sure that the Dido figure, Janie, survives, but Janie cannot overcome patriarchal attitudes and cultural chauvinism. In Hurston's sharpest critique, Tea Cake ventriloquizes White people's arguments against Black intellectual ability when he attacks Indigenous knowledge (*Eyes*, 156):

> "Dey don't always know. Indians don't know much uh nothin', tuh tell de truth. Else dey'd own dis country still. De white folks ain't gone nowhere. Dey oughta know if it's dangerous. You better stay heah, man. Big jumpin' dance tuhnight right heah, when it fair off."

Tea Cake's speech represents the same kind of racializing thinking that underlies Calhoun and Arnold's dismissals of Black intellectual ability, as well as Wright's critique of Hurston's novel and the attitudes of the White women who visited Hurston's elementary school.[46] Hurston recognizes the harm of this type of thinking, and however much one might be charmed by Tea Cake because of Janie's love for him, he is punished for this kind of thinking. The hurricane, representing racialized thinking, breaks the chains holding it back, unleashes havoc, and leads to his death.

Final lines

Throughout this chapter, I have attempted to show that Zora Neale Hurston reinscribes key moments of Vergil's *Aeneid*, especially around the relationship of Dido and Aeneas, in order to explore the boundaries of epic paradigms for a Black heroine. I want to conclude by looking at the final sentence in *Their Eyes Were*

Watching God, since it acts as the keynote to my argument that she is shifting the *Aeneid*'s focus.

The *Aeneid* ends with a famous contradiction. Aeneas, who was supposed to avoid fury, sees Turnus wearing the sword belt of the dead Pallas and, instead of performing *clementia*, strikes him down (*Aen.* 12.950–2, my translation):

> *hoc dicens ferrum adverso sub pectore condit*
> *fervidus; ast illi solvuntur frigore membra*
> *vitaque cum gemitu fugit indignata sub umbras.*
>
> Having said this, burning, Aeneas buries his sword in the upturned chest. Cold releases Turnus' limbs and his reproachful life flees with a groan beneath the shadows.

Or, as Dryden put it: "And the disdainful soul came rushing thro' the wound." Dryden's translation of *vita* as "soul" is important because of the final line of Hurston's novel. At this point, Janie has concluded her story, and the narrator has taken over (*Eyes*, 193):

> He [Tea Cake] could never be dead until she herself had finished feeling and thinking. The kiss of his memory made pictures of love and light against the wall. Here was peace. She pulled in her horizon like a great fish-net. Pulled it from around the waist of the world and draped it over her shoulder. So much of life in its meshes! She called in her soul to come and see.

Whereas the *Aeneid* ends with an indignant soul fleeing a dying man, Hurston's novel concludes with Janie drawing the world into her: her soul returns rather than vanishes. She has emerged from her epic with a sense that she is a deliberate product of her experiences. Her final verb "see" contrasts completely with Vergil's shadows and looks with a positive light into the future.

Notes

1 I am grateful to my colleague Dr. Joshua Walker for first suggesting I write about Hurston and Vergil, to Dr. Alex Lessie for being a generous first reader, to the audience at the Bard Early Colleges Dean Hour for their questions, and to Dr. Hannah Čulík-Baird and Bet Hucks for their interest in the project. Thank you as well to the editors, Drs. Rigoni and O'Neill, for making contributing to this volume a pleasure. I dedicate this piece to all my Year One Seminar students.
2 Hurston 1942: 131.
3 Hurston 1942: 131.
4 Michele Ronnick coined the phrase *Classica Africana* for studying African American engagement with the classical world. For a discussion of its utility as a phrase, see Walters 2007: 1–5; Rankine 2006: ch. 1.
5 Kaplan 2002: 533–4.
6 Hurston 1942: 34.
7 For further analysis, see Valkeakari 2005: 198–9. Hayes 1994 and Pondrom 1986 note references to the Persephone myth in Hurston's works. Neither mention that Hurston cites the myth again in a letter to Charlotte Osgood Mason (Kaplan 2002: 188).

8 Hurston 1942: 37.
9 Hurston 1942: 38.
10 For instance, Matthew Arnold's surprise that Mary Church Terrell was able to sight-read and translate Greek (Hairston 2013: 9–10) and John C. Calhoun's better known statement (reported by Alexander Crummle): "That if he could find a Negro who knew the Greek syntax, he would then believe that the Negro was a human being and should be treated as a man" (Ronnick 2005: 342, fn. 29). See also Walters 2007: 6–7.
11 Hurston 1942: 39. Hurston returns to the Herculean *exemplum* in a1938 letter to Jane Belo (Kaplan 2002: 416–7).
12 Boyd 2003 elegantly reconstructs Hurston's education.
13 Boyd 2003: 75. Hurston's date of birth is inconsistently given because she herself provided several different dates. "Hurston never reveals her birth date in the autobiography, perhaps because she had misstated her age for most of her adult life, often citing 1901 as the year of her birth instead of the 1891 date recorded in census records" (West 2005: 171).
14 Hurston 1942: 123.
15 Hurston 1942: 137.
16 Barnard Center for Research on Women 2005.
17 See Boyd 2003: ch. 17. Rankine has noted the similarity of folklore, including African American folklore, and classical mythology (Rankine 2006: 110).
18 Authors have suggested such engagement without developing any examples. See, for example, Hairston 2013: 197. Hurston's name has been largely left out of conversations dominated by Ralph Ellison and Countee Cullen. See Rankine 2006. Interestingly, both Hurston and Theodore Browne wrote adaptations of Aristophanes' *Lysistrata* in the 1930s. Hurston does not mention the project, and the text does not survive. See Hill 2015; Dué 2016: 40, 52–3.
19 Hurston's skill with complex allusions is most notably discussed in Gates Jr. 2014, where Hurston's work is used to demonstrate the intertextual technique of "signifyin(g)." This chapter thus adds to the evidence of Hurston as a master of sophisticated allusion.
20 Collected in Hurston 2020: 19–40. The story's typescript contains the address of the barbershop where Hurston worked as a manicurist and with which I opened this chapter, thus dating it to when she was reading Greek regularly (Hurston 2020: xxvi).
21 Hurston 2020: 19–20. I suspect "Cicero Omega Butts" is a joke about Hurston's own Professor Lightfoot (one of the earliest African-American professors of Latin) at Howard (Ronnick 2010: 386). In her memoir, she relates that she enjoyed gently (and sometimes not-so-gently) mocking her teachers with name changes (Hurston 1942: 128).
22 Hurston 2020: 26.
23 Hurston 2020: 199.
24 Hurston 2020: 199.
25 For one of the few extended discussions of this text, see Plant 2007: ch. 5.
26 Hurston 2011: 122.
27 Tracey Walters observes that when African American writers engage with myth, the result is "a syncretism where the individual myth is deconstructed and becomes unrecognizable as it is recreated into a new narrative" (Walters 2007: 12).
28 Gates Jr. 2014.
29 Ronnick 2010: 390.
30 I want to thank Bet Hucks for her lecture on the "Flying African" and Afrofuturism that helped me think through this section. See also Lavender 2016.
31 McDaniel 1990: 29–30.
32 Lowe 1997: 172.
33 See Jennings 2013, which builds on earlier research such as Southerland 1979; Lamothe 1999.
34 Hurston 1938: 131.

35 Logan 2013: 181.
36 Lamothe 1999: 157.
37 Pondrom 1986; Kubitschek 1983.
38 In asserting a classical engagement, I am conscious of Patrice Rankine's comment that

> [w]ithin the context of twentieth-century aesthetics in African American influence, any claim of classical influence on black authors is noteworthy. At the same time, appropriation of the classics by African American writers, despite opposing cultural forces, is a natural result of personal culture that includes a broader literacy as well as an idiomatic local experience.
>
> (Rankine 2006: 18)

39 Kaplan 2002: 304. Emphasis mine. Hurston would surely have learned about oral poetics and the Homeric question in her Greek courses if not in general conversation. Her Barnard transcript referenced earlier reports that she read Xenophon and Homer in the Greek courses that transferred. The course description for Greek 4 as it appears in the Howard University catalogue reads: "Homer's *Iliad*. The reading of six books, with a study of the Homeric Question, the Civilization of the Heroic Age, and the influence of the Homeric Poems. Scansion" (Howard University 2021). Early in her friendship with Langston Hughes, she compared him to Homer (Kaplan 2002: 131).
40 Wright writes, "The sensory sweep of her novel [*Their Eyes Were Watching God*] carries no theme, no message, no thought. In the main, her novel is not addressed to the Negro, but to a white audience whose chauvinistic tastes she knows how to satisfy. She exploits the phase of Negro life which is 'quaint,' the phase which evokes a piteous smile on the lips of the 'superior' race" (quoted in Gates Jr. and Appiah 1993: 17). June Jordan later critiqued Wright for creating a false binary between African American writers (Jordan 1974). See also West 2005: ch. 3.
41 Wright as quoted in Gates and Appiah 1993: 17.
42 For another reading of Vergible's name, see Gates Jr. 2014: 206.
43 Winterer 2010: 367. While at Howard, Hurston took a fair amount of Latin, as we saw in her transcript. The Howard Catalogue at that time reveals the popularity of the first six books of the *Aeneid*, as they are included in the basic entry requirements (Howard University 2021: 59). Further, her studies in English would have exposed her to the requirements for "Classics in Translation," which recommended, "The *Odyssey* and the *Aeneid* should be read in English translations of recognized literary excellence," of which Dryden's is certainly one (Howard University 2021: 56).
44 For "proems in the middle" see Conte 1992.
45 In *Res Gestae* 13, Augustus claims that the Senate voted to close the door three times during his reign.
46 See *supra* note 37.

References

Barnard Center for Research on Women. 2005. "Documents on Zora Neale Hurston from the Barnard College Archives: Zora Neale Hurston's Transcript from Barnard College (1928)." *The Scholar and Feminist Online*. http://sfonline.barnard.edu/hurston/bcarchives/ZNH_transcript.pdf.

Boyd, V. 2003. *Wrapped in Rainbows: The Life of Zora Neale Hurston*. New York: Scribner.

Conte, G.B. 1992. "Proems in the Middle." *Yale Classical Studies* 29: 147–59.

Dué, C. 2016. "Get in Formation, This is an Emergency: The Politics of Choral Song and Dance in Aristophanes' *Lysistrata* and Spike Lee's *Chi-raq*." *Arion* 24, 1: 21–54.

Gates Jr., H.L. 2014. *The Signifying Monkey: A Theory of African American Literary Criticism (25th Anniversary Edition)*. Oxford: Oxford University Press.

Gates Jr., H.L., and Appiah, K., eds. 1993. *Zora Neale Hurston: Critical Perspectives Past and Present*. New York: Amistad.

Hairston, E.A. 2013. *The Ebony Column: Classics, Civilization, and the African American Reclamation of the West*. Knoxville, TN: University of Tennessee Press.

Hayes, E.T. 1994. "'Like Seeing You Buried': Persephone in the *Bluest Eye, Their Eyes Were Watching God, and the Color Purple*." In E.T. Hayes (ed.) *Images of Persephone: Feminist Readings in Western Literature*. Gainesville, FL: University Press of Florida. 170–94.

Hill, L. 2015. "A New Stage of Laughter for Zora Neale Hurston and Theodore Browne: Lysistrata and the Negro Units of the Federal Theatre Project." In K. Bosher, F. Macintosh, J. McConnell, and P. Rankine (eds.) *The Oxford Handbook of Greek Drama in the Americas*. Oxford: Oxford University Press. 286–300.

Howard University. 2021. *Howard University Record: 1919–1920*. https://hustorage.wrlc.org/disk1/2021 catalog flipping books/1919-20/mobile/.

Hurston, Z.N. 1938. *Tell My Horse: Voodoo and Life in Haiti and Jamaica*. New York: Amistad.

———. 1942. *Dust on the Tracks*. New York: Harper Perennial Modern Classics.

———. 2011. "Herod the Great." *Callaloo* 34, 1: 121–5.

———. 2020. *Hitting a Straight Lick with a Crooked Stick: Stories*. Edited by G. West. New York: Amistad.

Jennings, L.V.D., ed. 2013. *Zora Neale Hurston, Haiti, and Their Eyes Were Watching God*. Evanston, IL: Northwestern University Press.

Jordan, J. 1974. "Notes Toward a Black Balancing of Love and Hatred." In C. Keller and J.H. Levi (eds.) *We're On: A June Jordan Reader*. Farmington, ME: Alice James Books. 189–93.

Kaplan, C. 2002. *Zora Neale Hurston: A Life in Letters*. New York: Doubleday.

Kubitschek, M.D. 1983. "'Tuh De Horizon and Back': The Female Quest in Their Eyes Were Watching God." *Black American Literature* 17, 3: 109–15.

Lamothe, D. 1999. "Vodou Imagery, African-American Tradition and Cultural Transformation in Zora Neale Hurston's 'Their Eyes Were Watching God'." *Callaloo* 22, 1: 157–75.

Lavender, I.I. 2016. "An Afrofuturist Reading of Zora Neale Hurston's Their Eyes Were Watching God." *LIT: Literature Interpretation Theory* 27, 3: 213–33.

Logan, M. 2013. "'Legba in the House:' African Cosmology in *Their Eyes Were Watching God*." In L.V.D. Jennings (ed.) *Zora Neale Hurston, Haiti, and Their Eyes Were Watching God*. Evanston, IL: Northwestern University Press. 175–90.

Lowe, J. 1997. *Jump at the Sun: Zora Neale Hurston's Cosmic Comedy*. Urbana and Chicago: University of Illinois Press.

McDaniel, L. 1990. "The Flying Africans: Extent and Strength of the Myth in the Americas." *Nieuwe West-Indische Gids/New West Indian Guide* 64, 1/2: 28–40.

Plant, D.G. 2007. *Zora Neale Hurston: A Biography of the Spirit*. Westport, CN: Praeger.

Pondrom, C.N. 1986. "The Role of Myth in Hurston's Their Eyes Were Watching God." *American Literature* 58, 2 (May): 181–202.

Rankine, P. 2006. *Ulysses in Black: Ralph Ellison, Classicism, and African American Literature*. Madison, WI: University of Wisconsin Press.

Ronnick, M.V. 2005. *The Autobiography of William Sanders Scarborough*. Detroit: Wayne State University Press.

———. 2010. "Vergil in the Black American Experience." In J. Farrell and M.C.J. Putnam (eds.) *A Companion to Vergil's Aeneid and Its Tradition*. Malden, MA: Wiley-Blackwell. 376–90.

Southerland, E. 1979. "The Influence of Voodoo on the Fiction of Zora Neale Hurston." In R.P. Bell, B.J. Parker, and B. Guy-Sheftall (eds.) *Sturdy Black Bridges: Visions of Black Women in Literature*. New York: Anchor Books. 172–83.

Valkeakari, T. 2005. "'Luxuriat[ing] in Milton's Syllables': Writer as Reader in Zora Neale Hurston's Dust Tracks on a Road." In J. Badia and J. Phegley (eds.) *Reading Women: Literary Figures and Cultural Icons from the Victorian Age to the Present*. Toronto: University of Toronto Press. 192–214.

Walters, T. 2007. *African American Literature and the Classicist Tradition: Black Writers from Wheatley to Morrison*. New York: Palgrave Macmillan.

West, G. 2005. *Zora Neale Hurston & American Literary Culture*. Gainesville, FL: University Press of Florida.

Winterer, C. 2010. "Why Did American Women Read the *Aeneid*?" In J. Farrell and M.C.J. Putnam (eds.) *A Companion to Vergil's Aeneid and Its Tradition*. Malden, MA: Wiley-Blackwell. 366–75.

3 Yehuda Amichai's "The Times My Father Died" (1959)

A Jewish Aeneas in flight from the Holocaust[1]

Giacomo Loi

An unexpected preamble: a Jewish Aeneas in the days of the pandemic

The year 2020 will remain in the memory of this generation as the year of the pandemic. Within a few months, a vast number of people were infected and died. In Italy, by the end of April, nearly 28,000 people had died, many more thousands had been infected, hundreds had undergone intensive care. Through the mass media, Italians became familiar with terms, symptoms, numbers to be obsessively checked. Those numbers would advise for or against future plans or even change the day of those who were allowed to step outside their houses to go to work—while everyone else was confined at home. If all of this was new and tragically unexpected, 2020 has also been the year of an Italian revival of Aeneas, as several books of different kinds put the Trojan hero center stage;[2] more than through books, Aeneas irrupted in the public discourse on two occasions. In late March, anthropologist Laura Marchetti published a dense newspaper article entitled "La civiltà è Enea che porta Anchise sulle spalle" ("Civilization is Aeneas carrying Anchises on his shoulders"), which became an instant sensation for its shocking ethical call.[3] In response to the Italian president's address concerning the "decimation" of the elderly generation, Marchetti reflected on the crossroads at which Europe found itself, the choice between saving elderly or young lives, a choice that "carries the indelible trace of a judgment of quality on a life, as if a life—the stronger, the more able—were worthier to be preserved for this reason only."[4] She proposed *pietas* as a fundamental value of civilization:

> Civilization is founded . . . and is born when Aeneas, in flight from the fire, carries the old father with him on his shoulders and, by hand, the young son. The *pietas*, which is his existential and social quality, pushes him to help, to include everyone, to cure everyone, even in spite of his own survival, of his own power.[5]

In the fight for survival that saw younger lives take precedence over older lives, Marchetti illuminates Aeneas' courageously uncompromising ethical choice.

DOI: 10.4324/9781003176145-5

Marchetti's reading of Aeneas resurfaced later on. In line with the policy of gradual re-openings, schools were scheduled to reopen in June only for a few days to allow the administering of the State Exam, the examination that marks the end of grade school. Once known as the "Maturity Exam," the final oral segment of the examination has inspired books and movies and is one of the most recurring nightmares of Italian adults. While a great deal of concern centered around safety measures in schools, many wondered about the students' way home: would they become vectors of infection in their families?

Over the last 30 years, Jewish Holocaust survivor Liliana Segre has developed a special bond with Italian students, whom she considers, in a way, her "grandchildren."[6] Expelled from state schools in 1938 with the passage of the racial laws, imprisoned in Italy, and later deported to Auschwitz, Segre has crossed the country as a witness to the Italian Shoah. Decorated and honored throughout Europe, in 2018 she was nominated senator for life, the highest Italian political honor, and has since become the national voice against discrimination and hate crimes. She wrote a letter to the students about to take the exam, where she draws on her long-standing, familiar relationship with them:

> As you know, I consider indifference the most insidious evil of our times. I felt on my skin and on the skin of my loved ones the results of indifference. It works just like in that story about Mithridates, that ancient king who made himself immune to poison by drinking always bigger doses. Except that indifference, drop after drop, leaves us alive from without, but kills within. . . . The ethics of responsibility is that one that obliges us not to be indifferent.[7]

The reference is here to the *Binario 21* memorial of the Italian Holocaust, the track from which her convoy departed to Auschwitz, where a gray-cement wall bears the word "indifference" in capital letters. While reflecting on her experience as a young child whose right to go to school was suddenly denied because of her Jewishness, she weaves together references to authors, texts, and historical figures that the students should know from school, from Mithridates VI of Pontus to Defoe's *Robinson Crusoe* and John Donne, from Horace to the Italian Constitution. As she recalls her studies after her return from the death camps, she highlights their great value in contrast to the words of poet Giacomo Leopardi: "But that 'crazy and most desperate studying,' which Leopardi said to have 'ruined' him, was, instead, a balsam on my wounds. . . . My own personal reconstruction ran parallel to the reconstruction of the country."[8] In the final address, she sets a clear model for her "ethics for responsibility":

> I know that for your age it has been a heavy burden [to pass] such a long time away from your friends, from your loves, from your schoolmates, not being able to do cultivate your passions for sport and many other passions. *It is a sacrifice that you had to do, much more than for yourselves, for the segment of society that is more exposed to the epidemic: the sick, the elderly, your grandparents. I very much like to think of you all as Aeneas, who rescues*

> *his father Anchises from Troy by putting him onto his shoulders: an image of great civility*. This has been an important maturity exam. And you already passed cum laude.[9]

As a loving yet firm grandmother, Segre acknowledges the sacrifices of the young generation during the strict lockdown months. As she remarks on the imposition of the sacrifice, when state laws imposed the lockdown, she contrasts it with the present situation, where the students are to make use of their freedom. Echoing Marchetti, Segre identifies Aeneas as a model of "civilization" and of an "ethics of responsibility," a new understanding of his *pietas*. Aeneas' traditional image is understood as demonstrating the ethical duty to protect the older generation, symbolized by Anchises, to the point that Ascanius is missing. To be sure, many youngsters would rather identify with Ascanius, but this tragic time calls for them to mature quickly. In choosing Aeneas as a role model, Segre is again drawing near to the students, as she calls them to an ethical re-appreciation of a mythical hero whom they have certainly studied in school.

Furthermore, she reappropriates Vergil's hero. Even today, references to the Roman past of Italy are inescapably bound to Fascist Italy, which saw the *romanità* as a Fascist founding myth and Vergil's *parcere subiectis et debellare superbos* as the justification for imperialist projects.[10] However, Segre bypasses the genealogical concept of Aeneas as the forefather of Rome, thus brushing aside any exclusivist reading of Rome and Italy as special heirs of that heroic past. By reimagining Aeneas' *pietas* as a universal ethical value, she claims for herself, a Jewish Italian Holocaust survivor, the cultural imagination of Rome that Fascism had appropriated, the very regime that, in alliance with Nazi Germany, persecuted and enslaved her and destroyed the lives of many of her loved ones. She posits, as an ethical model, the forefather of Rome, of the ancient empire that dispersed the Jewish people around the world. Thus, the child who could not save her father, Alberto Segre, from dying in Auschwitz reclaims Aeneas from her oppressors as a heroic role model, perhaps the hero she would have liked to be in the days of the Holocaust.

In this chapter, I discuss another 'Jewish Aeneas,' that of Israeli writer Yehuda Amichai.[11] While Segre's call resonates loud and clear in the public sphere, Amichai's work apparently retains the tone of a private elegy in which Aeneas enters as an oblique shadow, unnoticed by commentators. After an outline of Amichai's "The Times My Father Died," I will explain the importance of Vergil's *Aeneid* to the work, with a particular focus on the significance of its last paragraph.

Yehuda Amichai's "The Times My Father Died"

> The memory of my father is wrapped in white paper
> like slices of bread for the workday.
>
> Like a magician pulling out rabbits and towers from his hat,
> he pulled out from his little body—love.
>
> The rivers of his hands
> poured into his good deeds.[12]

"The Times My Father Died" (in the original Hebrew *Mitot Avi*, literally "the deaths of my father") tells the many different 'deaths' of the narrator's father.[13] The short story was published in an Israeli literary journal in 1959 and became part of Amichai's only short story collection, *In This Terrible Wind*, which came out in early 1961.[14] All these stories revolve around a single narrator and his episodic experiences, mostly set in a puzzling, riddle-like context. The narrator "remains as enigmatic to the reader at the end as at the beginning, the only certainty being his derivation from selected facts of the author's own biography."[15] This particular story allows the reader to follow the narrator from his childhood days to his maturity. Indeed, the story can be divided into two parts, separated by an authorial typographical break, a little star at the center of the page. The first part recounts the numerous *metaphorical* deaths of the father during the narrator's childhood; the second part concentrates on the *actual* one, when the narrator is already grown up and married. The two parts also correspond to different geographical settings, with the first one set in Germany and the second in Israel. In total, seven 'deaths' are recounted, a number usually associated with plenitude in Jewish culture.

In the first part, each metaphor, as Robert Alter noted,

> begins to assume a life of its own, so that the imaginative action of the story is less the external events than the rapid movement from metaphor to metaphor, every figure of meaning constituting a little explosion of revealed possibilities of meaning.[16]

The narrator particularly emphasizes the first two deaths; one is noticeable for its intensity, the other for its duration in time. Indeed, the first of the metaphorical deaths happens during the ritual of Yom Kippur, the Day of Atonement in Jewish liturgy. The child is astounded at observing his father perform the rituals of repentance that characterize the liturgy and compares that moment to death:

> One Yom Kippur, my father stood in front of me in synagogue. I climbed up onto the seat to get a better view of him from behind. . . . When they got to the Alenu prayer, my father went down on his knees like all the other people and touched the floor with his forehead. . . . Then he came back to life again.[17]

The narrator recounts that his father "died many more times, and kept on dying from time-to-time. Sometimes I was there, sometimes he died alone."[18] The death on Yom Kippur is exemplary because the child is present to describe the event, and is also intense yet brief. The narrator also discusses his father's death before his own birth, in a wearing long-lasting death: "For four whole years my father died in the war. He dug a lot of trenches. . . . My father dug a lot of trenches and dug himself a whole lot of graves."[19] His metaphorical death in World War I becomes a prefiguration of his biological death:

> When he really died, much later, all the bullets and shrapnel that had missed him got together and smashed his heart all at once; and that's how he never got out of the last trench, which others had dug for him.[20]

While the first two deaths are presented at length, in a continuous superimposition of past, present, and imagination, the series of deaths intensifies in the 1930s. The narrator recounts,

> once, just before Hitler came along, my father's former brothers-in-arms invited him to a regimental reunion. . . . My father didn't accept the invitation and this, too, meant death for him, because his comrades liked him very much and used to call him David. During the war, they used to give him some of their rations before the Day of Atonement so that he would have strength for his fast. They would gather stars for his prayers and moments of silence for his quiet devotions.[21]

The narrator does not tell us why the father refuses the invitation. Yet the allusive mention of Hitler's coming to power might indicate that the father feels uneasy among his fellow World War I fellow veterans, a segment of the population where Hitler enjoyed wide support. The Nazi party presented itself as the party of the war veterans, who had been treated—so ran Nazi propaganda—as second-class citizens under the Weimar Republic.[22] This new state of affairs contrasts with the conduct of his fellow soldiers in the war, where they cared so much about him as to provide food for him before the religious fast and quiet for his prayers. The reference to the name David is not coincidental: instead of the assimilated German name of the father, Friedrich, which is not mentioned in the story, the soldiers called the narrator's father by his Jewish name. The father's Jewishness does not impede his perfect integration in the Army, and these memories underscore the change in attitudes toward Jews at the rise to power of the Nazis in the early 1930s. Indeed, "after that he died a great many times."[23]

As the Nazis come to power, the deaths of his father happen much more often, until the family decides to flee:

> He died when they came to arrest him for throwing the Nazi pin I found into the garbage. . . . He died when they stationed pickets outside his shop to keep people from buying there because it was a Jewish shop. He died when we left Germany to emigrate to Palestine, and all the years that had passed died with him.[24]

The father's composite identity as a German Jew undergoes a deep change: as he flees to Mandatory Palestine, he keeps loyal to his Orthodox Judaism, while he must relinquish his German identity. The country for which he fought four long years had turned against him.

The second part of the story focuses on the father's biological death: "When he really died, God didn't know whether he was actually dead or not."[25] The narrator describes the father's need for oxygen, his convalescence in the hospital and his sudden death. Yet the story does not end with the 'real' death. The narrator goes on to tell about the cemetery in which the father lies, and the aftermath of his death: "The cemetery lies near the border. When things get rough there, the dead are left to themselves, with only a few soldiers turning up from time-to-time."[26] Just as the dead are a real presence in the cemetery, the father fills the imaginative dreams of the son: "my father still keeps dying. He comes to me in my dreams and I am afraid for him and say: take your coat, walk more slowly, don't talk, you mustn't get excited, take a rest from this awful war."[27] The "awful war" is likely a reference to the frictions at the border with Jordan, in Jerusalem, where the cemetery lies.

The narrator cannot let go of his father. He imagines him as if he may still die; somehow, paradoxically, as long as the father keeps dying, he is present to the son. In the last scene, a dream-like vision, the son carries the father on his shoulders along the Via Appia in Rome. There he calls a taxi for his father, who seems near death once more. As he fails to get a taxi, he sees his father far away in the arches of Porta San Sebastiano.

Although the title leads the reader to concentrate on the father, the story ends up being a *Bildungsroman* 'in the mirror' of the son. Very early on we know that at least the son would later move to Palestine. In fact, as he describes the furrow in his father's neck during the Yom Kippur ritual, the narrator comments: "A deep furrow, practically a *wadi*, ran right across it. It was the first time I had seen this deep, sun-scorched creek, though I was still far away from that country."[28] "That country" is unmistakably the Land of Israel, identifiable by the reference to the *wadi*, an Arabic word used in Hebrew to indicate valleys shaped by ephemeral torrents typical of the Middle Eastern landscape. He moves constantly between past and present, as for example when he tells us that he served in the British Army, as opposed to his father, who served under the Kaiser.[29]

He identifies his father's arrest as a central moment in his own growth: "It was terrible for me to see my father no longer able to defend our house against the enemy's onslaught. That was childhood's end. How could they just burst into our house like that against father's wishes!"[30] As Glenda Abramson acutely noted,

> these "deaths" may also refer to the growing maturity of the son and his ironic perception of the father's fallibility in critical life situations. The child's belief in the invincibility of his father is eroded by the father's confusion and helplessness.[31]

As the father is consumed more and more by death, the son grows more mature. After the father's death, the son realizes that his father was like a quarry: "he gave me all his stone and depleted himself. Now that he was dead and I was built up, he remained gaping, void and deserted."[32] By confronting his reflection in his father's mirror-image, the son underscores his independent choices: "I, for my part, go my way, developing some of my father's qualities and some of his facial features and traits. I develop some, and discard others."[33] Among the ones he discards is the father's religious Orthodoxy. While several times throughout the story God is disparaged or parodied, toward the end the very symbol of Jewish religious practice, the phylacteries, are put away: "I lay my phylacteries, not on my arm or on my forehead, but in the drawer which I never open anymore."[34] The son's distance from his father's zealous faith lies at the center of the story, as will become clear.

Far from being merely an exercise in first-person narration, "The Times My Father Died" must have been a deeply personal accomplishment for Amichai. Indeed, much of the material that makes up the story can be traced to Amichai's biography. While this is true of the whole collection *In This Terrible Wind*, in "The Times My Father Died" it is even more apparent.[35] Among many real elements incorporated into the story, there are of course the family's German origins and years spent there, the Orthodox Judaism of the father, his military service in the First World War, the flight to Palestine in the summer of 1936, some years after Hitler's rise to power, and the son's military service in the British Jewish Brigade. The episode of the father's arrest for throwing the Nazi pin into the trash is based on a real incident.[36] In the story, "when the train went past the Jewish Old-Age Home, which my father had supported, all the old people stood waving their bed sheets from windows and balconies."[37] This is a trace of the warm ties that the Pfeuffers enjoyed with the residents of the Jewish Würzburg old-age home, whom they would visit every Saturday afternoon.[38]

The Roman scene or the Roman riddle?

In reflecting on the text, I believe that an important interpretative key lies in its last paragraph. Throughout the story, "Amichai's lavish use of imagery, while embellishing the text with verbal fioritura and poetical interest, effectively destroys narrative continuity."[39] Moreover, the continual shift between the narrator and the father, the past and the present, external acts and internal reflections, make it difficult to give sense to his chaotic prose. In the last paragraph, however, a different setting and a peculiar image of the father and the son together may assist the reader in interpreting the story, as they offer a unifying model to reconsider its events and images. In translation, the close to *The Times My Father Died* reads as follows:

> *Once I was walking along the Via Appia in Rome. I was carrying my father on my shoulders*. Suddenly his head sagged down and I was afraid he was going to die. I laid him down at the side of the road, with a stone under his head, and went to call a taxi. Once they used to call on God to help; now you call a taxi. *I couldn't find one, and as I went searching I got further away from my father*. Every few steps I would turn round to see if he was still there, and plunge on toward the stream of traffic. I saw him lying at the roadside, his head turned in my direction, watching me. *I saw him through the ancient Arch of San Sebastian.* Passersby stopped for a moment to bend over him and then went on. I finally got into a taxi, but it was too narrow and looked like a snake. I got another one, and the driver said: We know him by now; he's only pretending to be dead. I turned round and saw my father still lying at the side of the road, his white face turned to me. But I didn't know if he was still alive. *I turned round again and saw him, a very distant object, through the ancient arches of San Sebastian's Gate.*[40]

The surreally enigmatic scene of the son's carrying his father in Rome has attracted much attention from critics, who have underscored the importance of the location and of the state of the father in the scene. In a short introduction to the story, Robert Alter notes:

> The dream of hallucination of a final encounter with the father is pointedly not differentiated from waking reality, for the effect of the whole story has been to break down the divisions between vision and factual experience. The father, who first died in Germany and last died in Jerusalem, is here seen in an ambiguous state between life and death in Rome, a location that may intimate the alienation of the son from his origins (Rome being traditionally a symbolic antithesis to Jerusalem).[41]

While Alter does not commit to a specific interpretation of Rome as a location, he recognizes the importance of place, a dominant theme in all of Amichai's production.[42] While Germany and Jerusalem are the real geographical settings of the story, Rome is understood as a symbol of alienation, while the liminal state of the father remains ambiguous.

Alter's lead was followed with greater detail by Glenda Abramson. Although critics have generally devoted less attention to Amichai's prose works,[43] Abramson examined Amichai's works across literary genres, identifying certain common core themes. Among these, the figure of the father is a dominating presence.[44] She also devotes several pages to "The Times My Father Died," where she too draws attention to the final paragraph:

> The story ends with a dreamlike incident of the son walking in Rome, carrying his father on his shoulders, an ironic view of the power he had wielded throughout his life and still wields after his death. The older man is stricken and the son goes for help. His last glimpse of his father through an archway sees him lying suspended between life and death, his face turned to the son, in Rome, the traditional antithesis to Jerusalem, the secular contrasted to the sacred. As the son's religious guardian he is unable to survive in Rome and is compelled to watch his son increasing the distance between them. This was the father's ultimate and most final death, the posthumous dying, after the son has already placed his phylacteries, not on his arm and forehead but in a drawer which remains firmly closed.[45]

Abramson better specifies the symbolism of Rome as the *secular* city opposed to the *sacred* Jerusalem. As the son enters Rome, that is, abandons Judaism for secular life, the father cannot but stop at the gate, where he finally dies. Abramson's interpretation correctly highlights one hinge of the story, the characters' opposite relationship with religion.

Yet the text is not explicit about the son's direction in his walk. As the distance between the two characters grows, is the son proceeding further into the city, as Abramson assumes, or is he instead walking away from the city? Moreover, while both commentators generally discuss Rome as a symbol, the story specifically identifies the settings as the Via Appia and the Porta San Sebastiano, the ancient gate at the end of the Via Appia. In general, Alter reads the scene as a simple "encounter" of father and son, while Abramson understands the son's carrying of his father as "ironic," that is as a metaphorical gesture to the father's burdening influence on his son's life—even after death. I argue, instead, that the son's carrying his father is a precise reference to Aeneas carrying Anchises, a myth that retrospectively illuminates meanings throughout the whole short story. Furthermore, the specific notations of place cooperate in creating different symbolic spaces. While I do not disagree with Alter's and Abramson's reading of Rome as an antithesis to Jerusalem, I propose a more nuanced interpretation. On one hand, the Via Appia configures an imagined underworld; on the other hand, the Roman Porta San Sebastiano represents the old European Jewish world that the son has abandoned.

Indeed, in Amichai's poetry, Rome is not a univocal symbol.[46] While the poet does make reference to the traditional religious antithesis in the poem "And That Is Your Glory,"[47] in the poem "I Feel Just Fine In My Pants" he points to a more complex relationship: "If the Romans hadn't boasted about their victory / on the Arch of Titus, we wouldn't know / the shape of the Menorah in the Temple."[48] As he draws attention to the Roman monument that memorialized Titus' victory in the First Jewish War, the monument becomes a precious piece of information about ancient Jewish culture that otherwise would be lost.

In this densely metaphorical story, I contend, Rome serves three different functions. (1) It throws into relief the allusion to the Aeneas myth, with Rome providing the cultural system of reference by which the allusion operates. In fact, the scene of the son carrying his father on his shoulders becomes an inescapably specific reference to the Aeneas myth once we recognize Rome as a cultural signifier. It is in connection with the Aeneas myth that (2) the Via Appia acquires the function of an imagined underworld. (3) Rome represents not the secular Rome in opposition to the sacred Jerusalem, as Abramson puts it, but rather the old European Jewry in opposition to the new Israeli community. Rome stands for the traditional world of Orthodox European Judaism, which stands in sharp contrast to secularly Zionist Israel.

A Jewish Aeneas in flight from the Holocaust

The reference to the Aeneas myth is dense in itself and has significant implications; it invites the reader to reconsider the events narrated in the story against the mythical vicissitudes of Aeneas and Anchises. Significantly, Amichai merges two different moments of Vergil's *Aeneid* into one—moments that, as we shall see, are connected by Vergil's Aeneas himself. These two moments, in turn, highlight different aspects of Amichai's (and Aeneas') personal story: his status (1) as a *refugee* and (2) as an *orphan.*

The very simple sentence "I was carrying my father on my shoulders" alludes directly to Aeneas' traditional iconography, which shows him literally carrying his father on his shoulders. The image appears in *Aeneid* 2, where Aeneas recounts to

Dido his flight from the destruction of Troy. After despairing of armed resistance against the Greeks, Aeneas returns to his house, where he tries to convince his father to leave. Only a portent persuades Anchises, initially determined to stay behind and die, to yield to his son's wish:

> Come then, dear father, mount upon my neck; on my shoulders I will support you, and this task will not weigh me down. However things may fall, we two will have one peril, one salvation.[49]

In the final line of Book 2, as daylight nears, Aeneas finally makes his way to the mountains after taking up his father.[50] Despite the death of Creusa, the light of the day suggests a new beginning for Aeneas' family.

Vergil's *Aeneid* would become available in Hebrew in its entirety only in 1962, thanks to Shlomoh Dykman, but Yehoshua Friedman had translated excerpts from Book 2 and 9, Joseph Gerhard Liebes had published a partial translation of the first four books in 1946, around the same time Yochanan Levy had translated and added a commentary to some passages from Book 1, 2, and 4,[51] and Mica Joseph Lebensohn's 19th-century translation of Book 2 via Schiller's German version had been printed in 1950.[52] While Amichai encountered the *Odyssey* in his high school years, it is harder to track down a textual encounter with the *Aeneid*.[53] He could have read Vergil in German, in the decades when the *Aeneid* was reappraised in Germany.[54] Besides, already in the 1930s Amichai enjoyed reading T.S. Eliot, a key figure in Vergil's reception in the 20th century, and was certainly familiar with a fundamental text in the reception of Vergil as a character, Dante's *Divine Comedy*.[55] Indeed, a reference to Vergil as Dante's "guide" appears in the story "Exodus from Egypt," which was published in the same collection as "The Times My Father Died." In that story, the narrator compares himself to a young man who stands next to his father in the dark present, like Dante next to Vergil in the *Inferno*.[56] Moreover, Amichai might have become aware of the Aeneas myth through iconography. In the 1950s, Amichai visited Rome, where he might have seen, among others, famous depictions of Aeneas' flight from Troy in Raphael's "Incendio di Borgo" in the Vatican's Stanze di Raffaello, and Gian Lorenzo Bernini's celebrated "Enea, Anchise e Ascanio," in the Galleria Borghese.[57]

Admittedly, in the story there is no character to be identified with Ascanius. Amichai focuses on the unshakeable bond between the father and the son only, to the point that other family members like the mother, the aunt, and the narrator's wife fade into the background. The Aeneas myth throws into relief not only the deep love that the son feels for his father; most importantly, this reference compels the reader to reflect on the myth more in general: Aeneas and Anchises leave burning Troy, their homeland, for a new, unknown homeland. While throughout his life Amichai dismissed episodes of Nazi anti-Semitism as "not deep traumas" and suggested that the family's move to Palestine in 1936 had been a "great happy event," the reference to the Aeneas myth illuminates the somber truth:[58] rather than voluntary *'olim*, 'ascenders,' the term traditionally applied to Jews who move to the Land of Israel, the Pfeuffer family fled Germany as refugees.[59] Amichai does not use the word 'refugee,' but the story makes it clear that the family had no desire to leave Germany for the Middle East and certainly no intention of taking part in the Zionist project. Indeed, Amichai's father decided to move to Palestine after he had seen two Jews beaten to death in the street and after Amichai himself had been attacked on his way from school.[60] Aeneas' burning Troy transfigures in a mythical aura the Pfeuffers' homeland, Germany, by now in the hands of the Nazi regime. Although the family did not suffer in the concentration camps, the Nazi persecution directly caused their flight. The Holocaust loomed on the horizon. In a later poem about a famous Israeli dancer, Amichai put it bluntly: "If he had continued to dance in Germany and had not come to Jerusalem he would / have danced to his death in the camps."[61] Even though it did not destroy their lives, the Holocaust destroyed their possible lives as German Jews. As Amichai looks back on his move to Palestine, his image is mirrored by Aeneas the *refugee*.

Via Appia: *Aeneas in the underworld*

To be sure, Amichai's biography does not replicate the journey of Aeneas: in his case it was the father who brought the son to salvation from the Holocaust. But this does not weaken the reference; it rather charges it with the frustration of an unattained past wish. Earlier in the story, when the father is arrested by the Nazis, the narrator expresses his wish: "If I had been bigger then, I would have covered up my father as Shem did when he walked despondently."[62] The narrator projects a similar wish in the reference to the Aeneas myth, as he suggests that if he had been bigger, he would have saved his father. Indeed, in the final scene the son shows deep, concerned preoccupation for his father as he looks for a taxi, presumably for the father to be taken to a hospital.

As I have noted, Amichai merges two different scenes, selecting different aspects of each. These aspects cooperate in a closing scene overcharged with meaning and references. While the pose of the father and the son references the finale of Book 2 of the *Aeneid* and the role of Aeneas as refugee, Amichai also recreates a dream-like descent to the underworld. Significantly, in the *Aeneid*, both the carrying away of Anchises and the descent into the underworld highlight Aeneas' love for his father, while presenting two different versions of Aeneas. Anchises' death marks the shift from the first to the second of these versions (*Aen.* 3.707–13): in Book 2 we encounter Aeneas the *son*, in Book 6 Aeneas the *orphan*. Even though Aeneas is the son of an immortal goddess, her presence in his life is evanescent.[63] His only real parent is his father. Although we are used to thinking of orphans as children, they can be understood as anyone who has lost both parents.[64] Even though Aeneas is a father himself, his desire to be with his own father is all the more striking in Book 6, where he enters the underworld to seek Anchises.[65]

I suggest reading the setting of the Via Appia as an oneiric underworld to which the son symbolically travels in order to meet his father. In fact, already in antiquity, monumental tombs, mausoleums, and catacombs characterized the Via Appia as a landscape of the dead, just as many ancient roads leading out of cities like Rome or Pompeii were lined with tombs. However, the modern Appia Antica constitutes a space especially consecrated to death: it is the cemetery of a *dead* civilization. The tombs are now, first and foremost, archaeological objects: rather than just tombs, they are *rovine antiche*, ruins of ancient tombs. This space is thus doubly consecrated to death—as a cemetery and as a remnant of a dead civilization.

Although tombs are not mentioned explicitly in the story, one of Amichai's poems might shed light on the Via Appia as a liminal space. Indeed, the Via Appia is central in the poem "Via Appia Antica," first published in 1968, in the collection *Now in the Uproar*. This collection contains poems that Amichai wrote between 1962 and 1968, but the poem clearly goes back to the same motifs that appear in "The Times My Father Died." As Amichai declared in an interview, "Prose and poetry are carved from a single block: sometimes it finds expression in one way, and sometimes in another. My prose tried to describe the conditions in which my poems were born."[66] The poems reads,

> What are they saying in the graves
> below the road from Rome?
> They are saying this: one of us is passing by
> who was given a few more days to live.
> . . .
> He arrives from St. Sebastian's Gate,
> the wind translates the language of the dead into his own tongue.
> His shadow collapses onto the gravestones as he walks.
> . . .
> He is ordained to return just as he came, he is ordained to lie when he speaks,
> so as to be even now silence like us. He is fated for what will not be.
>
> These are the days of kindness toward the dead;
> these dead who do not want it.
> As in the moments after the end of the last broadcast,
> when a gentle whistle persists briefly in the air.
> After it, stillness.[67]

While "The Times My Father Died" centers on the liminal state of the father in the loving son's imagination, the poem, by way of the indefinite identity of the protagonist, explores more in general the relationship between those who are alive and those who inhabit the land of the dead.[68] While the poem is interspersed with references to the spoken word, sounds, and silence, in the final lines the poet categorically excludes any possibility of communication with the dead. Perhaps only those who are in between life and death, the moribund, are able to communicate with both sides. For the poet, after death, there is nothing but "stillness." Beyond the common setting, the reference to the "last broadcast" is another thread to be found also in "The Times My Father Died," where the death of the father is described in the very same terms: "My father was looking like a broadcasting station, what with that jumble of wires and antennae. That day he transmitted his last broadcast."[69]

Thus, the walk in the Via Appia represents the son's encounter with his father at the boundary of death, in a reprisal of Vergil's *Aeneid* 6. Like Aeneas, the narrator is now an orphan who seeks his father. Just like Aeneas' father, his father populates his dreams: "My father still keeps dying. He comes to me in my dreams."[70] Indeed, Aeneas tells Dido of his dreams (*Aen.* 4.351–3) and sees his father in *Aen.* 5.722–39. In this latter episode, the reader can feel Aeneas' desperate call on his dead father for a comforting embrace: "He spoke, and passed like smoke into thin air. 'Where are you rushing now?' cries Aeneas. 'Where are you hurrying? Whom do you flee, or who bars you from our embraces?"[71]

In Book 6, Aeneas specifically seeks out Anchises. Speaking to the Sibyl, he persuades her to show him the way to his father:

> Aeneas the hero begins: "For me no form of toils arises, O maiden, strange or unlooked for; all this have I foreseen and debated in my mind. *One thing I pray: since here is the famed gate of the nether king, and the gloomy marsh from Acheron's overflow, be it granted me to pass into my dear father's sight and presence*; show the way and open the hallowed portals! *Amid flames and a thousand pursuing spears, I rescued him on these shoulders, and brought him safe from the enemy's midst.* He, the partner of my journey, endured with me all the seas and all the menace of ocean and sky, weak as he was, beyond the strength and portion of age. He it was who prayed and charged me humbly to seek you and draw near to your threshold. *Pity both son and father*, I beseech you, gracious one; for you are all-powerful, and not in vain did Hecate make you mistress in the groves of Avernus. If Orpheus availed to summon his wife's shade, strong in his Thracian lyre and tuneful strings; if Pollux, dying in turn, ransomed his brother and so many times comes and goes his way—why speak of Theseus, why of Hercules the mighty—I, too, have descent from Jove most high!"[72]

Aeneas mentions other heroes who visited the underworld. Notably, he is the only one who would endeavor into the land of the dead in order to see his father, his only request (*unum oro*, 106). His speech leads us back to the aforementioned rescue of his father as they fled Troy, the other moment of the *Aeneid* that Amichai merges together in the story. Aeneas also mentions Anchises' requests, a reference to his dreams. At the end of the book, when Aeneas finally meets his father in the underworld (6.679–898), he tells him: "Your shade, father, your sad shade, meeting me repeatedly, drove me to seek these portals. My ships ride the Tuscan sea. Grant me to clasp your hand, grant me, father, and withdraw not from my embrace."[73]

Even though Aeneas reaches the Underworld and demands the embrace he has been denied in Book 5, Anchises remains unreachable to his weeping son. Death is a change of state that cannot be undone: "Thrice there he strove to throw his arms around his neck; thrice the form, vainly clasped, fled from his hands, even as light winds, and most like a winged dream."[74] The same frustration pervades Amichai's Roman scene. While Anchises offers a prophecy of Roman future glory to his son and accompanies his son to the twin gates of Sleep, Amichai's dream scene is more enigmatic; it closes on the growing distance from his father.

Anchises in the Arches of Porta San Sebastiano

So far, we have encountered Aeneas as a *refugee* and as an *orphan*, but of course he is also a *founder*. While Anchises is ready to die in Troy as the city burns and is persuaded only by a portent not to stay behind, he does not live long enough to see his new homeland. Instead, despite the difficulties along the journey and the war in Italy, Aeneas succeeds in founding a new community for his Trojan people. In Amichai this polarization gestures toward the opposition between the Old Jew and the New (Israeli) Hebrew, a core theme in Zionist thought. While the Old Jew is the Jew leading a religious life in the Diaspora, the New Hebrew is the Jew native of the Land of Israel. Their opposite connotations were best expressed by Gershon Shaked: "The terms 'exilic' and 'Israeli' became two poles that characterized the thinking of Israeli society, in which 'Israeli' signifies the new, healthy and erect, while the 'diasporic'—the old, sick and bent-over."[75] Moreover, the active/passive dichotomy reflected different attitudes toward religion: while the "Israeli" was characterized by staunch secularism, the "diasporic" was identified with traditional Judaism. According to Zionist doctrine, "life in exile turned the Jews into oppressed, submissive, weak, and fearful people who passively accept their fate, hoping to be saved by God or by Gentiles' help."[76] As Nili Gold notes, in Amichai certain individuals become "representatives" of ideas.[77] Just like "Little Ruth," a childhood friend who was deported by the Nazis and killed in the Sobibor death camp, becomes his "representative of the Holocaust" and Dicky, Amichai's friend and commander in the Israeli Army who fell in battle during the 1948 War, becomes his representative of all the soldiers who die in war,[78] in this story the father may be read as the representative of the Old, Exilic Jew—from which the narrator (and Amichai) detaches himself.[79]

The Porta San Sebastiano constructs this opposition in spatial terms. As the son looks for a taxi for his moribund father, he feels he is getting further away from him: "I saw him through the ancient Arch of San Sebastian. . . . I turned round again and saw him, a very distant object, through the ancient arches of San Sebastian's Gate."[80] The Porta San Sebastiano is the gate where the Via Appia stops and Rome begins. Abramson interprets this detail as a sign of the father's inability to follow his son into Rome. However, the Roman setting may be interpreted as a symbol of Europe. The "ancient gate" itself, mentioned twice by its traditional, post-classical name, aptly summarizes European identity. Indeed, the gate was built in 275 CE as part of the Aurelian Walls of the city. In this respect, the gate might represent the ancient civilization of Rome. On the other hand, the gate is referred to by the name of a saint, which highlights the Christian identity of Rome. Thus, the Roman gate symbolizes Europe as the center of both classical and Christian heritage, two threatening forces for the Jewish people. The Roman Empire itself caused the Diaspora; Christianity actively persecuted or assimilated the Jews throughout the centuries of Exile. In the words of Uri Zvi Greenberg, a prominent

Israeli poet, Europe is "the kingdom of the Cross," a promise of suffering for the European diasporic Jews.[81]

Amichai's father did not want to relinquish his composite identity as a German Orthodox Jew. The country he had fought for in World War I had turned against him, as the story recounts. Even after the family arrived in Palestine, they moved from Petah Tikvah to Jerusalem in order for the children to grow in a more European, Orthodox Jewish atmosphere. He was instrumental in founding a German rite synagogue and kept in touch with Würzburg friends.[82] Throughout the story, the son ironically mocks his father's God, marking his distance from religion: "God, in whom he believed, hovered over him like a white protective umbrella, up above the path of the shells";[83] "when he really died, God didn't know whether he was actually dead";[84] "God, who is very high up, filled my father to the brim";[85] "once they used to call on God to help; now you call a taxi."[86] Not coincidentally, the first time we see the father he is "completely absorbed in his grown-up God," prostrated in the repentance ritual of Yom Kippur.[87] And what do his 'deaths' show, if not his continual sickliness? All of these traits make the father a recognizable stereotype of the Old Jew.

According to Nili Gold, in his early production Amichai fashioned "his Israeli persona."[88] The construction of this persona depended on the minimization (if not negation) of his diasporic past. As I showed, although in this story he does touch on his German past,[89] the Aeneas–Anchises comparison betrays a widely held, Zionist, polarized view of Jewish identities. The old Anchises of Amichai does reach the shores of Palestine but remains a European diasporic Jew; the Aeneas-like son suggests the heroic beginning of a new homeland.

Aeneas and Anchises also provide an apt point of contrast for the narrator and his father's treatment of family religious relics. Aeneas, when carrying away Anchises, requests that he "take in [his] arms the sacred emblems of our country's household gods" in order for Aeneas not to desecrate them with blood.[90] While in the *Aeneid* Anchises carries the *penates* at Aeneas' request, Amichai's narrator puts away his phylacteries in a drawer that he never opens. From the very first lines we know that the son will move to Palestine, and throughout the story we see him distancing himself from Judaism. In the end, the father, the guardian of the religious tradition, remains as if suspended just beyond the gate of Rome, forever in between life and death, past and present, Israel and Exile.

Conclusion

"The Times My Father Died" exemplifies well the overwhelming richness of Amichai's prose. In this chapter, I tried to disentangle and analyze some aspects of his use of the Aeneas myth. The whole story is a homage to Amichai's father and a monument to his love for him. Aeneas, in his characterizations as *refugee*, *orphan*, and *founder*, throws into relief the experiences of the narrator of the short story and of Amichai himself and engages in a dense symbolic dialogue with Rome, the Via Appia, and the Porta San Sebastiano. Significantly, the reference to Aeneas is not explicit. In contrast with Liliana Segre, who explicitly mentions Aeneas and forcefully asserts her sharing in a common Italian and European cultural patrimony ("I very much like to think of you all as Aeneas, who rescues his father Anchises from Troy by putting him onto his shoulders: an image of great civility"—she writes to the students),[91] Amichai leaves it to the reader to detect the allusion: in a text organized around a chronological opposition before/after the migration to Palestine and conceptual Diasporic/Israeli, an overt, positive reference to a Roman founding hero could read as a remnant of that diasporic culture.

Indeed, the story is permeated by—significantly—explicit references to the Bible and to Jewish liturgy,[92] and only in the end does Amichai turn to Greco-Roman mythology. It is the Roman setting that allows the reader to identify the classical allusion. Two cultural systems, the Jewish and the classical, are combined in the story, according to a strategy that Glenda Abramson has identified in a poem by Amichai, "Takis Sinopoulos, a Greek Poet."[93] The poem, about a visit to a Greek poet living in present-day Rome, combines the *Odyssey* with repeated allusions to Biblical formulae. The poem was published in the same collection as the poem "Via Appia Antica" and "Three Times I Came to Rome" in a sequence of poems inspired by Italy, in a *fil rouge* that goes back to "The Times My Father Died."[94]

In Jewish culture there is no such thing as a *katabasis* to meet the beloved dead; Amichai thus turns to classical myth for an imaginative depiction of his interactions with his dead father.[95] Glenda Abramson, in her article on Greek mythology in Hebrew poetry, analyzes Israeli poet Nathan Zach's use of the Orpheus myth in a poem about the prophet Daniel. By way of the Orpheus myth, Daniel's descent into the lions' den is transfigured into a descent to the underworld. She notes that "the dramatic instant of mythical Orpheus' descent for the sake of obsessive love has no equal in the Bible, except, perhaps, for the case of King David's moral plunge for love of Bathsheba."[96] The case of King David illustrates moral decay but certainly not a descent to the underworld. Even the witch of Endor's evocation of the dead prophet Samuel at the request of King Saul is far from a lovable or even legitimate encounter; it does not conjure up a special setting.[97] In contrast, Greco-Roman mythology affords a host of heroes who travel between the world of the dead and that of the living, such as Odysseus, Theseus, Heracles, Orpheus, and Aeneas.[98] Some of these myths are evoked by Vergil himself in Book 6, as we have seen. Together with Aeneas' filial *pietas*, it is perhaps this communicability between the two worlds that makes the Aeneas myth so especially appealing and relevant to Amichai, despite its cultural otherness.

As "The Times My Father Died" and many of his poems show, the distant figure of his father haunted Amichai for most of his life.[99] In "The Times My Father Died," Amichai sets his own story against his father's: as he proclaims his new identity as a member of the founding generation of the new Jewish state, he cannot but look back to his father in loving nostalgia. Aeneas encapsulates Amichai's retrospective and prospective looks: behind him, the destruction of Troy, that is the European Jewry annihilated culturally and demographically in the Holocaust; in front of him, the newly born State of Israel. Amichai's allusion to Aeneas captures well the dilemma of many European Jews who escaped from the Holocaust and struggled to reconcile their diasporic past with the newly acquired identity as Israelis. Even if they shed their old identity, memory continued to haunt them—even in their dreams, just like Amichai's father.

In the end, the growing distance between father and son marks not only the separation of death but also Amichai's detachment from his father's religious and cultural world. The father remained loyal to his Orthodox, European Judaism in a world that was irrevocably changed by the Holocaust. The son, born Ludwig Pfeuffer, chose a new life: upon arrival to Palestine, in 1936, he became Yehuda Pfeuffer, dismissing his assimilated first name; in 1946 the surname Pfeuffer yielded to a new Hebrew surname. By now, he was an entirely New Hebrew, who carried in his surname the promise of a new national beginning: "Amichai," that is, "my people lives."[100]

Notes

1 I would not have written this book chapter without the support and encouragement of a number of people: I am especially grateful to Neta Stahl, for introducing me to the beauty of Hebrew literature; to Shane Butler, who taught me what 'classical reception' means; to Tamar Sovran and Sidra DeKoven Ezrahi, for their careful reading and pointed suggestions. I also want to thank the department of Classical Studies at Bar-Ilan University and the organizers of the "Behind the Texts" series at Sorbonne Nouvelle–Paris 3 and at Durham University, where I presented some of my thoughts on Segre and Amichai and received precious feedback.

2 Among the different books, one is a critical work on the reception of Aeneas in the poetry of Giorgio Caproni (Caproni 2020; see Giannotti in this volume, Chapter 4), two are essays on Aeneas as the 'foreigner' (Guidorizzi 2020) and as the 'defeated hero' (Marcolongo 2020), and one is a political essay-manifesto written by former Prime Minister Matteo Renzi, which even exhibits Bernini's *Aeneas* on its cover in reference to the migratory crisis (Renzi 2020). Interestingly, Marcolongo, now a popularizer of classical culture, used to be Renzi's speech writer.

3 Marchetti 2020.

4 Marchetti 2020.

5 Marchetti 2020.

6 Segre often underscored her being "like a grandmother" to Italian and European youths; for example, she directly addressed her "future grandchildren" as she concluded her speech at the European Parliament on January 29, 2020, in the ceremony commemorating the liberation of the Auschwitz death camp. On Liliana Segre's biography and public persona see Greco 2019.

7 Segre 2020. Segre's letter was widely reported in the media. The translation is mine.

8 Segre 2020.

9 Segre 2020. Emphasis added.

10 Nelis 2018 and, in general, the whole volume. For the different trends in the interpretation of the *Aeneid* in Italy in 1930s, see Thomas 2009; Piperno 2020: 104–6.

11 Yehuda Amichai was born as Ludwig Pfeuffer in Würzburg, Germany, in 1924 into a Jewish Orthodox family. His father was a traveling salesman who then opened a

business in their town. He attended a Jewish school before moving to Mandatory Palestine in 1936, as Nazi anti-Semitism raged in Germany. The family first settled in Petah Tikvah for a short while, then moved permanently to Jerusalem. He served in the British Jewish Brigade during World War II, then fought as an Israeli soldier in the 1948 War, the Sinai War (1956), and the Yom Kippur War (1973). He studied literature at the Hebrew University of Jerusalem and taught Hebrew literature and Bible in schools. Later on, he lectured at the Greenberg Institute, at Berkeley, at New York University. His first poetry collection, *Now and in Other Days* (1955), was a groundbreaking novelty in Hebrew poetry. He went on to publish 25 poetical collections, the last one in 1998, *Open Closed Open.* He wrote a book of short stories (*In This Terrible Wind,* revised and expanded in 1973), a monumental novel (*Not of This Time, Not of This Place*, 1963) and other shorter prose pieces. He died in Jerusalem in 2000.

12 Amichai and Alter 2015: 43.

13 The English text can be read in Alter 1975: 316–25 and Amichai 1984: 185–97. I will be quoting, with modifications, from Alter's volume; the page numbers refer to this translation.

14 For the reviews of the collection, see Harel 1961; Cohen 1961; Dor 1961; Shaked 1961; Blat 1961.

15 Abramson 1989: 178.

16 Alter 1975: 314.

17 Alter 1975: 316–7.

18 Alter 1975: 318.

19 Alter 1975: 318.

20 Alter 1975: 319.

21 Alter 1975: 320.

22 See Diehl 1987, 705–15.

23 Alter 1975: 320.

24 Alter 1975: 320.

25 Alter 1975: 321.

26 Alter 1975: 324.

27 Alter 1975: 324.

28 Alter 1975: 324. Schachter's translation in Alter 1975 opts for a smoother English rendering, which reads 'groove' instead of '*wadi.*'

29 See Alter 1975: 318:

> And it's also good I wasn't in that war [World War I], otherwise we might have been killing one another; because he wore the uniform of Kaiser Wilhelm, while I wore the uniform of King George the Fifth, with a gap of twenty-five years in between.

30 Alter 1975: 320.

31 Abramson 1989: 183.

32 Alter 1975: 324.

33 Alter 1975: 324.

34 Alter 1975: 325.

35 For Amichai's autobiographical inspiration in poetry, see Abramson 1989: 13–27. Particularly on this story, see Gold 2008: 40; 169.

36 Gold 2008: 43.

37 Alter 1975: 320–1.

38 Gold 2008: 31–2. The visit to the old-age home is reimagined also in Amichai's radio skit "Bells and Trains," and in his novel *Not of This Time, Not of This Place.* See Guy 2004: 28.

39 Abramson 1989: 179.

40 Alter 1975: 325, with modifications and emphasis added.

41 Alter 1975: 325.

42 See, for example, Abramson 1989: 124–43; Shemtov 2005.
43 A notable exception is Shaked's study on the Israeli *New Wave*, in which Amichai the prose-writer is identified as an innovator, together with A.B. Yehoshua, A. Appelfeld, A. Kahana-Carmon, and A. Oz (Shaked 1971: 89–124). See also Abramson 1989: 147–195, Abramson 1997: 152–79 and Gluzman 2020.
44 See especially Abramson 1989: 50–70.
45 Abramson 1989: 183–4.
46 Rome and ancient Roman culture recur in Amichai's works. Apart from the poems that will be cited, Roman decadence pervades the short story "Nina from Ashkelon," translated in Amichai 1984: 87–109, and the novel *Not of This Time, Not of This Place* (see Ben-Dov 2018: 343–4).
47 The poem is a hard reflection on God: "I've been in Jerusalem, in Rome. And perhaps to Mecca anon" (Amichai, Bloch, and Mitchell 2013: 11). For a discussion, see Kronfeld 2016: 198–204.
48 Amichai, Bloch, and Mitchell 2013: 135.
49 *Aen.* 2.707–10, translated in Fairclough 1999: 365.
50 *Aen.* 2.804.
51 Friedman's translations were first published in the Hebrew magazines *Moznayim* and *Hatkufah* in the early 1930s and were later collected in a book printed in 1952, after his death. I thank Vered Lev Kenaan for the precious information on these translations.
52 Lebensohn's translation was entitled *Harisot Troya* (*Ruins of Troy*). See Dykman 1965: 96 and Holtz 1984 (Hebrew edition with English abstract). For a comparative study of Liebes's and Dykman's translations, see Aslanoff 1997: 204–5.
53 About the *Odyssey*, see the anecdote reported by Gold 2008: 157.
54 Schmidt 2008.
55 See Gold 2008: 304–7. Gold frequently underscores Eliot's continued influence on Amichai.
56 Amichai 1961: 249 (to my knowledge, the story is not available in English).
57 For a short account of Aeneas' iconographical reception see Canciani 1981 (in antiquity) and Lentano 2013: 333–7.
58 Gold 2008: 21.
59 The abstract term *'Aliyah*, pl. *'Aliyot* (עלייה/עליות) literally means 'ascent'—originally to mountain-high Jerusalem, later used as a metonymy for the entire Land of Israel. The related terms sing. *'oleh* and pl. *'olim* (עולה/עולים), often spelled without the apostrophe, identify the Jews who move to the Land of Israel. In fact, the different waves of Jewish immigration before Israeli statehood (1948) are usually referred to as First (1882–1903), Second (1904–1914), Third (1919–1923), Fourth (1924–1929), and Fifth Aliyah (1929–1939), each one with its own characteristic demographics, historical context, and ethos.
60 Gold 2008: 7.
61 See quote in Guy 2004: 27. I have modified the translation.
62 I follow here the translation in Amichai 1984: 191. Alter 1975: 320 offers a slightly different translation.
63 See *Aen.* 1. 405–10. Aeneas talks to Venus without knowing her identity, until she ultimately reveals herself, prompting Aeneas to manifest his disappointment: "and in her step she was revealed a very goddess. He knew her for his mother, and as she fled pursued her with these words: 'Why, cruel like others, do you so often mock your son with vain phantoms? Why am I not allowed to clasp hand in hand and hear and utter words unfeigned?' Thus he reproaches her and bends his steps towards the city." (translated by Fairclough 1999: 291). On this episode see Reckford 1995.
64 For a short survey of the figure of the orphan in modern Hebrew literature, see Cohen 2014. Orphans are a major theme, thematically or symbolically, in Israeli literature. See, for example, Amos Oz's *Fima* and *Story of Love and Darkness*.

65 On Aeneas as son of a mortal and of a goddess, see Bacon 2001.
66 Cole 2008: 166. On the common inspiration for prose and poetry in Amichai's works see also Abramovitz-Retner 1995.
67 For the complete poem, see Amichai 2015: 141.
68 From the same collection, see also the poem "Three Times I Came To Rome" on the notion that the Via Appia pertains to the dead: "And the gates are open to death all around. / Even the Porta San Sebastiano / I love" (Amichai 2015: 143).
69 Alter 1975: 322.
70 Alter 1975: 324.
71 *Aen.* 5.740—2, translated in Fairclough 1999: 523.
72 *Aen.* 6.103–23, translated in Fairclough 1999: 541, with modifications and emphasis added.
73 *Aen.* 6.695–8, translated in Fairclough 1999: 581.
74 *Aen.* 6.700–2, translated in Fairclough 1999: 581.
75 Gold 2008: 12.
76 Zerubavel 1995: 19.
77 Gold 2008: 93–4.
78 On "Little Ruth" (Ruth Fanny Hanover), her biography and her presence in Amichai's later poetry, see Gold 2008: 74–100. On Dicky's symbolic figure in Amichai's works, see Gold 2003: 60–1; in particular, see Amichai's story "Dicky's Death" in Amichai 1984: 111–9 and Gluzman 2020.
79 For a similar assessment of the father in Amichai's poetry, see Kronfeld 2016: 13: "This figuration of the father provides the poetry with a decidedly diasporic ideal of an alternative, 'soft' masculinity that is very different from the normative Israeli one."
80 Alter 1975: 325.
81 For an analysis of Greenberg's poem, see Stahl 2008.
82 Gold 2008: 153–5.
83 Alter 1975: 319.
84 Alter 1975: 317.
85 Alter 1975: 324.
86 Alter 1975: 325.
87 Alter 1975: 317.
88 Gold 2008: 20.
89 See also the story *Venice—Three Times*, where he recounts the family's stop in Venice on the way to Palestine (Amichai 1961). To my knowledge, the story is not available in English.
90 *Aen.* 2.717–20, translated in Fairclough 1999: 365.
91 Segre 2020.
92 "No one knows where Moses was buried, but we know where he lived and we still know all about his life" (Alter 1975: 324); "did I just want to bring him back as Elisha had done?" (Alter 1975: 322; cf. 2 Kings 4:32–5); "I would have covered up my father as Shem did when he walked despondently" (Amichai 1984: 191; cf. Gen 10:23).
93 Abramson 1990: 245–6.
94 Amichai 2015: 140–3.
95 For a different artistic solution, see Amichai's poem "A Second Meeting with My Father," where the meeting with the dead father takes place in a Haifa café, in a contrastive re-evocation of his previous poem "A Meeting with My Father." See Abramson 1989: 67–70.
96 Abramson 1990: 247.
97 1 Sam 28:7–20.
98 For an exhaustive collection of studies on the descent to the Underworld in Greek antiquity see Bonnechère and Cursaru 2014 (it includes a chapter on Vergil's *Aen.* 6). On the core texts of classical descents to the Underworld see Fletcher 2019: 13–46. Bernabé 2015

offers a schematic summary of *katabasis* myths, including those from ancient Near Eastern cultures. For its contemporary reception, see Falconer 2005; Fletcher 2019.

99 Abramson 1989: 50–70.

100 Gold 2008: 2–3.

References

Abramovitz-Retner, T. 1995. *Bein hamesaper levein shiro. Hakorrelatzia shebein shirah levein sifrut besifrut ha'ivrit ledoroteha*. Tel Aviv: Tel Aviv University.

Abramson, G. 1989. *The Writing of Yehuda Amichai: A Thematic Approach*. Albany, NY: State University of New York Press.

———. 1990. "Hellenism Revisited: The Uses of Greek Myth in Modern Hebrew Literature." *Prooftexts* 10, 2: 237–55.

———. 1997. *The Experienced Soul: Studies in Amichai*. Boulder, CO: Westview Press.

Alter, R. 1975. *Modern Hebrew Literature*. New York: Behrman House.

Amichai, Y. 1961. *Ba-ruaḥ Ha-nora'ah Ha-zot*. Le-khol. Merḥavyah: Sifriyat Po'alim.

———. 1984. *The World Is a Room and Other Stories*. Philadelphia: Jewish Publication Society of America.

Amichai, Y., and Alter, R. 2015. *The Poetry of Yehuda Amichai*. New York: Farrar, Straus and Giroux.

Amichai, Y., Bloch, C., and Mitchell, S. 2013. *The Selected Poetry of Yehuda Amichai*. Berkeley: University of California Press.

Aslanoff, C. 1997. "Les voies de traduction des œuvres de l'Antiquité classique en hébreu." *Les Études classiques* 65: 193–210.

Bacon, H.H. 2001. "Mortal Father, Divine Mother: *Aeneid* IV and VIII." In S. Spence (ed.) *Poets and Critics Read Vergil*. New Haven: Yale University Press. 76–85.

Ben-Dov, N. 2018. "The Vengeance of the Skull in Yehuda Amichai's *Not of This Time, Not of This Place*." *Prooftexts* 37, 2: 328–53.

Bernabé, A. 2015. "What Is a *katábasis*? The Descent into the Netherworld in Greece and the Ancient Near East." *Les Études Classiques* 83: 15–34.

Blat, A. 1961. "Sipurei hatoda'ah hapnimit." *Hatzofeh*, March 31.

Bonnechère, P., and Cursaru, G. 2014. *Katabásis dans la tradition littéraire et religieuse de la Grèce ancienne. Actes du colloque de Montréal et de Québec (2–5 mai 2014)*. Namur: Société es Études Classiques.

Canciani, F. 1981. "Aineias." In *Lexicon Iconographicum Mythologiae Classicae*, vol. 1. Zurich: Artemis Verlag.

Caproni, G. 2020. *Il mio Enea*. Edited by F. Giannotti. Milano: Garzanti.

Cohen, A. 1961. "Baruah hanora'ah hazot." *Haboker*, March 24.

Cohen, D. 2014. "Minorities in Modern Hebrew Literature: A Survey." *Jewish Literature: Textual Studies* (Kyoto University) 1: 89–127.

Cole, P. 2008. *Hebrew Writers on Writing*. San Antonio: Trinity University Press.

Diehl, J.M. 1987. "Victims or Victors? Disabled Veterans in the Third Reich." *Journal of Modern History* 59: 705–36.

Dor, M. 1961. "Prozah shel piyyut." *Ma'ariv*, March 24.

Dykman, S. 1965. "Checklist of Greek and Latin Classics Rendered into Hebrew." *Ariel* 12: 94–6.

Fairclough, H.R., and Goold, G.P., tran. 1999. *Virgil: Aeneid I-VI*. Loeb Classical Library. Cambridge, MA: Harvard University Press.

Falconer, R. 2005. *Hell in Contemporary Literature: Western Descent Narratives since 1945*. Edinburgh: Edinburgh University Press.

Fletcher, J. 2019. *Myths of the Underworld In Contemporary Culture: The Backward Gaze*. Oxford: Oxford University Press.

Gluzman, M. 2020. "Moto shel Dicky": hatekst hatraumati shel Yehuda Amichai." *Mehkarei Yerushalaim besifrut 'ivrit* 31: 453–488.

Gold, N.S. 2003. "Notes on Love and War in the Life of Yehuda Amichai." *Israel Studies Forum* 19: 57–71.

———. 2008. *Yehuda Amichai: The Making of Israel's National Poet*. Waltham, MA: Brandeis University Press; University Press of New England.

Greco, S. 2019. "Liliana Segre, or the Courageous Struggle Against Indifference and for Social Recognition." *Academicus* 19: 9–23.

Guidorizzi, G. 2020. *Enea, lo straniero: Le origini di Roma*. Torino: Einaudi.

Guy, H. 2004. "Amichai, Yehuda." In E. Sicher (ed.) *Holocaust Novelists*. Dictionary of Literary Biography; v. 299. Detroit: Gale.

Harel, T. 1961. "Meshorer benetiv haprozah." *Al mishmar*, May 5.

Holtz, A. 1984. "Harisot Troya me'et Micah Yosef Lebensohn bektav-yado." *Tarbiz*, Nissan-Sivan: 431–64.

Kronfeld, C. 2016. *The Full Severity of Compassion: The Poetry of Yehuda Amichai*. Stanford, CA: Stanford University Press.

Lentano, M., and Bettini, M. 2013. *Il Mito Di Enea: Immagini e Racconti Dalla Grecia a Oggi*. Torino: Giulio Einaudi Editore.

Marchetti, L. 2020. "La civiltà è Enea che porta Anchise sulle spalle." *Il Manifesto*, March 24.

Marcolongo, A. 2020. *La lezione di Enea*. Bari: Laterza.

Nelis, J. 2018. "Fascist Modernity, Religion, and the Myth of Rome." In H. Roche and K.N. Demetriou (eds.) *Brill's Companion to the Classics, Fascist Italy and Nazi Germany*. Leiden: Brill.

Piperno, M. 2020. *L'antichità "crudele". Etruschi e Italici nella letteratura italiana del Novecento*. Roma: Carocci.

Reckford, K.J. 1995. "Recognizing Venus. I: Aeneas Meets His Mother." *Arion: A Journal of Humanities and the Classics* 3, 2–3: 1–42.

Renzi, M. 2020. *La mossa del cavallo. Come ricominciare, insieme*. Venezia: Marsilio.

Schmidt, E. 2008. "The German Rediscovery of Vergil in the Early 20th Century." *Vergilius* 54: 124–49.

Segre, L. 2020. "Liliana Segre ai maturandi 2020: 'Lo studio fu balsamo per le mie ferite di sopravvissuta'." *La Repubblica*, June 16.

Shaked, G. 1961. "Baruah hanora'ah hazot shel Yehuda Amichai." *Ha'aretz*, April 6.

———. 1971. *Gal ḥadash Ba-siporet Ha-'Ivrit*. Sidrat Da'at Zemanenu. Merḥavyah: Sifriyat Po'alim.

Shemtov, V. 2005. "Between Perspectives of Space: A Reading in Yehuda Amichai's 'Jewish Travel' and 'Israeli Travel'." *Jewish Social Studies* 11, 3: 141–61.

Stahl, N. 2008. "Uri Zvi Before the Cross. The Figure of Jesus in the Poetry of Uri Zvi Greenberg." *Religion and Literature* 40, 3: 49–80.

Thomas, R.F. 2009. "Beyond the Borders of Eboli: Anti-fascist Reception." In *Virgil and the Augustan Reception*. Cambridge: Cambridge University Press. 260–77.

Zerubavel, Y. 1995. *Recovered Roots Collective: Memory and the Making of Israeli National Tradition*. Chicago: University of Chicago Press.

4 *Forsan et haec olim meminisse iuvabit*

Contemporary Italian writers remembering the *Aeneid*

Filomena Giannotti

Revocate animos maestumque timorem / mittite; forsan et haec olim meminisse iuvabit (Verg. *Aen.* 1.202–3).[1] With these words, Aeneas tries to hearten his men after the deadly storm that wrecked their fleet and forced them to make landfall in Africa. One day, not only will they remember their misfortunes, but they will do so with pleasure. The memory of Aeneas' misfortunes during his voyage across the Mediterranean is still alive in the literature of the 20th century. In this chapter, we trace Aeneas' difficult journey from Troy to the mouth of the Tiber, mapping out allusions to the *Aeneid* by some of Italy's most prominent contemporary writers who attempt to find some solace in the memory of their suffering over this most recent tumultuous century.

* * * *

The starting point of this survey, of course, is Troy, where Aeneas' journey begins. But before leaving Troy, Aeneas must face the fire that destroyed the city, witness the killing of many of his friends, and convince his father, Anchises, to escape from Troy.

These famous episodes are recalled by Giorgio Caproni, who is considered one of the most talented Italian poets of the 20th century, as well as one of the most intense and meaningful voices of modern European poetry. In order to understand his poetry fully, it is necessary to explore his background in brief. Caproni was born in Livorno in 1912. He moved first to Genoa and later settled in Rome, where he died in 1990. He was an accomplished violinist, and it was perhaps his gift for music that made his verses so melodic and rhythmical. Caproni fought in World War II and took part in the partisan resistance. He published several translations of European literature into Italian and wrote both poetry and prose, including journalistic pieces, short stories, and a novel, which he never finished.

One of his main works is *Il passaggio d'Enea* (*The Passage of Aeneas*), which has been partially translated into English by Ned Condini and published as one of several selected poems. *Il passaggio d'Enea* came out in 1956 and is divided into three parts. The first part, "Caption" ("Didascalia"), is a sort of introduction that explains where and when the *Passage of Aeneas* happens. The location is a "red

DOI: 10.4324/9781003176145-6

house," more specifically a "Custom House" on a road with lots of traffic. It takes place during a "bleak night," and the poet, lying sleepless in his bed, is looking at "skeletons of rare lights," headlights of passing cars, on the ceiling. All these "wandering flashes" lead him to the idea of the "passage of Aeneas":

"Caption"

It was in a red house,
the Custom House.
I happened to be there
on a bleak night, my mind
outwardly shaken by
an endless transit, like the sea.
I listened to dry leaves,
crackling in darkness.
Sneaking through slats of blinds
skeletons of rare lights
had the resplendence of the sea.
They were wandering flashes
of motorized *turistas*
giving me the idea
it was the passage of Aeneas.[2]

The second part of the poem is composed of five stanzas, but only in the last two does Aeneas return. Here the scene is apocalyptic—Aeneas is alone in this big catastrophe ("stranded" is Portnowitz's translation), and it is possible to identify some points of contact with Book 2 of the *Aeneid*, where Vergil describes the sack of Troy.[3] Special attention should be given to the fourth stanza (with "your," Caproni is referring to himself):

"Verses" IV

In the beating blood of your Aeneas,
stranded in catastrophe, the shore
a smoldering red smoke, now blistering
around his bony foot—Aeneas, trying
to bear a crumbling past upon his shoulders
toward safety, and amid the rolling snare
of the toppling city walls, gripping the hand
of a future still so frail it cannot stand
on its own strength. And in this mournful
flare of an escape, along these sands
still hot with blood, what refuge do you hope
to find out in the sea (that dark green moth
with white headlights) when you, like him,
suddenly find yourself out at the farthest

stretch of solitude, at that most precise
and yet uncertain point of our dark years?[4]

Six lines of this stanza ("Verses" IV 4–9) recall *Aeneid* 2.721–5, when Aeneas puts his father Anchises on his shoulders, holds his son Ascanius by the hand and escapes from Troy: *haec fatus latos umeros subiectaque colla / veste super fulvique insternor pelle leonis, / succedoque oneri; dextrae se parvus Iulus / implicuit sequiturque patrem non passibus aequis; / pone subit coniunx.*[5] For Caproni this is a symbolic image because in Aeneas he recognizes himself, a survivor of the Second World War, suspended between "a crumbling past," represented by Anchises, and "a future still so frail it cannot stand on its own strength," represented by Ascanius. This can also be considered the poem's climax, and as we shall see, Caproni will return to its imagery throughout his life.

Another contemporary Italian author, Attilio Bertolucci (1911–2000), was inspired by the same image. He was born near Parma and lived in Rome at the same time as Caproni. And like Caproni, he was a translator and a prolific writer of poetry, a novel in verse, essays, and documentaries. Our focus is on *Viaggio d'inverno* (*Winter Journey*), in particular on the poem "Towards Casarola" ("Verso Casarola").[6] In two long strophes, Bertolucci recalls the tragic moment when he was forced to escape the Nazis with his family on September 8, 1943. They hurried to take refuge in Casarola, a tiny village in the mountains near Parma. In this way Bertolucci managed to save himself and his family. The last words of "Towards Casarola" (lines 54–7):

Now, I suppose
it must be time to hoist my child on my shoulders,
so, emerging from the thick, he'll see with wonder
the swirl of smoke and stars above our destined Casarola.[7]

The similarities with lines 2.801–4 of the *Aeneid* cannot escape the reader's attention: *iamque iugis summae surgebat Lucifer Idae / ducebatque diem, Danaique obsessa tenebant / limina portarum, nec spes opis ulla dabatur. / cessi et sublato montis genitore petivi.*[8] By having the father carry his son, Bertolucci inverts Vergil's image of Aeneas carrying Anchises. Some years later, Bertolucci returned to these words again in a review he wrote for *La Repubblica* in 1978 of the first volume of a new Italian translation of the *Aeneid*, which he entitled "Col padre in spalla verso gli alti monti" ("Carrying the Father on my Shoulders Towards the High Mountains").[9]

* * * *

The first stop Aeneas makes after leaving Troy is in Thrace, where his intent to found a new city there is thwarted by a horrific miracle: the removal of some branches of myrtle cause the plant to bleed. Aeneas discovers this was the burial ground of Priam's son Polydorus, who was murdered with spears that then took root and produced the myrtle. Petrified with fright, Aeneas and his men decided to keep going. Vergil describes their departure thus (3.69–72): *Inde ubi prima fides pelago, placataque venti / dant maria et lenis crepitans vocat Auster in altum, / deducunt socii navis et litora complent; / provehimur portu terraeque urbesque recedunt.*[10] Caproni reshapes the last line into an enigmatic couplet:

> Little did I know that setting sail
> would mean the earth itself would drift away.[11]

The couplet is preceded by prose and by another couplet, both about Aeneas standing in front of Troy as it burns. These passages were unknown to the public until 2016, when Adele Dei, an influential Caproni scholar, published them on the basis of a copy she had made before Caproni's papers were transferred to the archives at the Gabinetto Viesseux in Florence, where they are now kept.[12] Although Luca Zuliani has questioned whether these verses were in fact that work of Caproni, I have recently tried to demonstrate that they are indeed authentic and were possibly composed between 1946 and 1948, that is, before Caproni began his work on *Il passaggio d'Enea.*[13] These debates notwithstanding, it is my contention here that these verses, like the *Passage of Aeneas*, are direct allusions to the *Aeneid.* It may have been the first time that Caproni saw Aeneas in a modern postwar context—as a survivor and an exile. If the couplet above does have its root in Vergil's *provehimur portu terraeque urbesque recedunt*, Caproni seems to have divided it into two parts, rendering *provehimur portu* into "setting sail" and *terraeque urbesque recedunt* into "the earth itself would drift away." Caproni's addition of "little did I know," and his omission of cities (*urbes*) are a function of his fusion of Aeneas leaving the wreckage of Troy, from Book 2, with his escape from Thrace in Book 3. "Little did I know" reflects the narrator's inexperience in "setting sail," which better fits with Aeneas' first decampment, his flight from Troy, not his second, his subsequent sailing away from Thrace. Similarly, as the only city Caproni's Aeneas has in mind is Troy, which has been destroyed, there are no *urbes* to left to "drift away from," but only *terrae*, "earth."

* * * *

Aeneas next heads to Buthrotum, in the western part of Greece, where he finds, to his surprise, Andromache, the wife of the fallen Trojan hero Hector. After Hector's death, she was taken to Greece by Pyrrhus, Achilles' son. She later married Priam's son Helenus. In Buthrotum, they built a small kingdom so similar to Troy that it is called "Little Troy" (*parva Troia*, 3.349). The meeting between Andromache and Aeneas provides the occasion for Valerio Magrelli to comment on the nature of art and its relation to lived experience. Born in 1957, Magrelli is a scholar and translator of French literature as well as a renowned contemporary Italian poet with a deep interest in philosophy.[14] It is perhaps Magrelli's work on Baudelaire that inspired his interest in Andromache. The erstwhile princess appears in Baudelaire's "Swan" as a symbol for all who have suffered loss.[15] Just as Baudelaire's swan, having lost its natural habitat, ended up alone on the streets of Paris, so

Andromache has lost her city and was carried away by Pyrrhus to a strange land. But Magrelli refocuses his attention on Vergil, and in particular, on the "Little Troy" that Andromache built with Helenus. According to Magrelli, Buthrotum's pale imitation of Troy is essential for Aeneas:

> Aeneas understands that salvation rests in the future alone. Which is why he decides to abandon Buthrotum, refusing a purely mimetic, imitative past. . . . While Helenus believes he's saved Troy by replicating it, Aeneas reincarnates it by founding Rome. . . . What is Buthrotum after all, but a clone cast from the same mold? . . . And yet, despite all, Aeneas needed Buthrotum in order to fully understand the principle of the law of transformation: the only way to repeat an experience is to alter it. The only true Troy will be Rome, the same as his lost homeland insofar as it is finally different.[16]

This passage is taken from *Il violino di Frankenstein. Scritti per e sulla musica* (*Frankenstein's Violin: Writings for and about Music*), which featured selections of Magrelli's previously published texts accompanied by musical interpretations of Magrelli's own work by contemporary Italian composers and performers. This particular passage comes from the act titled "Buthrotum" and reveals Magrelli's interest in art's mimetic property—the relationship between imitator and antecedent—and the salvific potential of art. In the same work, Magrelli asserts that "a true classic is a text that is capable of transforming itself into a pretext" in every sense of the word.[17] So in this case, the episode of Andromache and Buthrotum is a pretext for a timely reflection on the nature and value of imitation, the lesson for Magrelli being that, although a Buthrotum might be constructed with good intention, it will never be but dull and disappointing because it is substantially dead. For Magrelli, transformation is the very essence of life.

* * * *

After Buthrotum, Aeneas eventually finds himself in Carthage, where Dido is building a city and establishing its laws. Aeneas and Dido fall in love, but Aeneas leaves after receiving a divine reminder of his duty to found Rome. Dido commits suicide. However, Aeneas' seafaring is not yet finished, and the gods decide to sacrifice one of his men to guarantee safe passage for the Trojans to Italy. The victim is an experienced navigator, Aeneas' pilot Palinurus. He is drugged by the god of sleep, falls overboard, and dies.

Both of these episodes are the basis for one of the most famous Italian reimaginings of the *Aeneid*, *La Terra Promessa* (*The Promised Land*) by Giuseppe Ungaretti. Although Ungaretti is best known for his poems about World War I, between 1935 and 1953, he worked sporadically on *La Terra Promessa*, which would remain unfinished. As the Ungaretti himself declared, "The *Aeneid* is present throughout *La Terra Promessa*, and all the places that belong to it."[18]

In the 1930s, Ungaretti was living in Rome. It was there that he began work on *La Terra Promessa*. He may have been inspired by the traces of ancient Rome being uncovered every day during extensive excavations throughout the city ordered by Mussolini. However, while travelling on the Tyrrhenian Sea, he had a chance to visit Cape Palinuro, the place where, according to the *Aeneid*, Aeneas' faithful pilot Palinurus died. He also visited nearby Salerno, where he noticed the head of a statue of Apollo that had been caught by fishermen in their nets. Inspired by these things, Ungaretti wrote an article "The Miraculous Catch" in 1932 and started composing some passages of what would become *La Terra Promessa*.[19]

In considering how Ungaretti reworked the characters of Aeneas and Dido, it is worth adding a few words about how he had conceived the ambitious project,[20] which he never managed to complete:

> Eternal beauty (though inexorably tied to death, to images, to earthly affairs, to history, and therefore only *deceptively* eternal—as Palinuro himself will say) took on the form of Aeneas in my mind. Aeneas is beauty, youth, naivety, ever in search of the Promised Land, where he's left smiling and swooning at the thought of his own, fleeting beauty. Though this isn't the myth of Narcissus: it is an inspiring union between the life of memory, imagination, and speculation: the life of the mind; it is a union of carnal life in the long succession of generations. . . . Many facts about my life and my nation's life have necessarily been expanding in the early stages of drafting *The Promised Land*. This, in any case, even now, should occur at the point when, Aeneas having reached the Promised Land, the depictions of his previous experience stir up and reveal to him, in his memory, the fate of his current experience, and so forth for all experiences, until humans, centuries from now, are permitted to know the true Promised Land.[21]

Therefore, in this project, the main characters of the *Aeneid* were intended to take on new, symbolic meanings and be inserted in a program in which Aeneas represents beauty in search of a stable and serene destination.

We can see Dido representing the feeling of love lived on the edge of her existence in one of the few completed parts of this unfinished work, "Choruses describing Dido's Feelings." Ungaretti writes:

> Dido has come to represent that moment when we cross through the threshold, into the autumn of our lives; that moment when living stretches out into a desert; that moment when, with one last, horrifying tremble, youth shakes itself free from our bodies.[22]

It is interesting to listen to Dido's voice in Ungaretti's poems introducing her. In the third of the 19 "Choruses describing Dido's Feelings," the fascinating queen is represented in her trembling sensuality and simultaneous awareness of her fragility as a result of those feelings:

> *III*
>
> The wind has gone silent, now,
and the sea is silent;

all goes quiet; but I'm screaming.
Alone, I'm screaming my heart,
screaming love, screaming shame,
my heart that's been burning
since the day I gazed on you and you looked back,
and I'm nothing now but the frailest thing.

Screaming, my heart burning without peace
since the moment I've been nothing
but a ruined thing, abandoned.[23]

Subsequently, in "Choruses" XIV–XVII, Dido speaks in the conditional, formulating a series of apodoses with the respective protases left to the reader's imagination. It is as if the existential situation in which she found herself did not allow her to trust in any future, much less, in a certain and stable future, and her whole existence had been veiled in precariousness. Mario Petrucciani, who focused his attention on this grammatical detail—so much so that he chose *Il condizionale di Didone* as the title of his main monograph on *The Promised Land*—has written about "a poignant fabulous orchestration of the impossible."[24] The following is a very short example:

XV

Deserted, you'd see nothing but your own wrongs,
not even a plume of smoke to graze the edge
of sleep, quiescently.[25]

Ungaretti turns to Palinurus and his tragic attempted devotion to his assigned task in "Palinurus' Recitative," another Aeneadic fragment of *The Promised Land.* In Book 6 of the *Aeneid*, Aeneas eventually arrives in Cumae, where he is guided by the Sibyl to the Underworld. It is there that Aeneas reunites with his father Anchises, who had died during the journey, and witnesses the future of Rome to come. On his way to see his father, Aeneas sees Dido, who refuses to speak to him, as well as Palinurus, who is unable to enter the underworld because he has not yet been buried. Palinurus explains that he arrived on land after surviving four days at sea only to be stabbed to death by cruel people (*gens crudelis*, 6.359) while he clung, weighed down by his wet clothes, to the edge of a cliff. He asks that Aeneas find and bury him, but the Sibyl denies his request. She consoles him by telling him that people from cities on the coast will build a tomb for him on a jut of land that will grant him an eternal name (*aeternum nomen*, 6.381).

In "Palinurus' Recitative," Ungaretti writes: "Cape Palinuro, right near Velia, beyond Paestum, is the giant mound that has for centuries given form to Palinurus' desperate loyalty."[26] The "desperate loyalty" that the "giant mound" near Paestum symbolizes is Palinurus' loyalty to his task and to the promised land that Aeneas and his men have to reach.[27] In order to keep this promise, Palinurus heroically fought against sleep before falling into the sea and dying (5.833–71).

Palinurus' story made a deep impression on another famous Italian novelist, Carlo Emilio Gadda (1893–1973). He was an engineer who dedicated himself to literature from the 1930s onwards. One of his early works is *Giornale di guerra e di prigionia*, a diary covering the three years he spent in World War I, including some months as a prisoner in Austria. Particularly interesting is the epigraph which opens the diary: *prospexi Italiam summa sublimis ab unda* (6.357).[28] Gadda chooses this line from the *Aeneid* to make a comparison between himself and Palinurus, since Palinurus, before dying, caught sight of Italy on the crest of a wave. In a similar way, Gadda caught imaginary sight of Italy on the crest of the Alps when he was a prisoner in Austria. As the text following the epigraph shows, Palinurus glimpsing his desired destination from the top of a wave was for Gadda an image of profound symbolic meaning: the emblem of what we desperately want, which is already in sight, not far away, and which perhaps we will never be able to conquer and possess.[29]

In order to complete our analysis of Palinurus, it is necessary to return to Caproni and to *The Passage of Aeneas* again. Here are the last verses of this poem, taken from "Epilogue" ("Epilogo") 23–6:

> At last I'd reached the sands
> but drained of all my strength.
> Perhaps from the weight of my clothes
> sodden with my years.[30]

Notably, Palinurus is not mentioned explicitly. Furthermore, Caproni, who, in my opinion, completely identifies with Aeneas in the *Epilogue*, passing from the third to the first person, combines the characters of Palinurus and Aeneas. Unlike the Vergilian hero, Caproni's Aeneas or, better, Aeneas-Caproni proceeds from the hinterland toward the sea shore and will not have a glorious future with an illustrious family like the *gens Iulia* and an empire. On the contrary, like Palinurus, he is weighted down by his wet clothes, though here they are "wet" with age, and arrives at the shore only to suffer: "Caproni is a Palinurus shipwrecked on the land, he lost his strength in a desperate attempt to approach the sea, not to get away from it."[31]

Alessandro Fo found the Vergilian model for Caproni's verses in Palinurus' episode, especially at the moment when Palinurus grasps the shore with difficulty, weighed down by his drenched clothing (*madida cum veste gravatum*, 6.359).[32] But another allusion may come into play in the verse "avevo raggiunto la rena," which hints at Aeneas' lamentation of Palinurus' fate: his body lying naked on the sands of an unfamiliar shore (*nudus in ignota, Palinure, iacebis harena*, 5.871).[33]

Now it is time to leave Palinurus and to follow Aeneas' arrival in Italy, at the mouth of the Tiber. Aeneas arrives an exile (*profugus*, 1.2), a war refugee, a foreigner without a home. He is also regarded as an enemy by the local people, especially by the Rutulians and the Latins, leading to his fateful duel with their champion, Turnus.

Tiziano Rossi tried to imagine Aeneas' feelings when he arrived in Italy. Born in Milan in 1935, Rossi was awarded the prestigious Italian literary prize, the Premio

Viareggio (like Caproni, Bertolucci, and Magrelli before him). His poetry can be defined as epic, but an everyday epic. This is especially true for his collection *Gente di corsa*, which portrays "people on the run" on the gray horizon of urban and industrial civilization. Aeneas peeps out in this short poem:

> ***Nader A.***
>
> The 'immigrant': who, with a cigarette
> and a wary gaze, uproots himself and moves
> to this strange west (this stretch of dripping tar),
> unknown Aeneas: who would sing of this man?[34]

In the everyday hustle and bustle, Aeneas, who is now named Nader A., is an immigrant of the present, "with a cigarette." He probably arrived in Italy from the East (because of his name, Nader, and because "he moves to this strange west"). But above all, he is an "unknown Aeneas" and nobody "would sing of this man."

Although this poem dates back 20 years, it is still of particular relevance for Italy today. For several years the Italian coasts have been the favorite destination of a large flow of African and Middle Eastern immigrants, who, due to catastrophic wars and economic crises, are trying to escape to the European continent hoping for a better future. All Italians know of the many shipwrecks and tragedies this phenomenon has caused and how bitter the political controversy regarding the reception of these migrants has been. In 2019, Vergil was brought into this debate. In the press and social media, the proponents of a welcome policy have repeatedly recalled (and are still recalling) verses from the *Aeneid.* In particular, an episode involving Aeneas and his comrade Ilioneus upon meeting at Dido's palace in Carthage has been much discussed. Here Aeneas and Achates, while wrapped in a cloud, see Ilioneus arrive at Dido's palace under escort with an embassy of Trojans. Ilioneus says (1.522–43):

> *o regina, novam cui condere Iuppiter urbem*
> *iustitiaque dedit gentis frenare superbas,*
> *Troes te miseri, ventis maria omnia vecti,*
> *oramus: prohibe infandos a navibus ignis,*
> *parce pio generi et propius res aspice nostras.*
> *non nos aut ferro Libycos populare penatis*
> *venimus, aut raptas ad litora vertere praedas;*
> *non ea vis animo nec tanta superbia victis.*
> *est locus, Hesperiam Grai cognomine dicunt,*
> *terra antiqua, potens armis atque ubere glaebae;*
> *Oenotri coluere viri; nunc fama minores*
> *Italiam dixisse ducis de nomine gentem.*
> *hic cursus fuit,*
> *cum subito adsurgens fluctu nimbosus Orion*
> *in vada caeca tulit penitusque procacibus Austris*

perque undas superante salo perque invia saxa
dispulit; huc pauci vestris adnavimus oris.
quod genus hoc hominum? quaeve hunc tam barbara morem
permittit patria? hospitio prohibemur harenae;
bella cient primaque vetant consistere terra.
si genus humanum et mortalia temnitis arma,
at sperate deos memores fandi atque nefandi.[35]

These words, and especially lines 539–42, have been cited by those advocating for refugees and have also elicited strong reactions from those that would like to close the borders and prevent landings.[36]

The philologist Maurizio Bettini—also a distinguished representative of today's Italian fiction—intervened in the heated controversy and, taking a cue from this debate, constructed a whole book arguing that Vergil's *humanitas* is nothing less than one of the bases for our understanding of human rights today.[37] He begins with the answer that Dido gives to Aeneas (1.561–78):

Tum breviter Dido voltum demissa profatur:
"solvite corde metum, Teucri, secludite curas.
res dura et regni novitas me talia cogunt
moliri et late finis custode tueri.
quis genus Aeneadum, quis Troiae nesciat urbem,
virtutesque virosque aut tanti incendia belli?
non obtunsa adeo gestamus pectora Poeni,
nec tam aversus equos Tyria Sol iungit ab urbe.
seu vos Hesperiam magnam Saturniaque arva
sive Erycis finis regemque optatis Acesten,
auxilio tutos dimittam opibusque iuvabo.
vultis et his mecum pariter considere regnis?
urbem quam statuo, vestra est; subducite navis;
Tros Tyriusque mihi nullo discrimine agetur.
atque utinam rex ipse Noto compulsus eodem
adforet Aeneas! equidem per litora certos
dimittam et Libyae lustrare extrema iubebo,
si quibus eiectus silvis aut urbibus errat."[38]

Soon after, the cloud dissolves and Aeneas gives thanks for her generosity (1.603–10):

di tibi, si qua pios respectant numina, si quid
usquam iustitiae est et mens sibi conscia recti,
praemia digna ferant. quae te tam laeta tulerunt
saecula? qui tanti talem genuere parentes?
in freta dum fluvii current, dum montibus umbrae
lustrabunt convexa, polus dum sidera pascet,

semper honos nomenque tuum laudesque manebunt,
quae me cumque vocant terrae.[39]

Dido's response culminates with these famous words (1.627–30):

quare agite, o tectis, iuvenes, succedite nostris.
me quoque per multos similis fortuna labores
iactatam hac demum voluit consistere terra;
non ignara mali miseris succurrere disco.[40]

In this regard, Bettini writes:

> We can say that for two thousand years Ilioneus, Dido and Aeneas have not simply interpreted (for Virgil's readers) one of the poem's finest episodes; but they have continued to convey to our culture the principles according to which a people who are not barbarians—but who respect good morals, humanity, the will of the gods and who have their own future fame at heart—must behave when a group of castaways, fleeing a terrifying war, lands on 'our' shores. The dialogue between these Vergilian characters and the story that takes shape around them have become part of our cultural encyclopedia, or of our civilization, if you prefer to use this word. . . . We can say that—together with many other works that come to us from the ancient world—also *Aeneid* 1 has contributed to the creation of the cultural awareness that led to the development of these principles of mutual respect and guarantee, which are basic for our coexistence and that today we call 'human rights.'[41]

* * * *

This chapter might have finished here. First, because the question raised in *Nader A.* is one of the most relevant regarding our modern *Aeneid*, as Bettini's touching words clearly show. This crucial point indicates the connection between the ancient figure of the Vergilian hero and a contemporary nameless Aeneas. But at the same time, through just a few verses, it gives an idea of all the vitality of the classics, all the universality and modernity of the *Aeneid*. Second, because Aeneas' journey, which we have followed so far, is finished with his arrival in Italy.

But there is an imaginary stop that one must add to Aeneas' journey to capture the range of its influence with Italy's greatest writers of the past century. This spot is in Genoa. Obviously, Vergil's Aeneas never arrived in Genoa, but Giorgio Caproni, who moved to Genoa when he was 10 years old, imagines a poetic 'meeting' with Aeneas in his hometown:

> It was last summer [1948], on a trip to Genoa, that I first came face-to-face with Aeneas son of Anchises. I looked up and there he was, in Piazza Bandiera. . . . Just think about that—Aeneas, who by *miracle* had escaped the destruction of Troy, right there, bearing his double cargo, smack beneath the

> bombs and rubble of one of the most heavily bombarded and ravaged piazzas in all of Italy! . . . For that group to leave Troy in flames, only to find themselves in the flames of this tremendous war, and then to escape it with almost no damage: just one chip out of Anchises' foot, the sole trace of damage in a narrow piazza where the bombs spared little else.[42]

Actually the statue is a fountain, as Caproni himself has the opportunity to clarify:

> The base of the monument is a stone platform, on top of which sits a polygonal prism. On the prism's sides are four lion's heads, each with water streaming from its mouth. . . . [T]he statue itself . . . representing Aeneas holding his young son by the hand, with his frail father draped over his shoulders, as a good shepherd would carry his lamb, is for me one of the most moving sights on this earth.[43]

The statue itself might be unremarkable, but for the poet it is "one of the most moving sights on this earth," so much so that he went back to this subject many times in his life over a period of 40 years.[44] In 1965, this meager statue gave birth to the masterpiece *Il passaggio d'Enea*, which, according to Caproni, would have never been written if he had not met Aeneas 'in person' in piazza Bandiera.[45] Not only had Aeneas survived the destruction of Troy and all the misadventures in the Mediterranean Sea, but he had also ended up in one of the most ravaged piazzas in all of Italy and escaped the bombs of World War II. After such a series of impressive fortuities, Caproni cannot help but reach this touching conclusion:

> In that poor Aeneas I see a clear symbol of the men of my generation, alone in the midst of war, trying to bear on his shoulders a past (a tradition) that is crumbling all around him, while trying to safely deliver a future that is so uncertain it can hardly stand up on its own, more in need of being led than he is capable of leading.[46]

Coming 'face to face' with Aeneas, in such a special situation, led Caproni to consider Aeneas as a symbol of modern mankind after World War II, suspended between "a past (a tradition) that is crumbling all around him" and "a future that is so uncertain."

* * * *

Several different examples of a contemporary reception of the *Aeneid* in Italian literature have been considered so far. On one hand, the *Aeneid*'s characters have symbolized human and eternal feelings, such as loyalty (Ungaretti's Palinurus) or crucial moments of life (Ungaretti's Dido). On the other hand, through these examples, attention has been focused, in particular, on traumatic events, such as wars (the comparison with Palinurus in Gadda's diary of World War I and Caproni's Aeneas in the rubble of World War II), colonizations and replications (the fake Buthrotum in Magrelli), migrations (the unsung Aeneas of the present in Rossi), and the search for new identity (Aeneas without a home and suspended between the past and the future in Caproni). Thus, these authors have borne out the claims of Alessandro Barchiesi, who wrote:

> In Vergil . . . the Romans seem to be the dynamic result of a series of contacts and fusions among people, in which Trojan ancestors acted like catalysts. . . . This is the reading of *Aeneid* in which it is still possible to make progress: by stripping the text of its canonicity and bringing it back to the material and historical forces at work in that period: colonizations, migrations, search for new identities, the invention of the Roman *humanitas* as a 'package of values' which accompanies the Romanization (and Hellenization) of the West.[47]

In this perspective, not only is the *Aeneid* ours and modern, that is, universally and presently applicable, but it is also still alive, still being reshaped and reinterpreted by new writers and readers.

Notes

1 "Call back / your courage, send away your grieving fear. / Perhaps one day you will remember even / these our adversities with pleasure" (all translations from the *Aeneid* are from Mandelbaum 2004; here 1.281–4).

2 Translated by Ned Condini in Caproni 2004. The original from Caproni 1998: 153:

> Fu in una casa rossa: / la Casa Cantoniera. / Mi ci trovai una sera / di tenebra, e pareva scossa/ la mente da un transitare / continuo, come il mare. / Sentivo foglie secche, / nel buio, scricchiolare. / Attraversando le stecche/ delle persiane, del mare / avevano la luminescenza / scheletri di luci rare. / Erano lampi erranti / d'ammotorati viandanti. / Frusciavano in me l'idea / che fosse il passaggio d'Enea.

3 For further explanation regarding the similarities between *The Passage of Aeneas* and *Aeneid* Book 2, see Caproni 2020 and Giannotti 2020a.

4 This translation into English has been specially prepared for this chapter by Todd Portnowitz. All following translations from the Italian are by him, unless otherwise stated. All my gratitude goes to him. Caproni 1998: 155–6:

> Nel pulsare del sangue del tuo Enea / solo nella catastrofe, cui sgalla / il piede ossuto la rossa fumea / bassa che arrazza il lido—Enea che in spalla / un passato che crolla tenta invano / di porre in salvo, e al rullo d'un tamburo / ch'è uno schianto di mura, per la mano / ha ancora così gracile un futuro / da non reggersi ritto. Nell'avvampo / funebre d'una fuga su una rena / che scotta ancora di sangue, che scampo / può mai esserti il mare (la falena / verde dai fari bianchi) se con lui / senti di soprassalto che nel punto, / d'estrema solitudine, sei giunto / più esatto e incerto dei nostri anni bui?

5 "This said, I spread a tawny lion skin / across my bent neck, over my broad shoulders, / and then take up Anchises; small Iulus / now clutches my right hand; his steps uneven, / he is following his father; and my wife / moves on behind" (2. 974–9).

6 Bertolucci 1978: 201–2.

7 Bertolucci 1978: 202: "*Allora / sarà tempo di caricare il figlio in cima alle spalle, / che all'uscita del folto veda con meraviglia / mischiarsi fumo e stelle su Casarola raggiunta.*"

8 "Now the star of morning rose / above high Ida's ridges, guiding the day. / The Danaans held the gates' blockaded thresholds. / There was no hope of help. Then I gave way / and, lifting up my father, made for the mountains" (2.1078–82).

9 Bertolucci 1978. See also Bertolucci 1997: 1061–4, 1743. For Bertolucci's Aeneas, see Schiavo 2010: 252–4.

10 "Then, just as soon as we can trust the sea, / as soon as the air allows us tranquil waters / and while the south wind, softly whispering, / invites to journeying, my comrades crowd / the beach to launch our fleet. We leave the harbor. / Our eyes have lost the cities and the land" (3.90–5).

11 Dei 2016: 61: "*Io non sapevo che a partir per nave / tutta la terra se n'andasse via.*"

12 For Dei's work on Caproni, see Dei 1992. On the publication of Caproni's unpublished work, see Dei 2016: 61.

13 Luca Zuliani is the editor of the fundamental critical edition of Caproni, in Caproni 1998. On the authenticity and dating of this passage, see Giannotti 2020b.

14 He translated works by Mallarmé, Valéry, Jarry, Char, and Ponge.

15 Baudelaire 2009: 174–9.

16 Magrelli 2010: 126–8:

> Enea capisce che l'unica salvezza è nel futuro. Perciò decide di abbandonare Butroto, rinnegando un passato puramente mimetico, imitativo. . . . Mentre Eleno crede d'aver salvato Troia replicandola, Enea la resuscita fondando Roma. . . . Cos'è Butroto se non un povero clone tratto dalla matrice? . . . Eppure, malgrado tutto, Enea aveva bisogno di Butroto per comprendere fino in fondo il principio della legge trasformativa: il solo modo di ripetere un'esperienza consiste nel cambiarla. L'unica vera Troia sarà Roma, uguale alla patria perduta, perché finalmente diversa.

17 Magrelli 2010: 127: "*Secondo me ogni vero classico è un testo capace di trasformarsi in pretesto.*"

18 Ungaretti 1969: 556: "*L'Eneide è sempre presente nella Terra Promessa, e con i luoghi che furono suoi.*"

19 The article *The Miraculous Catch*, which is about this journey between Salerno and Capo Palinuro, came out for the first time in *La Gazzetta del Popolo* on May 5th, 1932 (see Ungaretti 2000: 148–53, 1125–9, 1151). It was Ungaretti himself who recognized the importance of this journey, on which Vergil was his guide, and of the emotions he felt as a starting point and deep root of the project *The Promised Land.* See Ungaretti 1969: 427–8; cf. Petrucciani 1985: 169; Petrucciani 1990: 392–3 and Fo 2007: 332.

20 See especially Petrucciani 1985; Petrucciani 1990; Petrucciani 2002; Guglielmi 1989; Fo 2007: 222–7.

21 Ungaretti 1969: 429–30:

> La bellezza perenne (ma inesorabilmente legata al perire, alle immagini, alle vicende terrene, alla storia, e quindi solo illusoriamente perenne—e lo dirà Palinuro) prese nella mia mente aspetto di Enea. Enea è bellezza, giovinezza, ingenuità in cerca sempre di Terra Promessa, ove fa sorridere e incantare nella bellezza contemplata e fuggente, la propria. Ma non è il mito di Narciso: è unione animatrice di vita della memoria, della fantasia e della speculazione: di vita della mente; è unione di vita carnale nel lungo susseguirsi delle generazioni . . . Molti fatti della mia vita e di quella della mia Nazione, sono andati necessariamente ampliando nella stesura il progetto primitivo della Terra Promessa. Esso, in ogni caso, anche oggi, dovrebbe svolgersi al punto in cui, toccata Enea la Terra Promessa, le raffigurazioni della precedente sua esperienza si desterebbero ad attestargli, nella memoria, di come andrebbe a finire l'attuale, e via di seguito tutte, sino a quando non sia dato agli umani, consumati i secoli, di conoscere la Terra Promessa vera.

See also the further statements collected by Leone Piccioni, the editor of the complete edition of Ungaretti poems, in his important essay *Le origini della "Terra Promessa"* in Ungaretti 1969: 427–64.

22 Ungaretti 1969: 430: "*Didone veniva a rappresentare l'esperienza di chi, nel tardo autunno, stia per varcarlo; l'ora in cui il vivere stia per farsi deserto: l'ora della persona dalla quale stia per separarsi, tremendo, orribile, l'ultimo fremito della gioventù.*"

23 Ungaretti 1969: 245:

> Ora il vento s'è fatto silenzioso / e silenzioso il mare; / tutto tace; ma grido. / Il grido, sola, del mio cuore, / grido d'amore, grido di vergogna / del mio cuore che brucia / da quando ti mirai e m'hai guardata / e più non sono che un oggetto debole. // Grido e brucia il mio cuore senza pace / da quando più non sono / se non cosa in rovina e abbandonata.

24 Author's translation. Petrucciani 1990: 393: "*Una struggente orchestrazione favolosa dell'impossibile.*"

25 Ungaretti 1969: 248: "*Non vedresti che torti tuoi, deserta, / senza più un fumo che alla soglia avvii / del sonno, sommessamente.*"

26 Ungaretti 1969: 566: "*Lo scoglio di Palinuro, quasi davanti a Elea, dopo Pesto, è quello scoglio ingigantito nel quale la disperata fedeltà di Palinuro ha trovato forma per i secoli.*"

27 Ungaretti 1969: 567; De Marco 2008: 65,155.

28 "High on a wave crest, I / saw Italy" (6. 468–9).

29 See Fo 2002: n. 62 for a list of the passages.

30 Caproni 1998: 157: "*Avevo raggiunto la rena, / ma senza avere più lena. / Forse era il peso nei panni, / dell'acqua dei miei anni.*"

31 Bettini 2002 quoted in Caproni 2020: 239: "*Caproni è un Palinuro naufragato in terra, la sua lena l'ha persa nel disperato tentativo di avvicinarsi al mare, non in quello di uscirne.*"

32 See Fo 2002: 210.

33 "O Palinurus, . . . you will lie naked on an unknown shore" (5.1150–2). Mandelbaum's translation here misses the word *harena* ("sand"), which is the anchor for Caproni's allusion. *Ignota . . . harena*, although it synecdochally stands for "unfamiliar shore," literally means "unknown sands," hence Caproni's "*rena*". For further discussion, see Caproni 2020: 183.

34 Rossi 2000: 19: "*Detto immigrato: sopra questo ovest / (strano catrame, bagnato impiantito) / fumando sigaretta guardingo si trapianta, / ignoto Enea, che mica lo si canta.*" See also Rossi 2003: 437.

35

> O Queen, / whom Jupiter has granted this: to bring / to being a new city, curbing haughty / nations by justice—we, unhappy Trojans, / men carried by the winds across all seas, / beg you to keep the terror of fire from / our fleet, to spare a pious race, to look / on with us kindliness. We do not come / to devastate your homes and with the sword / to loot the household gods of Libya or / to drive down stolen booty toward the beaches. / That violence is not within our minds; / such arrogance is not for the defeated. / There is a place the Greeks have named Hesperia, / an ancient land with strong arms and fat soil. / Its colonists were the Oenotrians. / Now rumor runs that their descendants call / that nation 'Italy,' after their leader. / Our prows were pointed there when suddenly, / rising upon the surge, stormy Orion / drove us against blind shoals; and insolent / south winds then scattered us, undone by brine, / across the crushing sea, the pathless rocks. / A few of us have drifted to your shores. / What kind of men are these? Or is your country / so barbarous that it permits this custom? / We are denied the shelter of the beach; / they goad us into war; they will not let us / set foot upon the border of their land. / If you despise the human race and mortal / weapons, then still consider that the gods / remember right and wrong.
> (1.735–66)

36 See Bartolucci 2019; Mocci 2016; Socci 2019.
37 See Bettini 2001; Bettini 2004; Bettini 2011; Bettini 2013; Bettini 2019.
38

> Then Dido softly, briefly answers him: / "O Teucrians, enough of fear, cast out / your cares. My kingdom is new; hard circumstances / have forced me to such measures for our safety, / to post guards far and wide along our boundaries. / But who is ignorant of Aeneas' men? / Who has not heard of Troy, its acts and heroes, / the flames of that tremendous war? We Tyrians / do not have minds so dull, and we are not / beyond the circuit of the sun's yoked horses. / Whatever you may choose—Hesperia and / the fields of Saturn, or the land of Eryx / and King Aceste—I shall send you safe / with escort, I shall help you with my wealth. / And should you want to settle in this kingdom / on equal terms with me, then all the city / I am building now is yours. Draw up your ships. / I shall allow no difference between / the Tyrian and the Trojan. Would your king, / Aeneas, too, were present, driven here / by that same south wind. I, in fact, shall send / my trusted riders out along the shores, / to comb the farthest coasts of Libya and / to see if, cast out of the waters, he / is wandering through the forests or the cities."
>
> (1.791–815)

39

> "May gods confer on you your due rewards, / if deities regard the good, if justice / and mind aware of right count anywhere. / What happy centuries gave birth to you? / What splendid parents brought you into being? / While rivers run into the sea and shadows / still sweep the mountain slopes and stars still pasture / upon the sky, your name and praise and honor / shall last, whatever be the lands that call me."
>
> (1.847–55)

40 "Thus, young men, you are welcome to our halls. / My destiny, like yours, has willed that I, / a veteran of hardships, halt at last / in this country. Not ignorant of trials, / I now can learn to help the miserable" (1.877–82).
41 Bettini 2019: 22–3:

> possiamo dire che per duemila anni Ilioneo, Didone ed Enea non hanno semplicemente interpretato (per i lettori di Virgilio) uno degli episodi più belli del poema; ma hanno continuato a trasmettere alla nostra cultura i principî secondo cui un popolo che non sia barbaro—ma rispetti i buoni costumi, l'umanità, il volere degli dèi e abbia a cuore la propria fama futura—deve comportarsi allorché un gruppo di naufraghi, fuggendo da una guerra spaventosa, approdi sulle "nostre" rive. Il dialogo fra questi personaggi virgiliani, e il racconto che attorno ad esso prende forma, sono entrati a far parte della nostra enciclopedia culturale, ovvero della nostra civiltà, se si preferisce usare questa parola. [. . .] Possiamo dire che—assieme a tante altre opere che ci vengono dal mondo antico—anche il primo libro dell'Eneide ha contribuito a creare la consapevolezza culturale che ha portato alla elaborazione di quei principî di reciproco rispetto e garanzia, basilari per la nostra convivenza, che oggi chiamiamo "diritti umani."

42 Caproni 1949:

> Fu l'estate scorsa [dunque del 1948] ch'io, trovandomi a Genova per una visita, m'incontrai la prima volta . . . con Enea figlio d'Anchise. Me lo vidi di soprassalto davanti in Piazza Bandiera . . . Pensate, Enea scampato per miracolo alla distruzione di Troia, e venuto a capitare, col suo duplice prezioso fardello, proprio sotto le bombe e i calcinacci d'una delle più bombardate e tartassate piazze d'Italia! . . . Un gruppo che partito così da Troia in combustione, così se n'è rimasto tra le fiamme di questa tremenda guerra, uscendone con un minimo danno: un piede

sbocconcellato ad Anchise, il quale è l'unico danno subito su una piazzetta angusta dove le bombe han risparmiato ben poco.

See Caproni 2020: 75–9, 160–3.

43 Caproni 1948:

> Lo zoccolo di questo monumento è una piattaforma di pietra su cui posa un prisma poligonale. Sulle facce laterali di questo prisma sono quattro teste di leone, dalle cui bocche esce, a fontana, l'acqua. . . . la statua vera e propria . . . rappresentando Enea che ha per la mano il figliolino e porta ciondoloni sulle spalle, come l'agnello del buon pastore, il fragilissimo padre, è per me quanto di più commovente io abbia visto sulla terra.

See Caproni 2020: 68–70, 155–7.

44 All the passages by Caproni about Aeneas are now collected with commentary in Caproni 2020.

45 See, for example, Caproni 1979. See also Caproni 2020: 98–112, 192–3.

46 Caproni 1979:

> In quel povero Enea vidi chiaro il simbolo dell'uomo della mia generazione, solo in piena guerra a cercar di sostenere sulle spalle un passato (una tradizione) crollante da tutte le parti, e a cercar di portare a salvamento un futuro ancora così incerto da non reggersi ritto, più bisognoso di guida che capace di far da guida.

47 Barchiesi 2006: XLIII:

> In Virgilio . . . il popolo romano appare come l'esito dinamico di una serie di contatti e di fusioni tra popoli, in cui gli antichi progenitori troiani hanno agito come catalizzatori. . . . È questa la lettura dell'Eneide in cui si può ancora fare dei progressi: liberando il testo dalla sua canonicità e riportandolo al gioco delle forze materiali e storiche di quel periodo: colonizzazioni, migrazioni, ricerca di nuove identità, l'invenzione dell'humanitas Romana come 'pacchetto di valori' che accompagna la romanizzazione (ed ellenizzazione) dell'occidente.

References

Barchiesi, A. 2006. "Le sofferenze dell'Impero." In R. Scarcia (tran.) *Virgilio, Eneide*. Milan: BUR. v–lii.

Bartolucci, F. 2019. "Enea non è un eroe 'pro migranti'. Insegniamo l'Eneide ai semicolti." *Il Primato Nazionale*, January 29. https://www.ilprimatonazionale.it/approfondimenti/enea-non-eroe-migranti-eneide-semicolti-102861/

Baudelaire, C. 2009. *Opere*. Edited by G. Raboni and G. Montesano. Milan: Mondadori.

Bertolucci, A. 1978. "Col padre in spalla verso gli alti monti [Review of Vergil's Aeneid, ed. E. Paratore, trans. L. Canali, vol. I (Books I-III)]." *la Repubblica*, May 30.

———. 1997. *Opere*. Edited by P. Lagazzi and G.P. Baroni. Milan: Mondadori.

Bettini, M. 2001. *In fondo al cuore, Eccellenza*. Turin: Einaudi.

———. 2002. 'Il passaggio d'Enea' di Giorgio Caproni." *Semicerchio* 26/27: 53–7.

———. 2004. *Le coccinelle di Redùn*. Turin: Einaudi.

———. 2011. *Per vedere se*. Genoa: Il nuovo Melangolo.

———. 2013. *Con l'obbligo di Sanremo*. Turin: Einaudi.

———. 2019. *Homo sum: Essere "umani" nel mondo antico*. Turin: Einaudi.

Caproni, G. 1948. "Monumento a Enea." *La Voce Adriatica*, October 20.

———. 1949. "Noi, Enea." *La Fiera Letteraria*, July 3.

———. 1979. "Genova." *Weekend*, October.

———. 1998. *L'opera in versi*. Edited by L. Zuliani. Milan: Mondadori.

———. 2004. *The Earth's Wall: Selected Poems 1932–1986*. Translated by N. Condini. New York: Chelsea Editions.

———. 2020. *Il mio Enea*. Edited by F. Giannotti. Milan: Garzanti.

Dei, A. 1992. *Giorgio Caproni*. Milan: Mursia.

———. 2016. *L'orma della parola. Su Giorgio Caproni*. Padua: Esteda.

De Marco, G. 2008. *Le icone della lontananza. Carte di esilio e viaggi di carta*. Rome: Salerno Editrice.

Fo, A. 2002. "Virgilio nei poeti e nel racconto (dal secondo Novecento italiano)." In F. Roscetti, L. Lanzetta, and L. Cantatore (eds.) *Il classico nella Roma contemporanea: Mito, modelli, memoria (October 2000)*. Rome: Istituto di Studi Romani. 181–239.

———. 2007. "Ancora sulla presenza dei classici nella poesia italiana contemporanea." In N. Borsellino and B. Germano (eds.) *L'Italia letteraria e l'Europa, III, Tra Ottocento e Duemila*. Rome: Salerno Editrice.

Giannotti, F. 2020a. "'Nel soffio del tempo'. Riferimenti classici letterari e mitologici nell'opera di Giorgio Caproni." In *Res Publica Litterarum. Studies in Classical Tradition*. In Press.

———. 2020b. "L'Enea ritrovato. Un appunto dattiloscritto di Giorgio Caproni." *L'Ulisse. Rivista di poesia, arti e scritture* 23: 121–37.

Guglielmi, G. 1989. "Giuseppe Ungaretti e la memoria dell' 'Eneide'." In *Mnemosyne: Studi in onore di A. Ghiselli*. Bologna: Pàtron. 311–24.

Magrelli, V. 2010. *Il violino di Frankenstein. Scritti per e sulla musica (con musiche di G. Baggiani, C. Boccadoro, L. Ceccarelli, e F. De Rossi Re)*. Florence: Le Lettere.

Mandelbaum, A., tran. 2004. *The Aeneid of Virgil*. Bantam Classic. New York: Bantam Dell.

Mocci, M. 2016. "Enea non era un 'profugo', il suo era un ritorno all'origine." *Il Primato Nazionale*, May 21. https://www.ilprimatonazionale.it/cultura/enea-profugo-origine-45275/

Petrucciani, M. 1985. *Il condizionale di Didone*. Naples: Edizioni Scientifiche Italiane.

———. 1990. "Ungaretti." In *Enciclopedia Virgiliana*. Rome: Istituto della Enciclopedia Italiana. V:391–4.

———. 2002. "Ungaretti e Virgilio: palinsesto alle origini della 'Terra Promessa'." In F. Roscetti, L. Lanzetta, and L. Cantatore (eds.) *Il classico nella Roma contemporanea: Mito, modelli, memoria (October 2000)*. Rome: Istituto di Studi Romani. I:61–70.

Piccioni, L. 1969. "Le origini della 'Terra Promessa'." In G. Ungaretti (ed.) *Vita d'un uomo. Tutte le poesie*, 427–64. Milan: Mondadori.

Rossi, T. 2000. *Gente di corsa*. Milan: Garzanti.

———. 2003. *Tutte le poesie (1963–2000)*. Milan: Garzanti.

Schiavo, P. 2010. "Tra memoria e pietas: l'Enea di Caproni e Ungaretti." In G. Sandrini and M. Natale (eds.) *Gli antichi dei moderni. Dodici letture da Leopardi a Zanzotto*. Verona: Fiorini. 237–54.

Socci, A. 2019. "Per attaccare Salvini usano pure Virgilio, ma è un clamoros autogol." January 28. www.antoniosocci.com/per-attaccare-salvini-usano-pure-virgilio-ma-e-un-clamoroso-autogol/?fbclid=IwAR0UPIDo4n9KVtU4xpCKjOb4KoSlgJIjBecXEpcOJjiqTqJmm9lGeYsARo.

Ungaretti, G. 1969. *Vita d'un uomo. Tutte le poesie*. Edited by Leone Piccioni. Milan: Mondadori.

———. 2000. *Vita d'un uomo, Viaggi e lezioni*. Edited by P. Montefoschi. Milan: Mondadori.

5 Philip Pullman's *His Dark Materials* trilogy and the *Aeneid*

Lyra as an anti-Aeneas

Babette Puetz

Introduction

Much recent scholarship has shown how children's literature tends to retell and refocus ancient epics.[1] Parry sums up that "children's literature has become a home for epic themes in a literary landscape otherwise often hostile toward their perceived simplicity and moral didacticism, and offers a possibility for the survival of the epic tradition in a modern world."[2] That said, children's books do not always allude to ancient epics uncritically but frequently highlight problematic aspects of their predecessors.

In this chapter I demonstrate how Philip Pullman's immensely popular *His Dark Materials* trilogy (1995–2000), henceforth *HDM*, falls squarely within this tradition by using the *Aeneid* as a source for depicting the extent of the humanity and sacrifice of its protagonist, Lyra, for the greater good. Critics have noted a "depth of humanity" in the *Aeneid*, especially in the Dido episodes, which bring to the fore an inner struggle between "passion and duty."[3] This struggle also proves to be central to the development of Lyra's character. Ultimately, this chapter will show how Pullman deploys and inverts features from the *Aeneid* in order to shape his modern heroine.[4]

The first section provides a summary of the *HDM* trilogy. The next four detail the important parallels and equally important differences between *HDM* and the *Aeneid*. The following section introduces a foundational similarity between Lyra and Aeneas: their strong sense of duty even in the face of sacrifice. It also discusses the critical differences between Lyra and Aeneas: she is very young, female, and from a time and place parallel to late 20th-/early-21st-century England. Additionally, it will be shown that, unlike Aeneas and Dido, Lyra works together with her first love, Will, until their break-up at the end of her journey. These differences lead Lyra to act upon her sense of duty in a different way than Aeneas; she learns, and her maturation shows in her compassionate actions toward others.

That brings us to two other significant allusions to the *Aeneid* in *HDM*: the underworld scene and Lyra and Will's tragic love story. Here Pullman strikingly reverses the order of his model: in the *Aeneid*, the love story precedes the underworld scene, so we can see the terrible consequences of the separation when

DOI: 10.4324/9781003176145-7

Aeneas meets Dido in the underworld. In *HDM*, the children first venture to the underworld, and it is here that they fall in love, even if they do not yet realize it.[5] Their terrible experience in the world of the dead binds them even closer together, the positive consequences of which are shown both in the love scene and in the mature way the children handle their eventual separation.

The next three sections provide the evidence for and detailed discussion of these claims. The first of these three covers the specific allusions made to and contrasts drawn between *HDM*'s underworld and Book 6 of the *Aeneid*. The analysis of the tragic love stories of Aeneas and Dido and Lyra and Will is a bit more involved and therefore split into two sections. The first of which examines how the two couples meet, while the last considers their unhappy endings. Again we see how Pullman cultivates his characters by careful divergence from the *Aeneid*. The final section offers concluding thoughts on Pullman's technique and the enduring relevance of Vergil's epic.

A brief summary of HDM

HDM tells of the journeys of 12-year-old Lyra Belacqua and Will Parry through parallel worlds. The first part of the trilogy, *Northern Lights/The Golden Compass* (*NL/GC*),[6] is set in Lyra's world, which is parallel and, in many ways, similar to ours, the greatest difference being that all humans have animal daemons. These are speaking animals that usually need to stay close to their human and, as physical manifestations of their human's soul, closely interact with and often advise them.[7]

In *NL/GC (as in Northern Lights/Golden Compass)*, Lyra, with the help of her truth-telling device (the 'alethiometer'), travels to the far North where she rescues kidnapped children, including her best friend, Roger, from a church-led research station that conducts experiments into "intercision," the forced separation of children from their daemons, in order to stop the sin ('Dust') associated with the start of puberty. After the successful rescue, Lyra is tricked by her father, Lord Asriel, to bring Roger to him. Asriel forcefully separates Roger from his daemon to create a burst of energy sufficiently large to blast an entrance into a parallel world. He succeeds, Roger dies, and Lyra follows Asriel into the world of Cittàgazze.

In the second book in the trilogy, *The Subtle Knife* (*SK*),[8] Lyra meets and befriends Will Parry, a boy of Lyra's age who has fled into the world of Cittàgazze from our own world, and the academic Dr. Mary Malone, who is researching conscious Shadow Particles, which are equivalent to the 'Dust' of Lyra's world. Will manages to obtain a special knife (the Subtle Knife) that can cut windows between different worlds.

The third part of the trilogy, *The Amber Spyglass* (*AS*),[9] is named after a spyglass, crafted by Mary Malone, in a world inhabited by creatures called the Mulefa, whom Mary befriends. The spyglass enables Mary to see what is called 'Dust' in Lyra's world. At the start of this part of the trilogy, Lyra is being held, drugged to sleep, in a cave by her mother, Mrs. Coulter, until Will frees her. The Church in Lyra's world, who have learned of a prophecy of Lyra as a 'second Eve,' plan to capture and kill her, but Will rescues Lyra and brings her to safety.

Lyra and Will travel to the underworld so Lyra can apologize to her friend Roger for her partial responsibility in his death. Lyra finds Roger's ghost, but out of pity for the dead, the children decide to set all ghosts free. This happens while the Church detonates a bomb to kill Lyra, which misses her and creates an enormous abyss instead, and while a large-scale battle is raging above ground between the Church's and Asriel's forces. Then Lyra and Will flee into the world of the Mulefa, where they meet Mary, who tells them a story about what it is like to fall in love ("the story of marzipan"), which leads Lyra and Will to realize that they are in love.

However, only shortly after hearing the story of the marzipan, Lyra and Will learn from an angel that they will need to live in separate worlds, as it is not possible to stay healthy when living in a world that is not one's own. Furthermore, all the windows between the worlds, except one, must be closed for all the worlds to be safe.[10] The children are devastated, but—bravely putting the greater good of all humankind before their personal happiness—decide that the one window to remain open must be the exit out of the underworld. This will free humans from their fear of death, which the Church uses to control them. Everyone returns to their world. Will breaks the Subtle Knife and Lyra agrees to go to school, both determined to live their lives to the fullest.

In the love and underworld scenes, in particular, Pullman reworks Vergil's *Aeneid.* As the next section shows, Pullman creates a heroine who is similar to Aeneas but possesses certain qualities that give her an advantage over the ancient hero: she has the vivid imagination of a child, which she uses effectively, and she keeps learning and maturing throughout the trilogy. Aeneas, in contrast, fails to learn, and so inflicts so much pain on others that his famed *pietas* may be doubted.[11]

Pietas, ancient and modern

Pietas is Aeneas' most celebrated character trait; it is his sense of duty, both to the gods and to the long-term survival of the Trojan people.[12] Like Aeneas, Lyra is driven by a wish to do what is right, which she repeatedly places before her own well-being. However, Aeneas' *pietas* is grounded in a strong sense of duty toward the gods, while Lyra is not driven by religious considerations, as religion is prominently criticized in *HDM*. Despite the existence of gods in Pullman's universe, it is always clear that Lyra's sense of duty originates from her own moral code. Even though Lyra has character flaws (she is an accomplished liar and is, at least early in the trilogy, easily manipulated by her parents), she instinctively seems to know what is right in important situations.[13] For example, when talking to Mary Malone about the Church's hatred of Dust, she says, "They think it's evil. But I think what *they* do is evil" (*SK* 100, emphasis in the original).

Additionally, both Lyra and Aeneas are loyal to their friends and companions, even though their missions are responsible for a number of deaths of those around them. Aeneas presses on despite his mission causing the deaths of Creusa, Palinurus, Misenus, Pallas, and of course Dido, to name a few. Roger, Lee Scoresby, Baruch, both her parents (Mrs. Coulter and Lord Asriel) and even God ("the

Authority") all die in the course of Lyra's mission. Despite these heavy costs, both heroes continue in their dutiful behavior.

Lyra's sense of duty is repeatedly depicted in the trilogy, most obviously in rescue scenes, such as the aforementioned rescue of kidnapped children in *NL/GC*. Her altruism goes a step further in the underworld scene of *AS* when Lyra and Will set the good of all humanity above their own love and happiness by resolving to live in different worlds (*AS* 520–2). Aeneas also sacrifices a great deal on his dangerous journey in order to create the best possible future for his fellow Trojans, but he also can appear callous, especially in his relationship with Dido.

In both works, duty is bound up with destiny. Although Lyra and Will have agency, Will realizes: "there was no arguing with fate; neither his despair or Lyra's had moved them a single inch" (*AS* 522). This is similar to destiny compelling Aeneas to coldly uphold his duty to proceed to Italy without Dido,[14] though, as we will see, there are crucial differences in how both couples handle the separation.

The underworld

Lyra's most profound learning experience happens in the underworld scene, which is arguably the most didactic part of the trilogy.[15] The influence of *Aeneid* 6 on this scene is obvious from the similarities in numerous details. However, Aeneas and Lyra each react very differently to the challenges they face during their respective *katabaseis*.[16]

Pullman's portrayal of the gloomy, joyless underworld plays on all the senses: "there was nothing but mist" (*AS* 303), "grey light," the damp and bitter air" (*AS* 303), "[t]he only sound was an endless drip-drip-drip of water (*AS* 303), "the silence was immense and oppressive" (*AS* 310), "cold" (*AS* 311). Likewise, Deiphobus in the *Aeneid* calls the underworld "our sad and sunless homes in this troubled place" (*tristis sine sole domos, loca turbida*, 6.534). Pullman provides details such as "stone blocks, green with ancient slime" (*AS* 303–4), reminding one of Vergil's hideous mud (*informis limus*, 6.416). *HDM*'s "sluggish stream" (*AS* 293), "filthy, stagnant pool" (*AS* 293) and "oily, scummy water" (*AS* 293) echo the *Aeneid*'s "sad swamp of the revolting (unlovable) waters" (*tristis palus inamabilis undae*, 6.438). *HDM*'s children hear "high mournful shrieks and wails that hung in the air like the drifting filaments of a jellyfish, causing pain wherever they touched," reminding one of Vergil's dead whose "suffering does not leave them even in death" (*curae non ipsa in morte relinquunt*, 6.444) and of Aeneas hearing "the groans and the cruel crack of the lash, then the dragging and clanking of iron chains" (*gemitus et saeva sonare / verbera, tum stridor ferri tractaeque catenae*, 6.557–8). Like Vergil's underworld, Pullman's includes a Charon-like ferryman and Harpies.[17]

Pullman even recalls a specific simile used by Vergil: the bodyless ghosts crowd around their living visitors, their voices "no louder than dry leaves falling" (*AS* 312). This clearly echoes Vergil's description of the ghosts: "as many as the leaves that fall in the forest at the first chill of autumn" (*Aeneid* 6.309–10).[18] The simile in the *Aeneid* points at both the ghosts' multitude as well as their insubstantial nature.

Pullman uses the same imagery, but with the focus on their soft voices.[19] Yet readers are likely to also associate the image of leaves with the fragility of life, the insubstantial nature of the ghosts, and possibly their large number, which is emphasized by Lyra feeling overwhelmed by them passing through her.

In her *katabasis*, Lyra shows incredible strength of character, especially when she endures the extremely painful separation from her daemon in order to cross to the island of the dead, and when she manages to befriend and strike a deal with the vile Harpies. The turning point in this scene is when Lyra talks about her life and notices how differently the Harpies react to her narrations of real-life events as opposed to fantastical stories.[20] The Harpies say they find true stories "nourishing" (*AS* 332). Lyra's ability to reason with the Harpies stands in marked contrast with Aeneas' own interaction with them on the Strophades in Book 3. Far from making a deal with them, Aeneas and his crew immediately engage them in armed combat and are cursed and driven off the islands as a result (3.209–77). In comparison with Aeneas' masculine hostility and its disastrous consequences, the success of Lyra's keen negotiation demonstrates the superiority of her more empathetic approach.

The Harpies scene also dramatizes *HDM*'s message that there is no need to be afraid of death, that one ought to enjoy life instead of living to win rewards in the afterlife. Notably, in the *Aeneid* a few special souls get to settle in Elysium (6.743–4), while in Pullman's version the same fate awaits everyone when they die.[21] This is important for the overall message of the trilogy regarding the focus on life rather than fear of what will happen after death.

Lyra decides to rescue all the dead out of pity, and at this moment the children fall in love (though they do not yet realize it, *AS* 319), which leads to Lyra's "Fall" and the downfall of the oppressive church of her world.[22] The creation of an exit for the ghosts of the dead has been interpreted as "a transition from the classical journey to the underworld, to the Christian Harrowing of Hell."[23] Admittedly, this part of the underworld scene does draw on this Christian theme (and subverts it), but Pullman also seems to draw on examples from Greco-Roman antiquity of characters freeing (or attempting to free) dead people from the underworld.[24] Greek heroes only attempt to resurrect certain people yet leave the workings of the underworld unchanged. Aeneas enters the underworld to speak with his father and, although he does not attempt to free anyone from death, he too makes no attempt to alter the order of the underworld. This contrasts significantly with Lyra and Will's decision to fundamentally change the nature of death by freeing all the ghosts of the underworld. Furthermore, the idea of the ghosts of the dead leaving through an exit reminds one of Vergil's gates of horn and ivory (*Aeneid* 6.893–6), but it is significant that in Pullman there is only one exit, not two.[25] When Pullman's ghosts of the dead leave the underworld, they turn "into the night, the starlight, the air . . . leaving behind a vivid little burst of happiness" (*AS* 382). They turn into nothing and everything in a moment of joy but do not influence the living, neither truly or falsely.

Aeneas travels to the underworld in order to speak to his father. He also meets a number of other shades known to him, including Dido and one of his crew, Palinurus. He feels sad for them yet does not consider freeing them from the underworld, even though their pitiful sight distresses him (*motus tumultu*, 6.317), especially when he sees Dido, who refuses to look at or speak to him (6.469–71).[26] In contrast with Lyra's exploits, Aeneas merely passively engages with the dead. Only Lyra shows enough pity, compassion, and bravery to improve the lot of all the dead.

To be fair, Aeneas never gets much of a chance to save Palinurus or anyone else. The Sibyl informs Palinurus that his prayers cannot help him, but soothes his grief by explaining that his name will endure as the name for the cliff where he died (6.337–83). The Sibyl hurries Aeneas along, exactly so as to not give him the chance to worry too much about the plight of the dead, as contemplation of the costs of his endeavor to found a new kingdom in Italy might keep him from completing it.[27]

There is, however, talk of rebirth in the *Aeneid*, though only for the select few allowed into Elysium (6.743–51), among them Aeneas' descendants.[28] Aeneas cannot understand why anyone would want to leave Elysium for a second life in "sluggish bodies" (*tarda . . . corpora*, 6.720–1): "Why do the poor wretches have this terrible longing for the light?" (*quae lucis miseris tam dira cupido?*, 6.721). Might Aeneas here be wondering if it is worth carrying on with his task to find a new home in Italy? This contrasts quite strongly with Pullman's positive outlook on life as preferable to death.

So the difference in the two actions of Lyra and Aeneas may result only partly from the differences in their characters, but just as much from Pullman's secular framework and the idea of an underworld where humans are not treated differently depending on their good deeds in life, as opposed to Vergil's underworld, which is structured according to divine justice.

The underworld scene is a memorable conclusion of the first part of the *Aeneid*, the journey from Troy to Italy, but even confronted with the consequences of his betrayal of Dido, Aeneas experiences no significant moral development.[29] In *HDM*, in contrast, the underworld scene is intensely didactic, as Lyra learns important lessons about compassion, determination, and effective storytelling. The Harpies change Lyra as Lyra changes them; they are the catalyst for Lyra's character development. She is able to apologize to Roger and set his ghost free. Aeneas, in contrast, even when he sees Dido's ghost in the underworld, is unable to make amends.

Mythical meet-cutes: falling in love in the *Aeneid* and *HDM*

Pullman places Will and Lyra on the doomed arc of Dido and Aeneas, using one of the most famous tragic love stories as a foil for the young lovers of his own work. Pullman lays the groundwork for this parallel by beginning Lyra and Will's relationship in a sylvan setting that is familiar from the hunt scene in *Aeneid* 4 (*AS* 491). Aeneas and Dido's relationship also blooms in the open forest but is consummated in a cave (*spelunca*, 4.165). The cave, with its underworld connotation, and the terrible thunderstorm from which Aeneas and Dido seek shelter foreshadow the dramatic end of this relationship,[30] while the beautiful sunny weather and setting in a *locus amoenus* do not prepare Pullman's readers for the brevity of Lyra and Will's relationship. In both works, the woodland settings suggest these relationships are natural developments for the characters. Still, whereas Lyra and Will emerge from this experience visibly elated and at peace with the world ("they were brimming with happiness" *AS* 492, see also *AS* 497), Dido feels guilt (*culpa*, 4.172), and rumors about her new relationship immediately start spreading through the entire region.[31]

Both couples are encouraged toward their relationships by third parties: Lyra and Will by Mary Malone and Aeneas and Dido by Dido's sister Anna and Aeneas' mother Venus.[32] Anna asks Dido, "are you going to waste away, living alone and in mourning all the days of your youth . . . ? Do you believe this is what the dead care about when they are buried in the grave?" (4.31–4). This sentiment of the importance of making the most of one's life, surprisingly, is not echoed in the love story in *HDM* but in the earlier underworld scene.

A comparison of the descriptions and similes used to depict Dido's and Lyra's falling in love is useful to show the differences between both relationships. Already in the second line of Book 4 of the *Aeneid*, Dido's love is likened to a wound and fire: *vulnus alit venis et caeco carpitur igni* (4.2).[33] The imagery of wounds and fire are strongly emphasized by their position as the first and last words of the line and the heavy alliteration. This foreshadows the tragic outcome of Dido's love: the metaphorical wound and fire symbolize the fatal wound that Dido will inflict on herself (4.689) and the fire of her funeral pyre (5.4). Fire imagery is frequent, with strong flames (4.54) and fire eating away at Dido (4.2). Dido's love is repeatedly compared to madness (4.65, 69, 101, 283, 298), and in her turmoil and pain, Dido is like a deer wounded by a deadly arrow (4.69–73).[34] This simile refers to Dido being "wounded" by love, her roaming through town and her vulnerability.[35]

Vergil also describes the more outwardly noticeable symptoms of Dido's love: Dido cannot stop thinking about Aeneas (4.3–4), she cannot find rest nor sleep and is troubled by fearful dreams at night (4.9). During the day she wanders through the city in her restless state (4.68–9). She sheds tears (4.30), cannot get enough of seeing and hearing Aeneas (4.77–9), and dreams of him when he is absent (4.83). She ignores the building projects in Carthage, her own appearance, and her reputation (4.88–9; 170).

In contrast, Lyra's awakening sexuality is described as new and exciting. When Lyra hears Mary Malone's story of marzipan, she "felt something strange happen to her body. She felt a stirring of the roots of her hair: she found herself breathing faster" (*AS* 467); the sensations she feels are "exciting and frightening at the same time" (*AS* 467); more and more parts of her body are affected until she sits quietly "trembling, hugging her knees, hardly daring to breathe" (*AS* 468). In the actual love scene in the woods Lyra's and Will's "hands were slow and clumsy, and they hardly tasted the food" (*AS* 491), Lyra has "a fast-beating heart" (*AS* 491), her fingers "tremble" (*AS* 492), "neither of them could look; they were confused; they were brimming with happiness" (*AS* 492).

Here Lyra's feelings are almost overpowering, but in the positive sense of her discovering a new and pleasant sensation, as opposed to Dido's feelings of pain and guilt. The story of marzipan uses an extended simile about a house which Lyra finds inside herself (*AS* 468) and the new discovery feels to Lyra "like a fragile vessel brim-full of new knowledge, which she hardly dare[s] touch for fear of spilling it" (*AS* 471). These similes stress how new, surprising, and precious the discovery of the sensation of falling in love is for Lyra, very much in contrast with the imagery of Dido as a wounded deer and the fire of love consuming her inwardly. Lyra's and Will's first kiss is described through a simile of two moths clumsily bumping together (*AS* 492), a gentle image, stressing the children's inexperience, the opposite of Dido's wild madness and pain.

Destined divorce: break-ups in the *Aeneid* and *HDM*

When Jupiter finds out about Aeneas' love affair, he sends Mercury to remind him of his destiny to found a city—in Italy, not in Carthage—who asks him, "Have you entirely forgotten your own kingdom and your own destiny?" (4.267). Dido's delaying Aeneas serves not only to explain the later enmity between Rome and Carthage but to characterize Aeneas.

It recalls the scene in *The Amber Spyglass*, when Mrs. Coulter keeps Lyra, allegedly out of love and protectiveness, drugged in a cave. Although the *Odyssey* is the most obvious allusion, Dido's cave at *Aeneid* 4.165 is especially significant here, as in both cases the selfish side of love is portrayed: Mrs. Coulter claims she was keeping her daughter in the cave out of love, but the fact that she has her drugged unconscious against her will shows that Mrs. Coulter is acting out of egotistical reasons. Considering how little interest she has shown in Lyra's life and well-being so far, it is not credible that she should suddenly feel so protective. Moreover, the fact that she has kidnapped Lyra and is keeping her prisoner in the cave reminds one of and is a step up from her extremely controlling parenting of Lyra during the very short period that her daughter lived with her in London in *Northern Lights/ Golden Compass*.

Aeneas and Dido consummate their relationship in the cave, where Aeneas makes Dido believe that he wants to stay with her permanently, knowing full well that he will sooner or later have to leave her to fulfil his mission to find a new home for the Trojans.[36] Unsurprisingly, the difference in the outcome of the cave scenes is telling: whereas Lyra is freed by her loyal friend Will, Dido is misled and ultimately betrayed by Aeneas, who only pretends to be loyal, so that Dido feels she only can help herself in this situation by committing suicide.

Aeneas' reaction to the gods' command to leave Carthage is to obey without hesitation or resistance (4.281–2, 345–7). He is mainly worried how to explain his departure to Dido (as shown through the series of rhetorical questions in lines 4.283–4) and decides to avoid the problem by making preparations in secret. It is obvious that Aeneas is not struggling with the decision itself, and his secrecy points to him being more worried about Dido's anger at him than any feelings of guilt on his part.[37] Dido finds out through the grapevine, and her reaction is like Will's when he hears that he will need to live apart from Lyra, a mixture of grief and anger. Will and Lyra are told this news together by an angel. Like Aeneas, they do not question the divine command, but unlike Vergil's hero, they both care more about the other than themselves, as is shown when they consider moving to one world together, even if one of them will become very ill and die within a few years. Lyra proposes: "*I'll* do it, Will! We'll come to your world and live there! It doesn't matter if we get ill, me and Pan."[38] And Will answers: "D'you think I could bear that, Lyra? . . . D'you think I could live happily watching you get sick and ill and fade away and then die. . . . Do you think I could bear to live on after you died?" (*AS* 516). Clearly, both Lyra and Will are more worried about the other's well-being than their own.

Both characters' distress at the impending separation are described in similes: Dido's reaction is compared to the behavior of a raving Bacchant (4.300–3), Pentheus in his delusion, and Orestes confronted by his mother and the Furies (4.469–73)—all tragic figures who experience or inflict madness (*furor*) brought on by *dolor*.[39] Her extreme external reaction reflects her inner state. The three short mythical comparisons at the same time remind one that Dido's predicament, like that of the characters in the similes, is caused by the gods. In contrast, Will's reaction, which is as strong as Dido's, is compared to the natural force of an enormous crashing wave in an extended simile, familiar from the beginning of the *Aeneid*:[40]

> Will felt a great wave of rage and despair moving outwards from a place deep within him, as if his mind were an ocean that some profound convulsion had disturbed. . . . He felt the wave build higher and steeper to darken the sky, he felt the crest tremble and begin to spill, he felt the great mass crashing down with the whole weight of the ocean behind it against the iron-bound coast of what had to be.
>
> (*AS* 521–2)

The choice of a natural force for comparison in this extended simile indicates the superhuman force of Will's emotion. We hear that Will gasps, shakes, and cries aloud in anger (*AS* 522), but the simile focuses more on his feelings than his physical reaction. Furthermore, Will's anger is strong, but, unlike Dido's and just like Lyra's, it quickly calms down enough for the children to be able to focus on what duty requires.

Dido confronts Aeneas about his planned departure, calling him a "traitor" (*perfidus*, 4.305, 366),[41] shedding tears (4.314), reminding him of how much she has given up for him (in particular her good reputation with her own and the neighboring peoples) and threatening suicide.[42] Echoes of this can be found in Lyra's tearful reaction when she finds out that she and Will can never live together (*AS* 512, 537) and the children's promises to each other to meet again in death (as atoms clinging together), though here the tears and thoughts of death are caused by grief, not anger. Death, moreover, is envisaged by Lyra and Will as a natural death much later in life, not suicide, and is seen as a hope to cling to as opposed to a desperate threat. Indeed, when Aeneas and Dido later in the epic meet in the underworld, Dido refuses to speak to him and turns away, still hurt and angry (6.469–74).

Aeneas offers feeble excuses: he had never promised marriage to Dido; the Fates compelled him to leave; and he could not unfairly cheat his men and especially his son, Ascanius, out of their future kingdom in Italy (4.333–61).[43] Dido, in her speech, remarks on his lack of tears and indifference to hers (4.370), which is very different from Will, who embraces his crying girlfriend (*AS* 513) and whose memory of Lyra's tears, later on, is so overwhelming that it causes the Subtle Knife to shatter in his hands.

The most important difference between these two scenes is that Aeneas makes the decision to leave without consulting Dido, and this betrayal is just as hurtful to her as the parting itself.[44] In contrast, Lyra and Will together make the hard decision to separate, united in their common sense of duty. Each is willing to sacrifice a long life in order to be able to stay together, although neither accepts the other's sacrifice, and both agree that leaving the window out of the underworld open is more important for all humanity than their personal happiness. Neither of them loses face in front of others through their decision. On the contrary, Pullman makes clear that this is a noble act. The angel Xaphania says: "Then you have already taken the first steps towards wisdom" (*AS* 525).

How much responsibility does Aeneas bear in Dido's death? How much is this the fault of the gods? First, he already started his relationship with Dido before Juno and Venus got involved, all the while knowing that the gods expected him to found a new city elsewhere and chiefly being concerned of his good reputation. Second, though Aeneas is commanded by a god,[45] humans and gods in the *Aeneid* have a certain degree of agency within what is prescribed by Fate.[46] Third, and more importantly, there is no reason why Aeneas could not have discussed the matter with Dido instead of making a one-sided decision and trying to scurry away in the night. This passage sheds a negative light on Aeneas as selfish, thoughtless, unfeeling, and even cowardly.[47] As much as he longed to soothe and console Dido (4.393–4), grief does not move him (4.438–9). Contrary to this, Lyra and Will emerge from their separation appearing unselfish and caring. Aeneas leaves a suicidal Dido in order to found his own kingdom, but Lyra and Will are determined to build the "republic of heaven," wherever they will end up living (*AS* 516, 548).

Pullman's choice of this (less than happy) ending reinforces his preference for real stories over fantasy,[48] just like when Lyra learns from the Harpies that narrations of real-life experiences are preferable to made-up stories and when Mary's real-life story of marzipan serves as the catalyst for Lyra's "Fall." Pullman, in fact, claims that this tragic ending is not what he wanted, but the story dictated it.[49] As a coming-of-age story, *HDM* shows Lyra's character development, and her willingness to make a great personal sacrifice reflects her increased maturity. Lyra and Will appear as much more steadfast than the epic hero Aeneas, who needs a scolding from Mercury to pursue his destiny (4.560–70).

Conclusion

The comparison of the romantic and underworld portions of the *Aeneid* and *HDM* reveals striking similarities in numerous details, especially in place-descriptions and style, in particular similes. However, it is clear that Aeneas and Lyra are different in important ways, and their differences are highlighted exactly because they contrast with all the similarities *HDM* shares with the *Aeneid*. Both Aeneas and Lyra need to decide on how to best tackle the obstacles to their destines. However, while Aeneas is eager (perhaps too eager) to obey the orders of the gods, no matter the human cost, Lyra learns crucial lessons about the importance of true stories, making the most of one's life, the rewards of loyalty and love, and the importance of autonomy in the face of (religious) authority. The focus on true stories seems to deliberately contrast Vergil's mention of the ivory gate of lies that Aeneas and the Sibyl walk through (6.895–8), implying that all that Aeneas hears in the underworld are lies.

Both Aeneas and Lyra are prepared to sacrifice an important personal relationship for the greater good, but as opposed to Vergil, who shows the terrible toll this unilateral decision of Aeneas' takes on Dido, Pullman outlines an alternative way of how to deal with this impossibly difficult situation: Lyra and Will part heartbroken but as lifelong friends, even if they can no longer see, touch, or communicate with each other once they are in separate worlds. Pullman does not seem to suggest here that Aeneas should have abandoned his task and settled down with Dido instead but rather that Aeneas should have included Dido in his decision and made sure they stayed friends.

The difference between Pullman's and Vergil's protagonists is most obvious when both feel pity for some of the ghosts in the underworld, but Lyra and Will decide to free the dead, even at mortal peril. This joint decision of cosmic importance indicates that the two of them are well matched in their great empathy and bravery. Hence, it is a fitting moment for Lyra and Will to fall in love. Since they start their relationship on an equal footing and possess the same impressive character traits, it is not surprising that they are much more successful than Aeneas and Dido in preserving their love, friendship, and respect for each other despite their necessary separation.

One reason for this difference between the ways in which Lyra and Aeneas handle their separations is Lyra's young age. This gives her the advantage of a child's vivid imagination, which allows her to see possibilities that would seem impossible to adults (like freeing the dead). C.S. Lewis famously claimed: "With Virgil European poetry grows up," viewing Homer's Achilles with all his passion as immature compared to Aeneas.[50] It is telling that Pullman chose a child protagonist who can be creative and flexible in her thinking in a coming-of-age story. Of course, some heroes from ancient epic learn and mature, such as Achilles, who himself is young in the *Iliad* (νήπιος, 9.440). However, Aeneas is quite rigid, striving to strictly obey the gods and destiny. Such obedience to authority (religious or other) is most unfashionable in contemporary children's literature, and in *HDM*, Pullman criticizes the authoritarian aspects of organized religion and their blind followers.[51] Blind obedience appears also to be criticized in the *Aeneid*: not only does Dido die, but Aeneas himself, as can clearly be seen in contrast with Lyra, has not learned from his trials and forfeits his *pietas* when he, against this father's command, does not spare the subjected Turnus.

The fact that Pullman made his protagonist a young woman is significant because ancient epics typically give female characters only minor roles and depict them from a male perspective. Dido has a larger role and is depicted with much sympathy by Vergil. In the end, however, Aeneas does not take her wishes into account, and she dies violently and prematurely. *HDM*'s female protagonist and her development, in contrast, are at the center of the trilogy. Lyra is very loyal and clever but is not used as a foil to other female characters and has more agency than Dido, who is constrained by concerns for her reputation.[52]

Thus, Pullman contrasts Aeneas' *pietas* with Lyra's attitudes toward obedience, loyalty, selflessness, and love. Even though Pullman strongly and obviously draws on the parallel passages from the *Aeneid*, he presents his readers with a protagonist who in many ways is an anti-Aeneas who can succeed where he fails.

Pullman in *HDM* clearly does not only employ references to the *Aeneid* in order to place *HDM* in a long tradition of epics but also in order to help characterize Lyra by contrasting her with Aeneas. Of course, *HDM* provides plenty to interest the many readers who do not know the *Aeneid* or the other literary sources that Pullman employs and subverts.[53] However, being able to see and understand how Pullman uses and subverts his sources illuminates the depth of his work. It also demonstrates the enduring relevance of the classics like the *Aeneid* to modern young adult fiction.

Notes

1 Parry 2016; Scally 2004; Stephens and McCallum 1998: 3; Anselm 2017: 199–200; Nikolajeva 1998; Martin 2005: 9–10.
2 Parry 2016: 9.
3 Kichwey 2010: 468.
4 Pullman has mentioned his familiarity with the *Aeneid* in interviews and has stated that he used to tell ancient Greek and Roman myths to his students when he worked as a teacher (Hodkinson 2016: 273, n. 21).
5 Aeneas' experience regarding love in the underworld is very different. As Boyle 1986: 153 notes, there his personal *amor* is repressed by an impersonal (goal-oriented) one, which is required for him to succeed.
6 Pullman 1996. In the UK publication the title *Northern Lights* is used, but in the USA *The Golden Compass*. See Parsons and Nicholson 1999: 126.
7 Anthropomorphized animal characters are popular in children's literature, so young readers are acquainted with the idea of symbolic animal characters, even if they are not aware of Socrates' *daimonion*, which has influenced Pullman's daemons (Squire 2006: 35).
8 Pullman 1997.
9 Pullman 2000.
10 The world of Cittàgazze is populated by frightening specters that attack adults and can use windows to travel into other worlds.
11 On Aeneas' failure to learn, see Boyle 1986: 96–8, 122 n. 75, 153–4, 172–3.
12 E.g. *insignis pietate vir* (1.10); *pius Aeneas* (1.220, 305); *sum pius Aeneas* (1.378); *Troius Aeneas pietate insignis et armis* (6.403). For definitions and uses of *pietas* see Binder 2019: I: 249–55. Syson 2013: 5 writes about the conflicts that *pietas* evokes in the *Aeneid*. The translations of the *Aeneid* used in this chapter are adapted from West 1990, though sometimes I have made changes to stay closer to the Latin original.
13 This character trait is reflected in her name, Lyra, which sounds similar to "liar," as is emphasized in the underworld scene when the leading Harpy angrily flies at her, shouting "liar"(*AS* 307–8).
14 For a thorough discussion of *fatum* in general and in the *Aeneid* in particular, see Binder 2019: I: 165–70, noting that here *fatum* and Jupiter's will are basically identical.

15 On didacticism in children's literature and in particular works engaging with the classical world, see Hodkinson and Lovatt 2018: 2–3, 11. On "map texts" and *katabaseis* in children's literature, see Nelson and Morey 2019: 94–143. They notice the didactic nature of these *katabaseis* for characters and readers.
16 The scene is also influenced by *Odyssey* 11. On the underworld scene and its influences, see Puetz 2019: 225; Williams 1990: 192.
17 On Pullman's and Vergil's Harpies, see Puetz 2019: 223–44.
18 See Hodkinson 2016: 275–6 for a short discussion of Pullman's epic similes.
19 See Thaniel 1971: 238–41 on Vergil's simile. On leaves/men similes in Greek poetry in general, see Griffith 1975; Sider 1996.
20 Pullman precedes this chapter with John 8:32, "the truth shall make you free" (*AS* 321).
21 On the different regions in Vergil's underworld, see Molyviati-Toptsis 1994: 33–46.
22 The ghosts' disintegration into atoms at exiting the underworld foreshadows Lyra's and Will's separation. See Russell 2003: 70. Loy and Goodhew 2004: 117 point out affinities with Buddhist principles.
23 Holderness 2007: 284.
24 E.g., Orpheus, Persephone, Hercules, Alcestis, Castor, and Pollux. Lyra has been compared to Persephone by Auxier 2009: 19–21 and to Orpheus by Bobby 2014: 147–9 and Hodkinson 2016: 273 n. 19, 276–9. Neither comparison is entirely convincing due to Lyra's agency (*contra* Persephone) and her success in freeing all the dead (*contra* Orpheus).
25 The idea of the two dream gates is based on *Odyssey* 19.560–7 about Penelope's dream of Odysseus' return.
26 See Binder 2019: II: 546–6 for a discussion of different interpretations of this scene and its similarities to Catullus 66.39–40 and *Odyssey* 11.541–6.
27 Cf. the foreshadowing of Aeneas' failure through Vergil's comments on Daedalus' failure as an artist (*Aeneid* 6.30–3) at the end of the descriptions of the doors of Daedalus on the temple that Aeneas contemplates right after he has arrived in Italy (Boyle 1986: 136–40). Here Aeneas is interrupted in his contemplation of the work of art by the Sibyl, who tells him to do something practical instead (a sacrifice) before Aeneas can think too much about how the panels of this art work relate to his own past and imminent future. This passage echoes Aeneas, right after his arrival in Carthage, looking at the mural of another temple (*Aen.* 1.446–93). Here, Aeneas does not realize that the depiction of Achilles' brutality toward Hector's body is a warning of Aeneas' own future behavior (Boyle 1986: 103n. 34).
28 On the inconsistencies in this scene, see Binder 2019: II: 609; O'Hara 1990: 166–7.
29 On Aeneas' lack of moral learning, see Boyle 1986: 150–4, 175.
30 The lightning has also been interpreted as symbolic for wedding torches (Binder 2019: II: 304). The fact that Aeneas and Dido's physical relationship starts during a deer hunt has been analyzed by Cormier 2020: 33–44, who notes that such scenes in the *Aeneid* (and in some of its receptions) carry a connotation of seduction.
31 Readers of the *Aeneid*, moreover, have overheard Juno and Venus planning to use Aeneas and Dido as pawns for their own purposes (*Aen.* 4.90–128). On Venus' use of Ascanius to win over childless Dido (*Aen.* 1.717–9), see Petrini 1997: 89–90.
32 However, Mary does not know that she is encouraging Lyra and Will through her story about what it feels like to fall in love: *AS* 464–9: cf. Colás 2005: 60–1.
33 See also *vivit sub pectora vulnus* (4.67). For an overview on similes in the *Aeneid*, see Binder 2019: I: 109–24. Boyle 1986, 90–4, 101–2, 106–7, 114, 119, 126–32 and 151 discusses in detail the association of fire imagery in the *Aeneid* with *furor* throughout the work. Boyle 1986: 132 interprets the many passages in which this imagery in association with furor appears in the *Aeneid* as Vergil portraying Aeneas' victory as one for "the forces of non-reason and the triumph, if of *pietas*, of *pietas* redefined as *furor*." Bartsch 1998: 334 outlines the "terrible cycle of history" regarding Aeneas telling the Carthaginians about the destruction of Troy as a catalyst for Dido's death in the flames of the pyre.

34 On this, see Clausen 2002: 80.
35 See Binder 2019: II: 291 for a detailed discussion of this simile.
36 Seen from this angle, the cave also stands for the potential to derail or, at least, delay missions: Aeneas' to sail to Italy and Will's to bring the Subtle Knife to Lord Asriel (as his dying father had instructed him to do: *AS* 12).
37 Binder 2019: II: 323–4 points out that *optima*, referring to Dido at 4.291, may be a first sign of Aeneas distancing himself from her.
38 Pan is Lyra's daemon.
39 See Boyle 1986: 85–132 on *furor* in the *Aeneid*. Binder 2019: II: 352 points out (quoting Mackail) that this passage is the *Aeneid*'s only direct allusion to "stage-representations."
40 On the similarly stormy first simile in the *Aeneid* (1.148–56), see Feeney 2014: 211–21. There Aeneas is helpless against the storm, which is calmed by Neptune. Here Will endures without divine intervention.
41 Binder 2019: II: 327 notes that *perfidus* not only alludes to a husband who has left his wife but also to "perjurious Troy" as well as the proverbial perfidy of Carthage held in Rome since the 2nd Punic War and the image of Hannibal as the cruel barbarian.
42 *Aeneid* 4.308, 4.386, here turning the fire of love imagery into "the black fires" of death, which can refer both to her impendent suicide as well as to her curse against Aeneas' men (*atres ignes*, 4.384). See Binder 2019: II: 338.
43 Page, quoted in Austin 1963 on *Aeneid* 4.331–61, notices "the cold and formal rhetoric" Aeneas is using when giving his excuses to Dido. Austin argues that Aeneas needed to use this tone so he would not break down in the emotional argument, but this lacks textual evidence in the face of the contrast between Dido's highly emotional speech and Aeneas' too rational and unfeeling answer. Binder 2019: II: 330–3 gives a summary of the various positions critics have held on Aeneas' speech. See also Oliensis 1997: 303–10; Feeney 1990: 169.
44 Clausen 2002: 84–5 rightly remarks on the hint at Aeneas' guilt in the verb *ambire* ('to circumvent by flattery or guile') at 4.283.
45 Feeney 1990: 189 calls Aeneas a representative for "the extreme case of the pressures and cruelties inflicted upon the individual who embodies in his own person the aspirations and future of a whole nation."
46 See Binder 2019: I: 169–70.
47 Of course, this bitter separation is mythologically necessary to serve as an etiological explanation for Carthage's later enmity toward Rome. We also see Aeneas' negative side when he kills Turnus, even though he begs for mercy, in Book 12. Binder 2019: I: 287–96 points out that even though Aeneas looks cruel here, his killing of his opponent and rival follows the classical pattern for a civil war: there is no place for a second strong character next to the (new) leader.
48 See Parsons and Nicholson 1999: 131. See also Colás 2005: 47.
49 Spanner 2002.
50 Lewis 1942: 37: "but a man, an adult, is precisely what [Aeneas] is: Achilles had been little more than a passionate boy."
51 In contrast, the *Aeneid*, in Turnus' death scene, seems to criticize Aeneas for now rejecting his *pietas* and instead giving himself over to rage (*furiis accensus et ira / terribilis*, *Aeneid* 12.946–7). On the different interpretations of this scene see Binder 2019: III: 679–81. On anger in the *Aeneid*, see Binder 2019: I: 224–8. Tarrant 2012 on *Aeneid* 12.946 notes that "neither *furiae* nor *accendere* is elsewhere applied to [Aeneas] in [Vergil]'s own voice." He finds this image of Aeneas "undeniably disturbing." He also notes the similar expression which Dido employs to refer to herself at *Aeneid* 4.376: *heu furiis incensa feror*.
52 It is striking that in the contemporary work, it is a male character, Will, who has the role of caregiver.
53 See also Parsons and Nicholson 1999: 122.

References

Anselm, S. 2017. "Zeitgemäße Helden als Modelle für morgen?! Überlegungen zur Rezeption von (antiken) Heldenbildern in einem (post)modernen Literaturunterricht." In M. Janka and M. Stierstorfer (eds.) *Verjüngte Antike. Griechisch-römische Mythologie und Historie in zeitgenössischen Kinder- und Jugendmedien*. Heidelberg: Universitätsverlag Winter. 117–34.

Austin, R.G. 1963. *P. Vergili Maronis Aeneidos Liber Quartus*. Revised ed. Oxford: Clarendon Press.

Auxier, R.E. 2009. "Thus Spake Philip Pullman." In R. Greene and R. Robison-Greene (eds.) *The Golden Compass and Philosophy: God Bites the Dust*. Chicago and LaSalle, IL: Open Court. 3–24.

Bartsch, S. 1998. "Ars and the Man: The Politics of Art in Virgil's Aeneid." *Classical Philology* 93, 4: 322–42.

Binder, G.P. 2019a. *Vergilius Maro: Aeneis. Ein Kommentar, Vol. 1: Einleitung, Zentrale Themen, Literatur, Indices*. Trier: Wissenschaftlicher Verlag Trier.

———. 2019b. *Vergilius Maro: Aeneis. Ein Kommentar, Vol. 2: Kommentar zu Aeneis 1–6*. Trier: Wissenschaftlicher Verlag Trier.

———. 2019c. *Vergilius Maro: Aeneis. Ein Kommentar, Vol. 3: Kommentar zu Aeneis 7–12*. Trier: Wissenschaftlicher Verlag Trier.

Bobby, S.R. 2014. "Persephone Ascending: Goddess Archetypes and Lyra's Journey to Wholeness." In C. Butler and T. Halsdorf (eds.) *Philip Pullman (New Casebooks)*. Basingstoke: Palgrave. 146–63.

Boyle, A.J. 1986. *The Chaonian Dove: Studies in the Eccolgues, Georgics, and Aeneid of Virgil*. Leiden: Brill.

Clausen, W. 2002. *Virgil's Aeneid: Decorum, Allusion, and Ideology*. Munich: Saur.

Colás, S. 2005. "Telling True Stories or the Immanent Ethics of Material Spirit (and Spiritual Matter) in Philip Pullman's 'His Dark Materials'." *Discourse* 27, 1: 34–66.

Cormier, R. 2020. "A Royal Chase in the Company of Three? The Hunting Scene in Vergil's Aeneid IV, Its Courtly Imitators and in Berlioz's Chasse Royale." *New Voices in Classical Reception Studies* 13: 26–44.

Feeney, D. 1990. "The Taciturnity of Aeneas." In S. Harrison (ed.) *Oxford Readings in Vergil's Aeneid*. Oxford: Oxford University Press. 176–90.

———. 2014. "First similes in epic." *Transactions of the American Philological Association* 144, 2 (September 1): 189–228.

Griffith, M. 1975. "Man and the Leaves: A Study of Mimnermos fr. 2." *California Studies in Classical Antiquity* 8: 73–88.

Hodkinson, O. 2016. "His Greek Materials: Philip Pullman's Use of Classical Mythology." In K. Marciniak (ed.) *Our Mythical Childhood . . . The Classics and Literature for Children and Young Adults*. Leiden: Brill. 267–90.

Hodkinson, O., and Lovatt, H., eds. 2018. *Classical Reception and Children's Literature: Greece, Rome and Childhood Transformation*. London and New York: Tauris.

Holderness, G. 2007. "'The Undiscovered Country': Philip Pullman and the 'Land of the Dead'." *Literature and Theology* 21, 3: 276–92.

Kichwey, K. 2010. "Vergil's Aeneid and Contemporary Poetry." In J. Farrell and M.C.J. Putnam (eds.) *A Companion to Vergil's Aeneid and Its Tradition*. Oxford and Malden, MA: Wiley-Blackwell. 465–81.

Lewis, C.S. 1942. *A Preface to Paradise Lost*. London: Oxford University Press.

Loy, D.R., and Goodhew, L. 2004. *The Dharma of Dragons and Daemons. Buddhist Themes in Modern Fantasy*. Boston: Wisdom Publications.

Martin, R.P. 2005. "Epic as Genre'." In J. Foley (ed.) *A Companion to Epic*. Malden, MA and Oxford: Blackwell. 9–19.

Molyviati-Toptsis, U. 1994. "Vergil's Elysium and the Orphic-Pythagorean Ideas of After-Life." *Mnemosyne* 47, 1: 33–46.

Nelson, C., and Morey, A. 2019. *Topologies of the Classical World in Children's Fiction: Palimpsests, Maps, and Fractals*. Oxford: Oxford University Press.

Nikolajeva, M. 1998. "Exit Children's Literature?" *The Lion and the Unicorn* 22: 221–36.

O'Hara, J. 1990. *Death and the Optimistic Prophecy in Vergil's Aeneid*. Princeton: Princeton University Press.

Oliensis, E. 1997. "Sons and Lovers: Sexuality and Gender in Virgil's Poetry." In C. Martindale (ed.) *The Cambridge Companion to Virgil*. Cambridge: Cambridge University Press. 294–311.

Parry, H. 2016. *The Aeneid with Rabbits: Children's Fantasy as Modern Epic* (PhD Dissertation). Victoria University of Wellington, Wellington, New Zealand.

Parsons, W., and Nicholson, C. 1999. "Talking to Philip Pullman: An Interview." *The Lion and the Unicorn* 23, 1: 116–34.

Petrini, M. 1997. *The Child and the Hero: Coming of Age in Catullus and Vergil*. Ann Arbor: University of Michigan Press.

Puetz, B. 2019. "'What Will Happen to Our Honour Now?': The Reception of Aeschylus' Erinyes in Philip Pullman's The Amber Spyglass." In M. Marciniak (ed.) *Chasing Mythical Beasts . . . The Reception of Creatures from Graeco-Roman Mythology in Children's & Young Adults' Culture as a Transformation Marker*. Heidelberg: Universitätsverlag Winter.

Pullman, P. 1996. *The Golden Compass*. New York: Knopf.

———. 1997. *The Subtle Knife*. London: Scholastic.

———. 2000. *The Amber Spyglass*. London: David Fickling Books.

Russell, M.H. 2003. "Ethical Plots, Ethical Endings in Philip Pullman's His Dark Materials." *Foundation* 88: 68–75.

Scally, L.A.M. 2004. *Miraculous Bridges: Crossing Genre Boundaries via His Dark Materials* (PhD Dissertation). Victoria University of Wellington, Wellington, New Zealand.

Sider, D. 1996. "As in the Generation of Leaves in Homer, Simonides, Horace, and Stobaios." *Arethusa* 29, 2: 263–82.

Spanner, H. 2002. "Heat and Dust: An Interview with Philip Pullman." *High Profiles*. https://highprofiles.info/interview/philip-pullman.

Squire, C. 2006. *Philip Pullman: Master Storyteller*. New York: Continuum.

Stephens, J., and McCallum, R. 1998. *Retelling Stories, Framing Culture : Traditional Story and Metanarratives in Children's Literature*. New York and London: Garland Publishing.

Syson, A. 2013. *Fama and Fiction in Virgil's Aeneid*. Columbus: Ohio State University Press.

Tarrant, R. 2012. *Virgil: Aeneid Book XII*. Cambridge: Cambridge University Press.

Thaniel, G. 1971. "Vergil's Leaf- and Bird-Similes of Ghosts." *Phoenix* 25, 3: 237–45.

West, D., tran. 1990. *The Aeneid*. London: Penguin.

Williams, R.D. 1990. "The Sixth Book of the Aeneid." In S.J. Harrison (ed.) *Oxford Readings in Vergil's Aeneid*. Oxford: Oxford University Press. 191–207.

Part II

The *Aeneid* and modern political discourse and culture

This section augments the literary methods deployed in Section I by applying theories of nationalism and political culture to demonstrate the value of the *Aeneid* in thinking about modern political discourse. The opening chapter by Paul Hay and John Hay provides an excellent transition, as it considers how a paradigm of classical reception, a translation of the *Aeneid*, functions as a political document, suggesting a new American origin myth and corresponding identity. Hay and Hay demonstrate that Christopher Pearse Cranch's 1872 translation articulates a sense of national unity after a bloody civil war, consciously modeling itself after Cranch's understanding of Vergil's project in Augustan Rome. Though Cranch's edition was first published slightly before 1900, its vision of a new American identity, focused on national unity, set the stage for American political ideals and debate in the early 20th century. The understudied Cranch translation is also quite relevant for another reason: it is used for the Barnes & Noble Classics Series *Aeneid* paperback, which means it is "the" *Aeneid* for a great many contemporary American nonspecialist readers.[1]

The subsequent chapter takes us into the 21st century with Tedd A. Wimperis's exposition of the value of the *Aeneid* in analyzing the modern political media that mobilizes the past to serve ideological goals in the present. Wimperis links interdisciplinary work on nationalism and cultural memory with Vergilian scholarship to emphasize the epic's continuing relevance to understanding the current political landscapes of China, the United States, Turkey, and Russia.

Following Wimperis's discussion of political media and cultural memory, J.R. O'Neill considers a particularly complicated instance of those very concepts: war memorials. O'Neill specifically focuses on the controversial Vietnam Veterans Memorial in Washington DC, and highlights how the *Aeneid* can explicate both the difficulties inherent in attempts to commemorate war dead and how they can be overcome.

Thus, this section segues from the familiar techniques in classical reception studies—examining the influence of the text on modern thinkers, artists, etc.—to methodologies focused less on identifying influence and more on how the *Aeneid*

DOI: 10.4324/9781003176145-8

can help us understand our present. These methods enable us to show the breadth and richness of the connections between the *Aeneid* and the modern world.

Note

1 As a point of comparison, its sales rank on Barnesandnoble.com is significantly better than the reissue of Mandelbaum's famed translation, Ahl's 2008 translation, and Ruden's acclaimed 2009 translation. See Barnes & Noble. 2021. "The Aeneid (Barnes & Noble Classics Series) by Vergil, Paperback." Accessed May 9. www.barnesandnoble.com/w/aeneid-vergil/1101708293?ean=9781593082376.

6 The patriotic singer

Christopher Pearse Cranch's American *Aeneid*

Paul Hay and John Hay

In 1872, nearly a hundred years after the founding of the new nation, the first full-length American verse translation of *The Aeneid* was published. The translator was Christopher Pearse Cranch (1813–92), a Transcendentalist poet and painter chiefly remembered today for his 1839 cartoon drawing of Ralph Waldo Emerson as a giant eyeball. Cranch's contribution joined a series of epic translations commissioned by the Boston publisher James R. Osgood and Company (formerly Ticknor and Fields). This series began with Henry Wadsworth Longfellow's celebrated 1867 rendition of Dante's *Divine Comedy* and followed with William Cullen Bryant's translations of Homer's *Iliad* (1870) and *Odyssey* (1871) and Bayard Taylor's version of Goethe's *Faust, Part One* (1870) and *Part Two* (1871). As Kirsten Silva Gruesz has noted, these were "the most ambitious and high-profile translation efforts attempted by US writers in the nineteenth century."[1] Christopher Phillips has suggested that the publisher used these new editions of world classics "to celebrate both the firm's reputation for elegant editions and the accomplishments of American poets who could harness the greatest poetry of all time."[2] Yet despite the significance of this venture, these texts, Cranch's in particular, have been consistently overlooked by scholars: a recent volume analyzing dozens of Anglophone and global translations of Vergil published since the early modern period failed to mention Cranch's *Aeneid* at all.[3]

But Cranch still has his readers: the popular "Barnes & Noble Classics" paperback edition of the *Aeneid*, which first appeared in 2007, uses his blank verse (unrhymed iambic pentameter) translation. The editor for this title, classicist Sarah Spence, has made some cosmetic changes to the vocabulary and syntax to update the text for 21st-century readers, but she promotes Cranch's 1872 version as "remarkably accurate."[4] It is likely that a sizable fraction of the *Aeneid*'s nonspecialist audience in America today encountered the text through the English verse of Christopher Pearse Cranch, which makes a study of his translation all the more valuable to scholars wishing to understand how the *Aeneid* is understood by modern readers.

This essay historicizes Cranch's translation of the *Aeneid* by considering its publication in the aftermath of the US Civil War (1861–65). Drawing on Joshua Matthews's argument that Longfellow's *Divine Comedy* should be understood as a wartime expression of a divided nation seeking unity, a "fitting epic of the Civil

DOI: 10.4324/9781003176145-9

War," we argue that Cranch's *Aeneid* similarly celebrates national union and offers hope to a shaken American political state.[5] This translation would have carried along with it the context of three different wars experienced by three different figures: Aeneas fighting in the exiled Trojans' battle with the Rutuli; Vergil surviving the decades of triumviral discord in the middle of the 1st century BCE, as Rome transitioned from a republic to the principate under Augustus; and Cranch witnessing the carnage of the US Civil War, in which his eldest son served. By reaching back to the *Aeneid*, Cranch was not looking to recover a forgotten classic; Vergil's epic had long been an American staple for Latin instruction. But by offering his full-length English verse translation, Cranch was suggesting that the poem might speak more directly to American readers in a new era of national rebirth. Previous scholars who treat Cranch's *Aeneid* translation as some sort of literary diversion, or who distinguish this project from the other topical, nationally conscious writings Cranch produced in the postbellum period, thus fail to properly contextualize this *Aeneid* as a distinctly American text.[6]

Our essay makes a case for the national politics of Cranch's American translation in three steps. First, we examine Vergil's evolving reputation in 19th-century America. What, after all, would Americans have thought of the *Aeneid*—both in Latin and in English? Second, we look more closely at the life and career of Cranch, a remarkably versatile intellectual too often dismissed as merely a minor Transcendentalist. And third, we analyze several passages in Cranch's translation to suggest how his text would have resonated for American readers in 1872. We suggest that this American *Aeneid*, which Cranch began working on in the 1860s, is an epic outpouring for a powerful postbellum political state—both a paean to the Union victory and an ironic warning to a potential "empire without end" (Ver. *Aen.* 1.279).

Vergil in America

From the 17th through the 19th centuries, Cicero and Vergil dominated the entrance examinations and freshman studies of English grammar schools and colleges in America.[7] Latin language comprehension was an essential aspect of secondary education, and Vergil was required reading for centuries. "Particularly in the colonial era," noted one scholar, "most men and women who later would make contributions to literary and/or intellectual discourse, knew the texts of Rome's epic poet about as well as the Bible (during the eighteenth century, perhaps better)."[8] So while Cranch may have been the first American to publish a full verse translation of the *Aeneid*, thousands before him had been parsing Vergil's Latin and rendering it privately into English. For instance, in the 1780s, John Adams boasted that his son John Quincy had converted the entire *Aeneid* into English as part of his studies. (William Cranch, father of the translator, was John Quincy Adams's classmate at Harvard as well as his first cousin.) And in 1796, a prose translation of Vergil's works by Yale alumnus Caleb Alexander was published in Massachusetts.[9] During the Revolutionary era of the "Founding Fathers" especially, Latin texts were revered for their insights into large-scale republican governance and philosophy, and their widespread use ensured familiarity among the US electorate in the late 18th century.

But the reputation of the *Aeneid* in the early US republic suffered in two respects. First, its use as a primer for Latin translation exercises often transformed it into an object of horror in the recollections of American men.

> Virgil is more generally read and less appreciated than any other classic. His poems are now used almost universally as a text-book, and at such an early period in the course of classical studies, that they appear to the pupil quite as difficult and uninteresting as the grammar and the dictionary.

Thus wrote the Boston intellectual Francis Bowen in 1842, in the preface to his own attempt at a new and improved Vergil textbook for schools. "Months, and even years, are bestowed upon the study of them, and the length of the task only adds to its wearisomeness," he continued.

> The associations formed at such an early period in one's education are retained with great tenacity through life, and the consequence is, that these elegant and delightful poems call up, in the minds of most persons, no other or more pleasant images than those of the spelling-book, the recitation room, and, perhaps, the rod.[10]

Read and recited purely as an exercise in Latin grammar and vocabulary, the substance of the *Aeneid* was often lost through a pedagogical approach favoring rote memorization and featuring corporal punishment.

Second, Vergil's *Eclogues* and *Georgics* were more often singled out for praise in the early republic and antebellum periods in US history. Vergil's pastoralism in these works was linked with republican virtue among civic agrarians like Thomas Jefferson.[11] The later "Augustan" Vergil of the *Aeneid* could appear anti-democratic. Writing in 1807, in the preface to his much-maligned epic poem *The Columbiad*, Joel Barlow observed that "Virgil wrote and felt like a subject, not a citizen. The real design of [the *Aeneid*] was to increase the veneration of the people for a master, whoever he might be."[12] The *Aeneid* was certainly appreciated as a classic, but the *Eclogues* and the *Georgics* were understood to be the more "American" of Vergil's works, and it was only after the US Civil War that the *Aeneid* was generally considered to be Vergil's masterpiece by American readers. Yet as one scholar has noted, it is striking that the *Aeneid* had not been more popular in the 17th, 18th, and early 19th centuries:

> Such potentially transportable themes as the birth of a new nation in a new land, the wandering of a divinely guided people, the struggle between the settlers and the native people, the transplantation of culture—these did not, in general, leave their mark on American thought and literature.[13]

The Latin classics had been of considerable importance to the generation of young men growing up in the Revolutionary era, but the succeeding generation, while still teaching Latin to its boys, was more skeptical of the value of ancient texts for a "new" nation.[14] As in Barlow's preface to the *Columbiad*, a suspicion that pagan texts of the distant past might not forward the progress of a modern Christian republic pushed students both toward utilitarian ventures and toward other academic subjects then in vogue, such as German Romanticism. Yet as Harvard graduates such as Edward Everett and William Emerson (older brother of Ralph Waldo Emerson) traveled to Germany in the 1810s and 1820s to continue their studies at the University of Göttingen, they were exposed to exciting new historicist scholarship, by German philologists such as Christian Gottlob Heyne and Friedrich August Wolf, that recontextualized Greek and Roman literature and reexamined the authorial status of figures from Homer to Vergil. The temporary decline in classical studies in early 19th-century America thus shortly gave way to a new rise in succeeding decades, as the academic and educational reforms taken home to the United States breathed new life into the study of ancient texts.

By the 1840s, the desire for a classical education had rebounded. American teachers had begun preparing their own Latin editions of Vergil for schools, responding to a growing need for updated classroom materials. The expansion of public education across the growing nation ensured that a knowledge of Latin literature was no longer the privilege of an aristocratic elite; "the middle class was introduced to the classics on a large scale for the first time, and the classics were carried to the very frontiers of American civilization," resulting in what one scholar has described as a "golden age" of the classics in America.[15] In fact, classicists today may be shocked by the confident optimism expressed by scholars in that era regarding the growing popularity of their field. "It is a much more common thing for young men to continue their classical studies beyond the time of the college education, than it has been in former days," asserted one publication in 1843.[16] A few years later, in 1849, John Larkin Lincoln, professor of Latin at Brown University, would remark that classical education "is at present, we think, in a rising and hopeful condition in our country."[17] The New England Transcendentalists, with whom Christopher Pearse Cranch was associated, were especially committed to a renewed study and appreciation of the classics in the 1840s. For them, perhaps paradoxically, "classical studies had intellectually progressive associations," suggesting the new perspectives tied to the historical scholarly practices at German universities.[18]

The antebellum era of the 1840s and 1850s even saw the emergence of the celebrity classicist: Columbia College professor Charles Anthon achieved national fame for his dozens of editions of Greek and Latin texts. Other classically trained scholars severely criticized the sloppiness of Anthon's publications, but middle-class readers eager to gain cultural capital propelled Anthon into literary stardom.[19] Anthon's long tenure in New York (he held his post at Columbia from 1820 to 1864) helped to solidify his national literary reputation; by 1851, Nathaniel Hawthorne was mentioning Anthon by name in his *Wonder-Book for Girls and Boys*. As most American readers handling the *Aeneid* would have been encountering the text in Latin, usually as preparation for college entrance exams, accessible editions were essential. Anthon's established text of *The Aeneid of Virgil, with English Notes, Critical and Explanatory*, which was part of "Anthon's Classical

Series" and first published by Harper and Brothers in 1843, was extremely popular.[20] Cranch noted in his preface that he used it as the basis for his translation.[21]

By 1872, when Cranch's *Aeneid* was published, the average American reader's comfort with Latin had deteriorated markedly. This was not because an interest in the classics was again on the wane—in fact, it was just the opposite. More mid-century middle-class readers, both men and women, were discovering the values of the classics, but this growing audience often lacked the language skills necessary to appreciate the Latin originals. In other words, Cranch was entering a literary marketplace in which familiarity with Vergil was rising among a readership less familiar with Latin. If we wonder why the first full American verse translation of the *Aeneid* was not published until 1872, we might do well to recall that such translations were in much less demand from earlier generations of gentlemen readers fond of passing over Latin texts in their leisure time.[22]

For those who wanted to read the *Aeneid* in English rather than in Latin prior to Cranch's work, two texts stood out for their popularity and availability. John Dryden's 1697 translation into heroic couplets remained the standard well throughout the 18th and 19th centuries.[23] In the novel *Changing Base; or, What Edward Rice Learnt at School* (1869), written by soon-to-be Harvard Professor of Latin William Everett, the young Rice confidently exclaims, when struggling with his own Latin translations, "I read lots of Dryden's Virgil with daddy, and he said it was the best translation ever written; and plenty of lines ran over. If I can do as well as Dryden, I'm content."[24] Also extremely popular was Joseph Davidson's 1743 prose translation, an American edition of which, prepared by Malcolm Campbell, first appeared in 1803. The London publisher Henry G. Bohn brought out a new edition of Davidson's translation, updated by Oxford's Theodore Buckley, in 1850, as part of "Bohn's Classical Library," and a few years later Harper and Brothers of New York arranged to reprint Bohn's Classical Library as "Harper's New Classical Library." The updated version of Davidson's *Aeneid* accordingly appeared in the series in 1857. It sold well; Harper's was still putting it through new printings in the 1890s. Cranch compared portions of his own translation to Davidson's before publishing it.[25]

Finally, it must be observed that the *Aeneid* had begun to replace the *Eclogues* and *Georgics* as America's favorite Vergilian text after the US Civil War. By the 1870s, a new American verse translation of the *Aeneid* would have been seen as appropriate following William Cullen Bryant's new verse translations of the *Iliad* and the *Odyssey*. A new generation of classicists helped to shift the tide. At the time Cranch's translation appeared, William Everett, then Tutor in Latin at Harvard, was known to his colleagues and students for having memorized the *Aeneid* in its entirety.[26] The epic's American reputation continued to grow steadily over the coming decades. By the end of the century, Helen Keller was reading it in Braille to prepare for the entrance examinations to Radcliffe College. It was one of her favorite books.[27]

Furthermore, Vergil's reputation vis-à-vis the *Aeneid* had improved in America as well. While Barlow could write in 1807 that the *Aeneid* taught readers to be subjects for autocrats, Vergil's love of Rome was received more favorably by the end of the

19th century. An 1897 "Students' Edition" of Cranch's *Aeneid* translation added an anonymously authored introduction characterizing Vergil as "the most national as well as the greatest of Roman poets" and as a "patriotic singer." The latter phrase specifically references Dante's reception of Vergil, but elsewhere the introduction praises Vergil's "ardent patriotism" and claims that "to produce a national epic had been [Vergil's] aspiration from his youth . . . to his maturity."[28] Readers were thus encouraged to approach Cranch's translation with the understanding that the poetry therein addressed not just mythological themes but national ones as well.[29]

Christopher Pearse Cranch: preacher, poet, painter, translator

Christopher Pearse Cranch came from an impressive family. Born in Virginia to a federal judge, he was distantly related to both Abigail Adams and Noah Webster (of dictionary fame). Having attended Columbian College (now George Washington University), Cranch went on to graduate from Harvard Divinity School in 1835. He then traveled west as a Unitarian "supply preacher," working as a pulpit substitute for regular pastors who might be traveling or otherwise unavailable. Cranch began with a brief stint in St. Louis, where he worked with his cousin William Greenleaf Eliot (grandfather of the poet T.S. Eliot). He also spent time in Peoria, Cincinnati, and Louisville; in this last city, he worked alongside James Freeman Clarke, the editor of *The Western Messenger*, a magazine sympathetic to New England Transcendentalism.

Transcendentalism is difficult to define. Typically associated with the elevation of individual consciousness, it was an American intellectual movement that built upon German Idealist philosophy, English Romantic poetry, and Unitarian Christian theology, popular among a coterie of ministers, writers, and artists living in Boston and Concord, Massachusetts, in the 1830s and 1840s.[30] No central principle anchored the movement, but adherents generally privileged spiritual truths over material phenomena, shared a faith that the spark of divinity was present within and accessible to all human beings, and favored progressive social reform politics. The text nearest to serving as a Transcendentalist manifesto was the short book *Nature* (1836), written by Ralph Waldo Emerson. Emerson was a former Unitarian minister who had left his pulpit to pursue a more secular intellectual life, and his popular lectures and essays encouraged Americans to look both outward to the wonders of the natural world and inward with a spiritual self-reliance in order to connect with a universal and unifying divine force that he called the Over-Soul.

Cranch came under Emerson's spell, and in the late 1830s he authored many poems and essays for *The Western Messenger* promoting the new movement. "The true Transcendentalism," he wrote, "is that living and always new *spirit* of truth, which is ever going forth on its conquests into the world, and leading all captivity captive."[31] Cranch also drew the cartoons and caricatures of Emerson that remain his most well-known works today. A drawing of an enormous human eye, with top hat and coattails, perched upon two long legs, has been reprinted endlessly in anthologies of American literature as a representative of the "transparent eyeball" from Emerson's 1836 *Nature*.

Figure 6.1 From Christopher Pearse Cranch, "River of Time," *Illustrations of the New Philosophy* (1837–1839), MS Am 1506, (21), Box 2, Houghton Library, Harvard University. Reproduced with permission.

Clarke collected Cranch's caricatures into *Illustrations of the New Philosophy*, a manuscript now housed in Houghton Library at Harvard University. In one illustration, designed to accompany Emerson's 1837 address "The American Scholar" (which Cranch had reviewed enthusiastically for *The Western Messenger*), a gigantic Emerson wades through the "River of Time," striding past Lilliputian scholars who rest dry above the water by sitting across the grounds of an institution built upon books. Two tomes—one labeled "ΟΜΗΡΟΣ" (Homer) and the other "VIRGIL"—act as pillars that reach above the river water and in turn support a volume of Shakespeare on which the college stands. In lines taken directly from Emerson's essay, a tiny scholar rests on these folios and exclaims, "This is good—let us hold by this," while the colossal Emerson walks by muttering, "They pin me down."

While the drawing initially suggests a disdain for the classics and a need to write one's own books ("the books of an older period will not fit this," claimed Emerson),[32] it also indicates that at least four authors—Homer, Vergil, Shakespeare, and Cicero ("Tully")—rest on solid ground and thus stand above the River of Time.

Cranch's cartoon vindicates at least these four classic artists as forming a stable foundation that remains timeless, if nevertheless obtrusive to Emerson's modern intellectual whims. It is tempting, in retrospect, to view the smiling shadow clinging to Vergil and waving to Emerson as a diminutive Cranch attempting to secure his own slice of literary immortality.[33]

Returning to the East Coast in 1840, Cranch finally met Emerson in person and fell in with the Transcendentalist circle in Massachusetts, where he was known for his sense of humor and his musical abilities. With Emerson as a mentor, he continued composing poems, many of which appeared in the short-lived but very influential Transcendentalist journal *The Dial*, culminating in the publication of his 1844 book, simply titled *Poems*.[34] But even as Cranch was developing a reputation as a leading Transcendentalist poet, his interests took him instead toward the visual arts. He married his cousin Elizabeth De Windt in 1843 and settled in New York, where he was deeply influenced by the Hudson River School of painting. This interest eventually took him to Italy in 1846 to paint landscapes, and he stayed there until 1849, when the Italian political revolutions forced him back to the United States for the safety of his family. In Florence he became good friends with the poets Robert and Elizabeth Barrett Browning, and in Rome he acquainted himself with the fashionable trends in the art world of that time. He also engaged in popular tourist activities, wandering through ancient ruins and paying his respects at the tomb of Vergil. "I think I can never over-estimate the immense advantages I enjoyed of a voyage to Italy in 1846 and a stay there of nearly three years," he later reflected.[35] He returned to Europe again, for a longer stay, from 1853 to 1863. He continued to contribute verses and essays to American magazines during this time, and he also authored several children's novels, which sold better than his paintings.

Cranch's next return to the United States was in 1863, in the midst of the Civil War. In fact, he stepped ashore in New York City just days after the city's horrendous draft riots. Horace Greeley, editor of the *New York Daily Tribune*, spotted Cranch in the street and invited him up to his office in the Tribune Building, where he showed him "the guns, hand grenades, etc., which had been in readiness all over the building in case of attack by the mob."[36] The war "brought out a sense of national pride" in Cranch, a staunch supporter of the Union cause who detested the institution of slavery.[37] The war hit home especially when his oldest son, George, enlisted upon turning 18 in 1865. (George was unharmed in the war but died of a lung infection two years later at Columbia College.) Cranch increasingly turned to patriotic themes in his poetry, and by the end of the decade he had started work on his blank verse translation of the *Aeneid*, which would appear in print in 1872.[38]

Cranch's postbellum *Aeneid*

Between 1867 and 1872, shortly after the termination of the US Civil War, the Boston-based publishing firm of Fields and Osgood brought out translations of the epics of Dante, Homer, Vergil, and Goethe by Longfellow, Bryant, Cranch, and Taylor, respectively. Cranch, it should be noted, socialized with these other men. These works were celebrated for what were then considered modern translation practices—chiefly, a more intense fidelity to the language of the original texts. Unlike earlier English translators, such as Alexander Pope, who focused more on the spirit of ancient texts than on the letter (and felt free to add superfluous new details, often to aid rhyme schemes), Cranch and his contemporaries focused intently on the specific language of the original. One critic of the 1870s thus referred to these poet-translators as "American literalists."[39] Upon reading his version of the *Aeneid*, William Eliot wrote to Cranch, "I read carefully, equally delighted with the poetry and the literal rendering. . . . Yours is Virgil and as exact almost as if you were making a school translation for students, while the verse is pure English."[40] This might sound like a backhanded compliment, but the accessibility of Cranch's translation would have been a significant selling point for American readers encountering the *Aeneid* for the first time. This was a popular rather than a specialist edition.

Cranch offered a prosaic poetry—the virtue of which was its straightforward style, and the vice of which was its unheroic tone. One contemporary claimed that Cranch's edition had "taken the foremost place among translations in English."[41] But despite the fact that it sold well and was reprinted several times over the ensuing decades, Cranch's text would find few ardent admirers. It came to be considered a pedestrian attempt. A later scholar labeled the edition "unmemorable" and observed that Cranch's "translation is literal, his language clear, his scansion unexceptionable, but there is a pervading lack of elegance; he banished the *heroic* with the couplet."[42]

To give just one example of Cranch's plain style, consider the very first three lines of his translation: "I sing of arms, and of the man who first / Came from the coasts of Troy to Italy / And the Lavinian shores, exiled by fate" (1; 1.1–3).[43] Cranch has rendered each of Vergil's Latin words with a basic, unsurprising English translation; a modern undergraduate student with a pocket Latin dictionary could easily have produced this translation for a homework assignment, identical in all respects but the line breaks.[44] This characteristic lack of poetic elevation in favor of a clear, unadorned translation appears again a few lines later, where he writes: "Many things also suffered he in war, / Until he built a city, and his gods / Brought into Latium" (1; 1.7–9).[45] These lines not only provide a straightforward translation but also nearly reproduce the word order of Vergil's original Latin verse.[46]

We might be tempted to view such a "literal" translation as exempt from the kind of historicist influences that often color a translation. But of course no work of art and no translation can ever completely escape the tenor of its time. Just as Joshua Matthews has suggested that Longfellow's Dante is a postbellum production, and just as Stephen Scully has argued that Dryden's Vergil reflects the political turmoil in England of his own time, we suggest that Cranch's *Aeneid* should be understood as the output of a Transcendentalist working in the wake of the Civil War.[47] Cranch surely grasped the reverse relationship—that the war might be understood in light of his classical education. In his Civil War poem "November 8th, 1864," he writes, "What record of the historian's pen, what poet's loftiest lays, / What parallel from out the grand and stern old Roman days, / What sculptured monument those lives, those deaths, can overpraise!"[48] Indeed, as Augustus sought to cultivate the idea of *res publica restituta* after his civil wars were over, so Cranch could declare at the Civil War's end that "the nation is re-born!"[49] His epic translation owes something to the historical context in which it was completed.

After his return to the United States in 1863, Cranch's writings increasingly returned to the Transcendentalist themes regarding spiritual truths that had fired his sensibilities in the late 1830s. For example, in a notable 1873 essay he argued for the need to understand the material world as a symbolic representation of the ideal world (following Emerson's argument in the 1836 *Nature*).[50] This Transcendentalist strain becomes notable in Cranch's translation of the *Aeneid* when the shade of Anchises reveals to Aeneas the future of the Roman race. When Aeneas asks about the process by which the dead become reincarnated as new human lives, Anchises replies:

> Know first, the heavens, the earth, the flowing sea,
> The moon's bright globe, and the Titanian stars
> By one interior spirit are sustained:
> Through all their members interfused, a mind
> Quickens the mass entire, and mingling stirs
> The mighty frame. Thence springs the life of men,
> And grazing flocks, and flying birds, and all
> The strange shapes in the deep and shining sea.
> (254–5; 6.904–11)[51]

This translation significantly differs from John Dryden's popular version. Dryden (in 1697) had rendered the speech as follows:

> Know first, that heav'n, and earth's compacted frame,
> And flowing waters, and the starry flame,
> And both the radiant lights, one common soul
> Inspires and feeds—and animates the whole.
> This active mind, infus'd through all the space,
> Unites and mingles with the mighty mass.
> Hence men and beasts the breath of life obtain,
> And birds of air, and monsters of the main.[52]

Here, Dryden's "one common soul," pervading a Newtonian universe like a gas ("infus'd through all the space"), attaches to the "mighty mass" mechanistically, as if guided by physical law; his words are reflective of a mechanical age that understood the universe in terms of mass and force. Alternatively, Cranch's "interior spirit" creates and sustains life, which grows and develops from such spiritual properties; his interpretation belongs to a Romantic era that saw organic life as being sustained by nonmechanical properties.[53] Cranch's version calls to mind Ralph Waldo Emerson's "Over-Soul," specifically in its gesture to a stream or river from which "springs the life of men."[54] In his 1841 essay "The Over-Soul,"

Emerson famously observed that "Man is a stream whose source is hidden. Our being is descending into us from we know not whence."[55] Indeed, in 1875, just three years after the publication of his translation, Cranch would get into an argument with Henry James about the validity of the very concept of the "oversoul."[56]

A further Transcendentalist aspect of Cranch's *Aeneid* emerges in the poem's descriptions of historical epochs. In his poetry volume of 1875, Cranch's "The Spirit of the Age" articulates a vision of the human race transitioning from one era to another. Cranch imagines the qualitative aspects of an "age" as a perceptible force (akin to electromagnetism) of which many are initially unaware but which eventually manifests itself as the "strong and free" spirit of the age, indeed "the soul of the nineteenth century." Such language was common among the Transcendentalists; in the first issue of *The Dial* (1840), for example, Emerson had written that the revolutionary "spirit of the time" was "felt by every individual."[57] This conception of the perceptible signs of the transition to a new era resembles the Roman understanding of the same phenomenon. For the Romans, obvious omens (such as the peal of trumpets in the clear sky) indicated the beginning of a new *saeculum*, or "age," and within the intellectual world of the Romans around the time of Vergil, it was understood that these *saecula* could possess qualitative characteristics or be connected to singular individuals.[58] Just as the Transcendentalists felt an impersonal power impelling the people and actions of their age, so did many Romans believe a new cycle in their organization of time brought with it a substantive spiritual change in human affairs.[59]

Cranch may have been drawn to the *Aeneid* because this very concept of a *Zeitgeist* appears in multiple places throughout the epic. Anchises describes Augustus to Aeneas in the underworld by saying that "the golden age in Latium he shall bring / Again" (184; 6.991–2).[60] Later, Evander shows Aeneas the site of the original golden age brought about by Saturn in Italy: "Beneath his reign / The golden age, so called, was seen. In peace / He ruled his people; till by gradual steps / There came a faded and degenerate age, / And love of war succeeded, and of gain" (326; 8.394–8).[61] And Jupiter, in his Book 1 prophecy to Venus, declares that "an age is coming in the gliding years" (17; 1.369)[62] in which the descendants of the Trojans—that is, the Romans—will come to control the Greek homelands of their heroic opponents in the Trojan War, and that this age will see the peaceful, benevolent rule of Augustus.

Cranch's translation does not impose any particular Transcendental interpretation on Vergil's own Latin words; even the degeneration of the original golden age in Book 8, made to sound like an impersonal force that crept into the world, reflects the syntax of Vergil's Latin. But the rhetoric of periodization in the *Aeneid* gains an additional accentuation for postbellum readers receptive to the other Transcendental touches Cranch placed on his translation, and it provides another resonant parallel between Vergil's Rome and America in 1872. (As we will see, the language of qualitative periodization also appeared in the poetry Cranch wrote after the assassination of Lincoln.) For Cranch, the qualities of a new era could be felt by those cognizant of the innovations and ideas suited to the time, and this phenomenon applied both to his literary Rome and to his contemporary America.

Readers of Cranch's translation thus might consider whether the nation had entered a new Golden Age of peace or whether the postbellum era would someday yield to another age characterized by changing fortunes for the American empire.

But in 1872, readers having experienced the tremendously devastating US Civil War would probably have been more deeply stirred by Anchises' remarks in the underworld on the battles between Pompey and Julius Caesar: "O sons, indulge not minds / For wars like these, nor 'gainst your country's life / Direct such valor" (260–1; 6.1044–6).[63] Anchises' prior exclamation "what carnage dire!" was all too germane to the bloodiest war in American history. Similarly, as the war climaxes in Book 12, the narrator exclaims, "Was it the will of Jupiter that thus / The nations whom eternal peace one day / Would join should clash in such a conflict dire?" (521; 12.642–4).[64]

Even Cranch's translation choices evoke a desire for a strong union in language that more fittingly suits postbellum America than Augustan Rome, as can be seen in several places. One of the many lapidary phrases of the *Aeneid* occurs at the end of the proem in Book 1, where, after detailing all the various impediments that the Trojans had faced and would face later, the poet writes *tantae molis erat Romanam condere gentem* (1.33). The word *gens* typically refers to people of the same familial descent, such as a "race," "people," or "clan."[65] Cranch translates this line as "Such task it was to found the Roman state" (3; 1.43), which instead gestures toward an organized political entity rather than a unified people. In fact, the word *gens* (and the closely related term *genus*) appears frequently throughout Book 1 of the *Aeneid*, and Cranch otherwise always uses the translation "race" for these appearances; for example, just a few lines later, Juno complains that she for "so many years with one sole race wage[s] war" (3; 1.61).[66] With such a verbal choice, Cranch steers away from considerations of ethnic bloodlines in favor of unity through a single government.

American readers in the 1870s would have found certain passages in Cranch's translation evocative of Abraham Lincoln. Neptune's calming of the waves during a storm is compared in a famous epic simile to a statesman, "some man of reverence and worth" (9; 1.191–2),[67] who through rhetoric and general authority quells a "sedition" (9; 1.188) among the people. The Latin word *seditio* (1.149), which Cranch renders with a term loaded with contemporary connotations, also appears later in the poem (11.340), but in that passage he renders it with the weaker phrase "strife of faction" (462; 11.449). The statesman simile, translated in this way, could call to mind for a postbellum American reader the leadership of Lincoln during the Confederacy's rebellion.

In addition, Cranch's description of the death of the helmsman, Palinurus, recalls the explicit comparison made by many Americans to the assassination of Abraham Lincoln in 1865. At the end of Book 5, as Aeneas sails the Trojans up to Italy, Jupiter assures Venus that they will reach their destined site, but one man will not make it there: the helmsman, Palinurus. Jupiter's declaration of "one life for many given" (213; 5.973)[68] and the extended passage in which Palinurus is lost to the waves would remind readers of how, immediately following Abraham Lincoln's assassination in 1865, many compared the president, the pilot of the ship of state, to the Trojan helmsman. The Rev. Charles S. Robinson, in an 1865 sermon, exclaimed, "Alas! we say, for the nation bereaved of its pilot, when out in the midst of such a sea as this! Palinurus has been suddenly swept, by a wave, from the helm."[69] Similarly, the Rev. Cephas B. Crane remarked, "We have lost our Palinurus, our helmsman, and our ship of state is adrift on stormy seas."[70]

Like many Americans, Cranch was particularly devastated by Lincoln's assassination. Just days after the event, he wrote two sonnets in memorial for the *New York Daily Tribune*, insisting that "not in vain he died."[71] In another poem, "The Century and the Nation," read for the Phi Beta Kappa Society at Harvard in 1874, Cranch mourned Lincoln as the "helmsman on the bark / Of state," who, "when thunders roared and lightnings flashed, / Steered us to port,—himself the assassin's mark." In this same poem, Cranch prophesies a glorious future for postbellum America, echoing Jupiter's promise (17; 1.369) that "an age is coming in the gliding years" when the Romans would achieve peace after the gates of war have been closed:

> For thee, our Country, may the advancing age
> Evolve a destiny more nobly vast
> Than ever stained with blood the antique page
> In blurred and lurid records of the past.[72]

But in many ways, the difficulties of the *Aeneid*'s conclusion mirrored the difficulties of the ending of the Civil War. The prudent advice offered throughout the poem seemed to apply to the politics of Reconstruction, such as Anchises' proclamation that Rome will "spare the vanquished, and subdue the proud" (262; 6.1072),[73] or Aeneas' proffered peace: "On equal terms let both the nations then,/ Unconquered, join and make eternal league" (503; 12.245–6).[74] Jupiter himself insists on political unity at the poem's close, prophesying that "all / Shall Latins be, one common speech to all. / Hence, mingled with Ausonian blood, shall rise / A nation above men and gods in worth" (539; 12.1061–4).[75] But the epic's final moment, the brutal killing of Turnus, suggests that reconciliation may not be easy. Cranch had demanded, in his memorial sonnets, that the Union should respond to Lincoln's assassination with brute force instead of clemency, advising (*contra* Anchises) that "We are stabbed whene'er we spare—strike in God's name!" When Aeneas, on the verge of extending mercy to the fallen Turnus, sees the belt of the slain Pallas and is filled with wrath, he kills Turnus as an act of vengeance; the final scene of the poem thus may have resembled to his readers the sort of avenging rage Cranch had advocated against the Confederacy.[76]

For Cranch, working in the 1870s, the sense that the larger nation (certainly much larger than the United States he left in 1846 to visit Italy) would become an "imperial power" (cf. 100; 3.210) was not without its worries. Cranch was no doubt familiar with the discourse of *translatio imperii* common in 19th-century American thought: a belief in the inevitable rise-and-fall cycle of supreme political power, then exemplified by *The Course of Empire* (1836), a famous series of paintings by the Hudson River School artist Thomas Cole depicting the development and devastation of an imperial society. This popular discourse may have influenced Cranch's decision to translate, in Aeneas' recounting of the fall of Troy, Vergil's phrase *Priami regna* (2.22) not in a straightforward rendering as "Priam's kingdom" but instead as "Priam's empire" (45; 2.30).[77] The word choice is notable given that the word "empire" only appears 11 times throughout Cranch's entire *Aeneid*, typically in relation to gods (and, except for one other instance, always as a translation for *imperium*, which occurs 40 times in Vergil). In the immediate downfall of Troy, Aeneas is told by a terrified Trojan that "Cruel Jove / To Argos now transfers the imperial rule" (63; 2.452–3);[78] this phrasing is striking, because the original Latin reads simply *omnia*, "everything" (2.326), which Cranch has expanded significantly with his translation "imperial rule." Later, Aeneas himself declares that "all the gods / By whom our empire stood have gone from us" (64; 2.483–4)[79] as Troy is being sacked by the Greeks. And at the epic's end, Aeneas insists that, should he be victorious in single combat against Turnus, "not then shall I command / The Italians to obey the Trojan rule; / Nor do I aim at empire [Latin: *regna*] for myself" (503; 12.242–4).[80]

The geographic expansion following the conquest of western lands in the Mexican–American War (1846–1848) was a major force contributing to the eruption of the US Civil War, as Americans fought over whether slavery would be practiced in the new territories. Aware as they were of the scholarly theory that the Roman Empire had collapsed after spreading itself too thin, Cranch and others of his generation were hesitant to speak positively of the imperial trend of territorial acquisition that was driving much American policy. Although Cranch knew that Vergil's epic was composed during a period of expansionary conquest under a leader whose various foreign wars to expand Rome's holdings throughout the known world received explicit praise within the poem, he nonetheless renders Vergil's Latin (or, as Richard Thomas has argued, interprets Vergil's subtextual ambivalence)[81] with moments of discomfort toward empire for an American audience grappling with these same geopolitical concerns.

The endurance of Cranch's translation

Cranch's translation of the *Aeneid* may not be canonical today, but its influence was significant. Widely hailed at its appearance in 1872, it was still being reprinted as late as 1914, over 40 years after its initial publication, by Houghton, Mifflin and Company (which had bought out James Osgood, Cranch's original publisher, in 1880). In 1899, the editor Frederick B. De Berard used Cranch's translation as part of his popular edition of the *Aeneid* in a multi-volume "Famous Tales" series for the New York publisher Isaac H. Blanchard. This series was then reprinted by the Bodleian Society of New York in 1902 and 1905. De Berard's prefatory materials explain that Cranch's was "one of the most accurate, scholarly and pleasing versions of the 'Æneid'" and was "among the very best of the many translations of the great epic."[82] At the beginning of the 20th century, Cranch's translation was thus poised to set the tone for the American reception of the *Aeneid*.

Indeed, we might consider Cranch's version to be the first influential modern translation of Vergil's epic. John Dryden's 1697 rendering had been the reigning standard when Cranch's work appeared in 1872. But whereas Dryden's translation is clearly an antiquated obstacle for today's readers, Cranch's continues to be extremely accessible, serving as the basis for the "Barnes & Noble Classics" edition of the *Aeneid* first published in 2007. Given the contemporary persistence of Cranch's translation, this work—and the historical context of its production—deserves to be better known. Aside from meriting scholarly attention due to its longstanding popularity in the United States, the translation and its history illustrate how the *Aeneid* has remained relevant as a "modern story" (with modernity broadly defined). The postbellum period in American literature fostered a national identity that could account for the country's new birth of freedom, and Cranch's *Aeneid* should take its place among the more familiar works of that period as an articulation of the new American origin myth.

Notes

1 Gruesz 2002: 85.
2 Phillips 2012: 245.
3 Torlone and Braund 2018. Joseph Dexter completely ignores Cranch's edition by falsely claiming that "no American verse translation of the whole of the *Aeneid* . . . was produced until the twentieth century." Dexter 2011: 41.
4 Spence 2007: xxxix. Spence wanted to avoid what she calls the archaic "Yoda-speak" of Cranch's original syntax. Spence 2007: xl.
5 Matthews 2013: 335.
6 It had once been fashionable to suggest that Cranch took on the translation merely as a "personal amusement." See Miller 1951: 22. Matthews explains that Longfellow's motivation in translating Dante was similarly long treated by scholars as a "personal escape from grief over the 1861 death of his wife." Matthews 2013: 326.
7 Richard 2010: 356–7.
8 Shields 2001: xli.
9 Alexander 1796. Two years earlier, Alexander had published a Latin textbook for US students; see Alexander 1794.
10 Bowen 1842: iii.
11 In *Lucy Howard's Journal*, Lydia H. Sigourney's 1858 loosely autobiographical fiction, the eponymous heroine translates for her grandfather, a Revolutionary War veteran, passages from the *Georgics* and the *Aeneid*. "I could not but observe that he gave more entire attention to the former than to the latter," she remarks. "This convinced me that, though he had been so long a military man, his tastes were peaceful. Doubtless he became a soldier from duty, when his country struggled for life, but his heart was with Nature and rural things." Sigourney 1858: 72.
12 Barlow 1807: ix.
13 Reinhold 1984: 227.
14 Americans in the early republic commonly compared the United States to Rome and were often on the lookout for would-be Caesars, anxiously anticipating a potential slide from republic to empire. But as Eran Shalev notes, such comparisons largely receded over the course of the 19th century (only to return at the end of the 20th). Shalev 2009: 217–8.
15 Richard 2009: x–xi.
16 Sears, Edwards, and Felton 1843: iv–v.

17 Lincoln 1849: 362.

18 Van Anglen 2010: 5.

19 In a review of one of Anthon's works, Cornelius Felton, Professor of Greek at Harvard, wrote this: "Haste is Professor Anthon's besetting sin. . . . Hardly one of his volumes is not deformed by mistakes, that seriously impair its usefulness as a work to be placed in the hands of young students." Fenton 1842: 180. "Dr. Anthon is a humbug," concluded another Harvard-educated critic. Dana 1845: 152.

20 Prior to the appearance of Anthon's text, students may have used a version such as J. G. Cooper's popular *Publii Virgilii Maronis Opera; or, The Works of Virgil*, which was republished many times. See Cooper 1827. Cooper's was the text that Emily Dickinson used when she was a student at Amherst Academy in the 1840s. See Habegger 2001: 141.

21 Cranch 1872: ix.

22 One early review of Cranch's *Aeneid* drew attention to the fact that many of his readers would be unfamiliar with the original Latin: "We are very sure that those who do not know the great Roman epic can not be introduced to it so agreeably, nor be so surely won to its enjoyment, as by this translation." "Two New Books" 1872: 891.

23 "Most Americans read Vergil in Dryden's translation, often reprinted in America well into the nineteenth century." Reinhold 1984: 224. As late as 1909, Berkeley professor George R. Noyes insisted that "Dryden's *Virgil* still remains practically without a rival as the standard translation." Noyes 1909: xxxiv.

24 Everett 1869: 173–4.

25 Cranch 1872: ix; henceforth cited parenthetically in the body text.

26 Irmscher 2017: 105.

27 Winterer 2010: 366. "Helen Keller's homemade Braille, Latin *Aeneid*," notes Winterer, "draws our attention to the shadow world of the *Aeneid* that flourished underneath the vast canopy of male translations and scholarly editions stretching from antiquity to the present." Winterer 2010: 366.

28 Cranch 1900: i–vii.

29 As one of his initial reviewers observed, "Mr. Cranch has, we believe, made a really valuable contribution to our national literature." "Mr. Cranch's Virgil's Æneid" 1873: 232.

30 For a good overview, see Gura 2007.

31 Cranch 1841: 407.

32 Emerson 1971: 56.

33 In another cartoon, Cranch includes a background character exclaiming in a speech bubble a line in Latin from the *Aeneid* (3.658) in order to describe a monster.

34 On Cranch's poetic apprenticeship to Ralph Waldo Emerson in the early 1840s, see Dowling 2014: 101–35.

35 Quoted in Stula 2007: 76.

36 Scott 1917: 254.

37 Stula 2007: 144.

38 Years later, following Longfellow's recommendation, Cranch also translated both Vergil's *Georgics* (in blank verse) and the *Eclogues* (in hexameters), but as he could not find a publisher for these works, they exist only in manuscript. See Miller 1951: 22.

39 Richardson 1878: 55. A notice in *The Literary World* observed that "the reader will be amazed by the literalness of Mr. Cranch's rendering of the poem, which is secured without sacrifice of rhetorical elegance or vigor." "Minor Book Notices" 1872: 91.

40 Letter from Rev. William Greenleaf Eliot to Mr. Cranch (St. Louis, January 8, 1873) in Scott 1917: 272–3.

41 Richardson 1878: 50.

42 Levenson 1950: 421, n. 10. It is worth noting that Dryden's celebrated version had been offered in what might have been considered a "plain style" for the 1690s; Dryden himself prefaced his translation by stating, "I have endeavoured to make Virgil speak

such English as he would himself have spoken, if he had been born in England, and in this present age."

43 Ver. *Aen.* 1.1–3.

44 While Dryden and John Conington, the only two poets whose translations Cranch says he had consulted, do take some liberties with their translations of the proem of the *Aeneid*, Anthon's rendering may have most influenced Cranch; in his commentary notes, Anthon's prose translation includes the phrase "came from the coasts of Troy to Italy and the Lavinian shores," just as Cranch's verse does. See Anthon 1843: 1 and Cranch 1872: vii, 1.

45 Ver. *Aen.* 1.5–6.

46 Of course, the word order can sound stilted to modern ears; this is the "Yoda-speak" that Spence complains of and changes, in her Barnes & Noble translation, to "Many things he also suffered in war, / Until he built a city, and brought his gods / Into Latium" (3; 1.7–9).

47 On Dryden, see Scully 2018.

48 Cranch 1875: 311.

49 Cranch 1875: 323.

50 Cranch 1873. Cranch also offers a Latin excerpt from the *Aeneid* in that essay.

51 Ver. *Aen.* 6.724–9.

52 Dryden 1870: 2.61–2.

53 In his source text, Cranch would have seen Anthon's note on the subject: "The poet is here describing what the Stoics called the 'Soul of the Universe,' or *anima mundi*, namely, a spirit or essence gifted with intelligence, and pervading and animating matter, and all things formed out of matter. The human soul is an emanation from this great principle, proceeding from it as a spark from the parent fire." Anthon 1843: 655.

54 In his poem "The Bird and the Bell," first published in 1866, Cranch had similarly described the divine presence as "the Central Good, the inflowing Power, / The Primal Life in which we live and move." Cranch 1875: 18.

55 Emerson 1979: 159.

56 Sargent 1880: 56.

57 Emerson 2013: 96. Perhaps more famously, Emerson had declared in "The American Scholar" that "each age . . . must write its own books." Emerson 1971: 56.

58 Hay 2019.

59 For the relationship between the chronological and the religious or sociopolitical aspects of the cycles of the life of Rome, see also O'Neill 2020: 233–6.

60 Ver. *Aen.* 6.792–3.

61 Ver. *Aen.* 8.324–7.

62 Ver. *Aen.* 1.283.

63 Ver. *Aen.* 6.832–3.

64 Ver. *Aen.* 12.503–4.

65 *Oxford Latin Dictionary*, 1st ed., gives six primary definitions, the first of which is "a race, nation, people" and the rest of which all refer to communities of people and not sovereign states. Glare 1983.

66 Ver. *Aen.* 1.47–8.

67 Ver. *Aen.* 1.151.

68 Ver. *Aen.* 5.815.

69 *Our Martyr President, Abraham Lincoln: Voices from the Pulpit of New York and Brooklyn* 1865: 92.

70 Crane 1865: 23. The tendency to link Lincoln with Palinurus continued long after the 1860s. In the April 1885 issue of *Harper's Monthly Magazine*, for example, William Phillips Garrison's poem "The Vision of Abraham Lincoln" characterizes "our martyr President" as "like Palinurus—in his hand / The broken tiller of the Ship of State— / Flung on the margin of the Promised Land." Garrison 1885. This poem was later reprinted in Crandall 1891.

71 Cranch 1865: 6. The poem was reprinted in several venues, such as *Poetical Tributes to the Memory of Abraham Lincoln* 1865, and Cranch retitled the verses as "The Death-Blow" and "The Martyr" for his own collection in 1875.
72 Cranch 1875: 267, 262. Similarly, in the sonnet "Our Country," Cranch remarks of a postbellum America bereft of its presidential hero, "our Ship of State / Repairs the chasm left by the fall of him / Who stood her mainmast." Cranch 1875: 326.
73 Ver. *Aen.* 6.853.
74 Ver. *Aen.* 12.190–1.
75 Ver. *Aen.* 12.837–9.
76 Cranch's insistence in that sonnet of the impossibility of reconciliation with the Confederacy ("no league, nor truce, save men with men") anticipates language in his *Aeneid*: "league" appears 18 times, and "truce" four times, in the last three books, as the Trojans seek peace with the local Italians. Elsewhere, the Fury Alecto enrages the Rutuli by encouraging friendly relations between the Trojans and Latins and tells Juno: "Behold, the work achieved / For thee, in discord and disastrous war! / Now bid them join in friendly truce and league, / While with Ausonian blood the Trojans reek!" (294; 7.677–80; Ver. *Aen.* 7.545–7.). Also, Dido curses the relationship between Romans and Carthaginians (and seems to pray for the future rise of Hannibal) by demanding, "No love, no league / between you!" (165; 4.822–3; Ver. *Aen.* 4.624) in revenge for Aeneas' departure. Cranch tends to use "league" when describing weak, failed, or impossible unions of communities in the *Aeneid*, whereas the stronger terms "state" and "nation" usually refer to successful groups; this verbiage perhaps reflects a belief that America could never have made a viable peace treaty with the Confederacy but instead needed to reunite the proverbial house divided.
77 Perhaps following Dryden: "While Fortune did on Priam's empire smile" (2.28).
78 Ver. *Aen.* 2.326–7.
79 Ver. *Aen.* 2.351–2.
80 Ver. *Aen.* 12.189–90.
81 Thomas 2001.
82 De Berard 1902: xi.

References

Alexander, C. 1794. *A Grammatical Institute of the Latin Language: Intended for the Use of Latin Schools, in the United States*. Worcester, MA: Isaiah Thomas.

———. 1796. *The Works of Virgil: Translated into Literal English Prose*. Worcester, MA: Leonard Worcester.

Anthon, C. 1843. *The Æneïd of Virgil, with English Notes, Critical and Explanatory, a Metrical Clavis, and an Historical, Geographical, and Mythological Index*. New York: Harper and Brothers.

Barlow, J. 1807. *The Columbiad*. Philadelphia: C. & A. Conrad.

Bowen, F. 1842. *Virgil; with English Notes, Prepared for the Use of Classical Schools and Colleges*. Boston: David H. Williams.

Cooper, J.G. 1827. *Publii Virgilii Maronis Opera; or, The Works of Virgil*. New York: White.

Cranch, C.P. 1841. "Transcendentalism." *Western Messenger* 8 (January): 405–9.

———. 1865. "A. L., In Memoriam." *New York Daily Tribune*, April 19.

———, tran. 1872. *The Æneid of Virgil, Translated into English Blank Verse*. Boston: James R. Osgood and Company.

———. 1873. "Symbolism and Language." *The Galaxy* 16 (September).

———. 1875. *The Bird and the Bell, with Other Poems*. Boston: James R. Osgood and Company.

———, tran. 1900. *The Æneid of Virgil*. Boston: Houghton Mifflin.

Crandall, C.H., ed. 1891. *Representative Sonnets by American Poets*. Boston: Houghton Mifflin.

Crane, C.B. 1865. *Sermon on the Occasion of the Death of President Lincoln, Preached in the South Baptist Church, Hartford, Conn., Sunday, April 16, 1865*. Hartford, CT: Case, Lockwood and Company.

Dana, C.A. 1845. "Rev. of *A System of Latin Versification*, by Charles Anthon." *The Harbinger* 1, 10 (August): 151–3.

De Berard, F.B., ed. 1902. "The Æneid of Virgil." In *Classic Library of Famous Literature*. Vol. 8. New York: Bodleian Society.

Dexter, J.P. 2011. "A Nineteenth-Century American Interpretation of the Aeneid." *Classical World* 105, 1: 39–56.

Dowling, D. 2014. *Emerson's Protégés: Mentoring and Marketing Transcendentalism's Future*. New Haven: Yale University Press.

Dryden, J., tran. 1870. *The Works of Virgil*. Philadelphia: Claxton, Remsen, and Haffelfinger.

Emerson, R.W. 1971. "Nature, Addresses, and Lectures." In R.E. Spiller and A.R. Ferguson (eds.) *The Collected Works of Ralph Waldo Emerson*. Vol. 1. Cambridge, MA: Belknap Press.

———. 1979. "Essays: First Series (1841)." In J. Slater, A.R. Ferguson, and J.F. Carr (eds.) *The Collected Works of Ralph Waldo Emerson*. Vol. 2. Cambridge, MA: Belknap Press.

———. 2013. "Uncollected Prose Writings: Addresses, Essays, and Reviews." In R.A. Bosco and J. Myerson (eds.) *The Collected Works of Ralph Waldo Emerson*. Vol. 10. Cambridge, MA: Belknap Press.

Everett, W. 1869. *Changing Base; or, What Edward Rice Learnt at School*. Boston: Lee and Shepard.

Felton, C. 1842. "Rev. of *A Classical Dictionary*, by Charles Anthon." *North American Review* 54 (January): 175–98.

Garrison, W.P. 1885. "The Vision of Abraham Lincoln." *Harper's Monthly*, April.

Glare, P.G.W., ed. 1983. *Oxford Latin Dictionary*. 1st ed. Oxford: Oxford University Press.

Gruesz, K.S. 2002. *Ambassadors of Culture: The Transamerican Origins of Latino Writing*. Princeton: Princeton University Press.

Gura, P.F. 2007. *American Transcendentalism: A History*. New York: Farrar, Straus and Giroux.

Habegger, A. 2001. *My Wars Are Laid Away in Books: The Life of Emily Dickinson*. New York: Modern Library.

Hay, P. 2019. "Saecular Discourse: Qualitative Periodization in First Century BCE Rome." In J. Osgood, K. Morrell, and K. Welch (eds.) *The Alternative Augustan Age*. Cambridge: Oxford University Press.

Irmscher, C. 2017. "'Larger the Shadows': Longfellow's Translation of Virgil's Eclogue 1." In K.P. Van Anglen and J. Engell (eds.) *The Call of Classical Literature in the Romantic Age*. Edinburgh: Edinburgh University Press. 103–25.

Levenson, J.C. 1950. "Christopher Pearse Cranch: The Case History of a Minor Artist in America." *American Literature* 21, 4 (January): 415–26.

Lincoln, J.L. 1849. "Rev. of Anthon's Cicero and Tacitus." *North American Review* 68 (April): 348–62.

Matthews, J. 2013. “The Divine Comedy as an American Civil War Epic.” *J19: The Journal of Nineteenth-Century Americanists* 1, 2: 315–37.
Miller, F.D. 1951. *Christopher Pearse Cranch and His Caricatures of New England Transcendentalism.* Cambridge, MA: Harvard University Press.
“Minor Book Notices.” 1872. *The Literary World*, November.
“Mr. Cranch’s Virgil’s Æneid.” 1873. *Old and New* 7, 2 (February): 223–33.
Noyes, G.R., ed. 1909. *The Poetical Works of John Dryden.* Boston: Houghton Mifflin.
O’Neill, J.R. 2020. “Claudius the Censor and the Rhetoric of Re-Foundation.” *Classical Journal* 116, 2: 216–39.
Our Martyr President, Abraham Lincoln: Voices from the Pulpit of New York and Brooklyn. 1865. New York: Tibbals & Whiting.
Phillips, C.N. 2012. *Epic in American Culture: Settlement to Reconstruction.* Baltimore, MD: Johns Hopkins University Press.
Poetical Tributes to the Memory of Abraham Lincoln. 1865. Philadelphia: Lippincott.
Reinhold, M. 1984. *Classica Americana: The Greek and Roman Heritage in the United States.* Detroit: Wayne State University Press.
Richard, C.J. 2009. *The Golden Age of the Classics in America.* Cambridge, MA: Harvard University Press.
———. 2010. “Vergil and the Early American Republic.” In J. Farrell and M.C.J. Putnam (eds.) *A Companion to Vergil’s Aeneid and Its Tradition.* Malden, MA: Wiley-Blackwell. 355–65.
Richardson, C.F. 1878. *A Primer of American Literature.* Boston: Houghton Mifflin.
Sargent, M.E., ed. 1880. *Sketches and Reminiscences of the Radical Club of Chestnut Street, Boston.* Boston: James R. Osgood and Company.
Scott, L.C., ed. 1917. *The Life and Letters of Christopher Pearse Cranch.* Boston: Houghton Mifflin.
Scully, S. 2018. “Aesthetic and Political Concerns in Dryden’s Aeneis.” In S. Braund and Z.M. Torlone (eds.) *Virgil and His Translators.* Oxford: Oxford University Press.
Sears, B., Edwards, B.B., and Felton, C.C. 1843. *Classical Studies: Essays on Ancient Literature and Art.* Boston: Gould, Kendall and Lincoln.
Shalev, E. 2009. *Rome Reborn on Western Shores: Historical Imagination and the Creation of the American Republic.* Charlottesville, VA: University of Virginia Press.
Shields, J.C. 2001. *The American Aeneas: Classical Origins of the American Self.* Knoxville, TN: University of Tennessee Press.
Sigourney, L.H. 1858. *Lucy Howard’s Journal.* New York: Harper and Brothers.
Spence, S., ed. 2007. *The Aeneid.* Translated by C.P. Cranch. New York: Barnes and Noble Classics.
Stula, N. 2007. *At Home and Abroad: The Transcendental Landscapes of Christopher Pearse Cranch (1813–1892).* Hanover, NH: University Press of New England.
Thomas, R.F. 2001. *Virgil and the Augustan Reception.* Cambridge and New York: Cambridge University Press.
Torlone, Z.M., and Braund, S., eds. 2018. *Virgil and His Translators.* Oxford: Oxford University Press.
“Two New Books.” 1872. *Harper’s Weekly*, November 16.
Van Anglen, K.P. Van. 2010. “Greek and Roman Classics.” In S.H. Petrulionis, L.D. Walls, and J. Myerson (eds.) *The Oxford Handbook of Transcendentalism.* New York: Oxford University Press.
Winterer, C. 2010. “Why Did American Women Read the Aeneid?” In J. Farrell and M.C.J. Putnam (eds.) *A Companion to Vergil’s Aeneid and Its Tradition.* Malden, MA: Wiley-Blackwell. 366–75.

7 The *Aeneid* and the politics of national history

Tedd A. Wimperis

As a commonplace of political rhetoric, cultural memory exerts a compelling persuasive and emotive influence in official communication. National capitals are filled with the media of commemoration, encompassing monuments, historic buildings, and other "sites of memory"; the words of founders and role models resound in stump speeches and televised addresses, lending weight to arguments predicated on communal identity and values. These ubiquitous expressions of memory in the civic sphere, alongside the myths, performances, holidays, and patriotic traditions that revive the national heritage in every generation, are not passive ornamentation but pointed rhetorical instruments. Mobilized in the service of diverse political agendas, national history is a didactic, protreptic tool for instilling norms, informing worldviews, and normalizing standards of conduct through the mythology of exemplary heroes and events. It also serves a crucial legitimating function, expressing a symbolic link between past and present authority that anchors contemporary government in its historical duties and represents current officials as the latest in a chain of sanctioned predecessors.[1]

Myths and memories of the community's past concretely affect the political sphere, underpinning entire ideologies, justifying domestic and foreign policies, and effectively shaping political reality through the organizing frameworks and principles they convey.[2] Owing to the importance of national history in guiding the discourse of the here and now, past and present exercise reciprocal force upon one another: as much as the past influences the present, the present constantly reinvents, reclaims, and reevaluates the past, constructing the meaning and value of that past after its own image, to answer its own contemporary needs.[3] Fifth-century Athenian dramatists fashioned the national hero Theseus into an ideal citizen on the tragic stage; the medieval British legend of an eponymous founder Brutus, descendant of Aeneas, wove Britain into the genealogy of Troy and the Roman Empire; in a show of Iran's storied past and cosmopolitan values, in 1971 the last Shah celebrated the 2,500th anniversary of the Achaemenid Empire's foundation with lavish spectacles at Persepolis and the tomb of Cyrus the Great.[4] National memories of heroes, traumas, achievements, and aspirations are a storehouse of effective rhetorical symbolism engineered, with varying fidelity to the actual facts of history, to rouse, persuade, and prescribe.

DOI: 10.4324/9781003176145-10

The ideologically charged exchange between past and present in political communication—what scholars often cite as the 'politics of memory'—grounds this chapter's approach to the *Aeneid*, a literary monument that engages cultural memory, and its overt politicization, with unique directness and nuance.[5] Vergil's song of Aeneas, the Roman 'national epic,' is an act of commemoration indelibly shaped by the ideological tides of the author's own era.[6] The story of the Roman people's first foundation in Italy renews and reconstructs the past in a way that responds to present concerns—the aftermath of endemic civil wars, Italy's integration into the Roman civic sphere, the installment of a new regime in the Augustan principate—while simultaneously ingraining the emperor's own authority and iconography into Roman cultural memory.

A classic (and long contested) case study in national history as political messaging, the *Aeneid* models the politics of memory not only in its external relation to the imperial regime but in its internal, fictive world, inhabited by Vergil's characters within miniature "nations" of their own. In what follows, this chapter will explore these outward- and inward-looking political contexts of the poem and expand on them to consider the value of the epic's ideological implications for its 21st-century readership. The *Aeneid*'s exemplum of the pervasive, mutually reinforcing influence of politics, memory, and identity still speaks volumes today, where governments the world over continue to apply the politics of memory to legitimate, discredit, sway, and mobilize groups of people.

The Augustan politics of the past

Ancient Rome's was a culture steeped in the purposeful cultivation of the past. Its civic media and landscapes, especially centers like the Forum, the Capitolium, and the Palatine, were replete, in Vergil's phrase, with "memorials of generations past" (*virum monimenta priorum*, *Aen.* 8.312). Honorific statuary and building projects; the ancestral *imagines* that imbued private households with ancient prestige; public festivals affirming the city's divine auspices; literary productions and theatrical performances that glorified the deeds of patrons and the entire *res publica*; all these provided venues of commemoration, fortifying continuity with tradition throughout what Hölkeskamp aptly calls a "cityscape of *memoria* in stone."[7]

Reliance on cultural memories to construct and inform the present is a cornerstone of Roman political communication, well articulated in the guiding paradigm of *mos maiorum*, "the ancestral ways." Programmatic in this connection are the speeches of Caesar and Cato, reported in the historian Sallust's *Bellum Catilinae*, on the proper punishment for the rebel Catiline's co-conspirators; each speaker supports his position with the argument that Roman values and the ancestors who embody them in collective memory would endorse a verdict for mercy or severity (51–52.36). Cicero, in many ways the model Roman orator, made studied use of appeals to *mos maiorum* to charge his rhetoric with the authority of ancestral sanction.[8] Julius Caesar's assassination in 44 BCE was inspired, at least in part, by loyalty to exemplary forebears, as his contemporary Brutus assumed the mantle of his tyrannicide ancestors Lucius Junius Brutus, founder of the Republic, and

Gaius Servilius Ahala, famed for slaying a would-be revolutionary who aspired to royal power. Proud of that lineage, a decade earlier Brutus had struck coins minted with these ancestors' portraits and that of personified Liberty. The goddess Libertas continued to appear on coinage of Brutus and Cassius minted after the Ides of March to advertise their Republican convictions.[9]

In the wake of the dictator's murder, Octavian stepped into this arena, and over the subsequent five-and-a-half decades of his public life proved himself an adroit practitioner of memory politics. In this he benefitted from the example of his adoptive father, a master of the art: Julius Caesar was an energetic propagandist whose program of self-representation laid much of the groundwork then taken up and furthered by his heir. It was during Caesar's lifetime, and largely through his own efforts, that the *gens Iulia* became especially famous for the myth of its Trojan origins. The family's descent from Venus, through the lineage of Aeneas and his son Ascanius (from whose cognomen "Iulus" the family traced its name; *Aen.* 1.288) was a mainstay of Caesar's public image, so well known that Cicero could refer to him as "Venus-born" (*Venere prognatus*, *Fam.* 8.15) in private correspondence in place of his actual name.[10]

Even before the climactic battle of Actium and the establishment of the principate, Octavian's own propaganda leaned heavily into the myth of Aeneas' Italian foundation, which simultaneously bound him to Caesar's family and memory in its Trojan pedigree and associated him, by the proxy of the famously "dutiful" Aeneas (cf. Vergil's *pius Aeneas*), with the chief Roman virtue of *pietas*: reverent dutifulness toward the gods, the community, and, most importantly in this context, one's father, a quality widely promoted as his moral mandate for avenging Caesar's killers.[11] The Julian conceit of Trojan ancestry and Octavian's appropriation of *pietas* as a defining virtue, combined in the propaganda of the late 40s BCE onward, elevated the figure of Aeneas to new prominence as a founding father of the Roman people, a paragon of Roman values, and a symbol of the *mos maiorum* that so animated Roman political ideology.

Aeneas' rising popularity as a preeminent cultural hero owed much to the deliberate cultivation of his myth. Before the 1st century (and especially before the principate), the tales of Aeneas had mostly been the provenance of Greek intellectuals, whose writings had generated an array of different accounts of Aeneas' story and his relation to Rome.[12] Though the mythologies surrounding the Trojan prince had a longstanding currency in the Greek world and Hellenized lands like Sicily and Southern Italy, plus a significant presence in Etruria, Romans themselves espoused this account of their origins only gradually, over a period of centuries that brought ever-increasing exchange with Hellenic cultures.[13] The common ground supplied by the Aeneas myth helped build bridges between the Romans and other Mediterranean communities, weaving Rome's national story into Greek mythological traditions. More concretely, it inspired several diplomatic bids with Rome from the 3rd through 1st centuries BCE, initiated predominately by communities from Sicily and the Troad who staked a claim to special favor on the basis of shared Trojan kinship.[14] The Roman embrace of Aeneas as a founding father—alongside the indigenous and longer prevailing founder Romulus—thus owed much to broader political developments: abroad, Mediterranean expansion and foreign policy; at home, the ascendancy of the Julians.

The founder Aeneas continued to gain stature in the post-Actian political landscape, whose memory was foregrounded not least through the literature of Vergil and his contemporaries, but also in coinage, official building projects, public rituals and performances, and installations like the Altar of Augustan Peace (9 BCE). Assimilation to the revered heroic founder ennobled Augustus' own image in turn; Aeneas was a model against which the princeps could be (favorably) measured and stood for a legacy that his notional heir would restore in the eyes of the public. The virtues of Aeneas became Augustus' virtues, *pietas* above all; an icon of sacred authority and devotion to duty, the founder emblematized *mos maiorum* and buttressed the Augustan program of cultural and religious revival.[15] The Forum of Augustus of 2 BCE, whose colonnades housed a "hall of fame" immortalizing Roman heroes and where Aeneas' statue stood among those of his Julian descendants, perhaps best exemplifies the principate's rhetorical mobilization of national history to shape not only the reception of the princeps but the very idea of Roman identity.[16]

Within the principate's first decade, the *Aeneid* deserves pride of place as a catalyst for the popularization of Aeneas, the fusion of his memory with Augustus' person, and the promulgation of an imperial ideology that would endure for centuries and inspire countless later emulators. The question of Vergil's own attitudes toward the regime—the willingness and genuineness of the epic as political propaganda—has occasioned a vibrant debate I will leave largely aside here; whatever the poet's own alignments may have been on a "pro-Augustan" or "anti-Augustan" axis (a binary whose poles are both detectable in the text and need not be mutually exclusive), it is arguably true that the poem was written, at least partly, "to praise Augustus through his ancestors," to quote the commentator Servius.[17]

Evidence in the *Aeneid* for its ideological messaging, including the key comparison of Aeneas with Augustus, is myriad but best represented by the three celebrated prophecies in which the princeps appears within the story *in propria persona*, as the future culmination of Aeneas' lineage and mission. In Book 1, as Aeneas faces death at sea, Jupiter reassures a distraught Venus with a grand prophecy guaranteeing not only the Trojans' survival but their destined global hegemony; the long reign of the Aeneadae in Latium climaxes in the extraordinary career of the "Trojan Caesar" (1.286), whose breadth of vision and military success, like Rome's divinely ordained empire, will be "limitless" (*imperium sine fine*, 1.279). When, in Book 6, Aeneas visits his father in Elysium and witnesses the parade of Rome's pre-incarnate heroes, Anchises announces Augustus' arrival with special fanfare (6.791–5):

hic vir, hic est, tibi quem promitti saepius audis,
Augustus Caesar, divi genus, aurea condet
saecula qui rursus Latio regnata per arva
Saturno quondam, super et Garamantas et Indos
proferet imperium . . .

> This is the man! Here he is—the one you've heard promised to you again and again: Augustus Caesar, born of a god, who will reestablish the Golden Age in Latium, in the lands once ruled by Saturn, and expand his power beyond the Garamantes and Indians.

A triumphant Augustus appears once more in Book 8, whose victory at Actium is the centerpiece of Aeneas' shield.[18] At the head of a united Italy, under the favor of Apollo and the other Roman gods, he enters battle against the Egyptian queen Cleopatra, her eastern hordes, and the monstrous gods who support them (8.671–713); in the aftermath of victory, the princeps stages the triple triumph amid the cheer of ecstatic crowds and the savor of sacrifices, sits enthroned before the Palatine temple of Apollo, and receives the tribute of peoples across the world (8.714–28).

A victor in war and peace; a global conqueror; a heroic savior of the nation from foreign aggression; a demigod descended from the founder's line who fulfills the nation's destiny to spread peace and prosperity over land and sea. Many aspects of Augustus' portrayal here—themselves adapted from longstanding tropes in Greco-Roman encomia—became fixtures of the imperial public image and were to echo through the ages in the propaganda of later regimes, notably the European exponents of colonial imperialism and fascism, who borrowed liberally from memories of the Augustan Age.[19]

Ideology in microcosm: communities and memory inside the *Aeneid*

As a premier document of early Augustan ideology, the *Aeneid* offers a blueprint for the newly fashioned monarchical, expansionist Roman mythology it had a key role in propagating. What makes Vergil's contribution to this nascent autocratic discourse all the more engaging is his apparent sensitivity to the communal and cultural dynamics on which that discourse relied: the ways in which political ideologies are formulated and promulgated within communities and derive their power from collective identity, tradition, and shared historical experience. Augustan propaganda depended heavily on Roman cultural memory to craft the emperor's image as the exemplar of a normative "national character"; this dialogue between political authority and national identity was evidently not lost on the poet Vergil, who inscribes it into the microcosm of his *Aeneid* in the civic landscapes inhabited by his characters.

His fictive Carthaginians, Latins, and Arcadians are represented as peoples with cultural memories of their own, especially involving founders, heroes, and leaders. Moreover, the power structures that govern these societies—headed by Dido, Latinus, and Evander, respectively—are shown to exist in close alignment with symbols, spaces, and practices evocative of those memories, from palaces decorated with statues of past sovereigns to annual festivals conducted by the royal house. In much the same way as Augustan media instrumentalized Rome's national history, the fictionalized regimes within the *Aeneid* link their image and authority with the community's formative traditions, most pointedly its memories of foundation.

Not yet a full generation past the founding of their city, the Tyrian settlers of Carthage already enshrine some of its earliest history, like Dido's famous ruse to purchase the land, now memorialized in the toponym Byrsa ("oxhide") that commemorates the event (1.365–8).[20] Within Carthage's cityscape, the prominently placed and richly adorned Temple of Juno constitutes a major site of memory, simultaneously a center of civic worship and a seat of government where Aeneas first encounters the queen (1.505–8):

> *tum foribus divae, media testudine templi,*
> *saepta armis solioque alte subnixa resedit.*
> *iura dabat legesque viris, operumque laborem*
> *partibus aequabat iustis aut sorte trahebat.*

> At that moment [Dido] sat at the doors of the goddess, under the temple's central vault, encircled with arms and seated high on a throne. She was giving laws and rights to her people, and assigning their tasks in equal measure or drawing them by lot.

The special veneration attached to this site is owed not only to Juno's prestige as the city's chief deity but also its direct connection with the city's founding.[21] It was here, the narrator reveals, that Juno had led the settlers to uncover the omen of the horse's head that foretold Carthage's power and prosperity (1.441–5):

> *lucus in urbe fuit media, laetissimus umbrae,*
> *quo primum iactati undis et turbine Poeni*
> *effodere loco signum, quod regia Iuno*
> *monstrarat, caput acris equi; sic nam fore bello*
> *egregiam et facilem victu per saecula gentem.*

> There was a grove of abundant shade in the middle of the city, where first the Phoenicians, tossed by waves and storms, unearthed a symbol that queenly Juno had revealed to them: the head of a vigorous horse, for thus their nation would be distinguished in war and prosperous throughout the ages.

"Central" to the city's life in its functions as well as its physical placement (1.441), Juno's temple stands at the intersection of memory, identity, and politics, a communal epicenter as well as a monument to a signal event in its foundation story.

As its name signifies, Carthage is a "new city," and its people still identify with their roots in Tyre; this includes the founder and monarch Dido, who maintains the icons and heirlooms of her Phoenician forebears.[22] Two moments during the diplomatic banquet in Book 1, a suitable context for political self-representation, witness her suggestive display of Phoenician lineage and political history. First, among the decorations set out for the feast, the narrator calls attention to silver plate richly chased with the deeds of Dido's ancestors, tales reaching back to the earliest days of her people (1.640–2):

ingens argentum mensis, caelataque in auro
fortia facta patrum, series longissima rerum
per tot ducta viros antiqua ab origine gentis.

On the tables was massive silver plate, and engraved in gold were the mighty deeds of her ancestors, an extensive narrative traced through countless heroes from the ancient origin of their nation.

Second, Dido makes a formal toast with a jeweled cup that once belonged to her father, Belus, and his line (1.728–30):

hic regina gravem gemmis auroque poposcit
implevitque mero pateram, quam Belus et omnes
a Belo soliti; tum facta silentia tectis.

Now the queen asked for a cup, laden with precious gems and gold—a cup which Belus and all his lineage had once used—and filled it with wine; then all fell silent in the hall.

These visual artifacts, the silver plate and the royal cup, advertise the illustrious antiquity of Dido's family and intimate her legitimate royal pedigree. Not unlike the *Aeneid*'s role (as Servius puts it) in "praising Augustus through his ancestors," the display of Dido's ancestral *res gestae* articulates a visual argument in support of political power, conveying continuity with the past and resemblance between early heroes and contemporary rule.

Vergil's Latins, portrayed with layered ethnographic detail, diligently preserve memories of their founding by the god Saturn, their early kings, and their military triumphs. In the poet's rendering, the very names the Latins use for themselves and their territory, *Latini* and *Latium*, are rooted in their foundation story; Evander bases the name of Latium on the verb *latere*, "hide," memorializing Saturn's refuge in the land after fleeing the heavens under Jupiter's aggression. Moreover, Evander claims that the god himself bestowed the name upon the new community he formed there (8.321–3):

is genus indocile ac dispersum montibus altis
composuit legesque dedit, Latiumque vocari
maluit, his quoniam latuisset tutus in oris.

He gathered together a people uncultivated and scattered across the high mountains, and gave them laws; and he willed that this land be called Latium, since he had *hidden* safely here.

Saturn defined the Latins, and the Latins in turn, chief among them their king, Latinus, define themselves in close relation to Saturn, whom they view as the founder and source of the royal bloodline (*sanguinis ultimus auctor*, 7.49); the descendant of Saturn, Latinus rules in continuation of this founding dynasty (7.45–9).[23] Even more broadly, Saturn's memory informs the identity and ideology of the whole Latin community, as a nation still enjoying the founder's Golden Age and embodying its values (7.202–4):[24]

ne fugite hospitium, neve ignorate Latinos
Saturni gentem haud vinclo nec legibus aequam,
sponte sua veterisque dei se more tenentem.

Do not shun our hospitality, nor be unaware that the Latins, Saturn's nation, are a just people—not owing to bond or laws, but by their own free will and abidance by the custom of our ancient god.

The paramount site of memory in Latium is the palace of Picus, where Latinus receives the Trojan embassy, and whose interior description bears quoting at length (7.168–89, 192–3):

ille intra tecta vocari
imperat et solio medius consedit avito.
tectum augustum, ingens, centum sublime columnis
urbe fuit summa, Laurentis regia Pici,
horrendum silvis et religione parentum.
hic sceptra accipere et primos attollere fascis
regibus omen erat; hoc illis curia templum,
hae sacris sedes epulis; hic ariete caeso
perpetuis soliti patres considere mensis.
quin etiam veterum effigies ex ordine avorum
antiqua e cedro, Italusque paterque Sabinus
vitisator curvam servans sub imagine falcem,
Saturnusque senex Ianique bifrontis imago
vestibulo astabant, aliique ab origine reges,
Martiaque ob patriam pugnando vulnera passi.
multaque praeterea sacris in postibus arma,
captivi pendent currus curvaeque secures
et cristae capitum et portarum ingentia claustra
spiculaque clipeique ereptaque rostra carinis.
ipse Quirinali lituo parvaque sedebat
succinctus trabea laevaque ancile gerebat
Picus, equum domitor . . .
tali intus templo divum patriaque Latinus
sede sedens . . .

[Latinus] bid them be summoned into the hall, and sat in its center upon his ancestral throne. The Palace of Laurentine Picus was a majestic and massive building, towering with a hundred columns over the city's heights, awesome

> in its groves and the veneration of forefathers. Here it was sanctioned for kings to receive the scepter and first take up the fasces; this temple was their senate house, and this was the site of their sacred feasts; here the fathers were accustomed to sit at long tables after the slaughter of rams. There, too, were images of the ancient ancestors standing in order, hewn from old cedar: Italus and father Sabinus, the vine-grower keeping his curved sickle under his effigy; old Saturn and the likeness of two-faced Janus were standing in the vestibule, and other kings from time immemorial; and those who suffered wounds in battle as they fought for their country. Many arms hung from the sacred posts, captured chariots, curved axes, crests of helmets, and the massive bolts of city gates, spears, shields, and prows seized from ships. Sitting with a Quirinal staff, gird in a short *trabea*, and carrying an *ancile* in his left hand was Picus himself, tamer of horses. . . . Within this shrine of the gods sat Latinus upon his ancestral throne.[25]

Alongside its more conventional functions as a civic space, the hall doubles as a museum of Latin national identity. The memorials of war heroes and showcases of spoils assert the nation's valor and strength, while the portraits of founders and ancestors adorning the space promote the ancient authority of the ruling house.[26] Vergil's description underscores Latinus' own participation in this visual program by bookending the *ekphrasis* with the same two images of the king atop his "ancestral throne"; the living display of Latinus himself, the latest representative of the founding dynasty, assumes the focal point of the palace's narrative history, personifying the crucial link between past and present.

Neighboring the Latins on the future site of Rome dwell the Arcadian refugees led by Evander, another community steeped in the remembrance of its past. The city's name of Pallanteum enshrines the memory of a founder, the Pallas who was Evander's ancestor (8.51–4) and whose name lives on within the dynasty in its young prince. The topography of Pallanteum contains the altar and gate commemorating Evander's prophetess mother Carmentis, who foretold their settlement's future glory (8.339–41), and the Argiletum, whose Vergilian etymology as 'Argus' Demise' casts the name and site as a memorial to the guest once hosted by the king (8.345–6).[27]

But pride of place among the Arcadians' collective memories belongs to the triumph of Hercules over Cacus, an act of communal salvation tantamount, in its centrality to civic identity and history, to an act of foundation.[28] Like the Carthaginian Temple of Juno and the Latin palace of Picus, the Herculean Ara Maxima is a site of memory that engages the religious and political structures of the whole city (8.102–6):

> *Forte die sollemnem illo rex Arcas honorem*
> *Amphitryoniadae magno divisque ferebat*
> *ante urbem in luco. Pallas huic filius una,*
> *una omnes iuvenum primi pauperque senatus*
> *tura dabant, tepidusque cruor fumabat ad aras.*

> It happened, on that day, that the Arcadian king was performing annual honors for Amphitryon's great son and the gods in a grove before the city. His son Pallas was there with him, and all the noble youth and a humble senate were offering incense; warm blood smoked at the altars.

As the ceremonies unfold, the salvific event is remembered through performance and narrative; the king's own dramatic recitation of the tale (8.185–275) is a centerpiece of the rites.[29]

Like other founder figures (the Augustan *pius Aeneas* included), Hercules emblematizes characteristic values within this community, and the Arcadians' memories of his combat with Cacus and other exploits celebrate his raw power and merciless suppression of evil above all; in this connection, the Vergilian Evander's appetite for violent imagery, retribution, and black-and-white justice—a marked tendency in his speeches, best exemplified by his bloody account of Cacus' death—may be rooted in a worldview shaped by the Herculean mythos.[30] The old king's tale of his own battle with the three-souled monster Erulus (8.560–7) strongly evokes Hercules' fight against the three-bodied Geryon, and his description of the gruesome torments plied by his Etruscan archnemesis Mezentius, in which the victim dies amid "bloody ooze and gore" (*sanie taboque*, 8.487) echoes his portrayal of Cacus' cave, where the heads of victims were hanging "with grim gore" (*tristi . . . tabo*, 8.197). The Herculean moral paradigm extends to the Arcadians' view of Aeneas as well: inviting another wandering hero into his home, Evander bids Aeneas to follow Hercules' example of generosity (8.362–5), and when Aeneas leads the army from Pallanteum, the Arcadians prepare for him a special steed fitted with a gilded-clawed lionskin (8.551–3), the token of their national hero.

Power and the past in the 21st century

The ideological investment in national history that suffused the Augustan Age, whose rhetorical underpinnings Vergil observantly replicates inside the *Aeneid*'s fictive polities, does not lack for historical comparanda. In Archaic Athens, Theseus' stature as a preeminent national hero gained rapid momentum during the 6th century, under the Peisistratid tyrants; the late antique Sasanian rulers of Iran demonstrated their continuity with the Achaemenid Persian Empire by embellishing the old royal necropolis at Naqsh-e Rustam with new monumental reliefs, joining those of Xerxes and Darius, that celebrated their victories.[31] In more recent contexts, Napoleon Bonaparte paid special homage to the memory of Charlemagne as a European unifier and founder, receiving a replica "crown of Charlemagne" in his imperial coronation and conceptualizing his reign as a renewal of the Frankish Carolingian Empire; Benito Mussolini famously idolized Julius Caesar as a role model, the ideological ancestor of a militant Italian populism whose rhetoric and spectacles were wrought in the likeness of the Roman Empire.[32]

No less in the 21st century, autocratic regimes continue to mine cultural memory for meaningful political symbols, following millennia of precedent. Nationalist programs and individual cults of personality alike rely on communal history for promotion and legitimation, leveraging emotive signs of collective identity and promising the restoration of past glories. Contemporary iterations of this chapter's guiding example, the ideological linkage of current leadership with national heroes, appear as today's headline news; events in China, Russia, and Turkey suffice to show the endurance and the breadth of adaptations of the same rhetorical toolkit exemplified by the Roman *Aeneid.*

Xi Jinping's tenure as paramount leader of the People's Republic of China has seen new assertions of executive control in tandem with a renewed emphasis on national identity, not least in the codification of "Xi Jinping Thought," Xi's own political philosophy, as an official governing platform, and the installment of the "China Dream," a program of cultural and economic rejuvenation, as a core policy tenet.[33] Xi has come to command an extensive cult of personality, buttressed by state-controlled media, through which his image and worldview have become ingrained into the national culture. His writings are standard in educational curricula, and a smartphone app titled "Study the Great Nation," launched in 2019, instructs users in Chinese history and Xi Jinping Thought, while doubling as a news service for media about the president.[34]

The nationalist politics of the China Dream have imbued the country's long past—a history poised tensely between an imperial heritage and modern communist ideology—with new resonance.[35] Xi's personal enthusiasm for Chinese history has focused on its literary and intellectual tradition, particularly the figure of Confucius, whose home in Shandong Province he visited in a widely reported tour in 2013 and whose classics are an avowed inspiration for the president's own thought and rhetoric.[36] More extensively, Xi's image has been fashioned after the memory of Mao Zedong, founder of the People's Republic, whose own personality cult is rivaled only by that of the current regime. Xi vocally embraces the founder's legacy, his policies evoking a return to the centralized party control of the Maoist era; comparisons between the two leaders abound in official media, including the increasing use of honorifics for Xi once recognizably linked with Mao.[37]

Under Vladimir Putin's administration, the Russian Federation has also attracted global attention for its authoritarian politics and offers an especially rich theater for the analysis of memory politics. Negotiating Tsarist, Orthodox Christian, Soviet, and post-Soviet pasts, defined both in relation to and in opposition to its western European neighbors, 21st-century Russia is plural in its ideological models and charged with the rhetoric of national history.[38] Under Putin's government, official efforts to promote Russian history in media and educational curricula have served to create a public discourse that "focused on nationalism, patriotism, imperialism, respect for authority, and the idea of the uniqueness of Russian historical development" to reinforce national identity and bolster support for the state.[39]

This revival of cultural memory has seen the growing rehabilitation of controversial figures from Russia's past. One of these is Ivan the Terrible, monuments of whom have begun appearing in Russian cities, including Moscow, since 2016; a contested figure, the tsar's legendary cruelty is remembered in counterpoint to his territorial expansion and centralization of the Russian state.[40] A similar case is the renewed popularity of Joseph Stalin, simultaneously the victor of the "Great

Patriotic War" who transformed Russia into a modern industrialized nation and the head of a famously repressive and bloody regime. Stalin's favorability ratings among Russian citizens (like those of Ivan the Terrible) have climbed during the 2010s, and, while Putin's government has stopped short of openly affirming Stalin's legacy, the celebration of his triumph over Nazism—a defining moment in modern Russian identity, inseparable from Stalin's leadership—has become under Putin a major patriotic holiday commemorated with military spectacles.[41] The rising profiles of authoritarian icons like Ivan and Stalin coincide suggestively with Putin's consolidating control of government and pursuit of aggressive foreign policy, notably in former USSR territories like Crimea and Ukraine, directives for which the nation's memories of state authority and conquest, both Tsarist and Soviet, provide historical context and exempla.

A different kind of contested memory implicates the legacy of Mustafa Kemal Atatürk, founder of the modern Turkish Republic, under the presidency of Recep Tayyip Erdoğan. Atatürk's cult of personality in Turkey remains predominant: his portrait, sometimes monumentally scaled, adorns spaces throughout the country; his Memorial Day on November 10 is observed as a national holiday; his colossal mausoleum complex in Ankara, richly endowed with national symbolism and historical artifacts, constitutes a premier site of memory and venue for political ceremony.[42] But for all the support Atatürk still enjoys, the politics of westernization and secularization he represents have run up against a rising tide of Islamist conservatism, whose views have been invigorated by Erdoğan's tightening grip on the Turkish state. The perceived opposition between Atatürk and Erdoğan has come to symbolize these diverging ideologies and ideals of national identity.[43]

Erdoğan has critiqued Atatürk's politics—condemning, for example, his westernizing language reforms as a detriment to the nation's "bond with its past"—and shown muted enthusiasm for his cult.[44] His approach to nationalism also differs markedly from Atatürk's in his embrace of Ottoman imperial history, attested by his desire to restore Ottoman Turkish language study to school curricula, as well as his more recent reestablishment of Hagia Sophia as an active mosque. Yet Erdoğan's relation to Atatürk's founding memory is in fact a delicate balance between the display of distance and continuity. The president has paid annual visits to the Atatürk mausoleum on November 10, leading remembrance ceremonies with a delegation of officials and affirming the founder's lasting legacy under his government.[45] Parallels with Atatürk are also pervasive in the rhetoric surrounding the attempted coup in July 2016, represented in official media as Turkey's 'second revolution,' in which Erdoğan's victory, like Atatürk's before him, saved and secured the nation. Classroom videos prepared by the National Education Ministry titled "The Triumph of Democracy on July 15 and Memorial of the Martyrs" feature juxtaposed images of Atatürk and Erdoğan, a reenactment of Atatürk's victorious Gallipoli campaign intercut with footage from the coup's suppression and audio of the president reciting the national anthem.[46]

To focus only on the rhetoric of illiberal regimes risks diminishing the manifold examples of memory politics at work in ideologically democratic systems as well. In the United States, appeals to national identity are a mainstay of presidential electoral messaging, an arena in which candidates regularly present themselves as the spiritual successors of past commanders-in-chief. While campaigning for his first term as 44th president, then-US Senator from Illinois Barack Obama famously drew connections between himself and another Illinois lawyer and legislator, Abraham Lincoln—a link that evoked, especially in the context of Obama's bid to become the first African-American president, Lincoln's legacy of emancipation and bridging national divides.[47] Obama's expressions of Lincolnian affinity included frequent quotations of and allusions to Lincoln, opening his presidential campaign in Lincoln's hometown of Springfield, Illinois, and swearing both inaugural oaths on Lincoln's personal Bible. The 45th president Donald Trump's campaigns and term of office saw the avowal of two role models that appealed, in somewhat contradictory ways, to different sets of voters: on the one hand Andrew Jackson, a pugnacious anti-establishment populist, whose portrait Trump installed in the Oval Office; on the other, Ronald Reagan, an icon of mainstream (establishment) conservatism, whose likeness appeared with Trump's on a commemorative coin set produced by his 2020 reelection campaign.[48] Several Democratic contenders in the primary election of 2019–2020—most prominently Senator Bernie Sanders and then-former Vice President Joe Biden—sought to align themselves with the New Deal politics of Franklin Delano Roosevelt to advance a program of progressive national reform amid economic crisis.[49] Once inaugurated, President Biden hung a large portrait of Roosevelt in the Oval Office, directly facing the Resolute Desk, as a centerpiece of the new décor.[50]

America's past, like that of any other nation, is a contested, fluid construct, subject to the currents of political discourse and the perspectives of diverse authors and audiences; variant readings of American history and its exemplary figures continually animate national debate on what America is or is not, should or should not be. In their respective campaigns, Donald Trump vowed to "Make America Great Again" by recapturing an idealized past, while Joe Biden framed the 2020 race as a "battle for the soul of America" to reclaim the values eroded during his rival's tenure.[51] In the final months of the Trump administration, a uniquely transparent example of the ideological policing of national history came in the form of the 1776 Commission, a presidential advisory committee formed, in Trump's words, to strengthen "patriotic education" in American schools, on the grounds that a perceived curricular emphasis on the country's history of enslavement and racism was indoctrinating students in anti-American beliefs.[52] The official *1776 Report*, released January 18, 2021, outlined such a "patriotic" approach to early American history, stating its goals as follows:

> The declared purpose of the President's Advisory 1776 Commission is to "enable a rising generation to understand the history and principles of the founding of the United States in 1776 and to strive to form a more perfect Union." This requires a restoration of American education, which can only be grounded on a history of those principles that is "accurate, honest, unifying, inspiring, and ennobling." And a rediscovery of our shared identity rooted in our founding principles is the path to a renewed American unity and a confident American future.[53]

The report drew intense backlash from scholars of US history, who decried the polemical partisanship and inaccuracies that laced its account of events, especially the notably optimistic appraisal of its core issues of race and slavery.[54] The commission was terminated in Biden's first day of office.

Like the evidence from China, Russia, Turkey, and ancient Rome explored in this chapter, the 1776 Commission embodies the drive to harness cultural memory for political ends, in the service not only of promoting national unity but of centralizing control over a hermeneutically unstable past. That said, the continual revival and reinterpretation of national heritage need not always be an instrument of ideological enforcement; shared myths and the identities they inspire also provide a space for valuable communal reflection and celebration. In a different and more positive context, the immense popularity of the Broadway musical *Hamilton*—a rendition of America's founding not so unlike the *Aeneid* in genre—exemplifies cultural memory's ongoing vibrancy in the public discourse and its constant reimagining in every generation to speak to new social realities.

For all the various media, unique national traditions, and diverse constitutions these examples encompass, the basic gestures and intentions remain consistent; the Augustan appropriation of Roman cultural memory offers one among countless expressions of a rhetorical practice originating long before, and still thriving long after, the composition of Vergil's *Aeneid*. Correspondences between the discourse of memory, identity, and politics inside and outside the poem, in ancient Rome and in the 21st century, highlight the epic's enduring value in discerning the tendentious use and abuse of the past, a value all the more immediate in an age of expanding nationalist and identitarian movements. Vergil's fictionalized reproduction of this discourse within the world of the *Aeneid*—strikingly self-referential in the context of his politically charged national epic—reveals the poet's attentiveness to the cultural, sentimental components of persuasion and the co-constructive exchange between ideology and memory that pervades the political imagination. We today, as readers of the *Aeneid*, students of history, and participants in our own civic communities enjoy a timeless resource in this Vergilian commentary as we navigate the crosswinds of political messaging both coercive and benign and evaluate critically the myriad ideations of our own national stories.

Notes

1 The nexus of cultural memory, identity, and politics engages fields across the humanities and social sciences. On cultural memory, see esp. Assmann 2011, whose model originates in Maurice Halbwachs's seminal work on collective memory (Halbwachs 1992). Pierre Nora influentially coined the term "sites of memory" for locations, objects, or even abstract concepts viewed as uniquely evocative of a communal identity; on this concept see especially Nora 1989, and Till 2003 on physical places as mediators of collective memory. Anthony D. Smith's studies of nationalism examine the foundational importance of communal myths and memories in the formation of ethnic identity, the basis of nation-states; see Smith 1997 and 2009, with further bibliography on identity and nation formation, notably Anderson 1983.

2 For contemporary examples of cultural memory's roles in political media and policy, see Hosking and Schöpflin 1997; Stråth 2000; Langenbacher and Shain 2010; Bottici and

Challand 2010; Bouchard 2013; for examples from antiquity, see Gehrke 2007; Derks and Roymans 2009; Gruen 2011: 223–307.

3 Cf. Halbwachs 1992: 46–51 and Assmann 2011: 71–2; in a series of modern case studies, Hobsbawm and Ranger 1983 examines the deliberate engineering of the national past (the "invention of tradition") to suit ideological goals.

4 On Theseus in 5th-century theater, see Mills 1998; the main source for the Brutus legend is Geoffrey of Monmouth's *Historia Regum Brittaniae* (1.3–18).

5 Verovšek 2016 offers a general view of this research paradigm and its methodological challenges. In connection with Augustan poetry, Nandini Pandey's 2018 examination of the principate's political iconography—specifically its co-invention, appropriation, and deconstruction by contemporary poets, including Vergil—offers an elaborative case study of ideological symbolism and power in the Roman cultural context; see too Habinek 2005, whose analysis of ritualized speech acts in the creation of culture and authority also pertains to this kind of discourse.

6 Literature on the *Aeneid*'s engagement with Roman politics and identity is extensive; representative works are Toll 1991; Stahl 1998; Johnson 2001; Syed 2005; Reed 2007; Nakata 2012; Seider 2013; Fletcher 2014.

7 Hölkeskamp 2006: 482; see also, for diverse approaches to memory culture in Rome, Walter 2004; Rea 2007; Bell and Hansen 2008; Rutledge 2012; Galinsky 2014; Ker and Pieper 2014, and Hölscher 2018; Langlands 2018 and Roller 2018 treat the use of exempla in Roman monuments and literature.

8 Kenty 2011.

9 Crawford 1974, nos. 433.1 and 433.2 (54 BCE); after the assassination, no. 500.2 (43–42 BCE), among a series of issues.

10 The substantial evidence of Caesar's Trojan affinities (for a fuller reckoning of which see Erskine 2001: 17–23) includes coinage minted with the likenesses of Aeneas and Venus, the staging of the dressage performance called the "Troy Game" (cf. *Aen.* 5.545–603), and his construction and dedication of the Temple of Venus Genetrix (in her aspect as mother of Aeneas and progenitor of the Julian family). For the ideological and mythological underpinnings of the *Aeneid*'s Iulus/Ascanius identification, see also Barchiesi 2016.

11 On Augustan *pietas*, see Zanker 1990: 201–10 and Galinsky 1996: 86–8.

12 See esp. Gruen 1992 and Erskine 2001: 15–43 on the Aeneas myth's Hellenic background and acceptance among Romans.

13 Roman references to the Trojan origin myth extend back to the third and second centuries—the majority of evidence comes from diplomatic encounters with Sicilian, Greek, and Troad communities—but gain steam in the 1st century. Sulla was the first known Roman to stage the dressage spectacle called the "Troy Game" (recorded in Plutarch, *Cato the Younger* 3.1; cf. *Aen.* 5.553–602), and the incipit of Lucretius' *De Rerum Natura*, which names Venus as the "mother of Aeneas' descendants" (*Aeneadum genetrix*, 1.1), is representative of increasing allusions in Latin literature.

14 Battistoni 2009; see also, more broadly, Jones 1999 on "kinship diplomacy" in Greco-Roman antiquity, with discussion of Rome's relations with the contemporary city of Ilium (94–105).

15 See Zanker 1990: 192–238; Evans 1992: 39–54; Galinsky 1996, *passim,* on the media for Aeneas' image in Augustan culture and its ideological significance, and Angelova 2015: 9–43 on the emperor's representation as a founder in the line of Aeneas.

16 The ideological messaging of the Forum is discussed by Lamp 2013: 60–7, in relation to rhetorical teaching, and Pandey 2014: 92–106, in relation to *Aeneid* 6; Harrison 2006 takes a wider view of the Augustan building program.

17 *Augustum laudare a parentibus* (*Serv. Praef.*). See Harrison's 1990 survey for the main positions and some core contributors to this 20th-century debate, which has at this point led to greater consensus around a nonbinary interpretive approach that reads in the *Aeneid* a tense polyphony of voices, both "optimistic" and "pessimistic," sometimes supporting, sometimes undermining the imperial narrative.

18 Gurval 1995 examines Augustan representations of the battle of Actium, which constituted a virtual foundation myth for the regime; on the ideological undertones of Vergil's Actium narrative, see Hardie 1986: 97–110; Quint 1993: 21–31; Syed 2005: 177–93; Miller 2009: 66–94; Wyke 2009: 345–54.

19 For various contexts of this ideological reception, see Quint 1993: 21–49; Thomas 2001; Hardie 2014: 93–126. On Vergil's use of literary topoi for monarchical power, see Cairns 1989: 1–28 on kingship in the *Aeneid*; models and comparanda for the Vergilian rhetoric of praise include Theocritus' Hellenistic Greek poetry in praise of Ptolemy II Philadelphus (*Idyll* 17; Hunter 2003) and the poet Horace's own encomia of Augustus (e.g. *Odes* 1.12, 1.37, 3.14, 4.5, 4.15), which themselves owe much to the example of Pindar (Race 2010).

20 Vergil adapted the account of Dido's trick from ethnographic sources; see Scheid and Svenbro 1985. Anthony Smith 2009: 46 discusses collective names (which are often based on memories of foundation) as a key component of ethnic identity formation.

21 See esp. Giusti 2018: 105–10 on the omen.

22 Phoenician *Qart Hadasht*, "new city," was Hellenized as *Karthago*. On Dido's ancestry in the *Aeneid* and the broader tradition, see Mackie 1993.

23 On Latinus' genealogy, see Rosivach 1980; Moorton 1988; Bleisch 2003; Casali 2020 probes ambiguities in the poem's varying accounts of the dynasty and Latin history (by the narrator, Latinus himself, and Evander) and roots the inconsistencies in these speakers' subjective, ideologically guided reconstructions of the past.

24 On Latinus' comments and Latin national identity, see Bleisch 2003: 101–2. The clear evidence for governmental authority and an active military in Latinus' kingdom (cf. the description of the palace of Picus) complicates this utopian picture, perhaps highlighting the statement's ideological rather than strictly factual nature; on the discrepant characterizations of Vergil's Latium, see Rosivach 1980; Bleisch 2003: 101–4; O'Hara 2007: 96–8.

25 Vergil refers in this passage (anachronistically) to aspects of Roman dress and ceremony: the "Quirinal staff" evokes the name of the deified Romulus, identified after death as the god Quirinus, and the *lituus*, a curved ritual staff associated with augury; the *trabea* was a ceremonial vestment worn by religious or political authorities; in Roman lore, the *ancile* was a sacred shield that fell from heaven and symbolized Rome's sovereignty. These attempts to ground Roman customs in a primeval Italian past are characteristic of the *Aeneid*'s representation of Latium, which also features such Roman institutions as the ritual opening of the Gates of Janus to signify a state of war (7.601–15).

26 Critics have long noted the resonance of this space with Roman sites of memory and have proposed various analogues; most recent is Crofton-Sleigh 2018. See also, as good context for the military displays in Picus' palace, the remarks of Smith 2009: 27–8 and Till 2003: 293 on war memorials and national identity.

27 On Arcadian and Roman memory in Aeneas' tour of Pallanteum, see esp. Papaioannou 2003: 688–91, 696–700; Rea 2007: 89–95; Seider 2013: 52–5.

28 Cf. Angelova 2015: 13–22 on the overlapping conceptualization of foundation and salvation in Augustan Rome and earlier Mediterranean practice.

29 Secci 2013 argues for Evander's deliberate elevation of Hercules as a national hero for his people; see also Schmitt Pantel 2013 on collective memory and identity in Greek state festivals, which the Herculean rites closely resemble.

30 On Evander's apparent taste for violence and its connection to Hercules, see Petrini 1997: 50–1, 62–5; O'Hara 2018.

31 On Theseus and the Peisistratids, see Anderson 2003: 136–42; on the Sassanid revival of Achaemenid sites and monumental art, Canepa 2010.

32 See Lentz 2008 on Napoleon and the legacy of Charlemagne; for Mussolini and Caesar, Wyke 1999.

33 Buckley 2018.

34 Hernández 2019.

35 Johnson 2016; Carrai 2020.

36 See Buckley 2014 on Xi's links with Confucius and other figures from the Chinese canon.
37 Gan 2017; Ding and Javed 2019.
38 On cultural memory and politics in modern Russia, see Liñán 2010; Brudny 2013; Bernsand and Törnquist-Plewa 2019; Wijermars 2019.
39 Liñán 2010: 168.
40 MacFarquhar and Kishkovsky 2015; Amos 2016; Nemtsova 2019; see Wijermars' 2019: 164–206 analysis of the multivalent discourse surrounding Ivan's image, focusing on the tsar's depictions in recent media.
41 Stalin's place in the national story has long been a fraught issue and epitomizes the general tensions around Soviet memory and modern Russian identity; see Malinova 2019; Kolesnikov 2020.
42 Glyptis 2008.
43 Ackerman 2016; Çağaptay 2020: 294–6.
44 Tharoor 2014; Tharoor 2020; Çağaptay 2020: 284–8.
45 For a recent example, see Tosun 2020, a report on that year's ceremony from the state-run Anadolu Agency; Akyol 2017 offers a political analysis.
46 Srivastava 2017.
47 Seelye 2009.
48 See Johnson and Tumulty 2017 on Trump's identification with and praise for Jackson, which attracted criticism in light of the latter's association with Native American genocide. During the sale of the commemorative coins, the Reagan Presidential Foundation and Institute called on the Trump campaign to discontinue its use of the former president's image in its fundraising, citing lack of authorization (Pengelly 2020); the putative link between the Trump and Reagan agendas has in fact been rejected by some conservative commentators (e.g., Lowry 2016).
49 E.g., Alter 2019.
50 For this decorative scheme see Linskey 2021, a feature that appeared in *The Washington Post*.
51 See especially Dias 2020 on this campaign rhetoric.
52 Crowley and Schuessler 2021.
53 The President's Advisory 1776 Commission 2021: 1; the quoted language is from the Executive Order (no. 13958, published November 5, 2020) that established the commission.
54 See Evelyn 2021 for an overview of the criticism.

References

Ackerman, E. 2016. "Atatürk Versus Erdoğan: Turkey's Long Struggle." *The New Yorker*, July 16.

Akyol, M. 2017. "Why Erdogan Now Embraces Ataturk." *Al-Monitor*, November 17.

Alter, J. 2019. "Which of the F.D.R. Wannabes Actually Understands New Deal Liberalism?" *The New York Times*, June 21.

Amos, H. 2016. "Russian City Inaugurates Statue to Bloody Ivan the Terrible." *Associated Press*, October 14.

Anderson, B. 1983. *Imagined Communities: Reflections on the Origin and Spread of Nationalism*. London: Verso.

Anderson, G. 2003. *The Athenian Experiment: Building an Imagined Political Community in Ancient Attica, 508–490 B.C.* Ann Arbor: University of Michigan Press.

Angelova, D.N. 2015. *Sacred Founders: Women, Men, and Gods in the Discourse of Imperial Founding, Rome through Early Byzantium*. Oakland: University of California Press.

Assmann, J. 2011. *Cultural Memory and Early Civilization: Writing, Remembrance, and Political Imagination.* Cambridge: Cambridge University Press.

Barchiesi, A. 2016. "Jupiter the Antiquarian: The Name of Iulus (Virgil, Aeneid 1.267–8)." In R. Hunter and S.P. Oakley (eds.) *Latin Literature and Its Transmission: Papers in Honour of Michael Reeve*. Cambridge: Cambridge University Press. 1–9.

Battistoni, F. 2009. "Rome, Kinship and Diplomacy." In C. Eilers (ed.) *Diplomats and Diplomacy in the Roman World.* Leiden: Brill. 73–97.

Bell, S., and Hansen, I.L., eds. 2008. "Role Models in the Roman World: Identity and Assimilation." *Supplements to the Memoirs of the American Academy in Rome 7*. Ann Arbor: University of Michigan Press.

Bernsand, N., and Törnquist-Plewa, B. 2019. *Cultural and Political Imaginaries in Putin's Russia*. Leiden: Brill.

Bleisch, P. 2003. "The *Regia* of Picus: *Ekphrasis*, Italian Identity, and Artistic Definition in *Aeneid* 7.152–93." In P. Thibodeau and H. Haskell (eds.) *Being There Together: Essays in Honor of Michael C.J. Putnam on the Occasion of His Seventieth Birthday*. Afton: Afton Historical Society Press. 88–109.

Bottici, C., and Challand, B. 2010. *The Myth of the Clash of Civilizations*. New York: Routledge.

Bouchard, G., ed. 2013. *National Myths: Constructed Pasts, Contested Presents*. New York: Routledge.

Brudny, Y.M. 2013. "Myths and National Identity Choices in Post-Communist Russia." In Bouchard. 133–56.

Buckley, C. 2014. "Leader Taps Into Chinese Classics in Seeking to Cement Power." *The New York Times*, October 11.

———. 2018. "Xi Jinping Thought Explained: A New Ideology for a New Era." *The New York Times*, February 26.

Çağaptay, S. 2020. *Erdogan's Empire: Turkey and the Politics of the Middle East*. New York: I.B. Tauris.

Cairns, F. 1989. *Virgil's Augustan Epic*. Cambridge: Cambridge University Press.

Canepa, M.P. 2010. "Technologies of Memory in Early Sasanian Iran: Achaemenid Sites and Sasanian Identity." *American Journal of Archaeology* 114: 563–96.

Carrai, M.A. 2020. "Chinese Political Nostalgia and Xi Jinping's Dream of Great Rejuvenation." *International Journal of Asian Studies*: 1–19.

Casali, S. 2020. "The Kings of the Laurentes: Contradictions and Points of View in Virgil's *Aeneid*." *Classical Journal* 115: 283–301.

Crawford, M.H. 1974. *Roman Republican Coinage*. 2 vols. London: Cambridge University Press.

Crofton-Sleigh, L. 2018. "The Curia in Aeneid 7." *Illinois Classical Studies* 43: 160–75.

Crowley, M., and Schuessler, J. 2021. "Trump's 1776 Commission Critiques Liberalism in Report Derided by Historians." *The New York Times*, January 18.

Derks, T., and Roymans, N., eds. 2009. *Ethnic Constructs in Antiquity: The Role of Power and Tradition*. Amsterdam: Amsterdam University Press.

Dias, E. 2020. "Biden and Trump Say They're Fighting for America's 'Soul.' What Does That Mean?" *The New York Times*, October 17.

Ding, I., and Javed, J. 2019. "Why Maoism Still Resonates in China Today." *The Washington Post*, May 29.

Erskine, A. 2001. *Troy between Greece and Rome: Local Tradition and Imperial Power*. Oxford: Oxford University Press.

Evans, J.D. 1992. *The Art of Persuasion: Political Propaganda from Aeneas to Brutus*. Ann Arbor: University of Michigan Press.

Evelyn, K. 2021. "Historians Rail Against Trump Administration's 1776 Commission." *The Guardian*, January 22.

Fletcher, K.F.B. 2014. *Finding Italy: Travel, Nation and Colonization in Vergil's Aeneid.* Ann Arbor: University of Michigan Press.

Galinsky, K. 1996. *Augustan Culture: An Interpretive Introduction.* Princeton: Princeton University Press.

———., ed. 2014. *Memoria Romana: Memory in Rome and Rome in Memory.* Ann Arbor: University of Michigan Press.

Gan, N. 2017. "What Do You Call XI Jinping? China's Elite Echo Language of Mao to Sing the Praises of Their 'Leader and Helmsman'." *South China Morning Post*, October 22.

Gehrke, H.-J. 2007. "Myth, History, and Collective Identity: Uses of the Past in Ancient Greece and Beyond." In N. Luraghi (ed.) *The Historian's Craft in the Age of Herodotus.* Oxford: Oxford University Press. 286–313.

Giusti, E. 2018. *Carthage in Virgil's Aeneid: Staging the Enemy under Augustus.* Cambridge: Cambridge University Press.

Glyptis, L. 2008. "Living Up to the Father: the National Identity Prescriptions of Remembering Atatürk: His Homes, His Grave, His Temple." *National Identities* 10: 353–72.

Gruen, E.S. 1992. *Culture and National Identity in Republican Rome.* Ithaca: Cornell University Press.

———. 2011. *Rethinking the Other in Antiquity.* Princeton: Princeton University Press.

Gurval, R.A. 1995. *Actium and Augustus: The Politics and Emotions of Civil War.* Ann Arbor: University of Michigan Press.

Habinek, T. 2005. *The World of Roman Song: From Ritualized Speech to Social Order.* Baltimore: Johns Hopkins University Press.

Halbwachs, M. 1992. *On Collective Memory.* Edited and translated by Coser. Chicago: University of Chicago Press.

Hardie, P. 1986. *Virgil's Aeneid: Cosmos and Imperium.* Oxford: Clarendon Press.

———. 2014. *The Last Trojan Hero: A Cultural History of Virgil's Aeneid.* New York: I.B. Tauris.

Harrison, S.J. 1990. "Some Views of the *Aeneid* in the Twentieth Century." In S.J. Harrison (ed.) *Oxford Readings in Vergil's Aeneid.* Oxford: Oxford University Press. 1–20.

———. 2006. "The Epic and the Monuments: Interactions between Virgil's *Aeneid* and the Augustan Building Programme." In M.J. Clarke, B.G.F. Currie, and R.O.A.M. Lyne (eds.) *Epic Interactions: Perspectives on Homer, Virgil, and the Epic Tradition Presented to Jasper Griffin by Former Pupils.* Oxford: Oxford University Press. 159–83.

Hernández, J.C. 2019. "The Hottest App in China Teaches Citizens About Their Leader—and, Yes, There's a Test." *The New York Times*, April 7.

Hobsbawm, E.J., and Ranger, T.O., eds. 1983. *The Invention of Tradition.* Cambridge: Cambridge University Press.

Hölkeskamp, K.-J. 2006. "History and Collective Memory in the Middle Republic." In N. Rosenstein and R. Morstein-Marx (eds.) *A Companion to the Roman Republic.* Malden: Blackwell. 478–95.

Hölscher, T. 2018. *Visual Power in Ancient Greece and Rome: Between Art and Social Reality.* Berkeley: University of California Press.

Hosking, G., and Schöpflin, G., eds. 1997. *Myths and Nationhood.* New York: Routledge.

Hunter, R. 2003. *Theocritus: Encomium of Ptolemy Philadelphus.* Berkeley: University of California Press.

Johnson, I. 2016. "The Presence of the Past—A Coda." In J.N. Wasserstrom (ed.) *The Oxford Illustrated History of Modern China.* Oxford: Oxford University Press. 301–24.

Johnson, J., and Tumulty, K. 2017. “Trump Cites Andrew Jackson as His Hero—and a Reflection of Himself.” *The Washington Post*, March 15.

Johnson, W.R. 2001. “Imaginary Romans: Vergil and the Illusion of National Identity.” In S. Spence (ed.) *Poets and Critics Read Vergil*. New Haven: Yale University Press. 3–16.

Jones, C.P. 1999. *Kinship Diplomacy in the Ancient World*. Cambridge, MA: Harvard University Press.

Kenty, J. 2011. “Congenital Virtue: *Mos Maiorum* in Cicero’s Orations.” *Classical Journal* 111: 429–62.

Ker, J., and Pieper, C., eds. 2014. *Valuing the Past in the Greco-Roman World: Proceedings from the Penn-Leiden Colloquia on Ancient Values VII*. Leiden: Brill.

Kolesnikov, A. 2020. “Facing a Dim Present, Putin Turns Back to Glorious Stalin.” *The Washington Post*, May 8.

Lamp, K.S. 2013. *A City of Marble: The Rhetoric of Augustan Rome*. Columbia: University of South Carolina Press.

Langenbacher, E., and Shain, Y., eds. 2010. *Power and the Past: Collective Memory and International Relations*. Washington, DC: Georgetown University Press.

Langlands, R. 2018. *Exemplary Ethics in Ancient Rome*. Cambridge: Cambridge University Press.

Lentz, T. 2008. “Napoleon and Charlemagne.” *Napoleonica: La Revue* 1: 45–68.

Liñán, M.V. 2010. “History as a Propaganda Tool in Putin’s Russia.” *Communist and Post-Communist Studies* 43: 167–78.

Linskey, A. 2021. “A Look Inside Biden’s Oval Office.” *The Washington Post*, January 21.

Lowry, R. 2016. “How Trump Killed the Reagan Mystique.” *Politico*, March 2.

MacFarquhar, N., and Kishkovsky, S. 2015. “Russian History Receives a Makeover That Starts With Ivan the Terrible.” *The New York Times*, March 30.

Mackie, C.J. 1993. “A Note on Dido’s Ancestry in the *Aeneid*.” *Classical Journal* 88: 231–3.

Malinova, O. 2019. “Constructing the ‘Usable Past’: The Evolution of the Official Historical Narrative in Post-Soviet Russia.” In Bernsand and Törnquist-Plewa. 85–104.

Miller, J.F. 2009. *Apollo, Augustus, and the Poets*. Cambridge: Cambridge University Press.

Mills, S. 1998. *Theseus, Tragedy and the Athenian Empire*. Oxford: Clarendon Press.

Moorton, R.F. 1988. “The Genealogy of Latinus in Vergil’s *Aeneid*.” *Transactions of the American Philological Association* 118: 253–9.

Nakata, S. 2012. “*Egredere O Quicumque Es*: Genealogical Opportunism and Trojan Identity in the Aeneid.” *Phoenix* 66: 335–63.

Nemtsova, A. 2019. “Putin Rehabbed Stalin, Now He’s Burnishing the Rep of Ivan the Terrible.” *The Daily Beast*, January 14.

Nora, P. 1989. “Between Memory and History: *Les Lieux de Mémoire*.” *Representations* 26: 7–24.

O’Hara, J. 2007. *Inconsistency in Roman Epic: Studies in Catullus, Lucretius, Vergil, Ovid and Lucan*. Cambridge: Cambridge University Press.

———. 2018. “Evander’s Love of Gore and Bloodshed in *Aeneid* 8.” In M.C. English and L.M. Fratantuono (eds.) *Pushing the Boundaries of Historia: Essays on Greek and Roman History and Culture in Honor of Blaise Nagy*. New York: Routledge. 232–45.

Pandey, N.B. 2014. “Reading Rome from the Farther Shore: *Aeneid* 6 in the Augustan Urban Landscape.” *Vergilius* 60: 85–116.

———. 2018. *The Poetics of Power in Augustan Rome: Latin Poetic Responses to Early Imperial Iconography*. Cambridge: Cambridge University Press.

Papaioannou, S. 2003. "Founder, Civilizer and Leader: Vergil's Evander and His Role in the Origins of Rome." *Mnemosyne* 56: 680–702.

Pengelly, M. 2020. "Trump Aims Barb at Reagan Foundation in Fundraising Coin Kerfuffle." *The Guardian*, July 26.

Petrini, M. 1997. *The Child and the Hero: Coming of Age in Catullus and Vergil*. Ann Arbor: University of Michigan Press.

The President's Advisory 1776 Commission. 2021. *The 1776 Report*, January 18. https://trumpwhitehouse.archives.gov/wp-content/uploads/2021/01/The-Presidents-Advisory-1776-Commission-Final-Report.pdf.

Quint, D. 1993. *Epic and Empire: Politics and Generic Form from Virgil to Milton*. Princeton: Princeton University Press.

Race, W.H. 2010. "Horace's Debt to Pindar." In G. Davis (ed.) *A Companion to Horace*. Malden: Wiley-Blackwell. 147–73.

Rea, J.A. 2007. *Legendary Rome: Myth, Monuments, and Memory on the Palatine and Capitoline*. London: Duckworth.

Reed, J.D. 2007. *Virgil's Gaze: Nation and Poetry in the Aeneid*. Princeton: Princeton University Press.

Roller, M.B. 2018. *Models from the Past in Roman Culture: A World of Exempla*. Cambridge: Cambridge University Press.

Rosivach, V.J. 1980. "Latinus' Genealogy and the Palace of Picus (*Aeneid* 7.45–9, 170–91)." *Classical Quarterly* 30: 140–52.

Rutledge, S. 2012. *Ancient Rome as a Museum: Power, Identity, and the Culture of Collecting*. Oxford: Oxford University Press.

Scheid, J., and Svenbro, J. 1985. "Byrsa: La ruse d'Élissa et la fondation de Carthage." *Annales: Histoire, Sciences Sociales* 40: 328–42.

Schmitt Pantel, P. 2013. "State Festivals and Celebrations." In H. Beck (ed.) *A Companion to Ancient Greek Government*. Malden: Wiley-Blackwell. 432–47.

Secci, D.A. 2013. "Hercules, Cacus, and Evander's Myth-Making in *Aeneid* 8." *Harvard Studies in Classical Philology* 107: 195–227.

Seelye, K.Q. 2009. "Evoking Abraham Lincoln." *The New York Times*, February 12.

Seider, A.M. 2013. *Memory in Vergil's Aeneid*. Cambridge: Cambridge University Press.

Smith, A.D. 1997. "The 'Golden Age' and National Renewal." In Hosking and Schöpflin. 36–59.

———. 2009. *Ethno-Symbolism and Nationalism: A Cultural Approach*. New York: Routledge.

Srivastava, M. 2017. "Erdogan Sews up Turkey's 'Second Revolution'." *Financial Times*, February 27.

Stahl, H.-P., ed. 1998. *Vergil's Aeneid: Augustan Epic and Political Context*. London: Duckworth.

Stråth, B., ed. 2000. *Myth and Memory in the Construction of Community: Historical Patterns in Europe and Beyond*. Brussels: P. I. E.-Peter Lang.

Syed, Y. 2005. *Vergil's Aeneid and the Roman Self*. Ann Arbor: University of Michigan Press.

Tharoor, I. 2014. "Why Turkey's President Wants to Revive the Language of the Ottoman Empire." *The Washington Post*, December 12.

———. 2020. "The Trouble with Making Hagia Sophia a Mosque Again." *The Washington Post*, July 13.

Thomas, R.F. 2001. *Virgil and the Augustan Reception*. Cambridge: Cambridge University Press.

Till, K.E. 2003. “Places of Memory.” In J. Agnew, K. Mitchell, and G. Toal (eds.) *A Companion to Political Geography*. Malden: Blackwell. 289–301.

Toll, K. 1991. “The *Aeneid* as an Epic of National Identity: *Italiam laeto socii clamore salutant*.” *Helios* 18: 3–14.

Tosun, M. 2020. “Erdogan Commemorates Ataturk’s 82nd Death Anniversary.” *Anadolu Agency*, November 10.

Verovšek, P.J. 2016. “Collective Memory, Politics, and the Influence of the Past: The Politics of Memory as a Research Paradigm.” *Politics, Groups, and Identities* 4: 529–43.

Walter, U. 2004. *Memoria und res publica: zur Geschichtskultur im Republikanischen Rom*. Munich: Verlag Antike.

Wijermars, M. 2019. *Memory Politics in Contemporary Russia: Television, Cinema and the State*. New York: Routledge.

Wyke, M. 1999. “Sawdust Caesar: Mussolini, Julius Caesar, and the Drama of Dictatorship.” In M. Biddiss and M. Wyke (eds.) *The Uses and Abuses of Antiquity*. Bern: Peter Lang. 167–86.

———. 2009. “*Meretrix Regina*: Augustan Cleopatras.” In J. Edmondson (ed.) *Augustus*. Edinburgh: Edinburgh University Press. 334–80.

Zanker, P. 1990. *The Power of Images in the Age of Augustus*. Translated by Shapiro. Ann Arbor: University of Michigan Press.

8 Daedalus in DC

Vergil and the Vietnam Veterans Memorial[1]

J.R. O'Neill

The Vietnam Veterans Memorial (VVM) in Washington, DC commemorates the men and woman of the United States armed forces who lost their lives in what to date has been America's most divisive foreign military engagement. Beginning in the late 1970s, Vietnam veteran Jan Scruggs lobbied Congress for a Vietnam War memorial, eventually winning approval—for land on the National Mall, not money for construction—in 1980. A competition for the design was announced in November of that year, and in May of 1981, Maya Lin was announced the winner out of 1,422 entrants. Her design consisted of two black granite walls nestled into the lawn of the Mall at a 125-degree angle to one another, forming an extended V nearly 494 feet from end to end. On the mirror-like granite face would be engraved the names of all the American servicemen and women (at that time, 57,939) known to have died in the Vietnam War.[2] Although Lin's design was selected because of its apparently apolitical design—manifest primarily in its lack of monumentalizing features typical of American war memorials—Lin's design set off a political firestorm that raged for years after the Memorial was dedicated on Veterans Day in 1982.[3] The most outspoken critics of the Memorial were career officers—graduates of the prestigious service academies—and conservative politicians, men who had been "fully exposed to the ideologies of national service and glory" and who saw the Memorial as a "black gash of shame."[4] Despite critics' often vitriolic attacks, the Vietnam Veterans Memorial has since been lauded by the general public and, most importantly, veterans. With nearly 5 million visitors each year, the Memorial has become one of America's most venerated public structures, a site of personal healing and national reconciliation.[5]

The conflict over the Vietnam Veterans Memorial was far more than a disagreement over a piece of public art, or even a renewed fight over the merits and legacy of US military intervention in Southeast Asia. Rather, it was a struggle over discourses of war and its costs—between the public versus the personal, the ideal versus the real, what war represents versus what it is really like. It is the very sort of conflict that lies at the heart of the *Aeneid*. By this I mean not simply Aeneas' own struggles with duty and sacrifice, or even Vergil's apparent ambivalence toward empire and what would shape out to be the Augustan project.[6] Rather, I see as a unifying theme of this enduring epic Vergil's own grappling with the failure of art and the fame it supposedly vouchsafes to compensate for the suffering and loss that

DOI: 10.4324/9781003176145-11

follow in empire's wake, or to offer solace to those who remain.[7] In what follows, I argue that an analysis of Vergil's exploration of art's incapacities and the inadequacies of fame offers an explanation of the ultimate success of Lin's controversial Vietnam Veterans Memorial.

Vergil's concurrent grappling with these issues is most clear in two of the *Aeneid*'s major *ekphrases*: Vergil's description of the Trojan War mural on the Junonian temple at Carthage (1.441–93) and the doors to the temple of Apollo at Cumae (6.14–33).[8] The *ekphrases*' ability to grant access to Vergil's apparent views on the limitations of art is suggested first by their cardinality, that each serves an important function in the organization of the *Aeneid* as a whole, with each introducing, as it were, a new narrative section of the epic. The *ekphrases* also bear thematic and symbolic relation to one another whereby each comments on a convergence of relationships: artificer and art, viewer and viewed, portrayal and portrayed. However, what we will see is that above all, Vergil's *ekphrases* all comment in some way on art's inability to compensate in any way for the loss of the people it attempts to commemorate or to relieve the suffering of the bereaved. Therefore, it is necessary to examine these *ekphrases* in detail in order to discover how the *Aeneid* can help explain the Vietnam Veterans Memorial's successes.

The Trojan War memorial

Aeneas encounters the Trojan Wall mural at a crucial juncture in the middle of the first *Aeneid*.[9] Appearing as it does after the destruction of the Trojan fleet yet immediately before Aeneas meets Dido for the first time, Aeneas' engagement and Vergil's description create a bridge between the 'old' Homeric world of Atreidae and Priamidae and the 'new' Vergilian one, at which a Romanized Aeneas is center.[10] At one level, Vergil uses the *ekphrasis* to root his Roman Aeneas (and his epic) in the Homeric tradition. The mural depicts vignettes Vergil's readers would recognize from the *Iliad*: general scenes of battle in which Greeks and Trojans each in turn take flight, the slaughter of Rhesus in his sleep by Odysseus and Diomedes, the supplication of the Trojan women to Minerva, and Priam ransoming Hector's corpse. Yet other scenes do not recall the *Iliad* directly: the death of Troilus, and Aeneas, Memnon, and Penthesilea in battle.[11] The mingling of Iliadic episodes with those that are not situates the *Aeneid*'s subjects in the Homeric milieu while simultaneously providing Vergil the opportunity to 'rehabilitate' Aeneas, whose place in the Hellenic canon was perhaps not as lofty as an elite Roman audience might have liked. In other words, Vergil deploys the *ekphrasis* to fashion Aeneas into a "fit ktistic hero" for a post-Actian Rome.[12] As such, the *ekphrasis* on the Junonian temple brings the Greek mythological world into contact with one whose teleological orientation Vergil's Roman readers would have recognized.

As mentioned earlier, the placement of Aeneas' encounter with the mural itself indicates its importance in interpreting the events of the first half of the *Aeneid*: Aeneas' own account of his struggles from the fall of Troy to his present landfall at Carthage and his subsequent arrival in Italy.[13] That is, the scene can serve as a cipher through which to interpret the narrative sections it bridges. For our purposes, perhaps the most salient feature of Aeneas' encounter with the Carthaginian mural is its double effect. As we shall see, Aeneas as leader sees an opportunity in the fact that events he himself has partaken in are depicted at all.[14] However, Aeneas as veteran experiences afresh the suffering he has already endured, while getting a foretaste of what he has yet to undergo. It is with this Aeneas that we begin.

Vergil sings of a *vir profugus*, an exile, tossed about by land and sea, a man who has suffered much and yet is driven to endure even more (*Aen.* 1.1–11). This man is not named for 92 lines. We first meet Aeneas himself in the midst of a shipwrecking storm. Frozen with fear, he groans and stretches his arms to the sky, crying that three- and four-times blessed are they who are already dead (1.92–101).[15] It is not simply that Aeneas has suffered and will continue to suffer. Vergil makes the suffering deeply personal, relatable. It is not the abstract suffering of an inscrutable heroic ideal. Here, the blessed dead are people Aeneas knew well, not least of all Hector, whom Aeneas will recall repeatedly in the first half of the *Aeneid*, never without tears.[16] And it is not that these men have merely died. Their deaths were violent and happened in full view of their loved ones (*ante ora patrum*, 1.95). Their deaths were terrible, the impact on those who survived them, traumatic.

As it seems he is going to drown, Aeneas does not bemoan the loss of some kind of heroic death. There is no evidence that Aeneas is at that moment concerned with glory, his own or that of his dead comrades. Aeneas' profound grief is suggested not only by the violence of the imagery he summons, but also his focus on the lifeless bodies of his friends. Aeneas wishes that his life had already been poured out and that he too were lying on Ilian fields (*occumbere*, 97) where Hector now lies (*iacet*, 99).[17] So many strong bodies (*fortia corpora*, 101)—not heroes or even men—are washed under the waves of the Simois along with shields and helmets. There is no mention of honor or glory, commemoration, monuments, or song—just corpses cast away like so much useless equipment.

Aeneas soon finds himself on the beach near Carthage, where he tries to encourage his men with a speech recalling all they had already endured. Here Aeneas, as the leader of his men, attempts to provide his fellow refugees some perspective: *forsan et haec olim meminisse iuvabit* (perhaps one day it will help to think back on even these events, 1.203).[18] Yet the poet lays bare Aeneas' own feelings (1.208–9):

> *Talia voce refert curisque ingentibus aeger*
> *spem vultu simulat, premit altum corde dolorem.*
>
> This is what his words convey. Sick with worry, he wears
> A hopeful face, buries his grief deep in his heart.

We see an Aeneas divided, leader and veteran, something Vergil will draw out even more when Aeneas is met with the surprising sight of the Trojan War mural in the center of Carthage, which will highlight, on the one hand, the vacuousness of the promise of future glory as compensation for suffering and loss and, on the other, the failure of commemorative art to provide solace.

In a grove consecrated to Juno, Aeneas finds amid this newly rising city a mural depicting events of the Trojan War, the first sign of relief for his fear in this strange land (1.450–2). Aeneas discovers an immediate practical use for the monument; not a remedy for trauma, not comfort, not compensation for all he has suffered and lost (1.459–63):

> *lacrimans "quis iam locus," inquit, "Achate,*
> *quae regio in terris nostri non plena laboris?*
> *en Priamus. sunt hic etiam sua praemia laudi,*
> *sunt lacrimae rerum et mentem mortalia tangunt.*
> *solve metus; feret haec aliquam tibi fama salutem."*
>
> Weeping, he wonders: "what is this place, Achates?
> Is there anywhere on earth our troubles are unknown?
> Ah, there's Priam! So even here, fame's reward. Even here,
> Tears for it all, impermanence strikes at the heart.
> Set aside your fear. This fame of ours just might
> Afford you some safety."

The events Aeneas sees depicted elicit a strong emotional response. They are events in which he himself was involved. Aeneas sheds tears for what he has been through, all he has lost. Vergil shows Aeneas struggling as he attempts to compartmentalize his two selves. His emotional response to revisiting his apocalyptic world is separate from the possibility of his exploiting *fama* to his, or rather, Achates', immediate benefit.[19] He tells Achates to set aside his *metus* (fear, anxiety, apprehension) but not his grief.[20] Aeneas is split between the traumatized participant in traumatizing events and a leader with immediate needs to meet.

As will be discussed below, the reader's experience of the mural is mediated entirely by Aeneas. That is, however the action might have appeared to an assumed Carthaginian viewer, what Aeneas sees is his apocalyptic world. So an apocalyptic world is what Vergil presents to his readers. Although Aeneas may find practical use for the monumental commemoration of his suffering—whatever protection *fama* might bring in the near term—far from alleviating his grief, the mural renews it. As he takes in the images, he groans repeatedly while a great river of tears wets his face (1.465). It is clear that the emotional response is the result of the viewing, not the hope that might be placed in *fama*, a sense of relief. As before, there is no evidence that Aeneas is suffering anything but grief at the waste of human life, the war that ultimately led to his city's destruction, and the suffering he has so far experienced in exile. His tears are tied to recognition. Crying, he recognizes the tents of Rhesus (*tentoria . . . / agnoscit lacrimans*, 1.469–70), just as he recognized himself fighting the Achaean princes (*agnovit*, 1.488). When he sees Hector, the first thing he notices is the "lifeless corpse" (*exanimum corpus*, 1.484), and then, among other lifeless objects (*spolia* and *currus*, 1.486) about to be ransomed, the "very corpse of his friend" (*ipsum corpus amici*, 1.486). Seeing Hector this way causes him to release a deep groan from the very pit of his chest (1.485). Hector is not called to mind a shining hero, his death fit for glorious song. Aeneas is seeing the mangled corpse of a dear friend all over again, as if for the first time.

Despite whatever short-term protection the commemoration of a heroized version of himself and his friends will afford, it fails to provide relief for his suffering or compensation for the lives lost. Aeneas sees dead people, friend and foe alike—Trojan youths, Achilles, Rhesus, Troilus, Hector, Priam, Memnon, Penthesilea. Vergil comments on the vacuousness of the artwork itself. The images are unreal, unsubstantial, lifeless (*pictura inanis*, 1.464). Vergil's description of what Aeneas takes in emphasizes suffering and death, adumbrates the imbalance between reward and cost that Aeneas will confront more acutely in Book 6. Furthermore, Vergil seems quite emphatic that the pictures of heroes in action do not bring comfort or promote healing. As each figure Aeneas sees is lifeless, so too is the monumental commemoration of those war dead. Memorializing the dead by heroizing them brings only suffering to the man who was there.

There is no indication presented as to why such a vivid depiction of the Trojan War should be in Carthage in the first place. It is reasonable to deduce that it has to do with Juno, patroness of Carthage, whose victory over the hated Trojans is rendered as an example of the goddess's power. Readers of the *Aeneid* in any era might also take for granted that the heroic feats of warriors depicted in such a way, despite there being no Carthaginian affiliation with the warriors who fought and died at Troy, could be used to inspire Carthaginian youth to glory. Dido and future leaders of Carthage can easily be imagined taking advantage of the heroic scenes depicted (a heroism which Aeneas does not or cannot see) to instruct the future warriors of Carthage in the discourse of national duty and sacrifice. The didactic or propagandistic capacity of war monuments is a function of the reader's experience of the same. Why Vergil expended so much poetic energy conjuring up the Trojan War memorial in Carthage seems to have more to do with the *ekphrasis* providing a screen through which to read other representations of death and glory in the rest of the epic.

An examination of Vergil's *ekphrasis* of the Trojan War mural reveals several problems inherent in monumental commemorative art, the most prominent of which is the potential for exploitation resulting from the depiction of heroic deaths of idealized warriors. We have seen that Aeneas, despite the renewal of intense grief at the sight of the graphic representations of events in which he was personally involved, finds that the fame his depiction on the monument bestows will afford him a measure of safety. His fame does not console, nor does it approach making his suffering worth the while. It is fleeting and tenuous. Venus recognizes this. She sends Cupid to swap places with Ascanius in order to tie Dido to Aeneas with the bonds of love, a surer guarantor (1.657–96). What is more, the fame of the depicted dead does not come close to compensating for their violent and premature deaths. We have also seen the mural's potential as propaganda. It is by no means difficult to imagine Carthaginian elders for generations to come pointing to the mural as an example for young warriors, using it to instruct them in the discourse of duty and glory—just as selective readings of Vergil's epic itself have so been used. But Vergil makes it clear that Juno's glory and a warrior's inspiration involves a double death for those depicted. First warriors must necessarily die on the battlefield. Then their identities as anything but warrior ideals are nullified in the lifeless rendering. Hector is no longer a friend, a father, a husband, or even a man. He becomes for the Carthaginians exactly what they see: an always already dead, always dying instantiation of duty and sacrifice. As Aeneas expresses with bitter sarcasm after seeing Priam's image: "Even here, fame's reward" (1.461). For all they have suffered and lost, the Trojans become a painting and a byword for duty to country.

The processes just described do have real-world consequences. Vergil's deployment of the *ekphrasis* situates his epic within the Greek cultural milieu, which helps to shape his Aeneas into a foundational figure fit for post-Actian Rome. An epic at which a suitably rehabilitated Aeneas is center came to suit the political needs of Augustus in fashioning his new Rome to the extent that, even today, it is nearly impossible to separate the *Aeneid* from its Augustan reception.[21] In other words, Vergil's description of an imaginary monument situates his fictional character in a literary tradition that ultimately was used to help legitimize an entire political order in Rome, and in those states which looked to Augustus' Rome as model.[22] In short, the Trojan War mural is recognizable today as a war memorial. As we shall soon see, it contains all of the pitfalls Maya Lin and Vietnam veterans like Jan Scruggs strove to avoid. Paradoxically, it was in Lin's attempt to avoid these pitfalls that much of the controversy arose, very nearly preventing the Vietnam Veterans Memorial from ever being built.

The Icarian memorial

The second major *ekphrasis* in the *Aeneid* is Vergil's description in Book 6 of the doors to the temple of Apollo at Cumae wrought by the legendary craftsman Daedalus (14–33). Aeneas' encounter with the doors serves perhaps an even more obvious organizational role than the Carthaginian paintings discussed in the previous section. Book 6 is the center of the *Aeneid*, structurally and thematically. It is the lynchpin between the Odyssean and the Iliadic halves of the epic that marks a significant transition for Aeneas: his own "strange journey" comes to an end as he at last reaches the hitherto elusive shores of Italy.[23] His descent into the underworld, through encounters with various shades of the dead and his lengthy interview with his father, Anchises, presents him with a clear articulation of the ideology of empire, after which he fully embraces his destiny as a founder of Rome. Yet it is also in Book 6 that Vergil most forcefully demonstrates the hollowness of the promises empire makes to those swallowed up in its wake.

Death and the inadequacies of commemoration and fame bookend the sixth *Aeneid*. Aeneas' landfall in Italy is overshadowed by the death of Palinurus, while the death of Aeneas' nurse, Caieta, inaugurates Book 7. Aeneas and Palinurus meet in the underworld. Aeneas' helmsman is forbidden to cross over Acheron because his body lies unburied. He begs Aeneas either to return to the place where his corpse lies to carry out final rites or use the powers apparently granted the son of a god to carry him across. Aeneas does not get the chance to respond. The

Sibyl interrupts. The place where his lifeless body now lies will grant Palinurus an eternal name (*aeternumque locus Palinuri nomen habebit*, 6.381). It will have to suffice—an honor never sought, nor an answer to his pleas.[24] Caieta is similarly honored, though here Vergil directly questions the value of eternal fame when stacked up against the nullification of the individual in death (7.1–4):

Tu quoque litoribus nostris, Aeneia nutrix,
aeternam moriens famam, Caieta, dedisti;
et nunc servat honos sedem tuus, ossaque nomen
Hesperia in magna, si qua est ea gloria, signat.

You too, Caieta, nurse of Aeneas, in death
Have given to our shores an everlasting fame:
Even now your reward preserves your resting place,
Your name marks your bones in mighty Hesperia—
If such a thing is glory.

If, in the other examples here cited, the promise of fame ought to compensate for nullification in death, here Vergil exposes the lie: Caieta does not receive fame, she grants it, but only by dying. The eternal toponym does nothing for the individual whose life is extinguished, nor for those who survive her.

The case of Misenus is also instructive.[25] Misenus' death is sudden and occurs unbeknownst to Aeneas and his men. His burial is one of two conditions necessary for Aeneas to descend into the underworld—itself unnecessary but for Aeneas' instruction in the practice of empire. As such, his death reads as an otherwise unnecessary sacrifice: Misenus, like Palinurus, here represents the waste of human life empire demands. Aeneas is stricken with grief upon learning of Misenus' death (6.175–6). That the place where he is buried shall forever be called Misenum brings no relief or joy (it certainly does not annul the man's premature demise). The line commemorating Misenus (*qui nunc Misenus ab illo / dicitur aeternumque tenet per saecula nomen*, 6.234–5) not only will be echoed by the Sibyl in her response to Palinurus' pleas but, as Segal has pointed out, is "heavy and formal" compared with the surrounding lines, suggesting "the pallid chill of the monument, of carved marble and the 'official' hero."[26] Commemoration brings no relief or joy to the living or the dead. Palinurus, Misenus, and Caieta lose their lives along the way to Aeneas' imperial destiny. In compensation, each receives an eternal name, something that offers no solace to the dead or those who mourn them.

The doors that open the sixth *Aeneid* encapsulate this lesson and appear to reveal Vergil's own views of art's limitations in a concentrated way. Vergil tells us that Daedalus built the temple to Apollo at Cumae to house the wings with which he made his escape from Crete to the place where Aeneas now stands.[27] Vergil draws a number of parallels between Daedalus and Aeneas that ultimately underscore the inevitable failure of art to compensate for loss or offer solace.[28] Both men are fugitives, each fleeing a kingdom in the east for a new home in the west.[29] Both men escape with their adolescent sons. Both have to contend with the fallout from a queen ruined by a cruel love.[30] Both are generally affected by grief and moved by pity.[31] Both make significant dedications to Apollo: Daedalus consecrated his wings and erected the temple that houses them, Aeneas praises Apollo's unfailing pity for Troy and vows a temple and festivals for him.[32] These parallels are reinforced by Vergil's choice to deploy seafaring language to describe Daedalus' flight from Crete: his wings are described as the "oars" (*remigium alarum*, 19) with which he "swam his unfamiliar path" (*insuetum per iter . . . enavit*, 16) through the sky.[33] An *insuetum iter* accurately sums up what Aeneas has gone through in the previous five books.

Despite much scholarly speculation, there is no way to reconstruct these entirely fictional doors.[34] Like the *ekphrasis* of the Trojan War mural, Vergil's description is not an account of a real object but a means to establish important themes and perhaps provide a cipher through which to read the book, if not the *Aeneid* as a whole.[35] In order to get a sense of what Vergil might be trying to convey with these doors, it is necessary to quote the *ekphrasis* here in full (6.20–33):

in foribus letum Androgeo; tum pendere poenas
Cecropidae iussi (miserum!) septena quotannis
corpora natorum; stat ductis sortibus urna.
contra elata mari respondet Cnosia tellus:
hic crudelis amor tauri suppostaque furto
Pasiphae mixtumque genus prolesque biformis
Minotaurus inest, Veneris monimenta nefandae,
hic labor ille domus et inextricabilis error;
magnum reginae sed enim miseratus amorem
Daedalus ipse dolos tecti ambagesque resolvit,
caeca regens filo vestigia. tu quoque magnam
partem opere in tanto, sineret dolor, Icare, haberes.
bis conatus erat casus effingere in auro,
bis patriae cecidere manus.

On the doors there's the murder of Androgeos;
Athenians, ordered to pay (how heartbreaking!)
Seven corpses from among their sons every year.
There stands the urn out of which all the lots are drawn.
Opposite stands Cretan land rising from the sea:
Here, the cruel love for the bull, mated through fraud by
Pasiphaë; here her mixed breed, biform son, the
Minotaur, monument to unspeakable lust;
Here, the suffering of that household and the maze
Unsolvable. But pitying a queen's great love,
Daedalus himself resolved its wandering ways,
The tricks of that house, guiding blind steps with a string.
You'd too have a role in such a great work of art,
Icarus, had only grief allowed it to be—

> Twice your father tried to depict your fall in gold
> Twice your father's hands fell.

There seems to be a correspondence in Vergil's description of the scenes between actions and the price paid for those actions. Even if Vergil meant for us to assume a symmetrical structure (one thinks of the bronze doors to the Curia Julia),[36] his description betrays an imbalance, with more poetic energy expended on the costs than on the actions that precipitate them. The elliptical *letum Androgeo* (20) contrasts with the significantly more elaborate description of the penalty paid by the Athenians for that murder. Vergil's description of the next set of scenes is only slightly more balanced than that of the first. Crete rising from the sea inaugurates the sequence, the central event appearing to be the *crudelis amor* of Pasiphaë for the bull (24–5). The result of this cruel love is described twice, an echo of the beast's double nature. The Minotaur is named just below his mother, emphasizing the sequence of evils while alluding to Daedalus' placing the creature's mother beneath the bull through his deceptive artistry. The creature's name is positioned next to the verb fixing its location in the reader's mind, both in the labyrinth Daedalus famously built to contain him and on the doors which memorialize his monstrous creation: *Minotaurus inest*.[37] The biform beast, that *Veneris monimenta nefandae* (26), is actually depicted, there for Aeneas to behold. The price paid for unspeakable lust is forever commemorated in gold, commemorated again in Vergil's epic.

The third set of actions and costs concerns Daedalus himself. The craftsman carved himself upon the doors, but rather than depict himself as the artificer of the *furtum* (24) by which Pasiphaë was able to mate with the bull and the *error* (27) wherein lurks the result of his artistry, the craftsman casts himself in a nobler role: pitying Ariadne, he solves the mystery of the Labyrinth for Theseus.[38] Vergil does not name the Labyrinth, although *Labyrinthus* not only scans into dactylic hexameter but is deployed in an elaborate simile in Book 5 to describe the action of the first Troy Game at the funeral of Anchises (5.588–93).[39] The omission underscores the polyvalence of the scene. That is, although the *doli tecti* refer primarily to the Labyrinth itself, the word *dolus* can mean any device or artifice, especially one constructed with malicious intent.[40] And the reader has already seen other artifices designed by Daedalus, namely the means by which Pasiphaë was able to mate with the bull. So, when Daedalus casts himself "resolving" the tricks of the House of Minos, he both literally solves the mystery of the Labyrinth for Theseus by means of the string and attempts to nullify his previous deceptions by an act of pity.[41]

The result of Daedalus' attempt at absolution is further tragedy. Casali argues that Vergil might have meant us to imagine the doors telling the rest of the story—how Theseus killed the Minotaur only to leave Ariadne to her demise for the sake of his own glory—but that Aeneas' viewing (and ours) is interrupted by the Sibyl.[42] Vergil's Alexandrian footnote at the outset of the *ekphrasis* (*ut fama est*, 14) signals that his readers were expected to know already the story of Daedalus' flight from Crete and perhaps the related story of Theseus's abandonment of Ariadne, one with rather obvious parallels to that of Aeneas and Dido.[43] That Theseus, Ariadne, and the Labyrinth go unnamed supports the notion that Vergil's readers are meant to fill in the gaps themselves while also allowing these well-known figures to take a back seat to the figures Vergil does name. But Aeneas, who mediates our engagement with the doors, lingers on a panel that is apparently left blank. It is the *casus* of Icarus—his fate, his fall.

If Vergil's audience were meant to know already that the *error* and *ambages* refer to the otherwise unnamed Labyrinth, and that the object of Daedalus' pity is the unnamed Ariadne, and that the person for whom the riddle of the Labyrinth was solved was the unnamed Theseus, then Vergil must have expected his readers to know already that Daedalus' story (*ut fama est*) is tied to the fate of his son, Icarus. But where is Icarus? There is no mention of the tragedy of his fall or the grief the father must have felt when the dedication of the temple and the forging of the doors is introduced. It is a significant omission. What we are left with is fugitive father reading fugitive father—the two men alone together, confronting the fruits of their pursuit of fame. It is not until the very end of the *ekphrasis* that the missing son is brought up at all. Not on the doors, nor by Aeneas; he is apostrophized by Vergil: *tu quoque . . . Icare* (30–1). Vergil inserts the absent son by explaining the apparently blank space on the doors where Icarus might otherwise have been carved, had only his father's grief allowed it.

Daedalus tried to compensate for the loss of Icarus, a loss for which he was responsible, by "bestowing upon him the deathlessness and eternity of embodiment in a work of art," but he failed.[44] Like Daedalus, loss has followed Aeneas every step of the way. The ideology of empire Aeneas will receive later in the book might perhaps come close to compensating for or justifying the wastage trailing in his wake, but like the image of Icarus' *casus*, it will remain "unrealised in history."[45] As Segal observed:

> Through Daedalus Vergil juxtaposes art with history as modes of escaping death's nullification of the individual life. But in him too he presents the tragedy of art, with all its magic unable to restore the life that has been lost, unable even to commemorate its deepest grief.[46]

In other words, it is an enduring and poignant irony that Daedalus' failure to render his son's fate in gold is what is ultimately capable of beginning to convey the depth of his grief. Moreover, realizing Icarus' fate in gold in the same way as Pasiphaë's love would have bled the representation of its communicative and commemorative power. There seems to be no more powerful monument to Icarus than the silence of that empty panel because upon seeing the blank space, the viewer is not presented with an instantiation, frozen in time, of filial duty, glorious youth, or any other abstraction. The viewer encounters the void on the otherwise busy monument as an instantiation of a father's profound grief, and the viewer cannot help but wonder at the source of that profound grief, a son who died young before the eyes of his father.[47]

The Vietnam Veterans Memorial

We have seen how the *ekphrases* discussed above complicate the commemoration of the dead. The *ekphrasis* of the Trojan War mural exposes the potential for exploitation inherent in monumental commemoration while simultaneously revealing the pain caused to survivors by depicting the deceased as idealized warriors, instantiations of duty and honor, always already dead, always dying. Daedalus' doors illustrate art's limitations in conveying grief. Art cannot effect the full expression of intense emotion, "where he comes up against the most personal and most excruciating . . . the artist hits a wall."[48] The cause of another's pain can be represented, and to some extent so can the effects of that pain, but the pain itself is as incommunicable as the experience of it.[49] As we shall soon see, Lin's design was selected and staunchly defended by a large number of Vietnam veterans because it did not attempt to render in stone a representation—realistic or allegorical—of collective suffering. The power of her design is in its monumental silence.

Vergil's art—not just the objects he describes, but the epic itself—reveals tensions between 'official' commemoration, which serves the material and rhetorical needs of those doing the commemorating (Dido's Carthage, Augustus' Rome), and the need of individuals to come to terms with personal loss. John Bodnar, writing on the Vietnam Veterans Memorial, examines the conflict between "vernacular culture," concerned with the needs of individuals who experienced loss and their challenge to "official" interpretations of the conflict in Vietnam, and the "official culture" of "national power [as] safeguarded by national political leaders" and those who seek to celebrate "the ideal of patriotic duty."[50] The VVM, despite the aims of those who worked for its realization, meets both needs (although it seems to privilege the former). I argue that the success of the VVM is its resolution of the conflict at the heart of the *Aeneid*—the struggle between empire's arms and the man—and that it accomplishes this by, in a way, bringing Daedalus to DC.

In order to get a better picture of this resolution, it is necessary to review the controversies that dogged the construction of the VVM and very often threatened its completion. From the outset, members of the Vietnam Veterans Memorial Fund (VVMF) insisted that any Vietnam War memorial be nonpolitical. It was later conceded that it was naïve to insist that any monument, let alone one commemorating America's most divisive foreign war, could in any way be nonpolitical.[51] But Maya Lin's design proved controversial precisely because of the lack of monumental features that made it attractive to the selection committee and the VVMF. Absent are the vaunting soldier and victorious general. There are no allegorical symbols of national glory; no eagles, stars, torches, palms, or wreaths. There are no classicizing features; no columns of white marble, nor anthropomorphized forms of Victory, Liberty, or Peace. The original design featured no flag, no human forms at all. The Memorial consists of mirror-like black granite panels on which are inscribed the names of those who died, listed in chronological order by date of their of death, without indications of rank or service branch.

The veterans wanted a memorial for veterans and those who care about them, and anyone else touched by the extensive conflict in Southeast Asia that boiled over into bitter antipathies at home. But stiff opposition arose from some career officers and conservative politicians who wanted a memorial that valorized the war and celebrated the nation that committed to it. As early as 1979, before Congress appropriated land for the construction of the Memorial, congressman John Hammerschmidt (R-AR) framed a proposed memorial as an act of revenge against those who had protested the war. Whereas news media had given the lion's share of attention to anti-war demonstrators during the 1960s and 1970s, a Vietnam memorial as Hammerschmidt envisioned it would grant permanent victory to those who supported the war. As the congressman triumphantly declared: "Now it's their turn."[52] West Point graduate and Pentagon lawyer Thomas Carhart was originally on the board of the VVMF. But after the selection of Maya Lin's design, he resigned in protest and became a leading opponent of the completion of the Memorial. He was looking for "a memorial to celebrate and glorify the Vietnam veteran."[53] But which veteran? Carhart and associates wanted a monument to celebrate an idealized warrior, a heroic instantiation of patriotic duty—precisely the thing Lin's design was not.

Although the vast majority of veterans and everyday Americans did support the Memorial as Lin had designed it (the majority of money for construction came from the general public), the few opponents were well connected, powerful, and had seemingly unlimited financial resources.[54] Their pushback continued to threaten the project well into 1982, as they energized allies in Congress and the Reagan Administration by spreading misinformation that a number of Americans soon started to believe.[55] No matter how many times the VVMF rebutted false claims by conservative activists (that the Memorial would be subterranean, that black is the universal color of shame and dishonor, that Maya Lin was a Chinese-born communist agitator, that this or that foreign power was actually funding the project to discredit the American military, and so on), the misinformation spread in publications such as the conservative *National Review*, in op-eds by conservative activists in newspapers across the country, and in memoranda circulated in the Reagan White House by anti-Memorial activists.[56]

An example of how misinformation spread from the small yet powerful opposition to the broader public is found in objections to the decision to make the Memorial out of black granite. Lin had chosen black granite because it would make the names perfectly legible in all manner of lighting conditions and because the highly polished granite would create a mirror effect: anyone viewing the names inscribed upon the Memorial will see themselves looking back at them, along with the sky, the grass, and the other monuments on the National Mall.[57] But the opponents saw in the color of the Memorial something sinister. Just after the selection of Lin's design, Carhart stated in a press conference that other monuments to America's war dead are "heroic," but that the Vietnam Veterans Memorial was a "black gash of shame and sorrow" that would humiliate those who fought in the conflict. He further said that "100 years from now, long after we're all dead and gone, visitors to the Mall will see only one thing: a black wall in a trench with a random scattering of names on it."[58] As much as Carhart misrepresented the actual design, the phrase "black gash of shame" caught on in the press and circulated widely.[59]

A month later, a memorandum from the office of Congressman Phil Crane (R-IL) inaccurately described the Memorial as a "pit with a black wall below ground level," and goes on to assert that "black is the universal color of dishonor and shame."[60] By January of 1982, Texas billionaire (and future presidential hopeful) H. Ross Perot orchestrated a protest of Lin's design at a meeting of the VVMF in which a dozen or so attendees read a list of demands from identical notecards. Of primary concern was that the Memorial had to be white, not black.[61] Admiral James Stockdale (who would be Perot's running mate in his failed bid for the White House a decade later) was the highest-ranking US officer captured by the North Vietnamese and had endured nearly eight years of torture in a North Vietnamese prison camp. He was one of the founding members of the fundraising arm of the VVMF but resigned in protest after his demand that white marble be substituted for the black granite was refused.[62] Criticism of the black granite then seeped into the public discourse and became much more blatantly racist. Senator Ted Stevens (R-AK) wrote to Jan Scruggs in October of 1982 regarding a constituent demand that the stone "be white instead of black because black is reminiscent of the Black Panthers."[63] A man from Des Moines, Iowa, wrote to the VVMF insisting that black was the most "ignoble" of colors by nature. A doctor from Lantana, Florida, suggested that the Ohio-born Maya Lin was not only a communist agitator but a "Chinese architect [who] did not feel that our engagement in this war was noble enough to warrant the employment of white or any other bright medium that might imply an allusion of honor."[64] Pointing out to critics that the much-revered US Marine Corps Memorial depicting the raising of the flag at Iwo Jima was also constructed of black granite did nothing to stem criticism of Lin's design.

Perot proved an exceptionally fierce opponent to the Memorial. Perot had originally supported the VVM, but his support seems to have been contingent on the Memorial serving the rhetorical needs of the military and political establishment. For instance, he suggested to Scruggs that the purpose of the Memorial should be to instruct children, "the future warriors of America," in the discourse of national duty and sacrifice.[65] Perot donated $160,000 to fund the memorial design competition. Infuriated with the selection of Lin's design, Perot exerted pressure on the VVMF (including the staged protest referenced earlier) to change it, even calling upon Texas-based artists and architects to send their own ostentatiously patriotic designs directly to the VVMF. Not making headway, in May of 1982 (just six months before the scheduled dedication of the Memorial) Perot wrote to the VVMF expressing vague concerns about the organization's finances and calling for an independent audit.[66] Perot later hired Roy Cohn, protegee of Senator Joseph McCarthy (R-WI) and mentor to Donald Trump, to pursue legal action against the VVMF. Ultimately, demands that the files of the VVMF be handed over to Perot and threats of lawsuits from Cohn came to naught.[67]

In an affidavit signed and notarized on September 23, 1983, Vietnam veteran David Christian, who was then under consideration for a position in Reagan's Veterans Administration, claimed that Carlton Sherwood, a conservative journalist and associate of Memorial opponents Tom Carhart and James Webb, said that Christian's support for the Memorial, a "black gash" designed by a "fucking gook," put him on the "wrong team," thereby threatening his chances at a political career.[68] Christian went on to run for Congress in 1984, but his campaign was broadsided by allegations of improprieties. An anonymous complaint had been filed with the US Inspector General alleging that Christian had illegally made use of Veterans Administration mailing lists to solicit campaign donations. The complaint was leaked to the press. The allegations were never proved and no charges ever laid, but Christian's 1984 campaign was sunk. Correspondence to and from the VVMF worried about a link between the allegations and Christian's support for the (by then complete) Memorial and his previous confrontation with Sherwood.[69] Whether or not these allegations were an act of political retribution against Christian for his support of the Memorial, the fear expressed in VVMF papers of such a possibility speaks to the intensity of the attacks from the small but powerful group of anti-Memorial activists.[70] So powerful was the drive to protect and maintain the "official" discourse of patriotic duty.

Resistance to Lin's design persisted well into 1982. Congressional authorization of the Memorial granted final approval to the Secretary of the Interior, at the time Reagan appointee James Watt. However, although he had never expressly stated that he was against the Memorial, Secretary Watt was late in signing the paperwork necessary for construction to begin. As late as January of 1982, Congressman Henry Hyde (R-IL) sent a letter to President Reagan, cosigned by 30 other members of Congress, urging the President to direct Watt to withhold his signature from any permits necessary to complete the "so-called Vietnam Veterans Memorial," writing that "we share the view that this alleged memorial is a black ditch that does not recognize or honor those who served."[71] To keep the VVM from being pigeonholed out of existence, a compromise was made. A flagpole and a statue would supplement the Memorial.[72] Only then did Watt sign the permits. Despite continued threats of lawsuits by Hyde and his allies, the VVMF broke ground on March 26, 1982, and the Memorial was completed and dedicated on November 13, 1982.

Daedalus in DC

On the Trojan War mural, the likenesses of dead warriors endure, but their identities as 'real' people—child, parent, sibling, spouse, lover, friend—are effaced. Misenus and Palinurus were each promised a *nomen aeternum* for their sacrifice. But as Vergil's eulogy of Caieta demonstrates, the fame a *nomen aeternum* is supposed to vouchsafe does nothing for the deceased. The toponym endures but the identity of the individual who lent the name disappears no less than that of the warrior emblemized as ideal duty and glory. As we have seen, commemorations like these always have in them the potential for ideological (re-)deployment. The vitriolic resistance to Lin's design by men deeply invested in the discourse of patriotic duty and national glory testifies to the difficulty of pressing the Vietnam Veterans Memorial into the ideological service of the state.

The response from the public to the completed Memorial was immediate and overwhelmingly positive.[73] At the dedication celebration, although there were the familiar trappings of any patriotic celebration, the experience for many of the attendees was deeply personal. Veterans and their families

> came to voice their personal sentiments: grief for fallen comrades, a desire to recognize the ordinary soldiers, and sorrow over the loss of loved ones. Expressions of national greatness, unity, and loyalty to the nation were not only infrequent, but often contradicted.[74]

In other words, the dedication events centered around the "vernacular culture," with the needs of individuals superseding the rhetorical demands of the polity.

Viewed at a distance, the Vietnam Veterans Memorial's panels appear blank. It is only upon drawing near that the names snap into focus. The viewer is met with James A. Lisenby, Antonio Jimenez, William D. Tolbert, and thousands of other names of individual people. Psychiatrist and author Jonathan Shay integrated trips to the Vietnam Veterans Memorial into therapies for veterans suffering from severe posttraumatic stress disorder (PTSD). He remarked that "the names . . . are a very powerful statement: each of these was a whole life. There are no et ceteras on the Wall."[75] In presenting the names of all US veterans who died in the Vietnam War, Lin immortalizes them without attempting to make them famous. Contrary to what Carhart wanted—a memorial that glorifies *the* Vietnam veteran—Lin commemorates each and every Vietnam veteran who died in the war.

Staring back through the name of the deceased on the Memorial's mirror-like walls is the viewer's own image, urging the viewer to wonder just who was Andrew L. Dawson, Sharon A. Lane, Gary R. Guest? Like the blank panel on Daedalus' doors where Icarus ought to have been, the viewer of the VVM is denied the mythologized external referent: there is no idealized hero to stand in for each of those 58,281 individuals. Like Icarus, "the men and women who died in the war . . . achieve an historically coded presence through their absence."[76] Confronting the void, it cannot be avoided: the person who bore the name is gone, nothing can replace them or justify their absence. Even if the person who bore the name is forgotten by the viewer, even if they were never known to begin with, the Memorial ensures that we cannot forget that they once lived and are now gone because of the war in Vietnam.

The Vietnam Veterans Memorial does not announce its own meaning; it invites contemplation.[77] It contrasts with the other monuments reflected on its surface: the Washington Monument and the Lincoln Memorial. The former "operates purely as symbol, making no reference beyond its name to the mythic political figure" it immortalizes.[78] The latter connotes a mausoleum and embodies Lincoln's political legacy by enshrining his words on the structure itself, the force of which is "its mythical reference" to the slain president.[79] In other words, these two structures, one by its eternal name, the other by its eternal words and likeness, leave little doubt as to what they are meant to convey, to celebrate, to perpetuate.[80] Vergil's Trojan War mural likewise attempts to foreclose interpretation by leaving little doubt as to its message by focusing on mythologized referents rather than real individuals. But as we have seen, Aeneas' reaction to it problematizes the notion of an imposed 'official' interpretation. The blank space on Daedalus' doors also invites contemplation.

Despite the Sibyl's attempts to hurry Aeneas along, he contemplates the void, and in doing so memorializes Icarus in a way no idealizing image could. The work of art in which both of these monuments are contained, the *Aeneid* itself, demonstrates that art cannot work "solely for the purposes of the ideology that produces it," that there is always room for new interpretations of old texts "that will foster a new kind of subjectivity in its viewers rather than enforce an existing one."[81] Lin's Memorial demonstrates that creating opportunities for the forever-changing subjectivity of individual viewers by focusing the viewer's attention on real individuals who lived real lives and died rather than mythologized instantiations of patriotic duty is a very effective tool for short-circuiting attempts to co-opt commemorative art for ideological purposes. National and individual healing happen in the silent spaces where the artist steps away and authority is silenced. Like Icarus's panel, the Vietnam Veterans Memorial resists being dragooned into ideological service because it cannot but demand quiet contemplation of real lives lost.

Notes

1 Funding from the Drescher Grant at Barrett, the Honors College at Arizona State University, allowed me to spend time at the Vietnam Veterans Memorial and to conduct research at the Library of Congress on its design and the controversy surrounding it. I would like to thank Tim Tetz from the Vietnam Veterans Memorial Fund for sharing his time and expertise. Thanks also to my research assistant, Ian Gill (Dartmouth, Class of 2023), and to Tom and Anne Sienkewicz, who read multiple drafts of this paper and offered suggestions for its improvement.

2 Names have been periodically added to the Memorial according to criteria established by the US Department of Defense (DOD). The Vietnam Veterans Memorial Fund (VVMF) regularly conducts audits of the names on the Memorial and compares them with data from the DOD. The VVMF published an audit in 2019 featuring detailed methodology and charts listing the number of additions by year. At that time, the total number of names was updated to 58,276 (VVMF 2019). Five more names were added in 2020, bringing the total, as of May 2021, to 58,281 (VVMF 2021).

3 Designs were chosen by a set of jurors consisting mostly of experts in public art and urban planning with complete independence from the Vietnam Veterans Memorial Fund, the organization established to fund and build the Memorial, although they agreed to be bound by a set of principles established in the VVMF statement of purpose which read, in part, that the "Memorial will make no political statement regarding the war or its conduct. It will transcend those issues. The hope is that the creation of the Memorial will begin a healing process" (Scruggs and Swerdlow 1985: 53).

4 Bodnar 1992: 9; Scruggs and Swerdlow 1985: 81–2; Shepard 1981.

5 Psychiatrist and author Jonathan Shay 2002 has written about the Memorial as an almost sacred space for veterans and their families. This has been reflected in the popular culture, for example, in Bobbie Ann Mason's best-selling novel about a Vietnam veteran struggling with posttraumatic stress disorder, *In Country* (1985), which was made into a feature film in 1989.

6 It must be remembered that Vergil was dead before the Augustan ideology as we today would define it was fully formed and articulated. The settlement of 27 BCE was its beginning, not its culmination. Although it is undeniable that there are elements of it present in the *Aeneid* (see Zanker 1988: 195), what might be the fullest expressions of Augustanism came after Vergil's death in 19 BCE. First is the Forum Augustum, which

Dio reports was begun in 17 BCE (54.8.3). The forum was dedicated in 2 BCE, despite its centerpiece, the temple of Mars Ultor, being as yet incomplete (Macrob. *Sat.* 2.4.9). Second is the *Res Gestae Divi Augusti*, which Augustus himself claims to have written down when he was 76 years old (*RG* 35.2), so in 13 or 14 CE. See Thomas 2001: xii–xvi.

7 If not his entire *oeuvre*, which, according to Boyle 1986, ought to be read as a unified whole—*Eclogues, Georgics, Aeneid.* Boyle goes farther still, arguing that Vergil's work testifies to the impotence of art in the face of history, that, in short, the sword is indeed mightier than the pen.

8 *Ekphrasis* is a vivid and elaborate description of an object within a poem. The description of the pictures on Juno's temple at Carthage, writes Williams, "is a remarkable example of Virgil's ability to use a traditional device (*ekphrasis*) in such a way as to strengthen and illuminate the main themes of his poem" (1960: 145).

9 For an extensive bibliography on the Carthaginian temple, see Bartsch 1998 and Pandey 2020.

10 However, after Vergil situates his epic in the Homeric world, he nevertheless moves away from it. Segal 1965: 644 points out the parallels between Aeneas' encounter with the Junionian temple in Book 1 and the Apollonian temple in Book 6, which, together with the Misenus episode in Book 6, further mark the "passing of the Iliadic world" (639).

11 Williams 1960: 145 argues that although "not Homeric," the Troilus myth was prominent in Greek and Roman art before the *Aeneid* was composed. He further argues (150) that the stories of Memnon and Penthesilea belong to the *Posthomerica* and therefore count as Vergilian innovation, along with other departures from Homeric episodes, such as Achilles dragging Hector's body around Troy rather than around the tumulus of Patroclus. Aeneas does appear in battle in the *Iliad* (20.156–352), but the emphasis on this episode is his flight from battle with Achilles.

12 Horsfall 1986: 17.

13 Additionally, the pictures on Dido's temple have parallels in the action of the *Aeneid*'s own Iliadic books, those recounting the Italian wars (9–12). See Lowenstam 1993: 38.

14 For example, Aeneas says to Achates: *solve metus; feret haec aliquam tibi fama salutem* (don't be afraid, this fame of ours will bring you a measure of safety, *Aen.* 1.463).

15 That we are catching a glimpse of the 'real' Aeneas is implied by Vergil having his exile's words tossed (*iactanti*, 102) just like the much-enduring exile himself (*iactatus*, 3).

16 On Hector and his role in the first half of the epic (i.e., the "mythical," pre-Roman *Aeneid*), see Segal 1965: 643–4.

17 Aeneas also calls upon Sarpedon, whose corpse in the *Iliad* (16.671–5) was whisked away to Lycia for burial. The first men to die in the *Aeneid* are Orontes and his Lycian crew (1.113).

18 In many an English translation of the *Aeneid*, *iuvare* is translated 'to please,' as if the painful experience, once firmly placed in the past, will serve as a source of pleasure. Judith Hallett 1991: 1 states that here Aeneas is attempting "to cheer a dispirited band of comrades by the observation that their painful present struggles may well become—over time and through memory—sources of pleasure," and that Vergil is furnishing "a model of collective remembrance." Dani Bostick (185–186) argues that *iuvabit* here could be read in light of Aeneas' and his men's traumatic experiences, that it never is 'pleasing' to recall traumatic events but that it might be helpful for them to reconsider their relationship with traumatic events, that one day "there will be *relief* in remembering" and that "it will be helpful one day to integrate these experiences into their personal and collective experience and identity."

19 Just above, Aeneas sees "Trojan battles set out in order, and the war now famous, known the whole world over" *Iliacas ex ordine pugnas / bellaque iam fama totum vulgata per orbem* (1.456–7).

20 *Metus* seems to take center stage in Book 1, with Jupiter and Dido echoing Aeneas' bid to set aside fear (*parce metu*, 1.257; *solvite corde metum*, 1.562). *Dolor* (grief) seems to take its place in Book 6.
21 As attested to by the ongoing debate about Vergil's optimism, pessimism, or ambivalence to empire and autocracy.
22 See Wimperis, this volume, Chapter 7.
23 Cf. *insuetum iter*, 6.16.
24 Although it is said that the Sibyl's words dispel Palinurus' concerns, whatever relief they bring is momentary (*parumper*, 382).
25 Misenus was closely associated with Hector (*Hectoris magni . . . comes*, 6.166), which is significant because, as Segal 1965: 643 notes, Misenus' death marks Aeneas' break with the "mythological" past, whereafter he will focus on the "historical," that is, Rome's imperial destiny.
26 Segal 1965: 637. The pointed echo of Ennius (Sk. 175–9) in this episode, itself an allusion to *Il.* 23.114–28, seems to comment on the cyclicality of death's nullification of young life and its commemoration in song.
27 This is a Vergilian innovation (see Galinsky 2009), a fact that emphasizes the parallels drawn between Aeneas and Daedalus and, hence, Vergil's complication of commemorative art.
28 Segal 1965; Pöschl 1975; Boyle 1986 comment on the various parallels. Staley 2002 goes into great detail.
29 *Daedalus fugiens* (6.14) recalls Aeneas, the *vir profugus* of 1.2. Hesperia (the land of the West) is Aeneas' destination. Daedalus heads north but somehow ends up in Italy (see Galinsky 2009).
30 Daedalus contends with the *crudelis amor* of Pasiphaë for the bull (6.24) that results in the *Veneris monimenta nefandae*, the Minotaur (26), from which he has to save Theseus, moved by pity for Ariadne's great love for him (*magnum reginae sed enim miseratus amorem*, 28). Aeneas must contend with the fallout from his love of Dido, whom he will encounter later in the Book (450–76). Rome, of course, will have to contend with Dido's Carthage.
31 Vergil's description of the doors is punctuated with words of grief and pity: an exclamation (*miserum*, 21) accompanies the description of the fate of the Athenian sons; Daedalus is *miseratus* on account of Ariadne (28), and grief (*dolor*, 31) is what prevents him from carving Icarus' panel. Throughout Book 6, Aeneas is likewise affected by grief and pity. For example, Aeneas is struck with pity for the unburied dead (332), including his men Leucaspis and Orontes (334); moved to tears himself, he pities Dido (476); and he forlornly refers to rebirth as a "mad desire" for the "miserable light" (*quae lucis miseris tam dira cupido*, 721).
32 Phoebus is described as *gravis Troiae miseratus labores* and as a reliable champion of the Trojans before and after the fall of Troy (56–61).
33 Boyle 1986: 140 identified several other verbal parallels, including the nautical language. Staley 2002: 138 points out that *remigium alarum* (19) is a rather common metaphor but is right to suppose that it is deployed here with purpose.
34 See Putnam 1987; Horsfall 2013: 85–7; Pandey 2014; and Pandey 2020: 145–6 for a comprehensive survey of scholarship on the Daedalus doors.
35 Boyle 1986: 133 refers to Book 6 as the "noetic core" of the poem, a "meta-book" that supplies a commentary of sorts for the rest of the epic. As such, the doors themselves provide instruction in how to read what follows.
36 The doors of the Curia Julia, which was completed by Augustus in 29 BCE, seem not to have been carved with pictures. However, the doors' balanced sets of discrete panels provide an example of the kind of symmetry Vergil might have had in mind.
37 That is, Daedalus created the door that permanently represents in gold the beast which through his artifice he had a hand in bringing into existence (by devising the contraption by which Pasiphaë could mate with the bull).
38 Pöschl 1975: 121; Fitzgerald 1984: 53 and Putnam 1987 point out that the Daedalus *ekphrasis* is unique in having an artist depict his own story. Although Helen does weave

the story of the Trojan War into a tapestry at *Il.* 3.125–8, the work is not described. Pandey 2014: 89–91; Pandey 2020: 146 discusses Daedalus' selective self-presentation, which would not have been lost on the reader and that demonstrates the "importance of audience subjectivity in constructing meaning" 2020: 147.

39 Staley 2002: 140 elaborates on this curious—though, I argue, purposeful—omission.

40 *OLD* s.v. *dolus* 1a.

41 *OLD* s.v. *resolvere* 1e: to unravel or solve a mystery or a puzzle; 7b: to make of no effect, cancel, undo, nullify. Staley 2002: 140 explores the connection between the *labores* and *errores* of Daedalus and those of Aeneas, although I share Horsfall's doubt that the Labyrinth of Daedalus necessarily prefigures Aeneas' descent into the underworld 2013: 88 but rather notionally ties Aeneas and Daedalus together as refugees whose attempts to bend the world to their designs results in traumatic loss.

42 Casali 1995.

43 Although the Alexandrian footnote points directly to the story of Daedalus' flight from Crete, it also accounts for the fact that neither Ariadne or Theseus is named in Vergil's description of Daedalus' actions leading up to his flight from Crete: readers would presumably be expected know already who Aeneas sees. The intertext is obviously Catullus 64, the lengthy description of the coverlet depicting, in part, the story of Theseus's slaying of the Minotaur and subsequent abandonment of Ariadne. The footnote also lends poignant force to the absence of Icarus, whose name is often inseparable from Daedalus in accounts of their flight. On the narrator's "empathy" with Daedalus' version of story, see Putnam 1987: 175–82.

44 Boyle 1986: 140. Pöschl 1975: 121 connects the illusion here to *Ody.* 11.206–7 (τρὶς μὲν ἐφωρμήθην . . . / τρὶς δέ μοι ἐκ χειρῶν σκιῇ εἴκελον ἢ καὶ ὀνείρῳ / ἔπτατ') with Vergil's attempt to communicate the incapacity of the artist to convey the depths of suffering.

45 Boyle 1986: 141. That is, the practice of empire according to the ideals laid out in Book 6 is impossible in real life, as will be exemplified by Aeneas' unmerciful slaying of the subjected Turnus.

46 Segal 1965: 644.

47 Cf. *ante ora partum* (*Aen.* 1.95), see above pg. 157.

48 Pöschl 1975: 121, responding to Goethe: "Zwar gilt weithin 'wenn der Mensch in seiner Qual verstummt, gab mir ein Gott, zu sagen, wie ich leide,' aber dort, wo das Persönlichste, Schmerzlichste zur Sprache kommt, stößt der Künstler—so will Virgil hier sagen—an eine Grenze."

49 On the "incommunicability" of Vietnam veterans' experiences and its effect on American art and popular culture, see Sturken 1991: 129–32. See also discussions in Shay 2002: passim.

50 Bodnar 1992: 13.

51 Scruggs and Swerdlow 1985: 80.

52 Scruggs and Swerdlow 1985: 17.

53 Scruggs and Swerdlow 1985: 81.

54

> The most meaningful statements of support continued to come in from the American people. Veterans organizations sponsored bingo games, bake sales, garage sales, dinner dances, and other activities that generated millions of dollars. Hundreds of thousands of veterans and their families had been exposed to considerable adverse publicity about Maya Lin's design, and yet they continued to donate their time and their dollars.
>
> Scruggs and Swerdlow 1985: 85

55 Scruggs and Swerdlow 1985: 88 estimated that there were less than a dozen committed opponents to the Memorial as designed by Lin. Documents from the VVMF archived at the Library of Congress, including extensive correspondence between VVMF board members and highly placed Reagan administration officials and members of Congress seem to bear this out. In just one example of the concerted effort, in a November 1981 memo,

congressman Phil Crane (R-IL) directed his staff to "activate the conservative network to make noise" in order to kill the Memorial (Vietnam Veterans Memorial Fund Records, Box 30: Congressional Reaction 1981–3. Library of Congress, Washington, DC).

56 Carhart himself seems to have invented the insidious lie that Lin was not an American and that the VVMF had been infiltrated by communists (Vietnam Veterans Memorial Fund Records, Box 29: Controversy and Criticism. Carhart, Tom 1981–4. Library of Congress, Washington, DC).

57 Sturken 1991: 121 refers to the effect as an "impromptu pastiche."

58 Associated Press, "Memorial Flap," October 13, 1981.

59 Sturken 1991: 123. She also notes that misogyny plays no small part in the popularity of the phrase. Maya Lin was seen by some of her critics to be intruding onto a male space, and that "a 'gash' is not only a wound, but slang for the female genitals" (*loc. cit.*).

60 Vietnam Veterans Memorial Fund Records, Box 30: Congressional Reaction 1981–83. Library of Congress, Washington, DC.

61 Scruggs and Swerdlow 1985: 100–1.

62 Scruggs and Swerdlow 1985: 84.

63 Vietnam Veterans Memorial Fund Records, Box 50: Congressional Correspondence 1983–4. Library of Congress, Washington, DC.

64 Vietnam Veterans Memorial Fund Records, Box 75: Files of the Project Director, May–October 1981. Library of Congress, Washington, DC.

65 Scruggs and Swerdlow 1985: 45.

66 Vietnam Veterans Memorial Fund Records, Box 30: Perot, H. Ross, 1981–3. Library of Congress, Washington, DC.

67 Vietnam Veterans Memorial Fund Records, Box 30: Perot, H. Ross, 1981–3. Library of Congress, Washington, DC. The involvement of a man like Roy Cohn further indicates the extent to which the conservative political establishment was involved in preventing a Vietnam War memorial that did not ostentatiously participate in the discourse of national glory.

68 Vietnam Veterans Memorial Fund Records, Box 29: Controversy and Criticism, Christian, David A, 1983–4. Library of Congress, Washington, DC.

69 Vietnam Veterans Memorial Fund Records, Box 29: Controversy and Criticism, Christian, David A., 1983–4. Library of Congress, Washington, DC.

70 An internal VVMF memorandum dated December 19, 1984, nearly two years after the Memorial's dedication, explicitly addresses the possibility of retribution and points to the claim that VA mailing lists were used as evidence that the anti-Memorial activists were behind the false claims (Vietnam Veterans Memorial Fund Records, Box 29: Controversy and Criticism: Christian, David A., 1983–4).

71 Vietnam Veterans Memorial Fund Records, Box 30: Congressional Reaction, 1981–3. Library of Congress, Washington, DC.

72 The compromise statue group and flagpole are set back about 50 yards from the VVM proper. The sculpture consists of a realist depiction of three young men in jungle battle dress. The sculptor, Frederick Hart, wanted to create an image that expresses "the bonds of love and sacrifice that is the nature of men at war" (National Parks Service 2020). The flagpole base contains the emblems of the five branches of the US Armed Forces. The flagpole and statue group were dedicated on Veterans Day 1984.

73 As Sturken 1991: 126 observes the "experience of Lin's work seems to have been so powerful for those who have visited it that negative criticism of its design has vanished." This is largely corroborated by my review of the records of the VVMF housed at the Library of Congress. Despite alleged reprisals against those perceived to have betrayed the anti-Memorial activists (e.g., David Christian), vitriolic attacks against the VVM (and the VVMF) seem to have evaporated by the spring of 1983. For an example of less-than-enthusiastic reception in the arts community of Lin's work, including the Civil Rights Memorial in Birmingham, AL (which shares a lot of the features of the VVM), see Abramson 1996: 679–709.

74 Bodnar 1992: 6.
75 Shay 2002: 170.
76 Sturken 1991: 127.
77 Sturken 1991: 123–4. On readerly subjectivity and Vergil's epic in general, his *ekphrases* in particular, see Bartsch 1998; Pandey 2014: 89–91; Pandey 2020: 146.
78 Sturken 1991: 120.
79 Sturken 1991: 120.
80 This is not to suggest that there is no room at all for subjective interpretation. Rather, I mean that subjective interpretation of structures like the Washington Monument and Lincoln Memorial is significantly circumscribed by the presentation of the work itself along with the declared purpose of its commissioning, funding, design, and construction, and its reception.
81 Bartsch 1998: 339.

References

Abramson, Daniel. 1996. "Maya Lin and the 1960s: Monuments, Time Lines, and Minimalism." *Critical Inquiry* 22, 4: 679–709.

Bartsch, Shadi. 1998. "Ars and the Man: The Politics of Art in Virgil's *Aeneid*." *Classical Philology* 93, 4: 322–42.

Bodnar, John E. 1992. *Remaking America: Public Memory, Commemoration, and Patriotism in the Twentieth Century*. Princeton: Princeton University Press.

Boyle, A.J. 1986. *The Chaonian Dove: Studies in the Eclogues, Georgics, and Aeneid of Virgil*. Leiden: Brill.

Casali, Sergio. 1995. "Aeneas and the Doors of the Temple of Apollo." *The Classical Journal* 91, 1: 1–9.

Fitzgerald, William. 1984. "Aeneas, Daedalus and the Labyrinth." *Arethusa* 17, 1: 51–65.

Galinsky, Karl. 2009. "Aeneas at Cumae." *Vergilius (1959–)* 55: 69–87.

Hallett, Judith P., et al. 1991. "*Nunc Meminisse Iuvat*: Classics and Classicists between the World Wars." *Classical World* 85: 1–27.

Horsfall, Nicholas. 1986. "The Aeneas Legend and the *Aeneid*." *Vergilius (1959–)* 32: 8–17.

———. 2013. *Virgil,* Aeneid *6: A Commentary*, Vol. 2. Berlin: De Gruyter.

Lowenstam, Steven. 1993. "The Pictures on Juno's Temple in the 'Aeneid'." *The Classical World* 87, 2: 37–49.

National Parks Service. 2020. *Vietnam Veterans Memorial*, April 20. www.nps.gov/vive/learn/historyculture/vvmoverview.htm.

Pandey, Nandini B. 2014. "Reading Rome from the Farther Shore: *Aeneid* 6 in the Augustan Urban Landscape." *Vergilius* 60: 85–116.

———. 2020. *The Poetics of Power in Augustan Rome: Latin Poetic Responses to Early Imperial Iconography*. Cambridge: Cambridge University Press.

Pöschl, Viktor. 1975. "Die Tempeltüren des Dädalus in der *Aeneis* (VI 14–33)." *Würzburger Jahrbücher für die Altertumswissenschaft*: 119–23.

Putnam, Michael C.J. 1987. "Daedalus, Virgil and the End of Art." *The American Journal of Philology* 108, 2: 173–98.

Scruggs, Jan C., and Joel L. Swerdlow. 1985. *To Heal a Nation: The Vietnam Veterans Memorial*. New York: Harper Perennial.

Segal, Charles Paul. 1965. "'Aeternum per Saecula Nomen', the Golden Bough and the Tragedy of History: Part I." *Arion: A Journal of Humanities and the Classics* 4, 4: 617–57.

Shay, Jonathan. 2002. *Odysseus in America: Combat Trauma and the Trials of Homecoming*. New York: Scribner.

Shepard, Robert. 1981. "Vietnam Vets Memorial Criticized." *UPI*, December 8.

Staley, Gregory A. 2002. "Vergil's Daedalus." *The Classical Outlook* 79, 4: 137–43.

Sturken, Marita. 1991. "The Wall, the Screen, and the Image: The Vietnam Veterans Memorial." *Representations*, no. 35: 118–42.

Thomas, Richard F. 2001. *Virgil and the Augustan Reception*. New York: Cambridge University Press.

Vietnam Veterans Memorial Fund. 2019. *Wall Audit Summary*, May. www.vvmf.org/wp-content/uploads/2019/05/Wall-Audit-Summary-FINAL.pdf.

———. 2021. www.vvmf.org/about-vvmf/.

Vietnam Veterans Memorial Fund Records. 1965–1994. *Manuscript Division, Library of Congress*. Washington, DC.

Williams, R.D. 1960. "The Pictures on Dido's Temple (*Aeneid* I. 450–93)." *The Classical Quarterly* 10, 2: 145–51.

Zanker, Paul. 1988. *The Power of Images in the Age of Augustus*. Ann Arbor: University of Michigan Press.

Part III

The *Aeneid* and contemporary trauma and identity

In this penultimate part, the chapters focus on a topic of tragic and immediate importance: trauma and fractured senses of identity. These chapters demonstrate that a poem more than 2,000 years old can indeed help us understand and manage trauma in the present day. First, Dani Bostick, drawing on her experience as a therapist working with patients with posttraumatic stress disorder, shows how Vergil's presentation and manipulation of time and memory in the *Aeneid* can help us better understand the temporal distortions experienced by victims of trauma.

Nancy Ciccone explores how the *Aeneid* can help us understand the suffering and needs of contemporary Syrian refugees, who must struggle with a fragmented sense of self (or senses of self) as result of the destruction of the basis for their communal identities. This chapter reads the literary epic and Syrian refugee testimony intertextually to outline the effects of trauma with a focus on the difficultly of constructing an individual identity with fragile cultural supports. By connecting the *Aeneid* with actual refugees' experiences, Ciccone's research completes a circuit begun with the linking of the *Aeneid* with modern fictional depictions of exiles in Part I (see Loi, Chapter 3, and Giannotti, Chapter 4). The *Aeneid* not only inspires artistic' portrayals of the anguish of exile, but it can help each of us understand the very real and fraught circumstances of present-day refugees.

The closing chapter combines the *Aeneid* with very notion of modernity itself and the difficulties of constructing an "authentic self." George Saad contemplates modernity within the tradition of Continental philosophy and argues that modernity is characterized by the virtue of authenticity, which requires a choosing of one's identity. He then explains how the *Aeneid* details Aeneas' quest for this very quality, making it one of the first works to describe what comes to define modernity, not only as an ongoing era but an ongoing human condition.

At the end of this section, we hope readers can appreciate the variety of insights that the *Aeneid* offers regarding the here and now, both inside and outside of academic interests. It is an epic that can speak to all of us.

DOI: 10.4324/9781003176145-12

9 A matter of time

Traumatic temporality in Vergil's *Aeneid*

Dani Bostick

"My mom told me this could change everything, like 9/11," a high school freshman told me as we left for what we all thought would be a two-week closure because of the growing threat of COVID-19. He was right. Some events are so destabilizing that they create a "before" and an "after" in terms of how we perceive ourselves and the world. "Trauma" is the term we use to describe such events. Sometimes trauma affects us as individuals, leaving us to cope with the "after" in isolation. During my interlude career as a mental health counselor, my office was a space where people could make sense of their suffering authentically before venturing out into the world, where they would pretend to be like everyone else. Trauma does not just affect individuals, however. It can disrupt entire communities, posing challenges related to collective identity and the stories we tell about ourselves as a group.[1]

The predominant vernacular about human suffering does little to help us navigate the "after." Superficial and monolithic, it is based on the constellation of symptoms that has been medicalized as posttraumatic stress disorder (PTSD) in diagnostic manuals.[2] Human suffering in the aftermath of trauma has largely been framed as an illness that can be mitigated by therapy, medication, and trigger-management. Representations of trauma in mainstream modern culture are born of this one-dimensional approach. Around the Fourth of July, for example, many people living in the United States are reminded about the potential of fireworks to cause flashbacks in veterans suffering from PTSD.[3] More generally, although the descriptor "trauma-informed" is found everywhere from classrooms to yoga studios, we nevertheless lack the tools to confront trauma in our own lives.

Navigating trauma involves more than the mitigation of individual symptoms because even in the absence of symptoms, trauma remains a destabilizing force. Trauma catalyzes a fundamental shift in life's basic structures and our place in them. As inescapable as gravity, it is an invisible force that pervades every aspect of life. Time is the mechanism through which trauma imposes its most drastic changes since it is the infrastructure of our lives and our foothold on the world.[4] Trauma shatters the predictability of time and replaces it with disorienting chaos, transporting the past into the present, disconnecting the present from all previous experience, and rendering the future unimaginable.[5] The result is a traumatic temporality, the compression of past and present, and the constriction or total

DOI: 10.4324/9781003176145-13

obliteration of the future. It results in an existence unmoored from linear narrative and chronology, which David Morris vividly described thus:

> [T]rauma destroys the fabric of time. In normal time, you move from one moment to the next, sunrise to sunset, birth to death. After trauma, you may move in circles, find yourself being sucked backwards into an eddy or bouncing about like a rubber ball from now to then and back again. August is June, June is December. What time is it? Guess again. . . . Another odd feature of traumatic time is that it doesn't just destroy the flow of the present into the future, it corrodes everything that came before, eating at moments from your previous life, until you can't remember why any of them mattered.[6]

Holocaust survivor Viktor Frankl spoke of "deformed time" and a "strange 'time experience'" among prisoners in concentration camps.[7] In the context of the collective trauma of the COVID-19 pandemic, Alison Holman and Emma Grisham wrote, "interrupting the flow of time creates perceptual distortions such as feeling like time has stopped or that everything is in slow motion, experiencing a sense of timelessness, confusing the order of time and days, and perceiving a foreshortened future."[8] This experience is so common that "a distorted relationship to time" has been called "the hallmark feature of trauma."[9] Obviously, universal structures of time remain intact for those who have not experienced trauma, with hours, days, weeks, and years passing as they always have. For this reason, traumatic temporality does not just confound, it traps those who have experienced trauma in an incommensurable world.[10]

Traumatic temporality not only disrupts perceptions of the world, but also of oneself. Jorge Borges asserted: "Time is the substance I am made of."[11] This claim has been repeated more recently: "[Time] is inseparably tied to our experience as a whole, to our self-consciousness—to life itself. We are time."[12] About the aftermath of war-related trauma, Morris wrote, "The man on the other side of [the trauma] is not me. In fact, he never existed."[13] Time is also a component of collective identity, which is formed and maintained by "facing the present and future, but also by reconstructing the collectivity's earlier life."[14]

Contemporary focus on the treatment of the symptoms of trauma not only ignores some of its most disorienting aspects, it pathologizes the "after" and positions it as a condition so aberrant that it requires a cure.[15] Where the medical model fails, literature can illuminate dimensions of trauma not fully captured through modern diagnostic criteria and ascribe meaning to traumatic events. On a more basic level, literature can attempt to represent phenomena that otherwise defy description.[16] Although literary trauma theory as an academic discipline is relatively new, human suffering is not. Modern readers often turn to contemporary works for such literary representations of trauma. It is perhaps unexpected that a Roman epic written over two millennia ago can speak to trauma in a way that is more "trauma-informed" and nuanced than the modern medical resources that pathologize it. Nevertheless, in the *Aeneid*, Vergil represents aspects of the human condition that are hard to capture in everyday language, namely, the collapse of time and loss of identity in the wake of trauma.

In this chapter, I will frame Vergil's treatment of time in the *Aeneid* as an example of traumatic temporality and the reestablishment of temporal order in the wake of trauma on an individual level for Aeneas and on a collective level for Vergil's contemporaries. I present Aeneas' speech to the Trojans at the beginning of Book 1 as a blueprint for integrating trauma into both personal and collective narratives that Vergil later leverages to assimilate contemporary trauma into the collective mythology of Rome. This chapter does not seek to apply modern diagnostic criteria to Aeneas or leverage the *Aeneid* as therapy for modern readers. Instead, my goal is to explore what Vergil communicates about trauma and its aftermath through his representation of time.

Trauma and time in the *Aeneid*

Trauma is a predominant theme in Vergil's epic, as it has been elsewhere with such frequency that Dominick LaCapra asked "whether all societies or traditions have trauma as at least a crucial component of a foundational myth of origins."[17] Indeed, the *Aeneid* is bracketed by its protagonist's capacity to suffer and cause suffering.[18] At the outset, Aeneas is defined by his trauma. In the first lines of Book 1, we learn that he has been "tossed about on both land and sea" (*multum ille et terris iactatus et alto*, 1.3), has suffered extensively in war (*multa quoque et bello passus*, 1.5), and was "forced to endure so much suffering" (*tot adire labores impulerit*, 1.10–1). When we meet him directly, we find him freezing, groaning, and wishing he had died in war (1.92–6):

> *extemplo Aeneae solvuntur frigore membra;*
> *ingemit et duplicis tendens ad sidera palmas*
> *talia voce refert: 'o terque quaterque beati,*
> *quis ante ora patrum Troiae sub moenibus altis*
> *contigit oppetere!*
>
> Suddenly Aeneas' limbs go limp with cold: he groans and, stretching both palms out to the stars, says: O three and four times blessed are those who managed to die before the faces of their fathers under the high walls of Troy![19]

Aeneas is not the first person to suffer in this way, nor is he the last. Vergil's passage echoes Odysseus's words in the *Odyssey*, an instance of intertextuality that affirms the universality of human suffering.[20] At the end of the *Aeneid*, the very last image is strikingly similar to our first encounter with Aeneas. Consumed by trauma-fueled rage, Aeneas kills Turnus, whose "limbs go limp with cold" and whose soul flees to the realm of the dead with a groan (*ast illi solvuntur frigore membra / vitaque cum gemitu fugit indignata sub umbras*, 12.951–2).[21] Vergil places Aeneas' individual suffering on a continuum that extends from the distant mythological past into the present.

Vergil's creative management of time is likewise a prominent feature of the *Aeneid*, examples of which bracket the story in the same way trauma does. Even before we meet Aeneas, we learn that Juno has been time traveling, so to speak, and has arrived on the scene to prevent the founding of the Roman people so that they will not destroy Carthage centuries later (1.12–22).[22] At the end of the epic, Jupiter and Juno predict the future (12.791–842). In between these episodes are other instances of temporal displacement and "vertiginous" layering of time,[23] along with an overall narrative sequencing whose "move forward is often made by a circuitous route, via inverted chronologies and repetitions in the narrative, and via setbacks and *deja vu* in history."[24] This description is similar to Morris' perception of traumatic time as "moving in circles" and "being sucked backwards."[25] Scholars have surmised that this treatment of time served to establish the Roman state as timeless and eternal.[26] However, Vergil accomplishes more. Through his representation of time, he replicates the way trauma—and people who have been traumatized—can seem to exist outside of linear chronology and hegemonic temporal structures.

This effort was undertaken with the backdrop of upheaval and uncertainty in Vergil's contemporary Rome. The poet lived amid constant strife, unrest, and civil war leading up to the definitive collapse of the Roman Republic and the establishment of the Augustan regime.[27] Although Augustus brought some degree of hope, internal and external conflicts continued to plague Rome. As Vergil was composing his epic, there was a broader cultural program aimed at situating Augustus' reign in a purported Golden Age, a task involving, generally, the segmentation of time that comes with any effort of periodization and a temporal reformulation to connect Augustus to heroic forebears.[28] It is impossible to know the impact of this historical context on Vergil personally, but it is evident that he has managed to craft an unusually nuanced representation of trauma throughout his work, especially through the words and experience of his hero, Aeneas.

Trauma and time in Aeneas' speech

In Book 1, during a speech to his comrades after their shipwreck and arrival at Carthage, Aeneas offers a vision for posttraumatic growth through the integration of traumatic memories into an expansive, linear narrative that establishes a sense of meaning and mastery over unsettling events. More broadly, his speech lays out a path to mitigate collective trauma and transform troubling events into a touchstone for national identity during what Catherine Toll called "a crucial formative phase" (1.198–207):[29]

> *'O socii (neque enim ignari sumus ante malorum),*
> *o passi graviora, dabit deus his quoque finem.*
> *vos et Scyllaeam rabiem penitusque sonantis*
> *accestis scopulos, vos et Cyclopea saxa*
> *experti: revocate animos maestumque timorem*
> *mittite; forsan et haec olim meminisse iuvabit.*

per varios casus, per tot discrimina rerum
tendimus in Latium, sedes ubi fata quietas
ostendunt; illic fas regna resurgere Troiae.
durate, et vosmet rebus servate secundis.'

"O friends—we are no strangers to earlier misfortunes—O you who have endured more burdensome things, god will bring about an end to this as well. You have approached rabid Scylla and her far-echoing crags, and encountered the Cyclopean rocks: restore your courage, cast off your despondent dread: perhaps one day it will be helpful to remember these things also. Through various misfortunes, and through so many crises, we are striving for Latium where the fates promise us peaceful lives: there, it is right for Troy to rise again. Endure, and save yourselves for prosperous times."

Aeneas' exhortation to the Trojans to restore their courage and cast off their despondent dread (*maestus timor*, 202) contain the two central foci of his speech: trauma and moving forward in its aftermath. To understand Aeneas' vision for the Trojans' future, it is first necessary to take a closer look at their current state.

Traumatic fear

From *maestus timor*, we know that the fear experienced by Aeneas and the Trojans goes so far beyond normal apprehension that "traumatic" is an apt rendering. *Maestus* is a word reserved for extreme grief. When paired with *timor*, it helps convey the essence of the reality of Aeneas and the Trojans, to which many of Vergil's contemporaries and readers across the ensuing millennia have been able to relate. It is significant that the word Aeneas chooses to describe *timor* in his speech is used in agonizing, uncertain circumstances both in the poetry of Catullus, whose influence on Vergil is well-documented, and elsewhere in the *Aeneid* itself.[30] For example, *maestus* appears four times to depict an anguished Ariadne after she was abandoned by Theseus (64.60, 130, 202, 249).[31] It also occurs in a powerful apostrophe Catullus directs toward his deceased brother: "What I will do is love you, and sing forevermore songs your death has made despondent" (*at certe semper amabo, / semper maesta tua carmina morte canam*, 65.11–2).[32] In the *Aeneid*, *maestus* appears in accounts of similarly heartbreaking loss, including the deaths of Dido (4.476) and Aeneas' father, Anchises (5.48). In the episode Michael Putnam calls "one of the poem's most emotional moments,"[33] Aeneas takes off the robes Dido made for him during happier times and, despondent (*maestus*, 11.76), puts them on the corpse of Pallas.[34]

In Books 2 and 3, when Aeneas recounts the events leading up to the shipwreck, he deploys *maestus* six times to express the depth of grief associated with significant losses before his arrival to Carthage. One instance involves the funeral of Polydorus (3.64). Two appear during his last interactions with his wife, Creusa: one describes both Aeneas and Creusa (2.681), the other Aeneas alone after he realizes Creusa is lost (2.769). Also in Book 2, Aeneas uses *maestus* twice discussing

Hector, whose death and mutilation haunt Aeneas, sometimes literally, throughout the epic.[35] First, Aeneas, describes the ghost of Hector as "very despondent" (*maestissimus Hector*, 2.270). A few lines later, his own words are despondent when he addresses Hector (*maestae . . . voces*, 2.280). Later in Book 3, as the Trojans are about to leave Chaonia, Aeneas notes that Andromache, Hector's widow, is "despondent because of their final departure" (*Andromache digressu maesta supremo*, 3.482).

Further supporting the idea that *maestus* has traumatic connotations in the *Aeneid* is the fact that all six of the episodes described here involve encounters with ghosts. Tormented Polydorus appears to ask for a funeral after Aeneas sees a bleeding tree. Creusa and Hector both appear to Aeneas when he is *maestus*.[36] Shortly before she is described as *maesta*, Andromache mistakes Aeneas for a ghost while she is making libations at Hector's empty tomb. Though alive, Aeneas is not where Andromache expects him to be in terms of time and place. The appearance of ghosts is a form of temporal distortion, the dead appearing where they do not belong. Death brings about the end of existence in the present, making the deceased a permanent part of the past. In modern Western culture, the concept of ghosts is considered irrational and experiences of past trauma in the present is medicalized as "flashbacks," or, in severe forms, "hallucinations."[37] Outside of this framework, it is more common for individuals who have experienced trauma to report encounters with ghosts.[38] Heonik Kwon noted that in Vietnam ghosts are used "as a means of historical reflection," particularly in the context of mass death and war.[39]

The *maestus timor* of Aeneas and the Trojans does not just evoke unpleasant emotions in the present, it creates a disorganized perception of time and obscures the future.[40] During his time in a concentration camp, Frankl observed this phenomenon: "The prisoner who had lost faith in the future—his future—was doomed."[41] After the attacks on September 11, there was a collective sense of grief along with the incessant worry that the attack was "possibly a preview of a more frightening future."[42] Despondent dread can infect the past as well because trauma changes the way reality is experienced, "coloring past, present, and future with the same dark ink of fear."[43] Traumatic fear has the power to collapse time, making the future hard to imagine and the past impossible to remember. What is left is often a perpetual present, devoid of context and possibility.

Restoring courage and casting off despondent dread

When Aeneas exhorts his comrades to restore their courage and cast off their despondent dread, his primary goal is not to evoke positive feelings.[44] There is much more at stake. Trauma can impede taking action, constructing meaning, and developing identity, both individually and collectively, tasks as important for the Trojans of Vergil's epic as they are for modern readers. Hence, in his speech, Aeneas does not just cheer up his men. Rather, he lays out a blueprint for mitigating *maestus timor* that elicits hope and a sense of purpose in order to inspire action, establish temporal order, and facilitate the construction of both meaning and identity.

Aeneas instills hope in the Trojans by promising them a future of peace and prosperity. Vergil's readers know the continued turmoil and trauma the future holds, so Aeneas' promise appears to go unfulfilled, as do other optimistic prophecies elsewhere in the *Aeneid*, particularly when they are delivered to boost morale.[45] Aeneas' objective is to create an opening to a future—any future.[46] Given the Trojans' circumstances, the significance of hope for mere survival should not be overlooked. Limiting the purpose of Aeneas' speech to encouragement ignores the strategy he presents for coping with trauma. When Aeneas uses the verbs *dabit* and *iuvabit* in his speech, future tense itself demonstrates hope. His vision for peace and prosperity is the mechanism through which he creates momentum toward that future. Aeneas also establishes a sense of purpose, which is reaching Latium and establishing a new Troy. Two millennia later, Frankl wrote about the importance of future orientation and purpose in concentration camps: "[A]ny attempt to restore a man's inner strength in the camp had first to succeed in showing him some future goal."[47]

The third element of Aeneas' blueprint is the reestablishment of order, which he expresses in one of the most famous lines of the *Aeneid*: "Perhaps one day it will be helpful to remember these things also" (*forsan et haec olim meminisse iuvabit*, 208). Here, Aeneas imagines a time when the Trojans will be able to recall distressing events and leverage them in a constructive way. In this scenario, past suffering is summoned through memory instead of invading the minds of those who have experienced it. The Nietzschean definition of future orientation best describes the task at hand: "exploring a situation with respect to how one can act in it in order to master it, instead of being mastered by it."[48]

This reading of Aeneas' speech involves a closer look at the meaning of *iuvare*, which can mean "to help" or "to please." Either Aeneas is saying that memories of the traumatic events will be pleasant or that the process of remembering will be helpful. The predominant interpretation over centuries has been the former, as if the mental representation of past traumatic events could inspire pleasure.[49] Aaron Seider summarizes the thinking behind this perspective: "Aeneas voices a belief that horrific events can be pleasantly remembered once they have receded into the past."[50] From an emotional perspective, trauma evokes a wide range of decidedly unpleasant emotions, which Vergil himself captures throughout his work and have been well documented in a wide range of other contexts over millennia. Aeneas does envision a more pleasant future for the Trojans, but it is not derived from mental images of the events that are the source of so much pain and anguish.

Supporting a reading of *iuvabit* as "will be helpful" is the way Aeneas leverages his own past trauma to motivate and inspire his men at the beginning of his speech when he mentions Scylla and the Cyclopean rocks. There is no indication that the recollection of this episode has been pleasant. In fact, there is evidence to the contrary: Aeneas' emotional state immediately after the speech is marked by hopelessness and pain. He is "sick with the weight of his heavy troubles" (*curis ingentibus aeger*, 208), carries a pain he stuffs deep into his chest (*premit altum corde dolorem*, 209), and only pretends to hope (*spem voltu simulat*, 209).[51] His reaction is aligned with Diomedes's words from Book 11: "I feel no joy in remembering evils from the past" (*nec veterum memini laetorve malorum*, 280). However, recalling the example of the Scylla and Cyclopean rocks has been helpful. Aeneas reminds his men of their ability to survive trauma and revisit it as a source of strength. If we construe *et* as "also" instead of "even," it is clear that Aeneas is pointing back toward the example of Scylla and the Cyclopean rocks as an example of how their present events could be used later in a positive way.

The future utility of traumatic episodes hinges on memory, which Vergil establishes as a central theme at the beginning of his work when invokes the Muse, telling her to remind him (*memora*, 1.8). Seider noted that in the *Aeneid*, memory "governs these transitions from past trauma to future paths."[52] Without memory, access to the future is blocked. The act of remembering is predicated on the reestablishment of linear temporal structures. No longer will the trauma infect the past, present, and future, effectively destroying the conventions of time; rather, it will be an episode firmly situated in the past that can be accessed voluntarily and deployed in the present as a source of hope and strength for the future.

The capacity to recall traumatic events is particularly helpful for both the Trojans and Vergil's Roman contemporaries, whose communities were in the process of negotiating identities in unsettled times.[53] LaCapra notes, "[a] crisis or catastrophe that disorients and harms the collectivity or the individual may miraculously become the origin or renewed origin of the myth."[54] Traumatic events that defy recall cannot be deployed in this way. Instead, temporal order—a cohesive perception of past, present, and future—is essential to this task.[55] Sequential time allows conceptualizations of past episodes to be transmitted to future generations to establish a sense of cultural continuity.[56] As Eviatar Zerubavel explained, "acquiring a group's memories and thereby identifying with its collective past is part of the process of acquiring any social identity."[57] Indeed, the blueprint Aeneas provides to the Trojans for integrating their trauma plays out on an individual and collective level elsewhere in the *Aeneid*.

Remediation of personal trauma

When Aeneas recounts the fall of Troy to Dido, it is obvious that it is a traumatic event. We know that he considers the fall of Troy to be an unspeakable sorrow (*infandus dolor*, 2.3), the retelling of which he equates with reliving it (*renovare*, 2.3).[58] Throughout his narrative, there are times Aeneas appears to relive events, floating back and forth between the present and past tenses, and even reacting physically to previous trauma.[59] This language is familiar even in modern contexts. Alice Seibold, for example, uses similar words to describe speaking about her sexual assault to a group of people: "I felt as if I had turned back the clock and was reliving the day."[60] Bree Bernwanger, an attorney who prepares immigrant women with trauma histories for their interviews with asylum officers, reports many clients have told her, "To tell it is to live it."[61]

The trauma of Troy is the driving force in the first five books of the *Aeneid*. In this section, I will look at two episodes involving Troy that align with Aeneas' representation of trauma in terms of both meaning and temporality: The search for Creusa in Book 2, which occurs chronologically before Aeneas' speech to his men, and his encounter with the visual depiction of Troy on the temple to Juno at Carthage, which comes shortly after the speech.

First, consider the loss of Creusa during Aeneas' flight from Troy, a traumatic, temporally disorganized event that ultimately provides purpose. After Aeneas notices he has lost Creusa during his flight, he has to reenter Troy and experience the same horrors he had just fled. As he is narrating the events to Dido, he is also reliving them (2.749–60):

> *ipse urbem repeto et cingor fulgentibus armis.*
> *stat casus renovare omnis omnemque reverti*
> *per Troiam et rursus caput obiectare periclis.*
> *principio muros obscuraque limina portae,*
> *qua gressum extuleram, repeto et vestigia retro*
> *observata sequor per noctem et lumine lustro:*
> *horror ubique animo, simul ipsa silentia terrent.*
> *inde domum, si forte pedem, si forte tulisset,*
> *me refero: inruerant Danai et tectum omne tenebant.*
> *ilicet ignis edax summa ad fastigia vento*
> *volvitur; exsuperant flammae, furit aestus ad auras.*
> *procedo et Priami sedes arcemque reviso . . .*

> I return to the city again and put on my shining armor. I am determined to relive every crisis, retrace the entirety of Troy, and risk my life again. I again seek the walls and dark gates from which I left, and retrace my steps throughout the night, lighting my way with a lamp: the ever-present horror in my mind and silence itself terrorize me. Then I go back home, in case by some chance she has gone there: the Greeks had taken over and were occupying the entire house. Fire, fueled by the wind, is consuming the gables of the house; flames are spreading, the blaze burns into the sky. I move on and see again the palace and citadel of Priam.

This scene captures the despondent dread of trauma discussed previously and mimics what sociologist Kai Erikson, in his work on the deadly Buffalo Creek Flood, called "repetitive drama in which the unsettled anxieties of the past and the newer anxieties of the present fuse together in a chronology that knows no time."[62] Aeneas' search for Creusa involves the repetition of risk and danger, as the use of numerous iterative words underscores: *repeto, renovare, reverti, rursus, retro, refero, reviso*. Aeneas articulates his fear using the present tense: "The ever-present horror in my heart and silence itself terrorize me" (*horror ubique animo, simul ipsa silentia terrent*, 2.755). Is he describing his reaction at the time of his search, or afterwards as it continues to haunt him? I would argue that it is the latter. When narrating his search, the *horror* is not just a part of the story. Likewise, the sounds of the wind, fire, conquerors, and conquered throughout the city would be far from silent. The events of that day appear to be a source of fear and ever-present horror for Aeneas, even as he later recalls it to Dido.

Similar to the way Aeneas attempted to provide relief to his comrades, the ghost of Creusa attempts to alleviate his cares by taking him out of the past and orienting him to the future (2.771–89). She, too, uses the word *iuvat*, telling her husband that feeding his sadness is not helpful ("How is it helpful to feed this insane grief?" *quid tantum insano iuvat indulgere dolori*, 776). She also contextualizes the tragedy in terms of divine will ("These things don't happen without the will of the gods," *non haec sine numine divum / eveniunt*, 777–8); presents a constructive task outside of Troy ("You have to plow through the vast sea," *vastum maris aequor arandum*, 780); and uses the future tense to instill a hopeful sense of purpose ("You will come to the land of Hesperia" *terram Hesperiam venies*, 781). She also gives Aeneas two directives. One involves his emotional state ("banish the tears shed for your dear Creusa," *lacrimas dilectae pelle Creusae*, 784), the other his purpose in the symbolic form of their son ("keep the love of the son we have together," *nati serva communis amorem*, 789). After his wife's speech, Aeneas pursues his future as he leaves Troy again, carrying his father, the symbolic link to his past.[63] Instead of being stuck in present trauma, he moves toward the future without abandoning his past. In addition to the association of Creusa and Hector with intense sadness, there is another commonality: they are the ones who first inform Aeneas of his destiny and instill in him a sense of purpose.[64]

A second example of traumatic temporality and the reestablishment of temporal order comes shortly after Aeneas' speech to the Trojans quoted earlier. The traumatic past encroaches on Aeneas' present as he wanders through Carthage and is confronted with visual images of the Trojan War depicted on the walls of a temple to Juno (1.446–93). Like so many affected by trauma, Aeneas faces his trauma while those around him remain oblivious—cloaked in mist by Venus, Aeneas is able to mingle with the people around him while remaining invisible (1.439–40). Throughout this episode, Vergil manages to capture the way trauma can invade the present, compressing time and defying the standard conventions of temporality. In general, *ekphrasis* lends itself to creating traumatic temporality because "the lack, or at least the weakness, of the linear links connecting these images creates a space for . . . a coexistence of past, present, and even future in the perception of the viewer."[65] Although Vergil tells us that Aeneas *sees* the battles portrayed in order (*videt Iliacas ex ordine pugnas*, 1.456), Aeneas recounts them out of order. Since this *ekphrasis* invites readers to view the representation as if they were part of the narrative, we experience the same disorientation as Aeneas when he scans the frieze crying (1.464–5).[66]

Aeneas' words after he views the frieze echo several components of the speech he had recently given to the Trojans. Here he tells his companion, Achates, to release his fears (*solve metus*, 1.463), which mirrors his instructions to the Trojans to cast off their despondent dread. Aeneas also provides a broader context for their trauma, seeing in retrospect that traumatic events will have a benefit in the future ("This fame will bring you [Achates] safety," *feret haec aliquam tibi fama salutem*, 1.463). Even though Aeneas did not willfully recall these events, the act of commemoration is still helpful. In fact, the entire episode is framed in terms of the benefits that this experience affords him. Before he sees the frieze, we learn that it will help him alleviate fear, have hope for the first time since the shipwreck, and perhaps most interestingly, have greater trust in his shattered circumstances (1.451–2). The sadness Aeneas experiences in the face of his past does not preclude him from trying to move forward with these events as a point of strength for his future.

Remediation of collective trauma

During the course of the *Aeneid*, it becomes clear that Aeneas' personal experience in Troy will not inform his personal identity or the collective identity of Rome. Even before he reaches Latium, Aeneas is addressed as "Roman" (6.851) by the shade of his father. Juno insists upon disconnecting Aeneas—and Rome—from a Trojan past when she tells Jupiter that the long-standing name of the Latins is not to change (12.823), they are not to become Trojans or be called Teucri (12.824), or change their language and clothing (12.825). As Juno says at the end of the narrative, "Troy is dead, and it will remain dead along with its name" (*occidit, occideritque sinas cum nomine Troia*, 12.828). This process plays out at the intersection of trauma and temporality. Aeneas' traumatic past is never situated as part of a past that can be accessed and used in his individual—or Rome's collective—future. There will be no collective memory or cultural continuity involving Troy because it is being forcibly erased by the gods.

Eventually, for Aeneas, as Pöschl notes, "[m]emory becomes hope; retrospective longing for Troy gives way to a visionary longing for Rome. He turns from his ancestors to his descendants."[67] The narrative point that brings about this change is Aeneas' underworld encounter with Marcellus, Augustus' recently deceased nephew and the last figure in a parade of prominent Romans who will live many years into Aeneas' future. Servius noted that the imperial family responded with such grief to this scene that Vergil could barely finish his recitation (Serv. 6.861). Sorrow over Marcellus's death is captured in the poem when Anchises tells Aeneas not to ask about "the immense grief of your people" (*ingentem luctum ne quaere tuorum*, 6.868). From these accounts, it seems this loss amounts to the same kind of "unspeakable sorrow" (*infandus dolor*, 2.3) that Aeneas recounts earlier in the work.

While the earlier traumatic memories of Troy centered on the individual suffering of Aeneas, the focus of this episode is on the collective. Marcellus' death in 23 BCE "threatens to overwhelm the magnificence of Roman achievement" and "deprives Rome of one of her (potentially) greatest leaders at a time when leadership is a cause for profound concern."[68] In having his protagonist encounter Marcellus, Vergil situates a destabilizing, traumatic current event in the distant past, simultaneously orienting Aeneas toward the future while providing instant historical and mythological context for the recent loss. What Aeneas experiences as a collapse of sequential time creates a sense of heightened chronological order for Augustan-age readers. In replacing his contemporaries' synchronic vantage point with a distant one, Vergil helps ascribe meaning to trauma. This tactic is similar to the one Frankl adopted in the concentration camp: "I succeeded somehow in rising above the situation, above the sufferings of the moment, and I observed them as if they were already in the past."[69]

Vergil's contemporaries can now look back on the recent death of Marcellus as if he were part of the more distant past when the shade of Anchises situates Rome's past as the distant future of his son's descendants: "Come now, I will disclose to you what glory is in store for the Dardan line . . . and I will show you your destiny" (*nunc age, Dardaniam prolem quae deinde sequatur / gloria . . . et te tua fata docebo*, 6.756–9). The parade of heroes along with Anchises's commentary "ignites [Aeneas'] soul with a desire for future glory" (*incenditque animum famae venientis amore*, 6.889). In this moment, the founder of the Roman people is motivated by Rome's future instead of his Trojan past. Here, Vergil not only facilitates a key transition for Aeneas, he does for the Roman state what Aeneas had envisioned for his shipwrecked crew in his speech in Book 1.

Just as *ekphrasis* allows the reader to share the perspective of the protagonist, this episode involves the audience as a participant. Zerubavel wrote, "a community's collective memory includes only those shared by its members as a group. As such, it invokes a common past that they all seem to recall."[70] In the case of the Marcellus episode, the community at hand is Augustan Rome, not the Trojans tasked with accompanying Aeneas in his quest to settle Latium. After all, Aeneas does not share anything about his trip to the underworld after he emerges, and because he exits out of the ivory gates, it is possible that Aeneas himself remembers nothing of the encounter.[71] In this case, Vergil's contemporaries would be the only beneficiaries of an episode that serves to ascribe meaning to the disorienting, potentially disastrous loss of Marcellus.

By placing Marcellus within reach of Aeneas, Vergil bridges a temporal gap between two circumstances of similar uncertainty: Aeneas' quest for Latium and Rome's quest for peaceful, stable succession. Vergil creates a similar effect at the end of Book 8 when Aeneas goes into battle carrying a shield depicting the history of Rome. Unlike the depictions of the Trojan War Aeneas sees in Carthage, the events on the shield are both depicted and recounted in chronological order (*in ordine*, 8.629), culminating in a description of the Battle of Actium and a triumphant Augustus. Aeneas' experience looking at his shield is different from his experience viewing the events of Troy on the temple frieze in Book 1. The events on the shield hold significance for the Roman reader, but not for Aeneas, whose disconnection from the events allows him to look upon them with joy.[72] Straddling two temporal landscapes, his future and the readers' past, Aeneas is unaware of the significance of these events. For his contemporaries, however, Vergil's treatment of Actium informed "public consciousness as a critical moment of collective history and national culture."[73] Again, Vergil has compressed the temporal distance between Aeneas and Augustan readers of the *Aeneid* so that they can look back on the trauma of prolonged civil wars and political uncertainty with a perspective that normally only comes with the passage of time.

Conclusion

Vergil does more than represent the atemporality of trauma. He also manages to create a temporal infrastructure for his contemporaries to contextualize traumatic events and reframe them as potential strengths, a lesson that resonates in modern times. With

Aeneas as the "embodiment of things Roman" and "the symbol of the mood existing between collapse and salvation, the chaos of the civil war and the advent of Augustan peace,"[74] it is through his experience that Vergil remediates Rome's collective trauma. And it is our encounter with the *Aeneid* that will perhaps provide insight into how our collective and individual experiences with trauma might be mitigated as well.

Trauma has been said to be "insulated from human dialogue" because it is "[t]orn from the fabric of time."[75] Through his treatment of trauma in the *Aeneid*, Vergil created the opportunity for dialogue that extends well beyond the confines of Augustan Rome. The *Aeneid* could easily be the subject of Katharina Donn's words regarding Jonathan Safran's novel about September 11, *Extremely Loud and Incredibly Close*: "The pathology of trauma itself here consists in the collapse of time and space, and in the subsequent disorientation of an individual who has lost the cornerstones of their identity."[76] The "after" of modern-day trauma, like September 11 and the COVID-19 pandemic, has all of the same features as Aeneas' "after."

Sociologist Kai Erikson noted that survivors of the 1972 Buffalo Creek flood "lost their navigational equipment, as it were, both their inner compasses and their outer maps" and were "unable to locate themselves in time and place."[77] Vergil provides a model for recalibrating our navigational equipment after trauma. The *Aeneid* gave Augustan-age Romans the ability to look back on the Marcellus's death and recent civil strife as if they had happened centuries prior. In the same way, the *Aeneid* can help modern readers situate their trauma in the past and locate themselves in a present time when it is already "helpful to remember these things also."

Notes

1 In the case of individual and collective trauma, the "after" can unfold in the midst of continued trauma.

2 See American Psychiatric Association 2013 for diagnostic criteria. For objections to common conceptualizations of trauma, see Visser 2011; Summerfield 2004.

3 See, for example, Marine Corps Community Services' announcements regarding fireworks (Marine Corps Community Services 2016).

4 For more on the role of time in society, see Nowotny 1992. Iparraguirre 2016 discusses the role of culture in constructions of time.

5 Iparraguirre 2016 notes that some Indigenous societies have nonlinear conceptions and constructions of time. In the context of trauma, distorted perceptions of time are disorienting because hegemonic perceptions of time are both linear and dependent on clearly defined conceptualizations of past, present, and future. Rosen noted that there is no way to "articulate a comprehensive, monolithic pre-modern or ancient conception of time and temporality" 2004: 3.

6 Morris 2015: xii. Here I define temporality as the "lived experience of time" (Stolorow 2015: 136). Hence, traumatic temporality is an experience of time caused by trauma.

7 Frankl 1959/2006: 70, 71.

8 Holman and Grisham 2020: 63.

9 Simko 2020: 54. Trauma has also been defined as a "jumbling of temporalities" (Paul, Banerjee, and Efferth 2015: 13).

10 See Stolorow 2015. The Covid-19 pandemic brought about a shared sense of distorted time since many people were no longer anchored by their usual routines. See Holman and Grisham 2020. Traumatic temporality is experienced by an individual, but the sense of alienation can be mitigated when it is shared by others.
11 Borges 1962: 233.
12 Wittmann 2016: xiii.
13 Morris 2015: xii.
14 Alexander 2012: 26.
15 PTSD has been linked to higher rates of suicide and other health problems, both mental and physical. See, for example, Sareen et al. 2007, and Stefanovics, Potenza, and Pietrzak 2020. Treatment for acute PTSD symptoms can save lives and increase the quality of life for people who suffer from trauma. My argument here is that the medical model oversimplifies and stigmatizes reactions to trauma.
16 Caruth 1996 defines trauma as an unclaimed experience and contends it is unrepresentable through linear narrative. Caruth tends to conceptualize trauma as an event affecting individuals, ignoring trauma that is embedded in daily life. Cvetkovich acknowledges that trauma can be "unspeakable and unrepresentable," but focuses on meaning, representation, and engagement with trauma both individually and collectively 2003: 7. For more on approaches to trauma theory, see also Balaev 2014; Forter 2011; Leys 2000.
17 LaCapra 2001: xii.
18 Barchiesi 1994: 109.
19 All translations are my own unless otherwise stated.
20 "Three and four times blessed are those who died at Troy" (τρὶς μάκαρες Δαναοὶ καὶ τετράκις, οἳ τότ' ὄλοντο / Τροίῃ ἐν εὐρείῃ χάριν Ἀτρεΐδῃσι φέροντες, 5.306–7).
21 For more on Aeneas' trauma and the killing of Turnus, see Panoussi 2020.
22 Cicero also hypothesized that the gods exist outside of traditional conceptions of time (*De Natura Deorum* 1.9.21).
23 Feeney 2007: 163.
24 Armstrong 2002: 328.
25 Morris 2015: xii.
26 See, for example, Mack 1978.
27 Born in 70 BCE, Vergil was 26 years old at the time of Caesar's death. See Johnson 1976: 135–54.
28 For more on periodization, see Zerubavel 1993 and 1998. For formulations of time in Augustan Rome, see Feeney 2007. Though his predecessor was more famous for his work with time via the Julian Calendar, Augustus also used time for propagandistic purposes (Wallace-Hadrill 1987). He consolidated the calendar and, if his horologium indeed functioned as a sundial, then he also provided temporal structure to the day, see Ker 2009: 281.
29 Toll 1997: 34.
30 On Catullus' influence, see Westendorp Boerma 1958; Lyne 1992; Napa 2010.
31 Later, after Theseus neglects to raise the flag indicating he is safe, his father is despondent, believing him dead (64.210). Ariadne specifically is a noteworthy intertext in the construction of the *Aeneid*'s Dido narrative and is a central theme of the Daedalus doors that open Book 6 (see O'Neill, this volume, Chapter 8).
32 See also Fourcade 1979; Bellandi 2003: 99; Armstrong 2013; Seider 2016. Catullus's influence on Vergil has been well documented; see Fourcade 1979: 86; Bellandi 2003: 99.
33 Putnam 2016: 88
34 See Anderson 1999 for more on *maestus* in Book 11.
35 In addition to these examples, in Book 1, Aeneas mentions Hector after the storm at the beginning of the Book (99–100) and is affected by a visual representation of Hector's death (483 ff.). At the end of the work, Hector is invoked before the fight with Turnus (12.438–41). See Pöschl 1962: 37.

36 Sugar 2019 associates Hector's apparition with Aeneas' trauma.
37 Wearne et al. 2020.
38 See, for example, Hinton 2021, who found that manifestations and frequency of hallucinations in people who have experienced trauma can vary by culture. For example, Cambodians report encounters with ghosts in episodes that researchers label post-traumatic hallucinations.
39 Kwon 2008: 2.
40 Sztomka 2004: 180 lists "bleak view of future" as a symptom of cultural trauma. For perspectives on the future in individuals affected by trauma, see Zimbardo and Boyd 1999.
41 Frankl 1959/2006: 83.
42 Hirsch 2003: 665.
43 Zimbardo, Sword, and Sword 2012: 6.
44 Frankl 1959/2006: 76. "Restoring inner strength" could be an alternate translation for *revocate animos*.
45 On temporal distortion and optimistic prophesies in the *Aeneid*, see O'Hara 1994.
46 LaCapra refers to "openings to the future" in the context of trauma (2001: 22). See also Simko 2020.
47 From a therapeutic perspective, "creating a future" is a primary task in recovering from trauma and is widely viewed as an essential task in establishing and maintaining a sense of well-being (Herman 2015: 196).
48 Stegmaier 2016: 388.
49 For a variety of examples of *iuvabit* translated, see Bostick 2019.
50 Seider 2013: 80.
51 Before Dido kills herself, she hides her plan while appearing calm and hopeful (*consilium volut tegit, ac spem fronte serenat*, 4.477). Even with suicidal ideation, which she eventually acts on, she conceals her distress so effectively that her own sister remains unaware of her suffering.
52 Seider 2013: 1.
53 The *Aeneid* was written during a time when a key task was "reconstructing the sense of Roman identity that had been shattered by the civil wars of the previous fifty years" (Orlin 2008: 244). On identity see also Toll 1997; Reed 2007; Seider 2013, and Wimperis Chapter 7, this volume.
54 LaCapra 2001: xii.
55 See Rappaport, Enrich, and Wilson 1985; Erikson 1968.
56 See Hirschberger 2018.
57 Zerubavel 2003: 3.
58 The only way to renew an emotion is to reexperience it.
59 Aeneas mentions that he bristles as he tells the story of Laocoon (*horresco referens*, 2.204).
60 Sebold 1999.
61 Fordham Law News 2016. Oscar Wilde wrote, "To tell it is to live it all again. Actions are the first tragedy in life, words are the second. Words are perhaps the worst" (Wilde 1998/1893: 42).
62 Erikson 1976: 244.
63 See Giannotti Chapter 4 and Loi Chapter 3 in this volume.
64 Kyriakou 1999 highlights the fact that both Creusa and Hector tell Aeneas his purpose and encourage him to move forward.
65 Schiesaro 2015: 165. Many scholars have written about this *ekphrasis*. For more, see Seider 2013; and O'Neill Chapter 8 this volume.
66 For alienation and trauma, see Gilmoor et al. 2020. Vergil also confounds the reader in Book 1 with a jumbled narrative that begins *in medias res,* provides a glimpse of recent past along with the distant future, and then continues with scattered references to the Trojan War before his encounter with the murals.

67 Pöschl 1962: 38.
68 Johnson 1976: 106. For more on this episode, see Reed 2007.
69 Frankl 1959/2006: 73.
70 Zerubavel 2004: 4.
71 For more on the ivory gate, see Tarrant 1982.
72 "He marveled at the things on Vulcan's shield, a gift from his mother, and rejoiced in the image, ignorant of the things on it" (*talia per clipeum Volcani, dona parentis, / miratur rerumque ignarus imagine gaudet*, 8.729–30).
73 Gurval 1995: 246.
74 Pöschl 1962: 34, 37.
75 Stolorow 1999: 160.
76 Donn 2017: 73.
77 Erikson 1976: 200, 209.

References

Alexander, Jeffrey C. 2012. *Trauma: A Social Theory*. Cambridge: Polity.
American Psychiatric Association. 2013. *Diagnostic and Statistical Manual of Mental Disorders*. 5th ed. Washington, DC: American Psychiatric Association.
Anderson, W. 1999. "*Aeneid* 11: The Saddest Book." In C. Perkell (ed.) *Reading Vergil's Aeneid: An Interpretive Guide*. Norman: University of Oklahoma Press. 195–209.
Armstrong, R. 2002. "Crete in the *Aeneid*: Recurring Trauma and Alternative Fate." *The Classical Quarterly* 52: 321–340.
———. R. 2013. "Journeys and Nostalgia in Catullus." *The Classical Journal* 109: 43–71.
Balaev, M. 2014. "Literary Trauma Theory Reconsidered." In M. Balaev (ed.) *Contemporary Approaches in Literary Trauma Theory*. London: Palgrave Macmillan. 1–14.
Barchiesi, Alexander. 1994. "Rappresentazioni del dolore e interpretazione nell'Eneide." *Antike unt Abendland* 40: 109–124.
Bellandi, F. 2003. "Ad Inferias: Ilc. 101 di Catullo fra Meleagro e Foscolo." *Materiali e Discussioni Per L'analisi dei Testi Classici* 51: 65–134.
Borges, J. 1962. "A New Refutation of Time." (J. Irby, Trans.). In J. Irby and D. Yates (eds.) *Labyrinths: Selected Stories and Other Writings*. New York: New Directions.
Bostick, D. 2019. "*Forsan et Haec Olim Meminisse Iuvabit:* Will Remembering Help or Please?" *Medium*, April 1. https://medium.com/in-medias-res/forsan-et-haec-olim-meminisse-iuvabit-will-remembering-help-or-please-d631c8829886.
Caruth, Cathy. 1996. *Unclaimed Experience: Trauma, Narrative, and History*. Baltimore: Johns Hopkins University Press.
Cvetkovich, A. 2003. *An Archive of Feelings: Trauma, Sexuality, and Lesbian Public Cultures*. Raleigh: Duke University Press.
Donn, Katharina. 2017. *A Poetics of Trauma After 9/11: Representing Trauma in a Digitized Present*. New York: Routledge.
Erikson, E. 1968. *Identity Youth and Crisis*. New York: W.W. Norton & Co.
Erikson, K. 1976/2004. *Everything in Its Path: Destruction of Community in the Buffalo Creek Flood*. New York: Simon and Schuster.
Feeney, D. 2007. *Caesar's Calendar: Ancient Time and the Beginnings of History*. Berkeley: University of California.
———. 2007. *Caesar's Calendar: Ancient Time and the Beginnings of History*. Berkeley, CA: University of California.

Fordham Law News. 2016. "Raising Funds for Friends." May 31. Accessed June 9, 2021. https://news.law.fordham.edu/blog/2016/05/31/2016-friendraiser/.

Forter, G. 2011. *Melancholy Manhood: Gender, Race, and the Inability to Mourn in American Literary Modernism*. Cambridge: Cambridge University Press.

Fourcade, Jacques. 1979. "*Dolor Catullianus* (II)." *Pallas* 26: 77–102.

Frankl, V. 1959/2006. *Man's Search for Meaning*. Boston: Beacon Press.

Gilmoor, A., et al. 2020. "'If Somebody Could Just Understand What I Am Going Through, It Would Make All the Difference': Conceptualizations of Trauma in Homeless Populations Experiencing Severe Mental Illness." *Transcultural Psychiatry* 57: 461–7.

Gurval, R. 1995. *Actium and Augustus: The Politics of Emotions of Civil War*. Ann Arbor: University of Michigan Press.

Herman, J. 2015. *Trauma and Recovery: The Aftermath of Violence—From Domestic Abuse to Political Power*. New York: Basic Books.

Hinton, D.E. 2021. "Auditory Hallucination Among Traumatized Cambodian Refugees: PTSD Association and Biocultural Shaping." *Culture, Medicine and Psychiatry* (January 1): 1–24.

Hirsch, I. 2003. "Reflections on Clinical Issues in the Context of the National Trauma of September 11." *Contemporary Psychoanalysis* 4: 665–81.

Hirschberger, G. 2018. "Collective Trauma and the Social Construction of Meaning." *Frontiers in Psychology* 9, 1441 (August 10).

Holman, Alison, and Emma Grisham. 2020. "When Time Falls Apart: The Public Health Implications of Distorted Time Perception in the Age of COVID-19." *Psychological Trauma* 12: S63–5.

Iparraguirre, G. 2016. "Time, Temporality, and Cultural Rhythmics: An Anthropological Case Study." *Time and Society* 25: 613–33.

Johnson, W.R. 1976. *Darkness Visible: A Study of Vergil's 'Aeneid'*. Chicago: The University of Chicago Press.

Ker, J. 2009. "Drinking from the Water-Clock: Time and Speech in Imperial Rome." *Arethusa* 42: 279–302.

Kwon, H. 2008. *Ghosts of War in Vietnam*. Cambridge: Cambridge University Press.

Kyriakou, P. 1999. "Aeneas' Dream of Hector." *Hermes* 127, 3: 317–27.

LaCapra, D. 2001. *Writing History, Writing Trauma*. Baltimore: Johns Hopkins University Press.

Leys, R. 2000. *Trauma: A Genealogy*. Chicago: University of Chicago Press.

Lyne, R.O.A.M. 1992. "Vergil's 'Aeneid' Subversion by Intertextuality: Catullus 66.39–40 and Other Examples." *Greece & Rome* 41: 187–204.

Mack, S. 1978. *Patterns of Time in Vergil*. Hamden, CT: Shoestring Press.

Marine Corps Community Services. 2016. "Fireworks and PTSD: How to Raise Awareness." Accessed April 25, 2021. https://usmc-mccs.org/articles/fireworks-and-ptsd-how-to-raise-awareness.

Morris, D. 2015. *The Evil Hours: A Biography of Post-Traumatic Stress Disorder*. New York: Houghton-Mifflin Harcourt.

Napa, C. 2010. "Catullus and Vergil." In M. Skinner (ed.) *A Companion to Catullus*. New York: Wiley. 377–398.

Nowotny, H. 1992. "Time and Social Theory: Towards a Social Theory of Time." *Time and Society* 1: 421–54.

O'Hara, J. 1994. "Temporal Distortions, 'Fatal' Ambiguity, and *Iulius Caesar* at *Aeneid* 1.286–96." *Symbolae Osloenses* 64: 72–82.

Orlin, E. 2008. "Octavian and Egyptian Cults: Redrawing the Boundaries of Romanness." *The American Journal of Philology* 129: 231–53.
Panoussi, V. 2020. "Combat Trauma in Vergil's Aeneid." In A. Karanika and V. Panoussi (eds.) *Emotional Trauma in Greece and Rome: Representations and Reactions*. New York: Routledge. 30–46.
Paul, N., Banerjee, M., and Efferth, T. 2015. "Life Sciences—Life Writing: PTSD as a Transdisciplinary Entity between Biomedical Explanation and Lived Experience." *Humanities* 5, 1 (December 30): 1–19.
Pöschl, V. 1962. *The Art of the Aeneid*. Translated by G. Seligson. Ann Arbor: University of Michigan Press.
Putnam, Michael. 2016. "The Sense of Two Endings: How Virgil and Statius Conclude." *Illinois Classical Studies* 41: 85–149.
Rappaport, H., Enrich, K., and Wilson, A. 1985. "Relation between Ego Identity and Temporal Perspective." *Journal of Personality and Social Psychology* 48, 6: 1609–20.
Reed, J.D. 2007. *Vergil's Gaze*. Princeton: Princeton University Press.
Rosen, R. 2004. "Ancient Time Across Time." In R. Rosen (ed.) *Time and Temporality in the Ancient World*. Philadelphia: University of Pennsylvania Museum of Archaeology and Anthropology. 1–11.
Sareen J., et al. 2007. "Physical and Mental Comorbidity, Disability, and Suicidal Behavior Associated with Posttraumatic Stress Disorder in a Large Community Sample." *Psychosomatic Medicine* 69: 242–8.
Schiesaro, A. 2015. "Emotions and Memory in Vergil's Aeneid." *Bulletin of the Institute of Classical Studies. Supplement* 125: 163–76. Accessed February 20, 2021. www.jstor.org/stable/44216714.
Sebold, A. 1999. *Lucky*. New York: Scribner.
Seider, A. 2013. *Memory in Vergil's Aeneid*. Cambridge: Cambridge University Press.
———. 2016. "Catullan Myths: Gender, Mourning, and the Death of a Brother." *Classical Antiquity* 35: 279–314.
Simko, C. 2020. "Marking Time Memorials and Museums of Terror: Temporality and Cultural Trauma." *Sociological Theory* 38: 51–77.
Stefanovics, E., Potenza, M., and Pietrzak, R. 2020. "PTSD and Obesity in U.S. Military Veterans: Prevalence, Health Burden, and Suicidality." *Psychiatry Research* 291.
Stegmaier, W. 2016. "Nietzsche's Orientation Toward the Future." *Journal of Nietzsche Studies* 47, 3: 384–401.
Stolorow, R. 1999. "The Phenomenology of Trauma and the Absolutisms of Everyday Life: A Personal Journey." *Psychoanalytic Psychology* 16: 464–8.
———. 2015. "A Phenomenological-Contextual, Existential, and Ethical Perspective on Emotional Trauma." *The Psychoanalytic Review* 102: 123–38.
Sugar, M. 2019. "The Shadows of Trauma: Ghosts and Guilt in Vergil's *Aeneid* 2." *Acta Classica* 62: 172–90.
Summerfield, D. 2004. "Cross-Cultural Perspectives on the Medicalization of Human Suffering." In G.M. Rosen (ed.) *Posttraumatic Stress Disorder: Issues and Controversies*. Hoboken, NJ: John Wiley and Sons. 233–45.
Sztompka, P. 2004. "The Trauma of Social Change: A Case of Postcommunist Societies." In J. Alexander (ed.) *Cultural Trauma and Collective Identity*. Berkeley: University of California.
Tarrant, R. 1982. "Aeneas and the Gates of Sleep." *Classical Philology* 77: 51–5.
Toll, C. 1997. "Making Roman-ness and the 'Aeneid'." *Classical Antiquity* 16: 34–56.

Visser, I. 2011. "Trauma Theory and Postcolonial Literary Studies." *Journal of Postcolonial Writing* 47: 270–82.

Wallace-Hadrill, A. 1987. "Time for Augustus: Ovid, Augustus, and the *Fasti*." In *Homo Viator: Classical Essays for John Bramble*. Oak Park, IL: Bolchazy-Carducci.

Wearne, D., et al. 2020. "Exploring the Relationship Between Auditory Hallucinations, Trauma, and Dissociation." *BJPsych Open* 6: E54.

Westendorp Boerma, R.E.H. 1958. "Vergil's Debt to Catullus." *Acta Classica* 1: 51–63.

Wilde, O. 1998/1893. *Lady Windermere's Fan*. Mineola, NY: Dover Publications.

Wittmann, M. 2016. *Felt Time: The Psychology of How We Perceive Time*. Translated by E. Butler. Cambridge, MA and London: MIT Press.

Zerubavel, E. 1993. *The Fine Line: Making Distinctions in Everyday Life*. Chicago: University of Chicago Press.

———. 1998. "Language and Memory: 'Pre-Columbian' America and the Social Logic of Periodization." *Social Research* 65: 315–30.

———. 2003. *Time Maps*. Chicago: University of Chicago Press.

Zimbardo, P.G., and Boyd, J.N. 1999. "Putting Time in Perspective: A Valid, Reliable Individual-Differences Metric." *Journal of Personality and Social Psychology* 77: 1271–88.

Zimbardo, P. G., Sword, R., and Sword R. 2012. *The Time Cure: Overcoming PTSD with the New Psychology of Time Perspective Therapy*. San Francisco: Jossey-Bass.

10 Dislocated identities

The *Aeneid* and the Syrian refugee crisis

Nancy Ciccone

War breeds traumatic events, compelling people to forgo all that they have known. Their experiences transform their identity. Abandoning homes, they leave behind material possessions, professional status, and sometimes family members. Whereas cultural trauma changes a group's consciousness, memories, and future identities,[1] individuals suffer trauma "as an event that shatters one's assumptive world, sense of self, and well-being."[2] As a foundational epic for the European West, the *Aeneid* offers a hero who becomes a war refugee. His reactions to unforeseen circumstances resonate with contemporary people. Today, Syrians fleeing their homeland undergo a crisis that extends back to ancient communities also made fugitive by war. In fact, parts of Trojan and Syrian migrations even overlap geographically. Although separated temporally and culturally, Aeneas' story and Syrian refugee testimonies illuminate each other.

While it may seem outrageous to investigate a fictional refugee in tandem with the suffering of actual people, all of their stories (fictional and factual) highlight strategies for survival. Reading Vergil's *Aeneid* alongside current studies in the disciplines of political science and psychological therapy underscores the endemic transformation of identity for all refugees. Vergil's narrative strategies complement testimonies in current case studies and interviews with Syrians. In addition, applying Cathy Caruth's literary theories to the *Aeneid* contributes insights into the ineffable aspects of trauma. Seeking safety and a home, Trojan and Syrian refugee migrations effectively entail remaking themselves. Their narratives enable a transition toward self-identification, even as they catalog loss.

Becoming a refugee first involves the decision to leave home. As the Greeks ravage Troy, the mutilated and dead hero Hector appears to Aeneas in a dream and tells him to flee (2.288–95). Aeneas does the opposite. He arms himself and joins the fray. In the middle of the carnage, his goddess mother stays his hand, reveals Troy's doom, and, echoing Hector, tells him to leave. Returning home, Aeneas eventually convinces his family to abandon Troy. In flight from the burning city, he shoulders his father and grasps his son's hand. This iconic image, indicating the past and future of Aeneas' family, also highlights his new responsibility for what he leaves behind and for the band of Trojans he will lead. Yet Aeneas' job is that of a warrior. As an epic hero, he is bound to fight, to protect his family and city, and he tries to do so until something stronger than he is, his mother, stops him. He

DOI: 10.4324/9781003176145-14

cannot do what he wants. He leaves despite his desire to remain, a desire entailed in his identity as a Trojan warrior.

Aeneas' reluctance to leave home is echoed in a case study conducted in Turkey by psychiatrist Barkil-Oteo and others.[3] In her refugee camp, the Syrian known as 'Ms. A' recounts the moment when she knew she had to leave her home. Although she had seen barrel bombs destroying her neighborhood, although she had seen dead bodies in the street and had known many people either tortured or disappeared, she stayed put until she saw a bomb hit her neighbor's house with the family still inside. Only then did she take her two children and flee. Like Aeneas, she forgoes that part of herself rooted in her location; she becomes responsible for the future of her family and the memories of their homeland. Ms. A moves to a refugee camp in Turkey, where Troy and Thrace, the first stop for Aeneas and his band of refugees, are thought to have been located. Like many modern Syrians, Aeneas seeks a nearby haven for safety, a Thracian people known for their friendliness to Trojans. Escaping the burning city in darkness, Aeneas' choice is practical. Yet it also indicates the familiar, the impulse to remain close to home. Unfortunately, he uncovers the remains of the last survivor of the Trojan royal line, who has been murdered by the Thracian king (3.19–68). Aeneas' discovery forces the Trojans farther from Troy. Ms. A's experience forces her across a national border.

The ongoing battles in Syria do not have the finality of a burning Troy, with the result that Syrian migrations occurred in waves.[4] At first, the majority relocated internally. Just as Aeneas tried to do, some refugees sought homes within the region but away from the fighting. Others stayed with relatives in nearby countries. Culturally and geographically connected to their homeland, both groups planned to return after their displacement. In interviews with Syrians in Turkey's refugee camps, Kristen Fabbe found that only 10% hoped to migrate to Europe; their first choice was to return to Syria, and their second was to remain in the neighboring countries.[5] For Aeneas, as for many Syrians, the return home becomes unfeasible. Those Syrian refugees living outside of camps in neighboring countries face other serious practical obstacles comparable to the Trojans' reception in Thrace. Although Syrians do not find a dead body, they deal with the "limitation of physical capacity and human resources in healthcare facilities, language and cultural barriers, the cost of transportation to facilities."[6] Those seeking safety within Turkish camps find their situation equally inadequate. According to Cantekin's interviews, they confront a host of insecurities in addition to the loss of family, home, and social networks:

> A considerable number of participants mentioned the difficulties concerning physiological and safety needs, such as unmet needs for non-food items, insufficient shelter, lack of privacy, intense feelings of fear and distress due to the proximity of the camps to the border. In particular, the camp location creates continuous levels of feelings of danger and fear amongst participants.[7]

Such recorded difficulties from the modern era highlight challenges Aeneas and his refugees endured as they sought a home. Temporary locations challenge security and safety.

In addition to practical challenges, Pearlman found that becoming a refugee involves a process of self-identification.[8] Several considerations determine the point at which people adopt that status. Circumstances change. News of increasing devastation, for example, demands a reassessment of the possibility of returning home. Pearlman reports on an international student whose revoked visa forced his decision as to whether or not to become a refugee.[9] Emigrating to Scandinavia, another Syrian roots his refugee status in self-recognition. Elaborating on the process, he advises: "forget who you used to be."[10] He then revises his statement, telling Syrians to remember the past but not to dwell on "past status, reputation, accomplishments, possessions. You are starting a new page . . . the page is not totally blank, but it's almost blank."[11] Some, however, reject the label of refugee altogether. Due to the negative connotations associated with the term, one Syrian insisted 'refugee' applies to a situation and not to a person.[12] Yet the rejection of the term paradoxically underlines the need for a person to find the resiliency to survive the trauma of war and displacement: labels and categories by themselves do not help. The loss of home stems from practical necessity, but the status of refugee evolves from an internalized realization no matter its name.

Unlike the Syrian examples, Aeneas does not need to identify his legal status. Troy is utterly gone. The Trojan diaspora consists of survivors who escaped and of those the Greeks captured as slaves. Vergil presents an emotional process for Aeneas similar to that of many Syrians. From the first lines of the *Aeneid*, we learn that his "fate / had made him fugitive" (*fato profugus*, 1.2).[13] But only when he sees a depiction of Trojans fighting Greeks does he seemingly realize the loss of his homeland resulting from the war, the *lacrimae rerum* (1.462), the "tears for passing things."[14] He recognizes Troy as "nothing but a picture" (*animum pictura pascit inani*, 1.464).[15] Like the mural, Troy is empty of life. In Turkey at her refugee camp, Ms. A hears news of attacks in her homeland. She seeks out YouTube videos to confirm the destruction. Despite the differences in medium, Ms. A and Aeneas both confront the ephemerality of homes.

Vergil suggests Aeneas' self-fragmentation even before he views the depiction of Troy's destruction. When we first encounter him, he weathers a storm and wishes he had been killed in his homeland "before their fathers' eyes" (*ante ora patrum*, 1.95).[16] In other words, Aeneas identifies with the already dead.[17] Recourse to Odysseus, Vergil's model for the introduction of his hero provides a contrast to underline Aeneas' despair and dislocation. For whereas Homer's hero also finds himself weeping, Odysseus longs for home, for his land, for his family (*Odyssey* 5.81–4). He aims to reclaim the material foundation of his identity, an untenable option for Aeneas. Yet despite their narrative similarities in being introduced as weeping epic heroes, in being victims of circumstances beyond their control, Roman Aeneas substantially differs from Greek Odysseus due to the different cultures informing their characterizations. Aeneas' identity, unlike wily Odysseus, centers on the piety for which he is famous. According to W. S. Anderson, the Roman concept of *pietas* entails duty to the gods, the nation, the family, and finally to oneself.[18] The concept hierarchizes obligation as if competing categories do not exist. For Aeneas, the notion of home is a fantasy. He aims to secure it but does not know where the gods, generally given to enigmatic information and to conflict among themselves, direct him. Vergil subsequently indicates a split in Aeneas' public and private representations once shipwrecked on Carthage. He climbs a crag, hunts for deer, and bolsters the spirits of his compatriots (1.180–207). Although "sick with heavy cares, / he counterfeits hope in his face; his pain is held within, hidden" (*spem vultu simulat, permit altum corde dolorem*, 1.209).[19] Hunting in Carthage further emphasizes his dislocation. He fails to recognize Venus, his mother, until she turns to leave him (1.405–10). Since she is disguised as a huntress, he takes her for Diana (1.329). Challenging his *pietas*, Aeneas' days demand actions in response to the unexpected.

As a refugee, Aeneas needs to rely on internal resources. In telling his story to the United Nations Refugee Agency, a Syrian named Maskoun articulates some of the challenges: "The refugee is a broken person when he arrives in a new country."[20] From an upper middle-class family by American standards, Maskoun makes the journey to Europe and struggles to recover himself. He describes moments characteristic of the refugee's dislocation: "Especially when he finds himself not understanding what's going on around him, not understanding the culture, not able to go outside to buy some bread or drinks. No connections."[21] Whereas Aeneas hunts near Carthage, obtaining necessities eludes Maskoun. Yet both are disoriented in a foreign land. Another refugee reports, "You lose the fact that you used to be a person. . . . I believe [everyone] forced to leave Syria is like us. We can't find ourselves."[22] Whether Trojan or Syrian, the trauma of leaving home couples with the strangeness of a new location. The experience alters the perceptions of mundane activities and of one's self.

While the Syrian Maskoun tirelessly works to learn, to rebuild a "life interrupted," others are less fortunate. Pearlman provides two contrasting examples of Syrians in Germany. A teacher finds he must learn the language and retrain to regain his profession. His job applications in "youth related fields" go unanswered until he finds work in a youth migrant hostel, only to lose that position due to his "performance."[23] Unable to assimilate in a foreign country, he sits at home and loses interest in all activity. In contrast to the teacher, a former doctor begins learning the German language in a refugee camp, volunteers in hospitals, and retrains for certification in his field.[24] A comparison between the teacher and the doctor points to a psychological component in their adjustments. Opportunities fail to present themselves to the teacher. Although unemployment is not his fault, he becomes socially isolated. The former teacher remains dislocated, while the former doctor accesses internal resources. These contemporary examples underscore the struggles affecting individuals in new environments. Adjustment requires fortitude already strained by migration.

Fleeing war, Syrians who decide not to return home need to find a new one. In the Kurdistan region of Iraq, for example, refugees have invested in permanent houses in a UN camp. Relying on cinderblocks and whatever is available, residents spend from $4,000–$7,000 to construct a house.[25] They build a community. In some camps, graffiti indicate the political affiliations of international refugees. Yet despite this investment, despite turning the camp into homes, they live on borrowed land. Sailing around the Mediterranean, the Trojans likewise seek settlement and community. They too build homes. At one point, they settle on Crete, establish the city of Pergamum, and plow the fields until a wasting pestilence and drought drive them back to the sea (3.135–42). Although not living on borrowed land as are those in the UN Kurdistan camp, the Trojans are not where they should be. They mistake Pergamum for home because Apollo's oracle tells them to find the "sons of Dardanus, the land / that gave you birth, the land of your ancestors" (*Dardanidae duri, quae vos a stirpe parentum / prima tulit tellus*, 3.94–5).[26] Anchises, Aeneas' father, directs them to Crete, "cradle of our people" (*gentis cunabula nostrae* 3.105).[27] Anchises, however, indicates the wrong lineage. Aeneas' search for stability depends on figuring out which ancestor the oracle means. Syrians encounter different obstacles. Economic deprivation and ever-changing policies undermine their plans to locate homes more permanent than in a camp.[28] Modern refugees face legal oracles no less inscrutable for them to interpret.

The progress of the journey offers other parallels between Syrians and Trojans. Some Syrians "reported traumatic experiences that occurred not only during the war in their home country, but also in the course of migration and relocation."[29] The journalist Alia Malek reports on a group of Syrians following a Facebook page titled "The Road to Germany: $2400."[30] For these refugees relying on unofficial channels, their journey involves a raft, van, trains, and buses while traveling from Syria to Greece to Macedonia, to Serbia, to Croatia, to Hungary, and finally to arrive in Austria. Along the way, they nearly drown in the Aegean. Each checkpoint presents a close arrest. Each step costs money. Malek's report focuses on Muhanid, who decided to leave Syria after he endured a month of daily beatings in jail due to mistaken identity; upon his release, he constantly feared being kidnapped to fight for the regime that had tortured him. Yet Muhanid agrees to take along a 14-year-old boy abandoned in Turkey by his chaperone. Although the parents pay him, Muhanid's sense of responsibility to the boy compels him to overcome difficulties blocking their passage. Landing in Athens, the group of refugees claim to be migrants, shifting their identity to gain access to Europe since migrants are temporary laborers rather than seekers of permanent asylum. Muhanid and his group are stopped at checkpoints, ushered into holding pens, and rely on their wits to move on. The rules and languages keep changing. At one detention camp in his journey, Muhanid declares, "It is better to die in Syria than to go through this humiliation."[31] His words recall Aeneas' death-wish: he had thought it better to die "before the eyes of his parents," given the chances of surviving his migration.

Malek's report provides insight into the danger in migrations, but equally as significant, it enables his interviewee, Muhanid, to come to terms with his experiences. This process works in much the same way as narrative therapy, a tool in the discipline of psychology and psychiatry to assist refugees. Stories provide a means to make sense of ourselves. In studying trauma victims, a professor of psychiatry, Mardi Horowitz, describes phases of rehabilitation. In phase four of this therapy, he finds:

> As intrusive emotional ideations about the trauma become less intense and the sense of episodic numbing is reduced, the narrative work of trauma evaluation

> leads toward attitude revisions, including new plans for adaptation. A sense of self-competence may gradually be reformed. Enhanced harmony between various self-attitudes may develop.[32]

Horowitz's work indicates the significance of recounting experiences to integrate the parts of one's self that have endured shifting and threatening circumstances. Even as narrations of experience catalog events, the process itself provides a path of adjustment to current situations, in part because the descriptions arise from a different temporal perspective than the trauma of the original experience. Intervening events alter memory, but more importantly, the narrative arises from the point of survival that necessitates a renegotiation of identity.

In Books 2 and 3 of the *Aeneid*, Vergil offers an example of narrative as therapy. Unlike many Syrian refugees in Europe and in camps, Aeneas is welcomed in Carthage and invited to recount his journey (1.753–6). In terms of narrative structure, the interlude of a back-story enables Vergil to explain how Aeneas came to be there after the storm. On another level, however, the events bear witness to the "traumatic experiences" occurring during his migration. Aeneas gathers these events into a single story. After he leaves Pergamum, his household gods reveal his destination to be Italy. Unreliable winds continue to detour him. Buffeted around Mediterranean harbors, Aeneas sometimes finds welcome, and at other times, hostility. As with Muhanid's group crossing Europe, the uncertainty stresses the Trojans' physical and psychological resources. At one harbor, the frightening Harpies, bird-like creatures with the faces of virgins, taloned hands, and disgusting discharge leaking from their bellies, attack the Trojans' food. As the Trojans fight back, the Harpy Celaeno revengefully prophesizes that they will eat their tables (3.255–7). Her words terrify the Trojans (3.259–60). They will later discover a benign meaning in the Harpy's words (7.116–9), but this surreal moment emphasizes the horror of being in a situation beyond their control and comprehension. An even more devastating incident resulting from a new location occurs once the Trojans are in Italy. Aeneas' son, Ascanius, slays a deer beloved of the Latium natives. He is ignorant of local customs. His routine activity of hunting incites the farmers to join in battle against the Trojans (7.475–510). Unwittingly, Ascanius provokes warfare.

Yet migrations also include reunion. The Trojans come across their compatriots, recently released from slavery and trying to rebuild their homeland in a foreign land (3.294–355). They hope to capture what has been lost. But the past cannot be reconstructed; this "Toy Troy" is a shadow of its original.[33] Comparable to the listless Syrian teacher, this group of Trojans are unable to move on. After a brief respite, Aeneas leaves them. The sea then tosses the Trojans to another harbor, home to the Cyclops (3.618–29). Their tendency to eat humans leads Aeneas to take on board a Greek abandoned by his compatriots (3.666–8). In picking up a refugee who is a Trojan enemy, Aeneas indicates to his Carthaginian audience that he retains his humanity in an inhumane world. He opts for mercy and civilization over the caves of the Cyclops. Like Muhanid with the boy in his care, Aeneas demonstrates responsibility for strangers.

Given the ineffableness of trauma, Aeneas' words alone fail to capture the experiences the Carthaginians invite him to tell. As a literary theorist, Caruth questions such narrations:

> Is trauma the encounter with death, or the ongoing experience of having survived it? At the core of these stories, I would suggest, is thus a kind of double telling, the oscillation between a crisis *of death* and a correlative *crisis of life:* between the story of the unbearable nature of an event and the story of the unbearable nature of its survival.[34]

According to Caruth, such stories entail a double-edged sword: the grief of loss and, with it, the cost of endurance. Yet revealing his escape from Troy, the loss of his wife, the death of his father enable Aeneas to integrate parts of himself into the single moment of storytelling before witnesses. It validates him and forces his traumatic experiences into a semblance of coherence. It personalizes the experiences, allowing him to own them, to become the main character in his own life. His welcome at Carthage and the narration of events allow Aeneas to settle in: "At last, he ended here, was silent, rested" (*conticuit tandem factoque hic fine quievit*, 3.718).[35]

Still, Aeneas is not where he needs to be. In addition to divine direction forcing him to Italy, rumor of his liaison with the queen has already surfaced among the Carthaginians. They resent Aeneas' intrusion because he is a Trojan, not a native; they see their nation neglected and heading toward ruin (4.113–8; 4.250–7). Their prejudice parallels that of some inhabitants of modern nations toward the Syrian refugees. Interviewing refugees in Germany, Pearlman quotes a man from Aleppo who reports that they are "blamed for everything": increased rents, overpopulation, rising crime; the media casts refugees as "lazy consumers of state welfare," "anti-Semites or religious fundamentalists bent on Islamizing Europe."[36] After the Paris terrorist attacks of November 13, 2015, the US governors rejected Syrian Muslim refugees and labeled them as "villains."[37]

Maskoun's interview aims to change narratives in the media. Asylum in France enabled him to pursue a master's degree, tutor fellow classmates, teach refugee children, and organize study in all things French for newcomers. His interview showcases his contributions to his new home to counter the negative stereotype. As in Aeneas' storytelling, the interview allows Maskoun to recount the events cataloging his survival. The process encourages the integration of his transformed identity. While he aims to focus on his contributions to combat prejudice, his interview also provides an antidote for other refugees' internalization of discriminatory bias assaulting their already fragile identities.

Furthermore, stories shared within the refugee community confirm for each other the 'what' of what happened to create social identity around their survival. In their essay on the Middle East conflict, Pace and Bilgic suggest that the shaping of "habitual memory" becomes "institutionalized in time, and constitutive of the group's identity."[38] Their work suggests shared narratives of experience eventually constitute 'the story' of survival. Individual narratives reinforce and merge with each other to put boundaries around trauma. However dislocated the people, the narrative itself establishes them in a community. In the same way, the *Aeneid* formulates a cultural history and a shared identity for Roman survivors of their civil war.[39]

Another example, from Barkil-Oteo's Turkish case study of narrative as therapy, shows similar outcomes to that of Aeneas' "resting" in Carthage. Going about her daily activities in her refugee camp, Ms. A suffers fainting spells.[40] They suggest the effects of trauma, which frequently presents as "uncontrolled repetitive occurrences of hallucinations and other intrusive phenomena."[41] Considering her symptoms physiological, she resists 'talk therapy' on the grounds that "We are all depressed, wouldn't you feel depressed if you lost everything?"[42] She attributes her anxiety to an uncertain future rooted in practical problems: an estranged husband in Germany and economic hardship in the camp. Recounting her life in Syria, she claims "others have seen worse things, I should not complain."[43] Yet narrating the events of her trauma uncovered the trigger for her fainting spells. They resulted from hearing news from home and keeping in touch with family members. Her reaction suggests that reconnecting with the life left behind upset her psychological balance. Narrative therapy revealed the connection and enabled her to consider her present situation and to display a range of emotions other than depression and terror.[44] Although her fainting spells had seemed disconnected from daily activities, the telling of her story modified Ms. A's physiological symptoms and reinvigorated her resiliency. Her "intrusive phenomena" quieted.

Aeneas' trauma manifest differently from that of Ms. A. He suffers from hallucinatory dreams and divine visitations. Aeneas considers himself unfortunate, victimized by circumstances and by events beginning with the loss of his homeland. As do many refugees, Aeneas justifies his actions by referring to future generations. He secures a home not for himself but for his son. Aeneas' advice echoes that of the Syrian refugee in Scandinavia "to remember the past, but not to dwell on it."

Aeneas battles his way to establish a homeland for the Trojans, but at the epic's conclusion, *pius* Aeneas brutally kills Turnus. Hesitating with his sword, he asks Turnus, "How can you who wear the spoils of my / dear comrade now escape me? It is Pallas / who strikes, who sacrifices you, who takes / this payment from your shameless blood" (*tune hinc spoliis indute meorum / eripiare mihi? Pallas te hoc vulnere, Pallas / immolat et poenam scelerato ex sanguine sumit*, 12.947–9).[45] The conclusion to the epic has produced controversy among scholars.[46] Interpretation of the moral implications of Aeneas' action reaches back to the 4th century, with Servius's commentary.[47] Aeneas has reasons for killing Turnus: he has instigated this chaos, and his survival might resurrect his resentment and rage, leading to additional warfare. Nonetheless, Aeneas hesitates. Turnus wears the spoils of Pallas, whose father entrusted him to Aeneas' guardianship. For Aeneas, Pallas is a surrogate son, and Turnus killed him in battle. Yet what has happened to the mercy Aeneas demonstrated when he rescued the Greek from the Cyclops? Although archaic heroes, most notably Achilles, kill out of revenge, Aeneas' action muddies the concept of the valor he had claimed in advising his son. His action also raises the question of how such slaying fits into the hierarchy of obligations and responsibilities entailed in *pietas*. Has his famous self-control been shattered or is it intact? As others have pointed out, Vergil's Latin suggests Aeneas moves from despair in being shipwrecked at Carthage to triumph over his despair. After all, he wins the battle. Indicating fear, the phrase *frigore membra*, cold limbs, that first described Aeneas in the storm of Book 1 (1.92) also describes Turnus's death in Book 12 (12.951).[48] According to this reading, Turnus switches places with Aeneas, whose limbs are heated by revenge. Yet the last lines reveal Turnus's "life, resentful, fled to Shades below" (*vitaque cum gemitu fugit indignata sub umbras*, 12.952).[49] In short, Vergil still ends the epic focusing on Turnus's final moments rather than on Aeneas' triumph.

Pallas's belt prompts Aeneas' killing of Turnus. The ethical implications of his action exceed the moment because they comment on the effects of trauma. Interpreting one of Lacan's commentaries on Freud, Caruth suggests "that the shock of traumatic sight reveals at the heart of human subjectivity not so much an epistemological, but rather what can be defined as an *ethical* relation to the real."[50] Her insight, applied to Aeneas, reinforces the collapse of his ethical integrity because reason, the "epistemological," fails to account for his actions. The sight of Pallas's belt causes Aeneas to misconstrue the reality that Turnus is already defeated and does not need to die. Aeneas seemingly acts from the psychological burden of survival. Allowing for the multiple interpretations of Vergil's conclusion, Aeneas' final words punctuate his dislocation: his experiences as a refugee culminate in the claim that his hand belongs to someone else, as if he has forfeited his previous identity.

Vergil's narrative suggests Aeneas' failure to integrate parts of himself. According to Horowitz:

> Traumatic events often lead to a sense of self with traits of incompetence, inferiority, degradation, depersonalization, or identity diffusion. By facilitating narrative structures about new aspects of the self and how existing self-schemas are harmonized, clinicians can help patients master symptoms, improve their emotional regulation, and achieve a sense of posttraumatic growth in identity and relationship capacities.[51]

To some degree, Horowitz touts the benefits of a profession unavailable to many populations. Yet the *Aeneid* suggests that even the telling of events offers an alternative to skilled counseling because it forces awareness. Following the work of psychologists Tracy and Robins, Michell Sugar has argued that feelings of guilt begin the process of narrating one's trauma because "it involves a series of cognitive and evaluative judgments that compel the experiencer to undergo an internal assessment of the 'self.'"[52] According to Sugar, Aeneas' frequent visions of ghosts demonstrate his sense of guilt. In effect, narrative as therapy enables some aspects of self-reflection already half-realized by guilt. Yet Aeneas' guilt remains unresolved. The last six books of the *Aeneid* illustrate a consequence of not making "sense of self." At best, Aeneas' final words and deeds illustrate Horowitz's "identity diffusion." In summary, the war calls Aeneas to immediate action. Hoisting his battle gear, he mirrors his response to the assault on Troy. However, he no longer defends his homeland: he now fights for a murky future. In Italy, the friendly King Evander provides a history of the Arcadians and a tour of the landscape (8.306–69), but no one asks Aeneas to tell his story, even if only to approximate its ineffability. Hence, Aeneas is disconnected; he struggles to marshal an identity, changed by his experiences, that "fits" with his location.

Syrians do not encounter a civil war when they arrive in a new country. Yet the prejudices many face create an atmosphere of hostility. Some confront a dislocation similar to that of Aeneas. His brutal slaying of Turnus, however understandable a response, illustrates a violent outlet to the unresolved conflict within himself. The episode points to the need for infrastructures to support modern refugees and for mediation between the native population and the newcomers to mitigate a cycle of resentments. Contemporary refugees require social, economic, and health supports. Their relocation, as strangers in a strange land, breeds frustration and adds to previous trauma, fracturing already dislocated identities. Aeneas' brutal slaying of Turnus also suggests unseen repercussions for ethical integrity. Trauma sets refugees adrift not only in practical terms but in their need to reframe understanding of themselves. The stress of survival may encourage the projection of unresolved conflict onto others and lead to irreparable harm.

At a time when higher education turns away from the humanities and toward science technologies, the *Aeneid*, as a cornerstone of Western epic, offers insights into surviving the unspeakable. One of the many enduring aspects of the *Aeneid* stems not from the details but from Aeneas' experiences of competing demands and uncontrollable disasters, experiences that challenge his identity. Yet at another remove, the *Aeneid* offers a paradigm and a warning to those who need to remake themselves. In Carthage, Aeneas tells the story of his experiences from his current perspective. He models ways to integrate a past with a present. In so doing, the epic itself offers narrative as therapy. At its conclusion, however, it also implies a cost for the failure to begin the healing of a dislocation that results from persistent trauma.

The adage 'winning is a lot like losing' captures the paradox embedded in the refugee's search for a new home but also an emotional reality for Trojans and Syrians. Perhaps unimaginable for native populations, the refugees' survival stands on a loss that frequently overwhelms the present. In "The Dry Salvages," T.S. Eliot writes, "That time is no healer: the patient is no longer here."[53] This raises a question: are the patients no longer here because they did not survive, given the vicissitudes of fortune, or are the patients no longer here because survival requires forging new identities? Despite all he endures, the character of Aeneas survives his migration to disprove the former interpretation while his alienation and fragmentation support the latter. It is, of course, the narrative of the *Aeneid* that enabled a fictional refugee, Aeneas, to overcome the eroding force of time. It is also, perhaps, narrative that will enable modern refugees to overcome the imploding force of dislocation.

Notes

1 Alexander 2004: 1.
2 Nagata, Kim, and Nguyen 2015: 357. Here they follow Caruth 1995.
3 Barkil-Oteo et al. 2018: 8.
4 For additional information, see Alhayek 2016: 10–1; Davis 2015: 65–76.
5 Fabbe 2018: 257.
6 Bilecen and Yurtseven 2018, quoted in Cantekin 2019: 202.
7 Cantekin 2019: 211–2.
8 Pearlman 2018.
9 Pearlman 2018: 304.
10 Pearlman 2018: 304.
11 Pearlman 2018: 304–5.
12 Pearlman 2018: 309.
13 Translated in Mandelbaum 2004: 1.1–2.
14 Translated in Mandelbaum 2004: 1.655.
15 Translated in Mandelbaum 2004: 1.659.
16 Translated in Mandelbaum 2004: 1.134.
17 For the significance of the phrase of dying "before their fathers' eyes" (1.95), see O'Sullivan 2009.
18 Anderson 1969: 21.
19 Translated in Mandelbaum 2004: 1.290–1.
20 Maskoun.
21 Maskoun.
22 Pearlman 2016: 30.
23 Pearlman 2018: 305–6.
24 Pearlman 2018: 306.
25 Hayes 2018: 90.
26 Translated in Mandelbaum 2004: 3.125–6.
27 Translated in Mandelbaum 2004: 3.139.
28 See, for example, Rygiel, Baban, and Ilcan 2016; Orchard and Miller 2014.
29 Barkil-Oteo et al. 2018: 316.
30 Malek, Van Agtmael, and Newfeld 2016: 40.
31 Malek, Van Agtmael, and Newfeld 2016: 49.
32 Horowitz 2015: 191.
33 Anderson 1969: 41.
34 Caruth 1996: 7.
35 Translated in Mandelbaum 2004: 3.931.
36 Pearlman 2018: 308.
37 Pope 2017: 55.
38 Michelle and Bilgic 2018: 508.
39 For readings of the *Aeneid* as a means to promote Augustan unity following the civil war, see, for example, Pogorzelski 2009; Wimperis 2020.
40 Barkil-Oteo et al. 2018.
41 Caruth 1996: 11.
42 Barkil-Oteo et al. 2018: 8.
43 Barkil-Oteo et al. 2018: 8.
44 Barkil-Oteo et al. 2018: 9.
45 Translated in Mandelbaum 2004: 12.1265–8.
46 Much has been written on the conclusion of *Aeneid*. For a recent overview and interpretation, see Putnam 2011.
47 Tarrant 2004: 117.
48 See for example, Mader 2015: 509; Quint 2011: 68–72.
49 Translated in Mandelbaum 2004: 12.1271.

50 Caruth 1991: 92.
51 Horowitz 2015: 193.
52 Sugar 2019: 173.
53 Eliot 1968: l. 3.8.

References

Alexander, J.C. 2004. "Toward a Theory of Cultural Trauma." In P. Sztompka, N.J. Smelser, B. Giesen, E. Eyerman, and J.C. Alexander (eds.) *Cultural Trauma and Collective Identity*. Berkeley, CA: University of California Press. 1–30.

Alhayek, K. 2016. "Syrian Refugees in the Media." *Middle East Report* 278: 10–11.

Anderson, W.S. 1969. *Art of the Aeneid*. Englewood Cliffs, NJ: Prentice-Hall.

Barkil-Oteo, A., Abdallah, W., Mourra, S., and Jeffee-Bahlou, H. 2018. "Trauma and Resiliency: A Tale of a Syrian Refugee." *American Journal of Psychiatry* 175, 1: 8–12.

Bilecen, B., and Yurtseven, D. 2018. "Temporarily Protected Syrians' Access to the Healthcare System in Turkey: Changing Policies and Remaining Challenges." *Migration Letters* 15, 1: 113–24.

Cantekin, D. 2019. "Syrian Refugees Living on the Edge: Policy and Practice Implications for Mental Health and Psychosocial Wellbeing." *International Migration* 57, 2: 200–20.

Caruth, C. 1991. "Unclaimed Experience: Trauma and the Possibility of History." *Yale French Studies* 79: 181–92.

———. 1995. "Recapturing the Past: Introduction." In C. Caruth (ed.) *Trauma: Explorations in Memory*. Baltimore, MD: Johns Hopkins University Press.

———. 1996. *Unclaimed Experience: Trauma, Narrative, and History*. Baltimore, MD: Johns Hopkins University Press.

Davis, R. 2015. *Syria's Refugee Crisis*. New York: Foreign Policy Association.

Eliot, T.S. 1968. *Four Quartets*. Boston: Mariner Books.

Fabbe, K. 2018. "Reflections on the Geopolitics of Refugees and Displaced Persons." *Review of Middle East Studies* 52, 2: 249–62.

Hayes, J.C. 2018. "Upon the Walls of the UN Camp: Situated Intersectionality, Trajectories of Belonging, and Built Environment Among Syrian Refugees in the Kurdistan Region of Iraq." *The Journal of Intersectionality* 2, 2: 59–102.

Horowitz, M.J. 2015. "Effects of Trauma on Sense of Self." *Journal of Loss and Trauma* 20: 189–93.

Mader, G. 2015. "The Final Simile in the *Aeneid*, Mechanics of Warfare and Textual Mechanisms." *Mnemosyne* 68: 588–604.

Malek, A., Van Agtmael, P., and Newfeld, J. 2016. "The Road to Germany: $2400." *Foreign Policy* 216: 38–53.

Mandelbaum, A., tran. 2004. *The Aeneid of Virgil*. Bantam Classic. New York: Bantam Dell.

Maskoun, S. "Refugees Are Not the Crisis. It's the Narrative We Tell about Them." *United Nations Refugee Agency-Innovation Series*. www.unhcr.org/innovation/refugees-are-not-the-crisis-its-the-narratives-we-tell-about-them/.

Michelle, P., and Bilgic, A. 2018. "Trauma, Emotions, and Memory in World Politics: The Case of the European Union's Foreign Policy in the Middle East Conflict." *Political Psychology* 39, 3: 503–17.

Nagata, D.K., Kim, J.H.J., and Nguyen, T.U. 2015. "Processing Cultural Trauma: Intergenerational Effects of the Japanese American Incarceration." *Journal of Social Issues* 71, 2: 356–70.

Orchard, C., and Miller, A. 2014. "Protections in Europe for Refugees from Syria." In *Forced Mirgration Policy Briefing*. Vol. 10. Oxford: Refugee Centre, Oxford University Department of International Development.
O'Sullivan, T. 2009. "Death Ante Ora Parentum in Virgil's *Aeneid*." *Transactions of the American Philological Association* 139: 447–86.
Pearlman, W. 2016. "Narratives of Fear in Syria." *Perspectives on Politics* 14, 1: 20–37.
———. 2018. "Becoming a Refugee." *Review of Middle East Studies* 52, 2: 299–309.
Pogorzelski, R.J. 2009. "Reassurance of Fratricide in the Aeneid." *American Journal of Philology* 130, 2: 261–89.
Pope, P.J. 2017. "Constructing the Refugee as Villain." *World Affairs* 180, 3: 53–71.
Putnam, M.C.J. 2011. *The Humanness of Heroes: Studies in the Conclusion of Virgil's Aeneid*. Amsterdam: Amsterdam University Press.
Quint, D. 2011. "Virgil's Double Cross: Chiasmus and the Aeneid." *American Journal of Philology* 132, 2: 273–300.
Rygiel, K., Baban, F., and Ilcan, S. 2016. "The Syrian Refugee Crises: The EU-Turkey 'Deal' and Temporary Protection." *Global Social Policy* 16, 3: 315–20.
Sugar, M. 2019. "The Shadows of Trauma: Ghosts and Guilt in Vergil's Aeneid." *Acta Classica* 62: 172–90.
Tarrant, R. 2004. "The Last Book of the Aeneid." *Syllecta Classica* 15: 103–29.
Wimperis, T.A. 2020. "Turnus's Tota Italia: Italian Solidarity and Political Rhetoric in Aeneid 7–12." *Transactions of the American Philological Association* 150: 143–79.

11 To know thyself in a world undone

Apocalypse and authenticity in the *Aeneid*

George Saad

Authenticity has been variously described as the radical freedom of the self-creating individual, as the expression of the true self (as opposed to an alienated facsimile), and as the self-responsibility of moral and political autonomy.[1] Rather than privilege one of these descriptions over the others, we should notice the common set of conditions that have enabled all of them to appear as possible articulations of the human experience. The authentic emerges through the apocalyptic, from the sense of a breakdown in the cosmic order that leaves us alone to find ourselves. The realization of the contingency of our historical moment separates us from the social awareness Heidegger termed "the they" (*das Man*) and reconstitutes us as individuals of personal conscience. Historically, modern individualism emerges from a post-Christian cosmology in which "the world" is finite, transitory, and always coming to an end, while human self-consciousness recognizes itself as unlimited and absolute. In Nietzsche's phrase, we stare into the abyss, and the abyss stares back into us.[2] The existential themes of modernity develop out of the problematic relation between the individual and world already established in early modern philosophy. Sean McGrath so describes this broken relation between self and world:

> The Cartesian subject did not find himself in any order, but rather ordered what it recognized as inherently disordered. The implication of this world-generating responsibility is that the subject itself finds itself without a place in the order that it has produced. The power of the Cartesian subject is contingent on its homelessness in the universe.[3]

Authenticity thus proceeds from the experience of ontological alienation. The Heideggerian articulation of authenticity emphasizes that a human being will always be between authenticity and inauthenticity, between the "ruinance" (later, "fallenness") of losing ourselves to an alien world, and the recognition of our potential for authenticity through this very loss.[4] The individual seeking to become her true self is an individual who looks backward to an original state of belonging, in which she did not experience her world as foreign and her person as synthetic. Nonetheless, in striving to redeem a loss that outstrips any possible restoration, we must avoid the instrumental logic of authenticity as a simple "curative" for alienation. The authentic does not present a solution to alienation but a way of coping with an essentially

DOI: 10.4324/9781003176145-15

tragic existential situation. Heidegger found an example of ruinance in ancient Greek tragedy, as it is only in the ruin of a turning-down (*kata-strophe*) that the human being discovers the "uncanny" capacity for authentic being.[5] To take one example, Oedipus, the self-confident destroyer of the Sphinx, discovered his true origin only through a series of self-destructive events. Fully self-responsible for both his transgressions and their punishment, Oedipus, "because of the crimes that he himself detected [*autophōrōn*], smashed both his eyes with self-blinding [*autourgō*] hand" (Soph. *Ant.* 51–2).[6] While we moderns celebrate our autonomy, tragedy posits the fracture of our world as the precondition for our finding ourselves and so recognizes calamities of self-ruin as a paradigm case of self-determination.[7]

Against this horizon of tragic self-ruin, the Greeks recognized our capacity for individuation while regarding it with caution. Christopher Gill describes the traditional Greek sense of the self as operating on an "objective-participant" model, in which "the ethical life of a human being is expressed in whole-hearted engagement with an interpersonal and communal role."[8] When the Delphic oracle bade the Greek to "know thyself [*gnōthi seauton*]," the oracle was generally interpreted as discouraging idiosyncratic deviations from social expectation.[9] It was an encouragement to temperate self-restraint, much like the saying that appeared alongside it, "nothing in excess [*mēden agan*]." This self-knowledge is the recognition of the self as embedded in and limited by the social order, a caution against the unwarranted self-assertion that led Oedipus to ruin. Another tragedy, Aeschylus' *Prometheus Bound*, presents this communitarian interpretation of the Delphic dictum when Oceanus urges Prometheus, his fellow Titan, to give up his headstrong rebellion against Zeus (Aesch. *PV.* 308–10):

> Know your limitations [*gignōske sauton*] and transform your ways to fit the times—for there is a new tyrant [*tyrannos*] among the gods.

Yet despite the conservative intention of this precept, it contains the dialectical seed of the modern interpretation of "know thyself" as "seek out and be true to your own person." The very act of encouraging an individual to harmonize with the social order recognizes their potential for disobedience, that is, their underlying individuality. If Oceanus can advise Prometheus to put down his rebellion, Prometheus already has a personal agency that can either resist or accommodate social limitations. Prometheus's recognition of his limitations does not negate his autonomy but rather confirms the freedom of an effective self-consciousness. As in the key Hegelian insight, only a consciousness unaware of its limitations remains entirely contained within them. When we are self-consciously aware of our limitations, they cease to function as absolute realities and are recognized as only relative barriers (limitations themselves limited).[10] Prometheus may choose to capitulate or to suffer on, but the very choice reveals his own agency as a potential countervailing force to the new Olympian tyranny. The war of the Titans and Olympians has broken the tapestry of social harmony, in which individual choice seamlessly aligns with collective expectation. In this postlapsarian coming to self-consciousness, the two interpretations of the Delphic dictum are dialectically interrelated.

Prometheus can accept or reject his limitations (the ancient communitarian reading of *gnōthi seauton*), but in the self-awareness of this choice he recognizes himself as a free individual actor (the existentialist modern reading of *gnōthi seauton*).

Social discord thus manifests the autonomy of individuals, as collective stability is now shown to be contingent upon their individual participation. Edward Jeremiah furnishes a further example of this phenomenon in the *Iliad.* After Antilochus and Menelaus dispute foul play at Patroclus's funeral games, they self-consciously mark their overtures of reconciliation with the *autos* morpheme (*Il.*23.591–2; *Il.*23.602–3). Each man emphasizes that he speaks on his own behalf, an emphasis on individual agency that becomes both possible and necessary only when interpersonal conflict has fractured social consensus. Jeremiah explains:

> Conflicts must be resolved as individuals, as a negotiation between one self and another, because they represent a breakdown or lacuna, even if it is only temporary, in the system of social regulation. In the absence of an automatic social solution the individual is for a time brought into starker relief and must assume responsibility. This autonomous self is marked with *autos*.[11]

This special recognition of the individual is central to epic heroism. The heroic individual is the individual who assumes the responsibility of self-determination in a crisis of authority. The *Iliad* opens with this assertion of self, as Achilles decides to become a recluse in mutiny, his will set against that of Agamemnon. The strength and independence of the heroic persona challenges failed conventions. The best of the Greeks must set himself against his fellows if he is to challenge a power hierarchy in which his contributions have gone underappreciated.

Greek tragedy and epic did not, however, conceive of a scenario in which the social order entirely passes away and leaves behind a self-sufficient individual. The Promethean figure and the epic hero learn (and thereby transcend) their limitations only through their ruin; they have no *Nachleben* in which they survive the cosmic order against which they struggled. Long underappreciated as a mere shadow of Greek originals, it was *Roman* literature that introduced the modern prospect of a self-sufficient individual radically cut off from their historical society. What I am suggesting here is not that modern individuality was a political or social reality for the Romans but rather that Vergil's *Aeneid,* the representative work of the Roman imagination, first expressed the problem of being an authentic individual in a fundamentally alien social body, a lone survivor after an apocalypse. Vergil's poetry expresses this anxiety of homelessness in the Hellenistic zeitgeist, the insecurity of the individual within a universal state that diminishes the bonds of local historical cultures.[12] Aeneas' lonesome wanderings mark the emergence of what Hegel describes as an abstract individuality, the painful replacement of Greek culture by a bare universality that leaves each alone to their own inner resources:

> In the wave of adversity which came across the Roman world, everything beautiful and noble in spiritual individuality was rudely swept away. In this condition of disunion in the world, when man is driven within his inmost self,

> he has to seek the unity and satisfaction, no longer to be found in the world, in an abstract way. The Roman world is thus the world of abstraction, where one cold rule was extended over all the civilized world. The living individualities of national spirit in the nations have been stifled and killed; a foreign power, as an abstract universal, has pressed hard upon individuals. In such a condition of dismemberment it was necessary to fly to this abstraction as to the thought of an existent subject, that is, to this inward freedom of the subject as such.[13]

The injunction of the Delphic dictum to "know one's limits" rings hollow in a world in which cultural distinction has been dissolved within the infinite empire (*imperium sine fine*) Vergil's Jupiter prophesies in Book 1 (1.279). To those seeking a boundary by which to know and limit the self, the endless empire offers only the loose forms of a world already undone. This apocalyptic world-feeling became the default of Christendom and continues in the secular universalism of modernity, as the abstract principle of market exchange governs a world stripped of the particularizations of historical and interpersonal experience. The United States, heavily inspired by neoclassical ideals at its founding, is just the latest revival of the Roman imagination dating back to the Holy Roman Empire of the 10th century, the latest attempt to find salvation from the travails of history in the formation of an idealized universal state. In the American dream, the authentic emerges from the apocalyptic, as we understand ourselves as both a society of exiles and as a society of rugged individualists. This association is hardly coincidental, as the essential relationship between exile and individuation can already be seen as the existential structure underlying the *Aeneid*—as the human experience that gives rise to empire.

It is looking backward from the present age of exiled individualism that we should read the *Aeneid* as the first expression of this our modern dispensation, of our bittersweet search for authenticity. Vergil introduces his hero Aeneas as a man ripped from his world—"a refugee in his fate" (*profugus fato*, 1.2). Unlike Odysseus, who longs to return to his homeland of Ithaca, Aeneas has only a distant ancestral attachment to Italy (3.147–72).[14] Buffeted by Juno's storm just before his first appearance in the epic, Aeneas can only turn backwards in remembrance, preferring a death witnessed by his elders at Troy to the prospect of an anonymous death at sea (1.92–101). While Aeneas is spared this end, he remains keenly sensitive to the empty nothingness of a wanderer's death. When the Trojans lose their helmsman Palinurus as a sacrifice to Neptune at the end of the fifth book, Aeneas laments that he will lie "naked on an obscure shore" (*nudus in ignota Palinure iacebis harena*, 5.871). The naked corpse is a corpse denuded of the recognition of culture, cut off from burial and communal memory. Stuck between the lost world of Troy and a still insubstantial Roman future, Aeneas is only intimately familiar with his immediate and temporary surroundings, with ships and camps on unfamiliar shores.

This is the existential sense of homelessness from which the *Aeneid* proceeds. Vergil sensed the grandeur of imperial Rome as emerging from a deep personal brokenness, the sort of brokenness Aeneas felt when he tearfully "fed his soul on the empty picture" of the Trojan War in Juno's temple (*animum pictura pascit inani*, 1.464). Art can only restore a pale imitation of a world lost even to those who died with it. The survivors suffer the same erasure of their humanity as the nameless dead, as the end of the city is also the end of their sense of personhood. The socially significant, meaningful individual degenerates into nothing more than a biological specimen. King Priam fought to defend his realm, yet in his soldier's death he shares with Palinurus the same fate of the anonymous corpse. "The proud ruler of Asia" becomes another "body without a name" (*superbum / regnatorem Asiae . . . sine nomine corpus*, 2.556–8). In his death, Priam loses the basic dignity even Achilles granted him when he recognized his foe's rightful claim to his son's body. For the survivor, Troy fades into memory and becomes a mere relic of the imagination. Aeneas' memory of Troy is collapsed into an individual possession and carried along the journey into an alien world, just as Aeneas carried his father and the Penates, the defeated guardians of Troy, out of the flames of Troy (2.707ff.). Relocating a lost world within himself, Aeneas copes with his circumstances in a way that prefigures the development of the interiorizing modern subject.

The events of the epic represent Aeneas' existential journey toward once more being at home in his world. Aeneas' initial narration of his wanderings and the tragedy of Dido capture the existential pain of the *broken self*, a self painfully and unsuccessfully grappling with its autonomy in the wake of social breakdown. The revelations of the underworld and Aeneas' shield mark the awakening of the *visionary self*, the self that has opened itself up to the truth greater than the immediate confusion of its circumstances. As Aeneas receives the "Roman idea" in moments of otherworldly inspiration, he partakes in the idealism Hegel read as the Hellenistic replacement of Greek communal life, the attempt to "recreate the lost harmony in the world of thought and replace the social order with an ideal one."[15] Finally, Aeneas founds this ideal world through a grisly conflict with the real world of Italy, ending the primordial age of Saturn and bringing about the self-consciousness of civilization. As his world falls apart, Aeneas' rival Turnus suffers the same abrupt individualization as his Trojan counterpart. Left alone to his own resources, he attempts to preserve the Italian world as his own, fighting on when all others have quit. Turnus thus represents Aeneas' *mirrored self*, a self reflecting back Aeneas' own struggle to reclaim authenticity from existential brokenness.

The broken self

Aeneas first appears in the epic as a passive victim of fate "tossed about by land and sea" (*terris iactatus et alto*, 1.3). Our hero has no personal presence, no continuous community, and experiences no direct positive association with the divine. Juno, forever remembering Trojan crimes, vengefully derails Aeneas' mission to reach Italy while he laments his distant relationship with his mother Venus, who appears to him only in disguise (1.307–9). Aeneas carries out a destiny that has already been authored by others, written in the scrolls of fate Jupiter reads aloud (1.262). Having wished that he would have died at Troy, his perspective remains graspingly retrospective. He depends upon the (often faulty) guidance of his father, Anchises, to navigate the Mediterranean in the third book, which concludes with his death (3.708–15). When the storm intervenes in the first book, Aeneas has just lost the last source of ancestral wisdom upon which he depends. He now tells Dido the story of a journey unwillingly undertaken to fulfill a destiny to which he has lost his only point of access. Even as he now assumes full responsibility for the survivors, he arrives at Dido's Carthage and presents himself and his men as merely passive survivors, "the leftovers of the Greeks" (*reliquiae Danaum*, 1.30; 1.598).

Dido becomes an anchor for this broken man, offering him succor born out of her own experience of an exile's grief (*non ignara mali miseris succurrere*, 1.630). Aeneas is in no position to turn down her sympathy in pursuit of a distant Italian destiny. Bouncing around the sea in the unfocused pursuit of a world-historical mission,[16] it seems inevitable that Aeneas should find himself in a purely incidental marriage. In Vergil's simile, he is the hunter who wounds his beloved in an accident, *nescius*, "unknowing" of his actions (4.68–73). Even after informing Dido of his plan to leave in a rousing speech, he falls asleep, and Mercury must once more return and rouse him to leave (4.554–8). He commits to Rome as weakly as he initially commits to Dido. Lacking a developed sense of self, the exile is driven by circumstance and incident. Adopting the casual noncommitment of a foreign visitor, Aeneas does not possess the resolute conviction to settle upon any course of action. Aeneas expresses this depersonalized loss of agency in his initial reply to Dido after she has learned of his plans to leave Carthage for Italy. He attempts to justify his actions by disowning them—his life is not his own (that was lost back in Troy), and so he is not responsible for his actions (4.331–44):

> Aeneas held his unshaken gaze on the decrees of Jove and fights his concern for her, pressing it beneath his breast. At last he responds in turn: "I [*ego*] will never deny that you, queen, who are able to list many (worthy) things in your speaking, are well justified in what you say. So long as I am mindful of myself [*memor ipse mei*] . . . it will not pain me to remember Elissa. . . . I [*ego*] did not expect to shroud this departure in secrecy. . . . If the fates would only let me to live my life by my own auspices and to order my affairs authentically [*sua sponte*], I would first tend to the Trojan city and the dear remnants of my people, the lofty walls of Priam would still stand, I would have, by this hand, reestablished a restored Troy for the defeated.

Revealing his self-understanding of his situation, Aeneas shows that he has not internalized his mission, acting only in deference to the wishes of Jove. He does not harmonize his own will with the divine but only executes a demand brusquely posited against his own wishes. Divided against himself, he must struggle against his concern for Dido, pressing it deep beneath his heart (*obnixus curam sub corde premebat*, 4.332). This language recalls Aeneas' repression and public concealment of his grief in the wake of the storm in the first book (*premit altum corde dolorem*, 1.209). His emotions in conflict with the abstract demand of duty, Aeneas speaks with an acute self-consciousness, beginning the speech with the emphatic first-person pronoun (*ego*) and then repeating it. Seeking to honor Dido, he situates her as belonging to an intensively remembering part of himself (*memor ipse mei*) that will endure despite his present actions. Aeneas now regards her as he regards Troy, as belonging to a set of effectively disowned "woulds" he clings to yet cannot fulfill.

Aeneas experiences his own agency as a painful contrast to an alien reality, as what would happen if he could act authentically (*sua sponte*). This sense of self-sufficient action as an unachievable ideal represents the turn from the negative Greek sense of the *authentēs* (the self-doing) as the destroyer of one's own kind—a suicide, family murderer, or tyrant.[17] Here, in the exile's attempt to reclaim a consistent and coherent personhood, we observe the beginning of a philological transition. The horrors of the tragic Greek *authentēs* are, in Edward Jeremiah's description, "sublimated as 'authentic' [and] somehow metamorphosed from designating socially dangerous agency to authenticity as the ambition of modernity and the individual."[18] For the exile Aeneas, self-agency would not imply a destructive stance taken against his world. Left to his own devices, he would restore Troy, where personal will and fate would align.[19]

Under his present circumstances, Aeneas' exile has rendered him unable to take moral ownership of his own actions. He cannot act as a fully invested, responsible person but only as a mere bystander who cannot accept his immediate existential reality. With Dido, his conduct now mirrors the caprice of fate, as he diffidently shuffles along while offering only a casual sympathy to those he hurts. His words are manipulative only insofar as his entire situation has arisen from deception. Sinon buried Troy with his lies (2.57ff.), leaving Aeneas no ground for earnest authenticity. Without Troy, Aeneas does not know what it would mean to honestly represent himself to the world. Knowing the sincere existential confusion underlying Aeneas' misrepresentation of himself, we see that the lies that brought down Troy have in turn made liars of the Trojans, rendering them alien and unrecognizable even to themselves.

Toward the conclusion of the speech to Dido, Aeneas attempts to personalize his Italian destiny (4.345–7; 4.353–9):

> But now Grynian Apollo and the Lycian lots have ordered me to snatch up [*capessere*] great Italy. This is my love [*amor*], this is my country [*patria*]. . . . The troubled ghost of my father Anchises disturbs me in my sleep and reminds me of my son Ascanius and the injustice laid upon his sweet head, whom I now cheat [*fraudo*] out of the kingdom of Hesperia and his destined lands. Now indeed a messenger of the gods sent by Jove himself (I swear this on both our heads) has brought down orders through the swift breezes: I myself [*ipse*] saw the god in plain light entering through the walls, and I clung to his voice with these ears.

Aeneas' depersonalized passivity is overcome by a fresh enthusiasm for a fate he does not understand. We may still question the veracity of this new narrative, as Vergil never narrates these dreams in which Anchises appears. Given the context of the speech, we may wonder if Aeneas is still seeking to persuade himself (as well as Dido) by recognizing his duplicity in the situation (*fraudo*) but identifying Ascanius as the victim of that duplicity in a more personally compelling narrative. But regardless of the unreliability of Aeneas' self-report, it is clear that he still understands nothing of the world-historical significance of his mission. He knows only that he is to snatch up Italy as his own bounty. This is the basic impulse to again have a world of his own, the *amor* of appropriating his own *patria*. Though he himself (*ipse*) excitedly testifies to Mercury's visit, Mercury will have to make a second visit, as the testimony of his own eyes remains only thin proof for Aeneas. Only an imagination invigorated by moments of vivid revelation can rebuild the broken self.

The visionary self

The broken Aeneas is perhaps the Aeneas most familiar to Latin students who have only focused on the start of the epic. *Pius* Aeneas, the man of devotion, gives himself over to a future he will never see toward a destiny dimly understood. Yet Aeneas' personal disengagement is conspicuous and problematic—his new Roman world cannot arise with its founder being dragged along as a reluctant spectator. The fifth book pivots away from the Trojan past as Aeneas holds funeral games for his father, Anchises, and buries his closest tie back to Troy. When the shade of Anchises advises Aeneas to visit him in the underworld via the Cumaean Sibyl, Aeneas reacts to the vanishing apparition with the same sense of betrayal he expressed when his mother Venus appeared to him in disguise (5.741–2).[20] Aeneas can no longer settle for fleeting glimpses of ghosts. He must now have a substantial encounter with his otherworldly parents and recognize, however dimly, the blessings of a future in which even his sufferings will be pleasant to remember (1.203).

His parents finally communicate a full, concrete vision of the Roman future to him at the conclusions of the sixth and eighth books. Anchises shows him the cyclical return of Roman souls in the underworld as a cosmological cycle underlying the enduring, eternal *Roma* Aeneas will inaugurate. Venus prompts her husband Vulcan to craft a shield for Aeneas that depicts the future events of Roman history. No longer constrained by his vanished Trojan point of reference, Aeneas is now presented with a global perspective in which his sufferings constitute a meaningful part of a larger historical whole. He is no longer the chance victim of an external order but a participant in history whose actions will manifest an eternally unfolding Roman idea.

Yet seeing himself in the light of history does not mean that he will fully repair the brokenness of Troy or resolve his confusion about his present circumstances. The broken self is not resolved but rather supplanted by a conviction in a new world. As in the modern ideology of American exceptionalism, the idealized new world represents a radical break with the historical past, a utopia unaffected by the grievous injustices of the old world. In Vergil's historical context, the strife of civil war is recast as a contingent, momentary human experience, the transient veil of an eternal order visible only to the initiated. While these visionary moments are revelatory—they are externally given to Aeneas and remain rationally incomprehensible to him—they come to him from a deeply personal source, from the parents he earlier sought in vain. Moreover, they speak directly to Aeneas as a lost individual and inform his new self-understanding as an historical agent. Though Rome will never exist in his present life, Aeneas grounds himself on the idea that his life is now part of a Roman eternity.

The established pattern of Aeneas lamenting his suddenly vanishing parents is reversed upon Aeneas' initial encounter with Anchises in the underworld. It is Anchises who is elated to see Aeneas and hopes that it may be possible for them to embrace (6.687–9).[21] Aeneas is no longer the one to whom fleeting images appear but is now a significant person in his own right. His longing to embrace his parent is now fulfilled with a bittersweet insubstantiality, as his father's ineffable shade (*imago*) passes through his hands "very much like a winged dream" (*volucrique simillima somno*, 6.700–2). For the living in the world above, this realm of the *imago* appears in *imag*ination, in the stock of impalpable but potent historical forms. In his hapless nostalgia for Troy, Aeneas had closed himself off from the transformative Roman immortality now laid before him. He has been unknowing (*inscius*) of the rebirth of the soul in the ceaseless cycles of an eternally unfolding history (6.711). Anchises's explanation of the transmigration of souls in the sixth book manifests an underlying spiritual reality that enables Aeneas to envision himself *sub specie aeternitatis*. This is not a personal afterlife, as souls drink from the river Lethe and forget their past lives before returning to the world above. Yet knowledge of this continuous community of souls enables the individual to locate himself in his unique historical destiny. The persistent memory of the insubstantial past transforms into the motivating vision of an imagined future. The world-weary Aeneas at first interprets the return of the souls to bodies as "a dread desire for life" (*lucis . . . tam dira cupido*, 6.721). Aeneas enters the underworld while disenchanted, experiencing his material existence as the imprisonment of the soul Anchises describes (*neque auras / dispiciunt clausae tenebris et carcere caeco*, 6.733–4). Yet this momentary capture of the divine seed in matter is the bittersweet source of all "fear and desire, grief and joy" (*hinc metuunt cupiuntque dolent gaudentque*, 6.733). Like the return of the liberated philosopher to Plato's cave (*Rep.* 519d ff.), the soul's reentry into the embodied world ennobles these blind corporeal forces with directed purpose.

The climax of Anchises's speech presents the Roman form of justice as a force operating through history. Addressed for the first time as a Roman, Aeneas learns that the law of his people shall be to "spare the defeated and beat down the proud" (*parcere subiectis et debellare superbos*, 6.853). While he may not recognize the figures of future Roman history parading before him, he can comprehend their movement as the building of an empire upon this principle. This moral imperative speaks directly to the experiences of Aeneas, a defeated refugee who will go on to found an empire. The mission of his life from this point forward can now be summarized as an enduring moral precept.

In extending Roman mercy to the defeated, Aeneas, a mighty man laid low, allows them to be equally reborn as participants in empire. The premodern sense of history as the endless return of recurring general forms morphs into a distinctively modern sense of history as a redemptive personal project. Aeneas is to become the world-historical actor who self-consciously shapes the course of events, acting upon abstract principles of conscience. Not content to merely act within the world, the new Roman hero aims to change it according to his vision of what it should be.

The eighth book concludes with Aeneas receiving a vision of Rome upon a shield sent down to him by his other parent, the goddess Venus. As with the procession of souls in the sixth book, Aeneas does not recognize the scenes of Roman history on his own shield. At the conclusion of the book, Vergil stresses this ignorance of fact as the awakening of imagination in the visionary self (8.729–31):

> Aeneas marvels [*miratur*] at all these things on the shield of Vulcan, the gift of his mother, and, unknowing of these matters [*rerumque ignarus*], he rejoices in their imagination [*imagine gaudet*], taking upon his own shoulder the fame and fate of his descendants.

For the visionary self, imagination trumps fact. When in the first book Aeneas saw the *pictura* of the Trojan war on Juno's temple in Carthage, the hollow image (*pictura inani*) recalls to his mind the all too factual trauma of the represented event, causing him to weep (1.464–5). By contrast, this Roman *imago* represents to him no veridical object or event but a fictive future. The image is presented purely as image and not as a painfully inadequate reflection of concrete reality. In this spirit, Aeneas takes up the *imago* upon the shoulder that once carried his father. After the exile has found himself in history, he replaces the confusion of his actual situation with the wonder of the ideal. He knows that he is more than what he has lost, that he, like Atlas,[22] is the hero upon whose shoulders the world rests.

Yet, as with Atlas, the awe-inspiring heroic vision becomes an overwhelming burden. When these Roman *imagines* meet the *res* of real Italian lives, Aeneas will no longer be able to comfort himself by contemplating lofty ideals. Ultimately, he must again face tragedy in his triumph, maturing to self-responsibility in his final conflict with Turnus, another broken man watching his world come to an end.

The mirrored self

As Turnus takes a stand against Aeneas and his own Italian rivals, his existential dilemma echoes the same dispossession Aeneas endured. In creating his Roman world, Aeneas will recreate for Turnus the alienating, isolating conditions from which he himself emerged; Turnus thus reflects back to Aeneas what he has gone through. Yet as a true mirrored reflection, Turnus inverts Aeneas' response to these conditions. He will die holding on to the culture with which he was born, becoming a self-conscious representative of his world as he loses it. His authenticity will not involve the world-building of Aeneas but rather a tragic fealty to the ancestral *mores* disregarded in the new Trojan world.

As in other moments in the second half of the epic,[23] the gods recede into the background as Aeneas and Turnus assume responsibility for their fates. At the start of the tenth book, Jupiter responds to the ongoing conflict between Venus and Juno by wiping his hands clean of any direct involvement in the war. While Homer's Zeus also makes such neutral proclamations, the *sua cuique* formula establishes the necessity of Turnus and Aeneas finally deciding the war in single combat, the epic confrontation between two exceptional individuals (10.111–3):

> Each man's own undertakings [*sua cuique*] will bring him both hardship and favor [*laborem fortunamque*]. Jupiter is the same king to all. The fates shall find their way.

Turnus is the deliberate source of his own misfortune, and this is precisely what makes his suffering genuinely tragic. Vergil's own narrative voice later laments Turnus's proud ignorance after the death of Pallas. The Rutulian exults "unknowing [*nescia*] of his fate and future lot," though a time shall come when he will rue this victory and its spoils (10.501–5).

From this apex of confidence, Turnus gradually meets his fate through an increasingly painful self-knowledge. As his doom approaches, he begins to recognize himself as its author. This particularly self-conscious aspect of Turnus's end becomes apparent when Aeneas begins rampaging on the battlefield following the death of Pallas. Juno tricks Turnus into avoiding Aeneas by conjuring up an apparition (*imago*) of his rival that leads him onto a ship rigged to sail away from the fighting (10.633–88).[24] Swinging at shadows as the apparition evaporates, Turnus despairs, "unknowing of matters [*ignarus rerum*] and ungrateful for the protection" (10.666). For Aeneas, the *imago* replaces *res* at the end of Book 8 in a moment of enraptured wonder, but when this same phrase appears for Turnus, to be "unknowing of matters" involves only an escape into hallucination. Now alone and forced to reckon with himself, he delivers a soliloquy expressing his understanding of his heroic role. He cannot once more face his people having abandoned them in battle and wonders what he might possibly do with himself in the face of such ignominy. He desires only escape from the shame of his own people and the "guilty reputation [*conscia fama*]" he fears will attend his desertion (10.679).

Turnus's existential dilemma elegantly brings out the double meaning of *conscius* in Latin, as it has both the English derivative sense of "conscious" and the sense here of "guilty." The two meanings have a profound unity. Turnus here becomes reflectively self-aware through an experience of guilt, a personal failure to protect his people that sets him apart from them. He speaks his own name and asserts his own will in bidding that the winds help him end his own life—"I, Turnus, willingly beseech thee" (*volens vos Turnus adoro*, 10.677). Like the Greek tragic figure, he suffers in his newfound autonomy, experiencing it as a titanic burden that prompts his attempted self-destruction. Acting within a society whose existence is immediately threatened with total ruin, Turnus experiences the pangs of inner conscience as it suddenly replaces the vanishing social regulation of his conduct in the shame and honor of a warrior's code. In this moment of individuation, he experiences what Heidegger terms "self-responsibility" (*Selbstverantwortung*), a responsibility independent from the expectations of the They (*das Man*).[25] The sharp guilt he feels arises from the "absolute guilt" that arises as a corollary to moral autonomy. The human being who has assumed self-responsibility has formed a conscience that is acutely aware of its own practical limitations, such that "every action is at the same time something marked by guilt" and so has become "guilty in an absolute sense,"[26] guilty in one's very being. A hero's death frustrated, Turnus can only seek to eliminate his torturously irredeemable self. His *consci*ous self-awareness is inextricably bound with the guilty *consci*ence of surviving in this isolated state as his people fight and die.

In the final book, Turnus's sister Juturna attempts to prevent the dual between Turnus and Aeneas by reigniting the conflict between the armies. Turnus puts a stop to the delays after he learns of Amata's suicide. The same feeling of self-conscious guilt which arose in his own suicide attempt returns (12.665–8):

> Turnus went numb, confounded by the changing image [*imagine*] of things, and he stood with a silent gaze—a great shame burns in his lonely heart [*uno in corde*] alongside a madness interlaced with grief, a love spurred on by rage, and his guilty courage [*conscia virtus*].

In his newfound self-responsibility, Turnus now experiences his courage paradoxically, like a mania near to despondency or tenderness close to fury. Like Aeneas unable to authentically address himself to Dido after the fall of Troy, Turnus flounders inconstantly between his emotions, challenged for the first time to choose his course of action as a self-conscious, authentic self. He has lost the naïve certainty of the "natural man" Hegel describes as "living quite unconsciously . . . in conformity with the morality of his town." Confronted by a foreign influence, he "immediately arrives at uncertainty as to whether his point of view or the opposite is wrong."[27] *Virtus*, the ethical ideal he could not betray in accepting Juno's salvation, now leads to the death and destruction of what it had intended to honor and preserve. As he realizes the failure of the heroic code in which he was socialized, the resulting cognitive dissonance further isolates the hero in a guilty self-*consci*ousness.

The ancient commentary of Servius emphasizes the solitariness Turnus experiences in his self-awareness. As the Trojans besiege and burn the city, a tower that Turnus himself (*ipse*, 12.674) had constructed goes down in flames (12.672–5). For Servius, the destruction of the city is illustrative of Turnus's grief "because we mourn deeply if we should see perish what we have made" (Serv. 12.674). As the Italian world burns, its flames reflect on Turnus and his deeds. He is both its author and its destroyer, its defender and its violator, its passion and its grief. What may have been a life of routine nobility has become an existential drama, with the hero struggling to affirm himself in a disappearing world. His mother-in-law, his people, and the gods are now gone from his view. In accordance with Heidegger, Turnus's inevitable death in defense of his world is the "ownmost [*eigneste*]" possibility of his being, the culmination of his being-as-self.[28] Authenticity requires that he choose himself as the author of his inevitable fate. However bad this fortune may be, "it is mine [*mea est*]; it is better that I alone [*me . . . unum*] on your behalf [*pro vobis*] . . . decide the matter with the sword" (12.694–5).

As Turnus finally faces death, his anxious self-consciousness gives way to dreamy self-surrender. First introduced into the epic while enjoying the unworried sleep of a comfortable prince (7.413–4), he dies in a nightmarish daze. In one last affirmation of his heroic self-identity, he attempts the Iliadic feat of hurling a great boundary stone at Aeneas (12.897–900).[29] But this dream of heroism is one more attempt to preserve the virtue of old against the facts of the present. Vergil echoes the Delphic dictum in describing how Turnus blindly runs up against his own limitations. Turnus "does not recognize himself [*se . . . cognoscit*] running or going or raising or moving the great rock in his hand" (12.903–4). As in a dream, the mind is willing but the body does not follow, however much Turnus may try to summon courage against this deadly lethargy. His surrender is, in this moment, his authenticity. Deprived of his weakening faculties, he must simply lie down and return to the ancestral Italian land flattened and disenchanted by the emerging Roman war machine (12.766–90).[30] As much as he struggles to personally take up the markers of his world, the massive boulders and sinewy rooted stumps, the Italian soil cannot be transported elsewhere. Confronted by the nontransferable substance of embedded nature, Turnus cannot start again.

Aeneas now stands and faces who he may have become at Troy, the tragic hero of the lost cause. His past suffering is reflected in the man he now destroys. Something of each belongs to the other. In a final inversion, the prideful Turnus embraces the self-sacrificing devotion of old while *pius* Aeneas will now kill with a passionate blade. When Turnus exhorts Aeneas for mercy, the burden of self-consciousness returns to our Trojan hero. Now it is he who must decide, "turning over his eyes [*volvens oculos*]" in a reflective pause (12.939). The epic will conclude with Aeneas' final decision as the fullest expression of his responsibility, as the general formula he has received for being Roman cannot account for the confused specificity he confronts in Turnus's plea. Left to his own judgement, Aeneas seems to favor leniency (12.938–41), perhaps remembering his father's Roman precept to spare those already humbled (6.853). Convincing arguments can, however, be made on the side of granting Turnus no mercy. The plausible accounts on both sides mean that the matter cannot be settled by the application of commonly accepted ethical precepts. In the moment of authentic judgement, as Denis McManus writes, we recognize that the They (*das Man*) "is not a unified agent that might decide which of these many norms matters most" and is ultimately "nobody."[31]

The final judgment will only arise within the situation, from his own experience of standing over Turnus, from the direct appearance (*apparuit*) of Pallas's baldric. The baldric speaks not to Aeneas' reason but his experience, recalling all the "memories of his fierce grief [*saevi monimenta doloris*]," an overwhelming appearance which he "absorbs in his eyes [*oculis . . . hausit*]" (12.945–6). A *monimentum* evokes an especially personal remembrance, and so Servius describes Aeneas' *dolor* as his own (proprie) (Serv. 12.945). This concluding *dolor* recalls the whole of Aeneas' suffering, his unrealized hopes alongside his abiding grief. Pallas had been his salvation in a strange land, the morning star who would clear away the darkness (8.589–91). Pallas fell and was buried in the intimate handiwork of the ill-fated woman who once listened to Aeneas' story of grief (11.72–5). Now the memory of Pallas throws Aeneas into a headlong rage heedless of any reasoned principle of justice. Deaf to Turnus's pleas, he remembers only his own suffering. His ideal of a merciful and just Roman world succumbs to the violence of a present reality laden with the weight of past suffering.

This vengeance is the authentic relation of Aeneas to the mirrored self before him. In his initial appearance, he lamented that it would have been better to die at Troy than to suffer on (1.94–6), and now he enacts this fate for another in a similar position. On one hand, the judgment that Turnus should die proceeds from Aeneas' own experience. His own tragedy of exile need not be repeated by his foe, who is being spared the pitiable life of an alien in his own land. On the other hand, executing Turnus represents the clearing away of Aeneas' own pre-Roman self, his own transformation from passive victim to a self-responsible authority. Aeneas' reaction to the baldric is thus a spontaneous manifestation of an emerging Roman personality that reflects his own psyche just as much as the facts of the situation. The visionary ideal of mercy need not be rejected entirely and weighs on Aeneas, who, like Turnus, will find guilt to be an indispensable aspect of self-responsibility. But the authentic decision is the decision that speaks to what is ownmost to Aeneas; it recognizes the plurality of norms and judges their weight and relevance, taking "all things considered."[32] For Aeneas, the memories stirred up by the baldric demand resolution and so represent an authentic spur to action.

The final dialog of the epic condenses the personal opposition of *Aeneas contra Turnum* into the simpler pronominal conflict of *ego contra te*. Turnus wants only to be restored to his own place and asks that his body returned to his own people (*me . . . redde meis*, 935–6). Echoing Priam's appeal to Achilles (*Il.* 24.485ff.), Turnus asks that Aeneas find empathy for him by considering his own father (*tibi talis Anchises genitor*). Aeneas responds by sharply inverting this pronominal logic—"Shall you [*tu*], clothed in the trophies of one of mine [*meorum*], escape me [*mihi*]?" (947–8). Each makes claims against the other with an utterly self-interested diction, yet this particular dispute between individuals is the founding moment of a universal Roman society. Turnus and Aeneas speak at once for themselves and for the world emerging out of their conflict. In speaking for his own (*meorum*), Aeneas speaks for Pallas, who exacts the capital penalty as the first punishment of Roman justice (12.948–9). Turnus shall be preserved in an Italian soil he affirmed as his own; the personal grief of Aeneas will motivate the universally avenging justice of Roman law. Historically, the Augustan age will be built upon the bodies of those who murdered Octavian's father.[33] Those who discovered themselves in the grief of an apocalyptic crisis have assumed the ultimate responsibility and remade the world in their image.

Conclusion

Our dissatisfaction with the end of the *Aeneid* reflects the enlightened conviction that a summary execution cannot be just. Justice arises not as an individual initiative but from communal deliberation. Civilization exists precisely to restrain this species of brutal authenticity. At its end, the *Aeneid* offers us no solution but rather the primordial problem from which modernity proceeds. Modernity begins where Vergil left off, recognizing the clash of bare individuals as the barbarism that politics aims to resolve. *Ego contra te* may be said to be the starting assumption of the modern polity since Hobbes's description of the pre-social ("natural") state of humans as a *bellum omnium contra omnes*. Like Hobbes's state of nature, the moral dilemma at the end of the *Aeneid* represents a moment in which traditional moral categories cannot apply because all social norms have vanished. Radical self-responsibility is the purest expression of conscience, and yet it must also be beyond good and evil, deciding without reference to any external law, to any social code or abstract rule or concept. The vanishing gods of the frontier go silent and offer no guidance.

The struggle of bare individuals arose only under exceptional circumstances for the ancients, yet it is understood as "natural" for a modern like Hobbes. Today, the unself-conscious life of traditional communities has been further replaced by a default individualism. As communities rapidly disappear amidst economic, technological, and social disruption, the ongoing apocalypse of modernity leaves the individual as the only survivor. The *ego* alone remains. Its boundaries have been institutionalized in the familiar architecture of modern liberal society—the person with legal rights firmly set against those of the state and other individuals. Where in antiquity the individual only appeared *in extremis*, as the heroic "one" arising in moments of extreme social stress, today the individual is prior to society. Yet the modern individual, like the ancient tragic figure, still suffers in this apparent liberation. The hubris of an inviolable private sphere cannot be maintained against the universal social forces (government, capital, mass media) that invariably overwhelm our petty sense of bourgeois ownership. United as a society only in the aggregate, alienation and conformism become the tragedy of the modern human being, however much freer we may be by political right.

The *Aeneid* can inform and enrich our individualized world by forcing us to reconsider the self in its original ancient appearance, one richer and more engaged with ambiguity than the abstract personhood of modernity, which seeks to reconstitute society on a merely contractual basis. The *ego contra te* of the final duel is equally an *ego contra me, tu contra te*. The other is a reflection of the self and the self a reflection of the other.[34] This truth of the mirrored self is lost in the immediate passion of conflict yet it is foundational for political life. It is not enough to see the state as a compact of otherwise unrelated individuals. A universal rule must have some ground in a substantially shared experience. The authentic state begins not in law but in the life of an individual who is, at the same time, everyone. Freedom begins as a subjective standpoint—as only *my* freedom—and yet it cannot remain so. This freedom ends with us asserting our rights in the face of another asserting their equally valid rights against us—in Aeneas facing Turnus, in Hegel's tragedy of two rights opposed to each other.[35] Only through this conflict do we fully recognize each other as free, moving from a jealous defense of particular interest to a universal respect for human autonomy.

Hard-won from the brutal realities of empire, this authentic universalism is the best and most enduring aspect of the Roman legacy, and yet it can only be appreciated from a first-person perspective. The universal becomes human reality through the experience of loss and restoration. The self that has become another self entirely is one liberated from its particularity. The survivor of the catastrophe has lost her past and yet abides. The *Aeneid* speaks to us as human beings who are always both *victor* and *victus*, always dispossessed in a foreign Roman world and yet always remaking it in our own image. Christianity shares this Vergilian lifeworld, responding to the same redemptive longing for kingdom or "empire without end" (*Aen.* 1.279) within the hearts of the defeated and the occupied. But where Christianity embraces Anchises's injunction toward mercy and lays stress upon the universal, forgiving even the proud, Aeneas falls back into the particularity of his own grief. The Roman empire will be eternal insofar as it draws upon this righteous outrage in constructing a universal state, recognizing the inexhaustibility of personal grief and demanding an unending commitment to secular justice. We may thus see the *Aeneid* as a parallel Gospel, one in which individual salvation occurs through a new kind of tragic afterlife: a life dead to itself becomes reborn in the universal significance of world history. As we attempt to reconcile Aeneas' personal fate with his historical destiny, we wrestle with the same question of authenticity familiar from the Gospels—what should it profit us to gain the world if we lose our own soul?

Notes

1 See discussion of how these various senses contribute to a general "ethic of authenticity" at Varga and Guignon 2020: § 1.2.

2 Nietzsche 1907: 97.

3 McGrath 2019: 119.

4 *Ruinanz* was the working term Heidegger used for what later became "fallenness" (*Verfallenheit*) in *Being and Time* (Heidegger 1962). This term better captures the catastrophic sense of an apocalyptic landscape that leaves the individual alone to confront the possibility of their authenticity. David Abergel argues that the "ruined" structure of average everydayness underlies a "confluence of authenticity and inauthenticity" (Abergel 2020: 74).

5 Campbell 2017: 84–5:

> [Heidegger's] readings of *Antigone* are meditations on Sophocles' claim in the first choral ode that there is nothing stranger than the human being, which Heidegger takes as saying that the human being is the uncanniest of all creatures. Strangeness and uncanniness do not on their own make the human being tragic, but in a remarkable passage in which Heidegger is discussing uncanniness, he says that "human beings themselves in their essence are a *katastrophe*," preferring the Greek in order to emphasize the way in which the human being is a turning (*strophe*) down (*kata*).

6 Translated by Sir Richard Jebb (1891). All other translations of classical texts are mine unless otherwise indicated.

7 Jeremiah 2010: 178:

> Tragedy delves into the negative implications of an emerging self, whether it be an individual who suffers for herself alone, the tension of individual self-determination with the sovereignty of the state, or the dangerous siren song of self-knowledge. It shows the self's reflexivity metamorphosing into various degenerate forms: self-destruction, incest, and the murder of kin.

8 Gill 1996: 12.
9 Eliza Gregory Wilkins provides a thorough discussion of self-knowledge in antiquity in his study of the Delphic dictum *gnōthi seauton*. Chapters 1–7 present the earlier interpretations of the saying as encouraging a sense of one's limitations. See Wilkens 1917: 12–59.
10 Hegel 2015: §60, 107:

> [S]omething can be known [*gewußt*], even felt to be a *barrier*, a lack only insofar as one has at the same time gone *beyond* it.

11 Jeremiah 2010: 54.
12 One may object that Romanization was not as universalizing as we may imagine, and that for the vast majority of persons within the empire, life went on without any appreciable disruption in their sense of personal or communal identity. To this objection, I emphasize that I am taking Vergil as an exemplar of the Roman imagination, which, of course, captures those under its ideological sway to a varied extent. While this Roman imagination originated with Roman elites and may have had only little impact in some locales within the empire, it could, as an ideology of homelessness, be universally adopted, for example, by northern Europeans for whom the concept of a nonlocal, geographically extensive state (i.e., the later Carolingian empire) first emerged from the disruption of their local cultures in contact with Rome. While not every life within the empire was immediately affected by Roman power, the ideal of a universalizing *Romanitas* was crucial to the ideological self-consciousness of the period and endures even into modernity.
13 Hegel 1955: II: 234–5.
14 The Penates tell him of his ancient Italian lineage in a dream.
15 Ferro 2018: 194.
16 It should be noted that there is a distinction between what Vergil has told us, the reader, about Aeneas' destiny and the extent to while this destiny has any tangible reality for Aeneas himself. While both Vergil's direct narration and the councils of the gods have given us a clear vision of Aeneas' destiny, Aeneas is only privy to this vision insofar as it is mediated by the Penates and his father Anchises, who only belatedly correct their route from Crete to Italy (3.121–208). When Anchises dies, he becomes predictably forgetful of his purpose in his relationship with Dido.
17 *LSJ*, s.v. "αὐθέντης."
18 Jeremiah 2010: 136.
19 Aeneas' visit to Buthrotum (3.294–462) provides a glimpse at the failure of a Troy rebuilt. Helenus's settlement at Buthrotum is called 'Little Troy' (*parva Troia*, 3.349) and a 'copy of great Pergamum' (*simulatum magnum / Pergamum*, 3.349–50) complete with a 'false Simois' (*falsus Simois*, 3.302). Fate and Helenus's own prophecy demand that Aeneas leave and continue seeking.
20 Compare *Aeneas 'quo deinde ruis? quo proripis?' inquit / 'quem fugis? aut quis te nostris complexibus arcet?* (5.741–2) to *'quid natum totiens, crudelis tu quoque, falsis / ludis imaginibus? cur dextrae iungere dextram / non datur, ac veras audire et reddere voces?'* (1.407–49).
21 The line closes with *reddere voces*, which directly echoes 1.449.

22 The image of the hero taking the world on his shoulders is deeply evocative of Atlas. Aeneas identifies Atlas as the common ancestor of the Trojans and Arcadians in speaking to Evander earlier in Book 8 (8.134–42).

23 Anchises explains that each shade below suffers a hell earned by their own deeds (*quisque suos patimur manis*, 6.743). Nisus wonders if the gods truly inspire our emotions or if each man's "dread desire [*dira cupido*]" becomes his own god [*sua cuique*] (9.184–5). See also Price, Chapter 13, in this volume.

24 Cf. Apollo saving Aeneas from the fighting by similar tactics in *Il.* 5.449.

25 See Heidegger's discussion of the call of conscience: "Conscience summons Dasein's Self from its lostness in the 'they'" Heidegger 1962: 319.

26 Heidegger 2002: 169. See discussion of this passage at McManus 2019: 1196.

27 Hegel 1955: II: 355.

28 Heidegger 1962: 294:

> Death is a possibility-of-Being which Dasein itself has to take over in every case. With death, Dasein stands before itself in its ownmost potentiality-for-Being. . . . When it stands before itself in this way, all its relations to any other Dasein have been undone. This ownmost non-relational possibility is at the same time the uttermost one.

29 The act of hurling the great stone is the act of a bygone heroic age which can no longer be replicated, even with the effort of seven men "such as the earth now brings forth." Diomedes also hurls a stone at Aeneas and hits him in the hip before the Trojan is spirited off the battlefield at *Il.* 5.303ff.

30 The Trojans removed an olive tree "sacred to Faunus and revered by sailors" to aid in the war effort, cutting down all impediments "with no distinction [*nullo discrimine*]." The stump of this tree provides Turnus momentary relief when Aeneas' spear is caught in it.

31 McManus 2019: 1198. Similarly, Campbell writes,

> For Heidegger, values belong to the register of calculative thinking, where one asks, "What is the best thing to do in this situation?" Antigone does not ask that question, nor does she appeal to a pre-existing set of standards that might help her make the decision to bury her brother. Rather, in Heidegger's terms, she dares to venture into the un-said and un-thought, into a 'place' that lacks familiar suggestions about how to act.
>
> (Campbell 2017: 97)

32 McManus 2019: 1192:

> Such [authentic] action is performed not merely to meet the requirements associated with occupying particular roles or to achieve particular purposes, but instead because it is judged best all things considered.

33 Augustus also builds a temple to *Mars Ultor*, Mars the Avenger, in his forum. See Rehak and Younger 2006: 11–2.

34 For a formal analysis of how Vergil sets up then dissolves boundaries, see Quint 2011. He writes, "Like warfare itself, chiasmus plots out distinctions and draws up sides, only to reveal an underlying reciprocity that undoes them or turns them into paradox" (Quint 2011: 295).

35 Hegel 1955b: I:446:

> In what is truly tragic there must be valid moral powers on both the sides which come into collision.

References

Abergel, D. 2020. "The Confluence of Authenticity and Inauthenticity in Heidegger's Being and Time." *Gatherings: The Heidegger Circle Annual* 10: 74–110.

Campbell, S.M. 2017. "The Catastrophic Essence of the Human Being in Heidegger's Readings of Antigone." *Gatherings: The Heidegger Circle Annual* 7: 84–102.

Ferro, B. 2018. "Hegel's Critique of Stoicism." In A. Magee (ed.) *In Hegel and Ancient Philosophy: A Re-examination*. New York: Routledge.

Gill, C. 1996. *Personality in Greek Epic, Tragedy, and Philosophy*. Oxford: Clarendon Press.

Hegel, G.W.F. 1955a. *Lectures on the History of Philosophy*. Translated by E. Haldane. Vol. II. London: Routledge & Kegan Paul.

———. 1955b. *Lectures on the History of Philosophy*. Translated by E. Haldane. Vol. I. London: Routledge & Kegan Paul.

———. 2015. *Encyclopedia of the Philosophical Sciences in Basic Outline, Part 1: Science of Logic*. Translated by K. Brinkmann and D.O. Dahlstrom. Cambridge: Cambridge University Press.

Heidegger, M. 1962. *Being and Time*. Translated by J. Macquarrie and E. Robinson. Oxford: Blackwell.

———. 2002. "Wilhelm Dilthey's Research and the Struggle for a Historical Worldview." In J. van Buren (ed.) *Supplements: From the Earliest Essays to Being and Time and Beyond*. Translated by C. Bambach. Albany: State University of New York Press.

Jeremiah, E. 2010. *The Emergence of Reflexivity in Greek Language and Thought: From Homer to Plato and beyond*. Melbourne: University of Melbourne. https://minerva-access.unimelb.edu.au/handle/11343/35437.

McGrath, S. 2019. *Thinking Nature: An Essay in Negative Ecology*. Edinburgh: Edinburgh University Press.

McManus, D. 2019. "On a Judgment of One's Own: Heideggerian Authenticity, Standpoints, and All Things Considered." *Mind* 128, 512: 1181–204.

Nietzsche, F. 1907. *Beyond Good and Evil*. Translated by H. Zimmern. New York: MacMillen.

Quint, D. 2011. "Virgil's Double Cross: Chiasmus and the Aeneid." *American Journal of Philology* 132, 2: 273–300.

Rehak, P., and Younger, J.G. 2006. *Imperium and Cosmos: Augustus and the Northern Campus Martius*. Madison, WI: University of Wisconsin Press.

Sophocles. 1891. *Antigone*. Translated by R. Jebb. Cambridge: Cambridge University Press.

Varga, S., and Guignon, C. 2020. "Authenticity." *The Stanford Encyclopedia of Philosophy*. https://plato.stanford.edu/archives/spr2020/entries/authenticity/.

Wilkens, E.G. 1917. *'Know Thyself' in Greek and Latin Literature*. Chicago: University of Chicago Press.

Part IV

The *Aeneid* into the future

While the previous sections have demonstrated the relevance of the *Aeneid* in the recent past and present, this final section reaches into the future. Beginning with an examination of Latin curricula in secondary schools, Frances Foster studies the perceptions of and reactions to the *Aeneid* of the next generation of readers. Her detailed empirical study investigates the ways in which Vergil's epic is taught in Latin classes in UK schools and finds that the often-narrow scope of the lessons—in this case centered on the Nisus and Euraylus episode in Book 9—affects students' perceptions of the epic, as well as Roman history and literature, in surprising ways. On the one hand, students indirectly inherit from their teachers—and the fact that Latin is taught only in university-track programs—the sense that the *Aeneid* imparts a kind of cultural capital, a belief often at odds with the desire to democratize the study of classical antiquity. On the other hand, since students are getting but a narrow slice of the text, they often miss the elements of the poem that make it worthy of further serious study—its literary register and the complex cultural and political contexts in which Vergil was writing. Foster's chapter, in sum, offers a word of caution to programs offering but a taste of this massively complex work.

In the closing chapter Evander Price contemplates a more spatially and temporally distant future as he considers Vergil's Golden Bough and Carl Sagan's Golden Records, which were placed aboard the Voyager space probes. The Golden Records are the farthest man-made objects from earth, currently gliding through interstellar space awaiting recovery by future space travelers. Price shows how studying the Golden Bough, which grants Aeneas safe passage into the depths of the earth, helps us understand the meaning and purpose of the Golden Records, which are soaring through the cosmos.

And so, at the end of our volume, we have a diverse set of answers from multiple disciplinary vantage points establishing the *Aeneid*'s relevance to our present moment—and the recent past that significantly informs our present—and a glimpse of its relevance into the far distant future. Yet, we have only scratched the surface; there are still so many things Vergil's poetry can elucidate today and, we expect, tomorrow. We hope that these chapters inspire others to join in that project, to see the *Aeneid* not just as a relic of the past, but as a vital part of our present and future.

DOI: 10.4324/9781003176145-16

12 The *Aeneid* for the next generation

An empirical study

Frances Foster

Introduction and context

The *Aeneid* has an extensively long history as a school text. It entered the curriculum in the Augustan era and has remained a feature of the curricula in many countries well into the 21st century. While Vergil's place on the curriculum of the Middle Ages and Renaissance has been well studied, the *Aeneid's* appeal to modern students and teachers has not been thoroughly investigated. This paper aims to address that gap with evidence from one country and from one angle, by examining the perspectives and attitudes of a group of UK school teachers and their 15–16-year-old students toward teaching and studying the text in Latin. I evaluate the empirical evidence gathered from students and their teachers at three state-maintained comprehensive schools in the United Kingdom. In so doing, I seek to establish how the *Aeneid* is perceived by 21st-century teenage students and teachers. I evaluate the ways in which the *Aeneid* is read as a modern story in 21st-century educational contexts.

Latin does not form part of the core curriculum prescribed by the UK government at the secondary level. Nonetheless, it is available as a curriculum subject in some maintained comprehensive schools and in many grammar schools (these are maintained schools that have an academically selective entrance policy). There is no coherent pattern behind which schools do and do not offer Latin as a curriculum subject, although Latin departments are more common in some areas of the country than in others. Many secondary school Latin departments have been created in the past 20 years by enthusiastic teachers, while other departments have been long established—both new and long-standing departments depend on supportive managers to keep them running. The managers of individual schools determine whether to offer students the option of taking Latin to examination level at age 16. Those students who do so have, on average, studied Latin for three, four, or five years before taking the examination. For this examination, Latin teachers must choose to teach at least one literary text (or anthology of short texts) from a list of texts by major authors, and an extract of Vergil's *Aeneid* is one of the most popular choices. The length of the extract (or frequently, set of extracts) from the poem is brief—around 100 lines of verse in total—and often it may be these students' only direct encounter with Vergil's epic.

DOI: 10.4324/9781003176145-17

This study examines how 15–16-year-old students relate to the experience of studying a short extract of the *Aeneid* and how they relate to what they read of the text. It also examines the teachers' rationale for choosing the *Aeneid* from the selection of available texts and investigates what teachers hope their students will gain from their engagement with such a short section of the *Aeneid.* While the teachers have studied Vergil's epic as a cultural artefact within the historical context of the Augustan world, their 15–16-year-old students do not. They encounter a small part of the story directly, in a language that they are still novices in learning, and in a register of language far more complex than they can handle without considerable support from their teachers. Thus, their impression of the poem is not based around a coherent and detailed understanding of Vergil's historical context and literary heritage but around an extract studied in isolation. An extract of the *Aeneid* is often students' first—and frequently, only—encounter with poetry written in another language, and the only experience they have with reading a literary text in unadapted Latin. In addition, 15–16-year-old students rarely have the broader knowledge of subsequent literary heritage to gain an understanding of the literary reception of the *Aeneid*, and nor are they ordinarily taught this. Therefore, these students may have a limited literary and cultural context within which to place Vergil's poem.

The *Aeneid* as a school text

As Butler has observed, Vergil's position on the curriculum has been and remains consistent.[1] He arrived on the school curriculum remarkably early—within his own lifetime, rather than long after his death. Suetonius records that in 25 BCE, a certain Quintus Caecilius Epirota was the first to teach the poetry of Vergil (Suet. *Gram*. 16.1), although he would have first taught the *Eclogues* and *Georgics* rather than the *Aeneid.* The use of Vergil's poems within the late antique curriculum has been studied in detail.[2] Horsfall has suggested that even in the Roman period many children would have studied just the first two books of the *Aeneid* at school, while only the more advanced students would have read further in the epic,[3] an idea that I have further investigated.[4] Vergil's place within the post-antique and medieval periods has been established by Orme, who notes that in the 7th century the *Aeneid* was read by scholars such as Aldhelm and Bede but was probably too difficult for most schoolchildren to read in its entirety.[5] Orme observes that by the 15th century, scenes from the *Aeneid*, such as the death of Dido, were read in schools,[6] and Basswell confirms that Vergil's effect on the Latin language is "virtually immeasurable."[7] Clarke has traced Vergil's position from the 16th to the 19th centuries, and he shows how boys from scholarly families demonstrated detailed familiarity with ancient literature, including the *Aeneid*, from a very young age. Clarke describes how John Connington could recite 1,000 lines of Vergil to his father at the age of 8.[8] This example demonstrates the elite extreme of schooling experience in the 19th century: only those attending the most expensive and ambitious schools read the whole *Aeneid* in this way. Stray notes that such experiences, particularly within 19th-century boarding schools, "led to the mutual reinforcement of male group solidarity and classical allusion"[9] by which elite males could identify others who had undergone similar (expensive) training. Stray illustrates that, by the late 19th and early 20th centuries, quotations from the *Aeneid* used in parliament usually came from the first two books of the epic,[10] suggesting that even these politicians had not read the epic in its entirety.

This brief overview demonstrates that young people have often experienced Vergil's *Aeneid* in chunks rather than as a totality. However, the vast majority of those who attended schools before the late 19th century came from privileged and wealthy families, who made an active choice to send their children to school. Various education acts from the late 19th century and 20th century enabled and required all young people in the United Kingdom to attend schools free of charge—in 1944 this was extended to include the 14–15 age group, and in 1975 it was extended again to include the 15–16 age group. Thus, 21st-century students of Latin in this age group do not all come from such elite backgrounds as their classically educated predecessors and may not be able to contextualize their experience with the *Aeneid* within that cultural milieu. Nonetheless, many may experience some level of privilege—even if only in attending a school that provides access to Latin.

Literature in the curriculum

Although Latin literature is not part of the mandatory curriculum, maintained secondary schools are required to provide opportunities for students to study English literature until the age of 16, and students study a range of texts variously labelled as "heritage,"[11] "high-quality," and "challenging."[12] Such terminology is inherited from political discourse. Shakespeare and poetry in general are regular features of this curriculum, in which the *Aeneid* seems to fit, but these texts are also those with which both students and teachers experience the greatest difficulty. Ray observes that a survey of trainee teachers' attitudes to poetry indicated that the trainees recalled negative experiences with poetry in their own secondary education and that few of them had read any poetry beyond that required at school.[13] In Australia, Weaven and Clark questioned why teachers appeared to be reluctant to teach poetry when presented with the option of doing so. They also investigated whether the absence of poetry in socioeconomically underprivileged schools might be reflected in teachers' perceptions of their students' capabilities. They were struck by a lack of confidence among experienced and well-qualified teachers toward the teaching of poetry.[14] Erricker has explored the ways in which different groups of students approach a "challenging" text (such as Shakespeare) in English, concluding that students require a level of academic confidence in order to take risks and tackle the material without fear of embarrassment.[15] While these challenging texts are taught to all students within the curriculum for English, regardless of attainment, teachers and students alike have reported low confidence when engaging with this material in a classroom context.

On the other hand, Pike has investigated how students in his English classroom responded to pre-20th-century literature, and notes that most of his students preferred the earlier texts. He argues that the teenage students valued the earlier poetry because these texts contained "a greater degree of indeterminacy," which allowed the young readers "more intellectual and personal space" to relate to the texts.[16] This historical gap between the time of the text and the present is much greater for students reading an ancient text like the *Aeneid*, which was already archaic even for students in the late Roman world. While Pike remains ambivalent about establishing a canonical set of works for the curriculum, he argues for the value of teaching earlier literature, since it encourages "diachronic reading." Such reading, he claims, provides "aesthetic distance" that allows the reader a closer interaction with the text, and this interaction is more likely to change adolescent readers' horizons.[17] There is a substantial safe "aesthetic distance" between Vergil and the modern student, but this is perhaps exaggerated by the fact that the *Aeneid* is set in a past that is also distant from Vergil's own time, and legendary rather than historical.

Publications by Latin teachers evaluating the practice of teaching ancient literature, and particularly the *Aeneid*, echo the language of "heritage literature" as "high quality" and "challenging." Butler notes that, anecdotally, students' early (and often only) encounter with an original Latin text "is seen as integral" to students' experience of the subject.[18] Davies evaluates the "sense of unease and frustration" students may experience when they first attempt to read the *Aeneid* in Latin because students are trained to read more straightforward prose, and Vergil's word order is very different.[19] Carr and Pauwels have examined attitudes to language learning in Australia to explore why language learning is perceived as unpopular among boys. They note that Latin seems to be an exception, in that boys opt to study Latin in the few (and predominantly elite) schools in which it is available. They show how the Latin teacher they interviewed felt that the subject matter presented in Latin lessons was more appealing to boys than that studied in modern languages, citing the "soldiers, heroes, battles, military campaigns"[20] that feature heavily in the *Aeneid*. The students studying Latin also spoke about the "military campaigns, heroic deeds, great leaders" that they enjoyed.[21] However, Carr and Pauwels also noted that studying Latin represents "highly valued curriculum capital, with an exclusive appeal" for those (few) students who have access to studying it.[22] This cultural capital lies at the heart of canon formation, as Guillory points out when he alludes to the way in which Vergil entered the educational canon as a model of language and style.[23] The change in language of instruction from Latin to a vernacular (in this case, English) has tempered the idea of Vergil as a model of style, but his value as curriculum capital holds for those who can place him in historical and cultural context. Students, however, may not be capable of making that placement: Connor notes that, as a result of reading the *Aeneid* in small chunks of 15 or 30 lines at a time, students "only see the metaphorical trees and never the forest that is the entire *Aeneid*."[24] How, therefore, do students who only read 100 lines of the epic, and generally much more slowly than Connor's 15- or 30-line chunks, perceive what they read of the *Aeneid*?

Sample and design

I collected the data for this study from three state-maintained comprehensive schools in the United Kingdom. All three schools offer Latin as an option on the mainstream curriculum, and it is taught by one or more specialist Latin teachers. I selected these schools from a larger pool of 26, following an initial questionnaire to 28 teachers during a training event designed for secondary-school Latin teachers. The initial questionnaire endeavored to discover how many of the teachers chose to teach Latin verse as an option to their 15–16-year-old students, and if they did teach Latin verse, which texts they chose to teach, in order to make the selection of case study schools. The three selected schools are situated in different areas of the country, and they are mixed comprehensives, meaning they do not charge fees or require entrance examinations but take all young people who live within a specified distance of the school gates. These schools are therefore representative examples of the type of education the majority of young people in the United Kingdom receive. The names of the schools and teachers have been fictionalized to protect their identity.

In order to situate the schools within a wider educational context, I present some basic demographic information about each school. Carrowdown College is situated within a large metropolis and has around 2,000 students aged 11–18. The school population reflects the local demographic: 7% of the students speak another language in addition to English at home, and the number of students receiving free school meals is close to the national average. Waywold High is situated in a relatively affluent small market town and takes around 2,000 students aged 11–18. The school population is more affluent than that of Carrowdown, and the number of students receiving free school meals is well below the national average. Very few students speak another language at home, and the demographic reflects a small town within easy commutable distance of several major urban centers with skilled employment. Fledden Academy is situated in a village with a predominantly rural community, some traveling a considerable distance to get to school. Fledden is smaller than Carrowdown and Waywold, taking around 1,000 students aged 11–18. The local area is less affluent with some deprivation, largely linked to the isolated nature of the rural environment. The number of students speaking another language at home is below the national average. The school is close to a military base, and thus a significant number of students have a parent serving in the armed forces. Carrowdown College has three Latin teachers, Waywold High has two, while Fledden has just one Latin teacher who also teaches modern languages.

Each of the three schools has selected a slightly different curriculum model for Latin, although all three have chosen the same options for national examinations at age 16. At Carrowdown and Fledden, students start learning Latin at age 11. Students aged 11–13 at Carrowdown are placed in "ability based" teaching groups according to a range of criteria, and Latin is taught to the higher attaining two-thirds of students, after which it becomes optional. By contrast, in Fledden students opt to study Latin (from a menu of four other languages) at the age of 11, and there are no minimum literacy requirements. At Waywold, students may elect to join an after-school Latin club at the age of 12, but it is only offered as a formal subject from age 13, and it is only offered to higher attaining students. Students between the ages of 14–16 at Carrowdown may also elect to study a course in classical civilization (a non-linguistic course about the culture, history, and literature of the ancient world), but there is no requirement for those taking Latin to do so. Neither Fledden nor Waywold offer such a course, and so for students at these schools, Latin is their only means of accessing the Roman world.

All three schools teach the language, particularly at the earlier stages, through the well-known *Cambridge Latin Course*, which was developed in the late 1960s and has been revised regularly (the most recent edition currently used in the United Kingdom dates from 1998). The stories in this course are set in the empire of the late 1st century and provide students with a fair insight into the social history and daily life in Pompeii, Roman Britain, and other areas of the Roman world during the Flavian dynasty, and in particular under the emperor Domitian. However, the course covers very little about the Augustan period during which the *Aeneid* was composed, and literary culture does not feature until very late—appearing only in the final sections of the course that are rarely covered in Latin classes in 21st-century schools.

Students thus embark on reading an extract of around 100 lines from the *Aeneid* with their teachers with little or no knowledge about Vergil's literary career, Augustan Rome, and the afterlife or reception of the *Aeneid* itself. This experience is likely to have been their first encounter with unadapted Latin and with a verse text in a language other than English. The linguistic capacity of students at this level in Latin is limited to a relatively small vocabulary: the language portion of the terminal examination requires the knowledge of around 450 words. While students at this level have encountered all cases, tenses, moods and voices, their confidence with the various permutations may be relatively weak. Students are required to translate complex sentences such as purpose and relative clauses, but their syntactical grasp of Latin tends to rely heavily on a familiar word order, which is employed by the textbook and the synthetic Latin they read for the language component of the course. The *Aeneid* is written in a highly complex literary register, one which was never spoken. Vincent points out that "classical" Latin is based on register and style, as much as on linguistic structure. It is therefore a form of language which is "diastratic (based on social class and education) and diaphasic (based on register and context)," rather than diachronic (linked to a historical period) or diatopic (linked to a geographical location).[25] This register of Latin had to be taught even to native speakers of the language. Evidence shows that Roman children struggled with Vergil's archaic vocabulary and particularly with his word order, since they were not familiar with the separation of noun and adjective pairs in everyday language.[26] It is not surprising, then, that Vergil's linguistic register is too complex for 15–16-year-old students in the 21st century to handle without considerable guidance and support.

I collected the data from these three schools from three angles. First, students in the target cohorts studying an extract of Vergil's *Aeneid* answered a short questionnaire (distributed and collected by teachers) asking which aspects of the text they enjoyed and what they found challenging. Secondly, I conducted extended semi-structured interviews with the teacher in charge of Latin at each school who is responsible for curricular decisions—in Waywold and Carrowdown, this was the head of department, while in Fledden this was the sole Latin teacher. Finally,

I arranged to observe a class of students studying the *Aeneid* in each of the three schools, although a variety of external factors at Carrowdown prevented this observation from taking place. My observations comprised taking field notes on the way in which students and teachers engaged with the text as a nonparticipant observer. The findings, based on the resulting data, offer a small-scale snapshot of how students and their teachers approach reading an extract of the *Aeneid.* These findings are not generalizable, since this study is localized, specific, and based around a relatively small number of students and teachers in one country. Nonetheless, they provide a glimpse into the classroom and the students' perspectives on what it is like to read an extract of the *Aeneid* without the larger cultural context that most adult readers of the epic in its entirety (even in translation) take for granted.

While Books 2, 4 and 6 are the most popular books of the *Aeneid* chosen for students to study, the fourth most popular for this age group is *Aeneid* 9 (the remaining books are rarely studied at this level). The students in all three schools were studying a set of short extracts from *Aeneid* 9 taken from the episode involving Nisus and Euryalus. The passages they studied introduced the two characters and their plan (9.176–96) before skipping ahead to a glimpse of the two Trojans killing sleeping Rutulians (9.339–56), and culminating in a slightly more extended extract narrating the discovery and deaths of both characters (9.369–445). These sections barely describe the Trojans' camp in Italy but not how they arrived, nor the tensions between the Trojans and the Rutulians. Reading such a short section of the epic, and from a book in which Aeneas himself never appears, provides a very disjointed view of the poem—not least because the gaps before and during the extracts require considerable glossing in order for the narrative to make sense. Isolating this portion of the epic focuses on the characters of Nisus and Euryalus but without any overall picture of the wars in Italy nor of the ways in which they reflect the literary wars at Troy or the historical civil wars in Rome.

Blood, spears, and verbs: students' responses

I received a total of 44 responses to my student questionnaire, with relatively similar numbers from Waywold and Carrowdown but a lower number from Fledden, since it is a smaller school with fewer students taking Latin. The numbers of respondents were proportionate with the overall student populations at each school and to the numbers taking Latin within each school. The questionnaire invited respondents to indicate, using a simple Likert scale, their overall impressions of various aspects of the text and those areas they found challenging. It also invited them to expand on these ideas in their own words if they wished. It asked them whether they enjoyed reading poetry in English lessons in order to establish basic attitudes toward reading literary verse texts without the additional barrier of Vergil's Latin.

Responses to this question about poetry in English were mixed: 17 (39%) indicated they enjoyed studying poetry, 19 (43%) were ambivalent, and 7 (16%) expressed a dislike of poetry in school. Many of those who felt ambivalent qualified their response, showing a more complicated relationship with poetry, such as,

"There are some I enjoy but most we learn in school I don't," and many cited either the choice of poem or the choice of task (particularly analysis and essay writing) as the reason for their ambivalence. With one exception, all respondents indicated aspects they actively enjoyed in the extracts from the *Aeneid* that they read. The subject matter of the *Aeneid* received the most attention from the students, and the most popular aspect they identified was mythology—37 (84%) said that they liked the mythology in the text, and one indicated that "like" was too mild a term. Mythology receives considerable attention in popular culture, forming the basic premise of books and games such as *Percy Jackson* and *God of War*. However, the extracts of *Aeneid* 9 these students studied contain very little well-known mythology, since none of the famous figures from the Trojan war are featured, the gods do not play a significant role, and there are no fabulous monsters. Nonetheless, most respondents still felt they were able to identify features of mythology that they enjoyed within the story. This may indicate something about how the students perceive the larger text of the *Aeneid* as a whole. If they have learned, from their teachers' contextualization, that the *Aeneid* is a long story about Roman and Greek gods and mythology, then this may color their perception of the text, even if it does not match with the short extract they read. They may be responding to their idea of the whole poem, even though they lack background to the *Aeneid* and its reception.

Other features that proved particularly popular were the plot, the adventure story, finding out what happens next, and the characters. Of these, 30 (68%) reported that they enjoyed the plot and the adventure story, while none indicated that they did not enjoy these features. The characters received less attention, although they were appreciated by 24 (55%) respondents, whereas the descriptions were only enjoyed by 14 (32%), and 19 (43%) liked the idea that they were reading a text which had been written a long time ago. The aspects that seem to appeal most to these young people are linked to the story and action, particularly the intense action of the dramatic episodes. Very few students felt comfortable in reading the text aloud (the question did not specify whether this meant reading the Latin aloud or a translation), with this activity gaining only four positive responses (9%). Carr and Pauwels note that the lack of a spoken element in Latin really appealed to the Australian students they spoke to,[27] and this seems to be reflected among these UK students. This response may be more closely linked to the self-consciousness of teenagers rather than a reaction to the *Aeneid* itself.

Respondents also commented on what makes reading the *Aeneid* challenging for them, and linguistic problems dominated here—34 (77%) identified word order as a major hurdle, 29 (66%) noted tricky vocabulary, and 15 (34%) found that long sentences were difficult. These three aspects were often linked together in students' comments—one pointed out that "sometimes verbs are far away from the nouns they describe" and another pointed to instances in the "word order where words that go together are on different lines." For these young people, the shape of the verse provides a visual indication of how sentences might be structured, and putting together words that are visually separated from each other presents a challenge. Some referred to the idea that the unusual word order creates "emphatic positioning" or "it's done for effect." One student noted that the idioms which Vergil uses are "more difficult" to understand, and another commented on the extended epic similes, but such comments were rare. Several respondents referred to the "complex," "new," "more abstract," and "high level" words that they encountered in extracts of the *Aeneid*, which they identified as distinct from the vocabulary they had learned for the language component of their Latin course. Although they do not articulate it fully, these students have identified aspects of Vergil's language that belong to the literary register of classical Latin rather than the Latin language as it was used for daily communication in the Augustan era. These same aspects of register marking out classical Latin were those that young people in the ancient world struggled with when reading Vergil,[28] particularly where adjectives are separated from the nouns they describe.

Most students found the plot or narrative of the extract straightforward, although six students suggested that they found this confusing, because the "situation sometimes changes a lot and is difficult to keep up with" or "there's so much going on." These responses reflect the nature of the fast-paced action in the sections of the Nisus and Euryalus story the students study—while they enjoy the action and drama, the disjointed and brief nature of the extracts means that for some students, following the story can be harder. In a similar way, most respondents found the characters engaging, but five students alluded to issues with the names of characters, since the "names have different forms" which they found more difficult to remember. The *variatio* in naming characters by patronymics and epithets as well as their usual personal name is another aspect of epic verse, although the majority of respondents did not consider this much of a barrier to understanding the text. For these students, the alternative names do not reflect the Homeric model, since they lack familiarity with it. They can form another barrier to their grasp of the story, although not an insurmountable one. For most students, this is another feature which falls into the various things Vergil might do "for effect" and on which they can comment in their examination responses.

In lessons, students' enjoyment of the plot and action of the passages was evident. They recalled the characters of Nisus and Euryalus easily, although they had limited awareness of the other Trojans. Since the extracts these students study are so short and isolated, characters such as Nisus and Euryalus, who hardly feature in a holistic view of the *Aeneid*, loom large in this extracted episode. Students were keen to volunteer information about the various ways in which the Rutulians die, and when invited by the teacher, one student understood that Nisus "hits someone who's not looking in the back and he vomits." This student has focused on the word *vomens* (9.414) as a particularly graphic description of what happens when Sulmo is struck by Nisus's spear. The teacher drew students' attention to the verbs in this sentence and asked why they were all positioned earlier rather than placed at the end of their clauses, as is usual in the synthetic Latin students read elsewhere in their course. A student replied that this is a sign of "speeding the action up," and they focused on the various action verbs in the sentence—*frangitur* (it breaks), *transit* (it—the spear—goes through), giving a sense of the speed of the violence. They also reacted enthusiastically to Vergil's image of Sulmo "vomiting a hot river from his chest" as he "rolls over cold" and "beats at his guts" with long moans (*volvitur ille vomens calidum de pectore flumen / frigidus et longis singultibus ilia pulsat*, 9.414–55). The visual nature of the scene and its action engaged the students, and they focused on the violence as they might encounter it in a graphic novel, comic book, or video game.

While much of their attention was understandably taken by the minutiae of the text in order to understand the unfamiliar vocabulary and word order, the students also looked at what for them was the "bigger picture" in their short extract. They debated questions about loyalty raised in the text, considering what they might do in Nisus's position and whether heroism is the best option. One girl suggested "I'd run, and maybe I could go and warn everyone," as she thought about the situation. The students identified closely with the characters of Nisus and Euryalus, partly because these are the main characters they read about and partly because Vergil presents them as young men, an age group these adolescent readers feel affinity with. The students were curious about the context of their short extract, and when they read about Euryalus's death, they asked "what happens after, does Aeneas come back?" Since Aeneas does not appear in *Aeneid* 9 as a whole, let alone in the 120 lines of text that they read in Latin, these students rely entirely on their teachers to provide context and to give an impression of the character of Aeneas and the other Trojans. However, students were most drawn by the fast-moving narrative and the action-packed elements of the epic. In the lessons I observed, there was no discussion about the main characters' homosexuality. Such discussion may have taken place in other lessons already and was as a result not a focal point for these lessons. It may also be an indication that these young people are so acclimatized to different understandings of sexuality through the PRIDE movement and the rainbow emblem that the presence of homosexual characters in a Latin text has become unremarkable. Either way, this is speculation arising from a lack of comment.

"Did enough kids cry?": teachers' responses

The three teachers in charge of Latin at each school—Marcellus at Carrowdown, Camilla at Fledden, and Silvia at Waywold—are the staff responsible for selecting the texts and options that their students study in Latin. Of the three, only Camilla had answered the initial teacher questionnaire, since Silvia and Marcellus had sent a junior colleague to the training day at which that questionnaire was circulated. All three are well-qualified and experienced teachers who had been working at their respective schools for at least five years when I spoke to them. They are all passionate about teaching Latin and regularly have to justify or defend Latin's place in the curriculum to parents, to students, and to the senior leaders at their schools, as do most secondary-school Latin teachers. These teachers all studied Latin at school themselves before completing an undergraduate and postgraduate degree in classics, followed by a subject-specific teacher training qualification. They are thus all well versed in study of the *Aeneid*, the Augustan context from which it emerged, and the epic's subsequent reception in ways which their students are not. Their rationale for opting to teach a section of the *Aeneid* and their impression of what their students gain from the experience are valuable, since they can reflect on the differences between their own understanding of the text and what their students can take away from it at the age of 16.

The teachers were all explicit about their own enjoyment of the *Aeneid* as a key motivator for choosing to teach it. Marcellus noted that his own positive experiences in studying the *Aeneid* at school aged 15–16 drew him to choose a specialist option in the *Aeneid* in the final year of his degree and therefore influenced his choice to teach it. Silvia enthused, "I'm in love with the *Aeneid*, I could teach it hopefully forever, in Latin as in English, and I know that whatever chunk they set I will enjoy, and I hope that will, you know, benefit the students." Her rationale is that the students are more likely to have a positive experience from her own personal engagement with the text. They also echoed statements made by a number of respondents on the initial teacher questionnaire, about the cultural capital that the *Aeneid* has accrued. Silvia referred to the *Aeneid* as "prestigious literature" and suggested that giving her students a glimpse of the *Aeneid's* influence raises its profile for her students. One respondent to the initial questionnaire stated this idea very plainly: "if there's one Latin author students should read, it is Virgil," although it was echoed by many others. These teachers seem to be motivated by passing on cultural prestige and privilege to their students, and they perceive the *Aeneid* to be a key part of that prestige.

The teachers were all very aware of those aspects of the text that they could use to engage their students and draw them further into the epic. Camilla explained that she tried to "stress the emotional side" of the narrative, since this helped the students relate to the characters more directly. Marcellus went further, saying that he tried to help his students gain a sense of what these characters might have been like. As a result, he reported that his students wanted to know what Nisus and Euryalus would do next, but also what happens to Euryalus's mother. He took pride in being able to share some of his knowledge of the reception of the *Aeneid*, suggesting things students could read and showing them Renaissance responses to the text. Silvia also described trying to get the students involved with the characters but in addition drawing their attention to "those little philosophical questions, the questions that cross the millennia," such as what might count as a noble death and whether Nisus was right to try and sacrifice himself to save Euryalus.

Marcellus explained how he uses contemporary culture to help his students draw links and gain a deeper understanding of the text. He spoke about the simile comparing the dying Euryalus to a flower bowing its head in the rain (9.435–7), and he described how he employs "lots of World War I imagery with that, using poppies as the dramatic link." This includes a version of the story of Nisus and Euryalus told through pictures from the First World War and clips from the UK television series *Blackadder Goes Forth* (a classic, with which many UK students are familiar). This topic is highly emotive, and Marcellus draws on cultural material that these students will have studied elsewhere on their curriculum. The final images of *Blackadder Goes Forth* are particularly moving for audiences who have followed the Blackadder household through the centuries, and so by drawing these parallels, Marcellus heightens the emotional appeal in ways his students can access. He described the success of this lesson in terms of the emotional response he was able to elicit from his students, referring to how many "kids cried" by the end of the lesson. This was an aspect of teaching the *Aeneid* that Marcellus identified as being one of the most rewarding for him, as he could see "how much they care about the characters," in particular when his class comprised students he has taught Latin to since they were 11 years old. He described how he remembers these students when he taught them to start reading Latin five years earlier and that he found it "beautiful" to watch the same students read Vergil themselves and discuss it with him.

Conclusion

In this chapter, I have examined the perspectives and attitudes of a small group of UK schoolteachers and their 15–16-year-old students toward teaching and studying Vergil's *Aeneid* in Latin at three schools. While the teachers have considerable knowledge and understanding of the text, with its historical and cultural context and afterlife, their students do not. They perceive the short section of the text that they study as a fast-paced action narrative—responding most to the plot and the characters. Many of the students identified strongly with the two young characters, who are central from their perspective. While the students are aware that they are reading a short extract of a much larger narrative text, much of that context remains distant for them. Some are curious about the remainder of the narrative, but this curiosity starts from the perspective of the portion of the poem that they read. Although this study is based on a small-scale study in only one country, these results may provide some indicators about the future reception of the *Aeneid*. The students noted that they particularly enjoyed the mythological elements, even though these elements do not feature in the extracts they read. This suggests that they may perceive the rest of the epic—which they have not read—as a mythological narrative, from the way in which their teachers have presented it to them. In a similar way, they may also absorb some of their teachers' views that the *Aeneid* is "prestigious literature" and a central part of cultural heritage, while adding their own understanding of antiquity and the Roman world. The students were able to identify those aspects of Vergil's language that form part of the poem's intensely literary high register, even though they could not articulate it as such. This implicit understanding may add to their perception of the epic as the preeminent classical work. The idea that the *Aeneid* is a piece of prestigious heritage literature authorized by its place on the curriculum and their teachers' respect for it potentially establishes its status as the standard of a privileged classical education for these students. On the other hand, what makes the *Aeneid* distinctive—even preeminent among ancient texts—is potentially lost on many of the next generation.

Both Carrowdown and Waywold offer Latin as a curricular option beyond age 16, and students at Fledden who wish to continue their study of Latin may do so at a school in a neighboring town. Since any of the students who choose to follow an academic (rather than a vocational) curriculum beyond age 16 usually choose to study only three subjects, the numbers who continue Latin are small. For the majority of the students in this study, therefore, this is likely to be their only encounter with the *Aeneid* in Latin—and potentially their only encounter with it within formal education. The Nisus and Euryalus story may be considered a narrative digression—it is hardly central to Aeneas' flight from Troy and establishment of a new kingdom in Latium—and as a result, these students have what some may consider a slightly distorted view of the context of the whole. These three teachers are motivated to convey some of their own passion for Vergil's *Aeneid* and to give a flavor of their knowledge surrounding Vergil's historical context as well as the epic's literary heritage and afterlife. They appeal to their students' enjoyment of the plot and characters and focus on making these aspects even more accessible for the students, such as by heightening the emotional strands of the narrative. In doing so, they provide their students with part of the cultural capital that they have gained and want to pass on. Students' responses suggest that their lasting memories of studying the *Aeneid* are likely to focus on the stories—the action and the characters. This is similar to the response of Augustine, who recalls how he enjoyed reading about the fall of Troy (*Conf.* 1.13). These students may be able to recall only the plot of the Nisus and Euryalus episode in the future, along with the knowledge that the *Aeneid* is a famous Roman poem. This does provide them with cultural capital on which to make sense of other cultural artefacts they may encounter.

Notes

1 Butler 2011: 14.
2 For example, Foster 2014; Foster 2017.
3 Horsfall 2013: 251.
4 Foster 2022.
5 Orme 2006: 30.
6 Orme 2006: 124.
7 Baswell 2006: 32.
8 Clarke 2014.
9 Stray 1998: 58.
10 Stray 1998: 66.
11 OCR 2016: 2.
12 Department for Education 2014: 5.
13 Ray 1999: 404.
14 Weaven and Clark 2013: 2006.
15 Erricker 2014: 92.
16 Pike 2003: 365.
17 Pike 2003: 367.
18 Butler 2011: 14.
19 Davies 2006: 173.
20 Carr and Pauwels 2005: 145.
21 Carr and Pauwels 2005: 99.
22 Carr and Pauwels 2005: 99.
23 Guillory 1993: 80.
24 Connor 2006: 171.
25 Vincent 2016: 5.
26 Foster 2014.

27 Carr and Pauwels 2005: 99.
28 Foster 2019.

References

Baswell, C. 2006. *Virgil in Medieval England: Figuring The Aeneid from the Twelfth Century to Chaucer*. Cambridge Studies in Medieval Literature. Cambridge: Cambridge University Press.

Butler, C.J. 2011. "Virgil in the Classroom." *Proceedings of the Virgil Society* 27: 14–25.

Carr, J., and Pauwels, A. 2005. *Boys and Foreign Language Learning: Real Boys Don't Do Languages*. London: Palgrave Macmillan.

Clarke, M.L. 2014. *Classical Education in Britain 1500–1900*. Cambridge: Cambridge University Press.

Connor, Donald E. 2006. "The Forest and the Trees: Teaching the *Aeneid* in High School." *The Classical World* 99, 2: 170–2.

Davies, D. 2006. "New Strategies for Reading Vergil." *Classical World* 99, 2: 173–6.

Department for Education. 2014. "English Programmes of Study: Key Stage 4 National Curriculum in England." https://assets.publishing.service.gov.uk/government/uploads/system/uploads/attachment_data/file/331877/KS4_English_PoS_FINAL_170714.pdf.

Erricker, K. 2014. "Taking Risks with Literature: An Exploration into the Resilience of Pupil Responses to the Study of a Challenging Text at GCSE." *Literacy* 48, 2.

Foster, F. 2014. "Reconstructing Virgil in the Classroom in Late Antiquity." *History of Education* 43, 3.

———. 2017. "Teaching Language Through Virgil in Late Antiquity Learning Languages in Late Antiquity." *Classical Quarterly* 67, 1.

———. 2019. "Teaching 'Correct' Latin in Late Antique Rome." *Language and History* 62, 2.

———. 2022. "'Alii dicunt . . . ' Servius and Virgil's Anonymised Readers." In U. Tischer, T. Kuhn-Treichel, and S. Poletti (eds.) *Sicut Commentatores Loquuntur*. Turnhout, Belgium: Brepols.

Guillory, J. (1993). *Cultural Capital: The Problem of Literary Canon Formation*. Chicago: University of Chicago Press.

Horsfall, N. 2013. *Virgil, "Aeneid" 6: A Commentary*. Berlin: De Gruyter.

OCR. 2016. "GCSE 9–1 Specification: English Language J351." https://ocr.org.uk/Images/168996-specification-accredited-gcse-english-language-j351.pdf

Orme, N. 2006. *Medieval Schools: From Roman Britain to Renaissance England*. New Haven: Yale University Press.

Pike, M.A. 2003. "The Canon in the Classroom: Students' Experiences of Texts from Other Times." *Journal of Curriculum Studies* 35, 3.

Ray, R. 1999. "The Diversity of Poetry: How Trainee Teachers' Perceptions Affect Their Attitudes to Poetry Teaching." *The Curriculum Journal* 10, 3: 403–18.

Stray, C. 1998. *Classics Transformed: Schools, Universities, and Society in England, 1830–1960*. Oxford: Clarendon Press.

Vincent, N. 2016. "Continuity and Change from Latin to Romance." In N. Vincent and J.N. Adams (eds.) *Early and Late Latin: Continuity or Change*? Cambridge: Cambridge University Press. 1–13.

Weaven, M., and Clark, T. 2013. "'I Guess It Scares Us'—Teachers Discuss the Teaching of Poetry in Senior Secondary English." *English in Education* 47, 3: 197–212.

13 Aeneas, Anthropocene, and apocalypse, or, Aeneas in space

Evander Price

sic itur ad astra

Vergil, *Aeneid* 9.641

In the midst of an environmental apocalypse that has inundated our world with a collective sense of existential dread, I find in the *Aeneid* something wonderfully and terrifyingly resonant in the story of a person who survives civilizational collapse—the fall of Troy—and manages, despite all of his flaws, to rebuild anew. Who at this moment can see the surrounding onslaught of mounting wildfires, wave upon wave of a worldwide pandemic, rising sea levels, accelerating species extinction, swelling hurricanes, heat waves, droughts, all compelling forced migrations from now uninhabitable homelands, and not feel a little like Aeneas? I mean the Aeneas we first meet in Book 1, a refugee on a ship fleeing his destroyed city, caught in a sudden violent storm that threatens to sink him and the last of his kind, a sobbing Aeneas, a praying Aeneas, his "limbs loosed by a chilly fear," (*solvuntur frigore membra*, 1.92). That is an Aeneas I can relate to. Aeneas is the hero for the Anthropocene. And so this essay does what Aeneas did when caught *in medio apocalypsis*. I will "stretch my two palms to the stars" (*duplicis tendens ad sidera palmas*, 1.93) or, rather, my ten fingers to the keyboard, to forward a hopeful reading of Book 6 of the *Aeneid*. I propose we search for Aeneas in space.

I do not mean to suggest a perfect mapping of Book 6 of the *Aeneid* anachronistically onto the endeavors of NASA in the 1970s. Instead, I suggest some striking parallels between Aeneas' retrieval of the Golden Bough and subsequent descent into the underworld, and Carl Sagan's creation of a Golden Record, the first human-made object to leave the solar system. In particular, I suggest that the descent into hell can be read as an analog for the ascent into space and suggest some ways that Aeneas' struggle is very much like our own. Aeneas is exactly the sort of hero we need to confront apocalypse: always sacrificing, suffering, flailing, despairing, losing, and often missing the mark; but when he is at his best, his eyes are firmly fixed on his obligations to the future generations who might follow him.

But first, some space exploration history.

DOI: 10.4324/9781003176145-18

Voyagers

On August 20, 1977, NASA launched the Voyager 2 into space. Its identical twin, the Voyager 1, followed a few weeks later, set for a different trajectory.[1] Each bore a Golden Record along with cartridge and stylus, a glittering gift to whoever might, in some distant future, retrieve one of these probes. Together, their mission was to take measurements and collect data on the Greco-Roman gods revolving around the sun: Mars, Jupiter, Saturn, Neptune, Uranus. It was the Voyagers' short-term aim to take photographs of the moons and snap planetary portraits of each god at stunning resolutions. Their path was delicate, tortuous, utterly precise, weaving through the planets as closely as possible, a journey fittingly called the "Grand Tour" of the solar system.[2] Their collected data would allow NASA scientists to gather new information about the solar neighborhood so that, through the study of the solar system, human beings might better learn of their place in the cosmos. After threading their fated flybys, the Voyagers traversed the very limits of the solar system, measuring the properties of the heliosphere. Thirty-five years later, Voyager 1 sailed into the heliopause, the outermost limit of the solar system, defined by the line at which the prevailing solar winds are overcome by cosmic winds. Soon, around 2025 or so, the compact nuclear reactors of both Voyagers will fizzle out, and these probes, triumphs of semiautonomous computer intelligence, will die.[3] From that moment on, the Voyager probes become protective shells, cosmic packaging for a gift from humanity to whoever might retrieve them. The Voyagers remain only the bearers of the Golden Record.

Slipping through the frictionless vacuum of space, the Golden Record is likely to be the most enduring object ever made by human beings. In its inaccessibility, its irretrievability, its temporal expansiveness, it becomes a remarkable thought experiment made real. It demands that one think of incomprehensible distances, unfathomable amounts of time. It impels its audience to think universally. It is monumental in its achievement of immortality, safe in the vacuum of space from the erosive forces of time. And it is monumental in the etymological sense of the word, which derives from the Latin verb *monere*, "to warn, to remind."[4] This 12-inch disk is arguably the most monumental of all monuments.

As such, it has been called many things: a time capsule, a cenotaph, a sarcophagus, a gift, a cocoon, a mixtape, a Rosetta Stone, a love letter, a long-play record.[5] There are more metaphors to add to this list: the Golden Record is a collective *memento mori*; a golden graven image meant to substitute for otherwise absent gods; a new Golden Bough. The Golden Record is temporally and spatially the most ambitious monument yet created, highlighting an imagination of what the future will be and endeavoring to define the purpose of humankind within that imagined future.

The strange and noble aspiration of humankind to throw some selection of its thoughts, dreams, discoveries, memories, and music into space is accompanied by the harrowing epiphany that just about anything NASA launches into space will outlast humanity itself, that rocket detritus and space trash might well be the most lasting vestige asserting the presence of human existence in this universe.[6] Much of what can be said about the Golden Record can also be said about all sorts of other abandoned space stuff: the Mars rovers, the moon buggy, cell phone satellites, Alan Shepard's golf balls, even packets of feces, urine, and vomit left on the moon by the Apollo missions, along with their footprints—each of these objects have an equal claim on eternity.[7] By one estimate, there are some 100 million miscellaneous objects bigger than a millimeter in orbit around Earth, threatening satellites and space stations with the possibility of their impact at 17,000 miles an hour. These bits of detritus will continue to assert the presence of humanity into the deep future, an archive of space miscellany, the fodder for some future space archeologist's research.[8]

To understand what it means to make things that are immortal, I turn to classical literature, particularly Vergil's story of the Golden Bough. Greek and Roman mythology, after all, is chock-full of sacred objects and immortal beings. Through these comparisons, I demonstrate the optimistic and pessimistic interpretations of this immortal object. I argue that the Golden Record is an effort, on the part of Carl Sagan, with the bullhorn of NASA, to set a common collective goal for all of humanity in a universe without the god or gods who had previously mythically and religiously defined this common purpose. The claim that NASA (through Carl Sagan) was inviting a mytho-religious dimension to a scientific mission is not a new one. In *Redeeming Culture: American Religion in an Age of Science*, historian James Gilbert delves into the many ways that the line defining religion from science has been frequently scrambled in American culture, from the Scopes trial to the Apollo 8 broadcasted reading of *Genesis* on Christmas Eve, 1965.[9] Kendrick Oliver's *To Touch the Face of God* more narrowly defines the religious dimensions of American space exploration. This essay adds to Oliver's work, while simultaneously expanding the correlation between religious transcendence and cosmic transcendence to the realm of mythology and monumentality.[10] Because monuments such as the Golden Record imply a belief or faith in effecting a particular future, they necessarily adopt a religious and moral dimension in the message they convey about what *should* be.

I argue that the creator of the Golden Record, the popular cosmologist Carl Sagan, was tapping into mythical paradigms in this project. Sagan's particular flavor of scientific moral prognostication invokes Vergilian antecedents. Sagan, wittingly or not, literalized the myth of the Golden Bough in space. In other words, by creating this strange golden object, Sagan and his team played the role of ancient Roman gods, creating a heroic challenge (the reception of the record) for some future group of heroes, either aliens or future humans, to strive to achieve. What would it mean to retrieve the Golden Record?—that is a difficult question. To answer it, let us instead ask an analogous and parallel question: What did it mean to retrieve the Golden Bough?

The Golden Record

The Golden Record is, quite literally, a long-play record, the ubiquitous musical medium of the 1970s, and, at that time, the most reliable way NASA could think of to store data for long periods. Rather than vinyl, however, it is made of copper electroplated in gold.[11] The idea to attach a message to a satellite had first been put forward in 1972, when NASA let Carl Sagan fix a small plaque to the Pioneer 10. The Golden Record was no mere plaque. As Sagan explains, the Pioneers 10 and 11 were mere "visual greeting cards" compared to the Golden Record, which contained some two hours of music and images spiraled into its golden grooves.[12]

The record was a result of a broad collaboration. Sagan consulted a wide range of thinkers. They included astronomers like Harvard's A.G.W. Cameron, Frank Drake, the founder of the Search for Extra Terrestrial Intelligence (SETI), philosophers like Steven Toulmin at the University of Chicago, biologists such as Leslie Orgel at the Salk Institute, businessmen like B. M. Oliver, Hewlett-Packard's president for research and development, ethnomusicologists like Alan Lomax, founder of the Cantrometrics Research Center, artists like Jon Lomberg, and science writers like Timothy Ferris, who writes about the Golden Record to this day. Science fiction masters Richard Heinlein and Isaac Asimov contributed ideas.[13] Careful delegation was necessary to compile a thoughtful, distilled portrait of humankind's greatest hits in just six weeks with a budget of $25,000.[14] The resulting record contained six and a half minutes of greetings in 59 languages (including a humpback whale song); "Sounds of Earth," an audio essay with Kepler's *Harmonices Mundi*; recordings of volcanoes, oceans, birds, heartbeats, and Morse code of the Latin phrase *ad astra per aspera*—"through hardships, to the stars."[15] Then there is the world music, a quartet of German composers, an Indian raga, Melanesian panpipes, a Navajo night chant, a Japanese bamboo *shakuhachi* (flute) piece, a Pygmy initiation song, a Javanese *gamelan* (orchestra), blues from Blind Willie Johnson, and even Chuck Berry's "Johnny B. Goode."[16] This would be a gift, Sagan told us, for aliens.

No such *lingua cosmica*

> A sad spectacle. If they be inhabited, what a scope for misery and folly. If they be not inhabited, what a waste of space.
>
> —Attributed to Thomas Carlyle by Carl Sagan[17]

Imagine: an alien plucks the Golden Record out of its protective case and looks at the directions for how to play an LP. Would an alien be able to decode the message on the Golden Record? A 2014 article in the *Atlantic* claims yes.[18] The answer, however, is a bit more complicated.

The problem of inventing a universal language is an old one that arose historically in the global context of finding a neutral medium for communicating foreign policy and trade relations among nations. Expanding the idea to the literal 'universal,' Hans Freudenthal wrote the seminal book *Lincos* (1960), short for *lingua cosmica*, in which he argued that mathematics is the only logical universal language for extraterrestrial communication.[19] The connection between music and mathematics, as Sagan well knew, can be traced back to the *musica universalis* of Pythagoras.[20]

Sagan, Drake, and the rest of the SETI team loved to play this game: what would a proper universal language look like? They would write their own mathematical codes, often in binary, and send them to one another.[21] A correct translation might be nothing more than an 8-bit picture of a martini glass, but the translatability would establish at the very least that within the universe of SETI scientists, a universal mathematical language could be conceived. The "depressing shock," Drake lamented, was that "almost none of the elite members of [SETI] were able to interpret this message."[22] Forget interstellar communication: inter-SETI communication failed.

Sagan and Drake both wrote up detailed explanations for how to read the Golden Record's directions in *Murmurs of Earth*. The essential first step for an alien to understand is the concept of "on" and "off," which is the basis of binary programming. Hydrogen, being the most abundant element in the universe, could operate as the key to this cosmic Rosetta Stone, a sort of galactic shibboleth.[23] If an alien species could recognize a diagram representing the hyperfine transition of a hydrogen diatom at its two lowest energy states, then the aliens would be able to determine both a measure of distance related to the wavelength produced and a measure of time relative to the speed of that transition (.7 billionths of a second), and thus have a key for understanding the rest of the diagrams on the record that describe, among other things, the Earth's position relative to a number of pulsars and the speed at which the record ought to rotate (16⅔ rpm) in order to play appropriately.[24] But who could?

The assumptions here are astonishing. To detect and retrieve a nearly one-ton satellite traveling at a velocity of 38,000 mph is a massive technological feat.[25] Voyager is travelling at 21 times the speed of your average bullet and is much, much larger. Then, presuming one could catch up to Voyager, the aliens would then need to have sensory apparatuses akin enough to humans to be able to see the diagrams on the Golden Record, logic similar enough to comprehend binary, and a nuanced understanding of hydrogen.[26] Next is the matter of playing the record in a medium capable of transmitting sound. To retrieve the Golden Record in space is a stellar technological accomplishment far outstripping the relatively simple process of strapping it to a satellite and rocketing it into space in the first place; it is the difference between firing a gun and catching a bullet mid-flight. Sagan was aware of this:

> There is a major difference between sending and receiving. We have only recently achieved the ability of doing either, and any civilization even a bit behind us technologically could do neither. Therefore, a baby civilization like ours is not a civilization that might be expected to transmit; the technology of other communicative civilization should be far in advance of our own.

Sagan and his team expected a lot from their imagined retrievers; most of all, they expected these hypothetical aliens to be of a sort far smarter and more skillful than the senders themselves.[27]

There is much more to be said about these hoped-for aliens. Trevor Paglen usefully categorizes aliens into two categories: alien-aliens, and alien-strangers. The alien-stranger is one that is "not human, but which shares many characteristics with human;" for example, think of the recognizably humanoid creatures from *E.T.*, *Star Trek*, *Star Wars*, *Close Encounters with the Third Kind*, and so on. The latter 'alien-alien' is "an alien that is truly and radically non-human, with few if any overlapping communication strategies, thoughts, or sensory experience." Imagine the buggers in *Ender's Game*, the monolith in *2001: A Space Odyssey*, or the heptapods in Ted Chiang's 2010 novella, *The Story of Your Life*. Paglen concludes that the idea of communicating with the alien-stranger that Sagan and Drake had in mind is ridiculous. Paglen asks, "Is it even theoretically possible to compose a message for extraterrestrials with 'a full picture of earth and its inhabitants?' Answer: 'Of course not.'"[28] He goes on to explain that, although the Golden Record was created with the "alien-stranger" category in mind, it is much more likely the record encounters an alien with no means of comprehending or communicating with any object that operates under the anthropocentric assumptions of Sagan and his crew. Paglen is not alone in his doubts. Aliens may have no interest in inspecting the Voyager,[29] they may be unable to hear or see, and they would likely have a language constructed in the context of an environment so dramatically unearthly and unhuman that translation may be impossible.[30] It is likely space is a Tower of Babel, that here is no such *lingua cosmica*.

Paglen discards any notion of the Golden Record's reception by an alien race, calling the idea of alien reception "a figment of human imagination." Nonetheless, it is a useful thought experiment, Paglen explains,

> because thinking about aliens is a way to think about ourselves and our relationship to the future. Symbolically, much is at stake . . . what relationship do we want to have to the cosmos, to the stranger and to the future? Should our disposition be pregnant with nihilism of silent indifference, or should we endeavor to develop an ethical relationship to those symbolic figures, and, by extension, ourselves?

For Paglen, any meditation on aliens is reciprocally a meditation on our future selves. As we saw, the probability of successful communication with nonhuman aliens is near zero. In addition, supposing that the human species were to endure on Earth for another 40,000 years, the closest living things to the Golden Record at that moment would nevertheless still be human beings. Our sun would still be the closest star to Voyager. To John Casani and others, the Golden Record exists as a concretization of the old anthropological device of the imagining how Martians would perceive a given human practice.[31] It acts as a nexus for the discussion of the values, ideals, failures, and social constructions of current humans.[32] The Golden Record asks us to project ourselves far, far into the future, so far that if we persist, those future humans will surely be aliens to us.

If no one is to retrieve the Golden Records, then the Golden Records will travel silently on in space, unperturbed except, perhaps, by periodic peppering with micrometeorites. Sagan thought about this deeply, and went so far as to make a mathematical prediction about the rate of degradation, estimating,

> two percent of the record should be micropitted by the time the spacecraft reaches a distance of one light year. This corresponds to about 4,000 tiny impacts before it leaves the cloud of cometary debris. Thereafter, in interstellar space, the abundance of micrometeorites should be much less, and the outward face of the record will degrade at the very slow rate of about 0.02 percent of its area for every 50 light years traveled. An additional two percent of damage will not occur until the spacecraft had traveled an additional 5,000 light years, which is one-sixth of the distance between the sun and the center of the Galaxy. It will take the Voyager spacecraft about a hundred million years to traverse such a distance.[33]

The records will remain recognizable (were there anyone to recognize them) long after the pyramids disintegrate like so many melting mounds of butter, long after the sun swells into a red giant and consumes the solar system. Some interminable amount of time after that, they will crumble into a whimper of their previous form. Seen from the perspective of eventual desuetude, the Golden Records are cenotaphs in space, empty golden sarcophagi carrying some slice of the memory of the Anthropocene beyond the brief time allotted on Earth.

Sagan and team knew that the Golden Record would never, beyond the realm of thought experiment, be retrieved. They further knew that if any communication with aliens were to happen, it would not happen via the snail mail of slow-moving space stuff. Radio waves travel at the speed of light, nearly 18,000 times the speed of Voyager—alien communication is the stuff of radio telescopes.[34] Why then go through all the trouble of constructing a Golden Record? One way to answer this question is thoroughly nihilistic. Sagan, when he wrote about the Golden Record, surrounded it with tons of positive, forward-thinking rhetoric. Looking, however, more widely at his popular writings, Sagan pragmatically forecasted the end of the planet in myriad ways. Asteroids, he said, have hit before, and will hit again, like "30,000 swords of Damocles hanging over our heads—ten times more than the number of stars visible to the naked eye under optimum atmospheric clarity."[35] He was a product of his Cold War moment, painfully aware of the threat of nuclear catastrophe. He wrote a book where he dubbed the term "nuclear winter."[36] The world, for Sagan, could just as easily end "in fire" as it could in ice, "if it had to perish twice," as Robert Frost put it.[37] In this reading, communicating with aliens and creating some sort of object for reflection for humankind are both ancillary impetuses for the creation of the Golden Record. When one considers the endless cold emptiness of space, the Golden Record is just another reminder, a *memento mori*, of the impossibility of getting off this rock. Ironically, Voyager was launched into space carried by a repurposed intercontinental ballistic missile (Titan IIIE)—the very same rockets that could propel warheads around the planet and end the world as we know it.[38]

With the imminent and probable demise of humankind, the Golden Record—safely bolted to the side of the Voyagers, sealed off from the erosion of wind, water, fire, and the most dangerous, erosive, destructive force of all: human beings—had the responsibility of bearing the last memory of humanity's brief existence into eternity.

A noble metal

> *"if gold ruste, what shal iren do"*
>
> —Chaucer[39]

Gold is the material of mythology. Of the noble metals—ruthenium (Ru); rhodium (Rh); palladium (Pd); osmium (Os); iridium (Ir); platinum (Pt); silver (Ag)—gold (Au) is the noblest.[40] It is the *rex metallorum*—the 'King of Metals.'[41] Here, nobility is defined by the relative inertness of the metal in comparison to other substances. Chemically speaking, to be noble is to be unreactive, which is not to say noble metals resist forming bonds. They can be mixed into all sorts of alloys that are common in jewelry.[42] Nobility here means it is difficult to impel gold to form a bond that creates new compounds (oxides or carbides, for example). Gold has the highest resistance to dissociation, that is, it is difficult to split its atoms from one another or dissolve them in acid. It also has the least stable chemisorption state, which means its outer surface offers a uniquely improbable, unstable place for another chemical—oxygen or water, say—to bond to.[43] Whereas other metals mix and meld with the world around them—oxygen corrodes them, acid dissolves them, water rusts them—the noble metals stand apart for their resistance to change. Atoms of gold simply refuse to socialize with any other substances.

Physically, however, it is extremely malleable. It can be flattened "to airy thinness" that can be applied to almost any surface.[44] Ultrathin translucent coats of gold are evaporated onto the visors of astronauts to augment their vision and protect against radiation. Neil Armstrong walked on the moon gazing through a thin, protective veil of gold.[45] Gold is an efficient and corrosion-resistant conductor of electricity.[46] It effectively reflects infrared light, which makes it an excellent tool for deflecting heat and controlling temperature in the radiation-filled vacuum of space; in a temperamental universe, gold always keeps its cool. Sheets of it blanket critical components of spacecraft, protecting them from exposure to the extremities of space.[47] Its unique combination of chemical stubbornness and physical malleability makes it an invaluable medium for grappling with the challenges of creating technology that can suffer the conditions of space.

Pressed into a record, gold is noble in the sense of being the vehicle through which humankind would make itself known to the universe; it is noble in the etymological sense of being a 'well-known' (*nobilis*) object here on earth; it is noble in the sense of being rare; it is noble in the sense of being utterly apart, physically and temporally, from the mundane; it is noble in the sense of representing an ideal, in this case, an effort to convey the very best face of humanity to the cosmos. Certainly, Sagan and his team built the record out of gold because of technical necessity, that is, its chemical stability, but he didn't anticipate just how fitting the medium and the message are. It is fitting, in a sense Marshall MacLuhan would appreciate, chemically, physically, etymologically, symbolically, and ideally, to its message.[48]

Cosmic alchemy

By considering the Golden Record as an object stemming from the esoteric alchemic tradition, I propose an Eliadian reading of the Golden Record: it is alchemy in space.[49] The alchemic shorthand for gold is simple, just a circle with a dot in the center. *Sol* it is called, or *helios*, the sun sign, ruled by Apollo, god of prophecy and music—the *prima materia*, the noblest metal, seemed the material of the sun itself.[50] Note the coincidence of the uncanny resemblance between this ancient glyph and the Golden Record itself, seen from above, even with a hole for its spindle. Further, the copper core of the record is the element of Venus, goddess of love, ♀. It is almost as if the object itself were an invocation of the Apollo and Venus. Foresight and Love united to form this object that will fly ever further into an infinite future.

These symbols come from alchemy, magical progenitor of chemistry, which took as its core belief the concept of universal correspondences: the idea that the revolutions of the planets and stars above somehow affected or reflected what would occur in the earthy sphere below. Alchemists believed that if a baser metal could be transmuted into a nobler one, so too could the human soul move from a fallen state to one of grace. Modern science has long since disillusioned these esoteric beliefs, yet the symbolism remains: this idealized snapshot of humanity is literally elevated to the stars: *musica mundi* to *musica universalis*, thanks to the star-shooting power of rocket science. Yet the Golden Record is not a work of scientific research—it holds no scientific merit whatsoever. If the Golden Record can be read as an alchemic attempt to move some idealization of humankind beyond the mundane and into the cosmos, it is reasonable to bring in related alchemic myths, such as the myth of the Golden Bough, an object Aeneas could only retrieve with the help of his mother, Venus, after visiting the Temple of Apollo at Cumae.

Discus Aureus: Ramus Aureus

The story of the Golden Bough is a Vergilian invention described in Book 6 of the *Aeneid*, marking the transition from the Odyssey-structured *nostos* epic to the Iliad-style war epic. Robert A. Brooks called the Golden Bough "one of the most critical and complex events in [the *Aeneid*'s] internal structure."[51] I argue here that the parallels between the Golden Bough and the Golden Record are uncanny, extending well beyond their shared materiality. Vergil's *katabasis*, the decent into hell, further becomes NASA's *anabasis*, the ascent into the heavens.[52]

Vergil tells us how Aeneas and the Trojans land at Cumae, following the advice of Helenus to seek out the wisdom of the oracle (3. 433–62). Vergil relates how the temple of Apollo was built by Daedalus, that ancient engineer who, among many other feats, was the first human being to achieve flight. We might imagine Daedalus as a sort of Ancient Greek version of the contemporary NASA engineer. Vergil then provides an *ekphrasis* of the golden doors of the temple. Aeneas meditates on these doors, which depict scenes from Daedalus' life, before Aeneas is interrupted by the Sibyl.[53] With the Sibyl's help, Aeneas learns to perform the rituals that will permit him entry into the underworld so that he might consult the shades of the dead and better understand his fated mission to found Rome. The descent, the oracle famously explains, is easy. Anyone can go to the underworld; it is coming back that is the privilege of very few heroes (6.126–9). To go to hell before your time and to return belies a foolish desire to die twice. To descend to the underworld with the possibility of return (i.e., without dying), one must bring a particular gift: the Golden Bough. Aeneas prays for divine assistance finding the bough, and two doves appear. These are the sacred doves of Venus, his mother, sent by her to show him the way. Once there, he greedily pulls the Bough down from the tree and brings it back to the oracle. With his golden passport, Aeneas and the oracle descend together into the underworld and consult the shades who foretell the entire history of Rome. The Bough is first described twice by the Sibyl setting out Aeneas' task (6.136–9; 145–8):

> In a dark forest, there lies
> A branch, gold leafed and gold stemmed,
> Said to be sacred to the Juno of the Inferno; the whole world
> Hides this branch and encloses it in the dark valleys of shades. . . .
>
> Therefore, look high with your eyes and by divine will, you find it,
> Seize it with your hand, for the branch itself will follow willing and easily
> If the fates call you; otherwise, with no amount of,
> Or any iron, will you be able to conquer it.

Just what is this Bough? The Golden Bough is described as "a branch golden both in its leaves and in its spry shoot" (6.137). It is delicate, crackling in the soft winds near the gateway to hell, foul-smelling Avernus (*olens Avernus*, 6.201). It is secreted away in a dark forest so well that the "whole world hides this branch and encloses it with dark valleys of shades" (6.138–9). It is a thing of metal growing from a thing of wood, an unnatural, divine object somehow growing from a tree—divinity springing from mortality.

Robert Brooks calls this phenomenon "life-in-death"—a fitting symbol of the paradoxical position of Aeneas, a living being, passing through the world of the dead. "The bough," Brooks explains,

> becomes a guarantee both of Aeneas' ability to enter the underworld and his protection while passing through it. . . . As he plucks the bough from the tree, death from life, so he departs from the underworld unharmed, life from death.[54]

The Golden Bough is a moral, mythical, and religious object. Not only is it impossible to find if one is not meant to find it, but it is impossible to pluck if one is not destined to pluck it. The medium of gold, as discussed earlier, is important to both these objects. It promotes these objects to the realm of the sacred. A vinyl LP is to the Golden Record what a wooden tree branch is to the Golden Bough. The Golden Bough is hidden deep in a grove in a dark valley of shades, just like the Golden Record is hidden by the whole universe in the dark depths of space. To find the Golden Bough is to find a needle in a haystack, a branch in a forest, a satellite in a cosmos. Any interpretation of the Golden Bough can be usefully translated to the Golden Record. We then return to the initial question: what would it mean to *retrieve* it?

In the 2,000 years of Vergilian hermeneutics and criticism, there have been many answers to this question. Anthony Ossa-Richardson outlines the major readings of the Golden Bough from the 4th-century Italian scholar Servius onward.[55] Servius's glosses locate the Golden Bough in pagan ritual, connecting it pseudomorphically with the Pythagorean mystical interpretation of the letter Y, representing the fork at which a youth chooses to live a life of virtue or vice.[56] The Golden Bough is the symbol of the life lived in pure virtue. It yields only to the moral hero whose pure heart and *pietas* allow him to retrieve it.

Adrian Parvulescu argues further that the Golden Bough is a symbol of peace.[57] Parvulescu notes that readers often overlook the frequency with which the Greek and Roman underworld is *invaded* by heroes, a point of particular concern to Charon, who is immediately upset that Aeneas has arrived in armor (6.388) and thus is dressed for battle, which is hardly what anyone wants from a guest. Charon has good evidence; the infernal kingdom has suffered many unwelcome guests, such as Theseus, Pirithous, and Hercules. "Hercules stole our dog!" laments Charon, who refers to the monstrous three-headed watchdog Cerebus, or in his opinion, a poor trembling creature (*trementem* 6. 396) unnecessarily abused by an uninvited intruder. Charon reminds us of the importance of perspective.

The Golden Bough is thus an infernal passport, indicating that the bearer has great piety and has been destined by the gods to make this trip. The bearer enters not by strength of brute force (as Hercules and Theseus did) but through the proper avenues, the agreed-upon bureaucratically signed-and-stamped route to hell. Aeneas can retrieve the Golden Bough because he has impeccable *pietas*, and we know he has impeccable *pietas* because he retrieves the Golden Bough. The bearer need only show it to say "we come in peace," and Charon diligently makes way. By extension, the Golden Record is a moral object—to retrieve it an act of *pietas*. The bough's message of peace, incidentally, is the foremost message on the Golden Record, a phrase that is etched by hand into the negative space between the grooves and the spindle:

> *To the makers of music—all worlds, all times.*[58]

It is for this reason that Charon looks upon the Golden Bough in the same way we might imagine a human of the distant future looking upon the Golden Record, "Marveling at a gift so venerable, the fateful branch [record], unseen for so many years" (*ille admirans venerabile donum / fatalis virgae longo post tempore visum,* 6. 408–9).

The 6th-century scholar Fulgentius observed that the Golden Bough is Aeneas' ticket to visions of the future Roman Empire. The Golden Bough represents the hero's achievement of so much knowledge (*scientia*) and learning (*doctrina*) that one is able to see beyond the fog of the present into the fated future.[59] So too with the Voyagers, which remain to this day an example of extending human perception deep into the universe. The classics scholar Maud Bodkin also reads the Golden Bough as a key to unlock a vision of the future, in other words, an object that allows a hero the visionary epiphany that is seeing the purpose and meaning of their life unraveled into a deep future.[60] Communication with aliens is the stuff of fiction: like Vergil's proleptic anachronism of having Aeneas speaking to the shades in the underworld; that is, what is the deep future for Aeneas is the past for Vergil's readers. So too with the Golden Record and Golden Bough, both objects that serve as a vehicle for imagining such deep futures, though the Golden Record puts us in the position of Aeneas (as opposed to the position of Vergil's readers), with a vision of the future too distant to experience. In other words, anyone reading this chapter will die as Aeneas does before the visions of the future that are made accessible by the record come to fruition.

Aeneas is granted the rare privilege of seeing the meaning of his life marched in front of him in ghostly procession, the whole history of Rome. Of course, ultimately, Aeneas leaves the underworld through the Gate of False Dreams. Vergil uses this device to suggest an interpretation of Roman history that emphasizes the horrors of war (*bella, horrida bella,* 6.86), compared to the pleasures of peace. This is fitting with the Golden Record encouraging an idealized vision of the future that remains, as always, a dream—the influence of the dream, we hope, nonetheless profits us with some sort of collective wisdom to make conscientious decisions for the future of humankind.

The Golden Bough is thus proleptically imagined by Vergil as a symbolic device to tell a complex Roman anti-war epic.[61] We will see that Sagan also imagined the Golden Record an anti-war symbol. Neither Vergil nor Sagan are particularly optimistic about these golden visions. Understanding the record as the analog of the bough casts Carl Sagan, the creator of the New Golden Bough, in the role of the divinity who places the Bough in the forest. Or rather, in the absence of gods to create Golden Boughs to define the goals for heroes, Sagan creates his own goal, his own purpose. But his goal is not for a single hero—it is a collective golden goal for all human beings. By putting the Bough into space, he aspired to create a defining symbol, a nexus for thoughts of what the cosmic future and purpose of humankind ought to be. Sagan set into motion half of a heroic cycle, establishing a heroic goal and posing it as a challenge to future generations: the *Discus* or *Ramus Aureus* is Servius's and Pythagoras's 'Y,' the split between realization of the Golden Record as either the nihilistic post-apocalyptic cenotaph or the optimistic challenge to future generations to persevere against all odds. This ability to see the future yet do nothing about it, this Cassandra-like power seems essential to the Anthropocene human condition: knowing what is going to happen, indeed, even having the powers to measure it, to predict it, to reckon it, and yet nonetheless being absolutely unable to prevent it.

Sagan thinks that the collective grasp of this humbling perspective is essential to achieving any sort of ethical relationship with one another here on Earth, as well as whatever might be out there in our ever-expanding universe, be it spatially or temporally distant. The lesson to take away from Voyager is not that human beings are smart, special, and justly privileged. The lesson is the opposite. The search for aliens is also a search for further evidence destabilizing any claims on the primacy of human perspective. To make a golden gift for aliens is to presume their existence and imagine a universe from their perspective. If human beings are the only sentient life in the cosmos, that is a type of specialness. However, as we noticed earlier, even the humans in the distant future who may recover the Golden Record may be well-nigh aliens to us. The Golden Record cautions against the parochialism of putting humans of this time period at the center of a system of 'universal' ethics. What Sagan would have audiences of Voyager ponder can be summed up in one of Sagan's most famous speeches, the "Pale Blue Dot," a narration introducing a photo taken when Voyager 1, skirting the outward bounds of the solar system, turned its camera back toward Earth, which appeared as barely more than a fleck of dust:

> Look again at that dot. That's here. That's home. That's us. On it everyone you love, everyone you know, everyone you ever heard of, every human being who ever was, lived out their lives. The aggregate of our joy and suffering, thousands of confident religions, ideologies, and economic doctrines, every hunter and forager, every hero and coward, every creator and destroyer of civilization, every king and peasant, every young couple in love, every mother and father, hopeful child, inventor and explorer, every teacher of morals, every corrupt politician, every "superstar," every "supreme leader," every saint and sinner in the history of our species lived there—on a mote of dust suspended in a sunbeam.
>
> The Earth is a very small stage in a vast cosmic arena. . . . Our posturings, our imagined self-importance, the delusion that we have some privileged position in the Universe, are challenged by this point of pale light. Our planet is a lonely speck in the great enveloping cosmic dark. In our obscurity, in all this vastness, there is no hint that help will come from elsewhere to save us from ourselves.[62]

Sagan's primary problem with anthropocentrism is the heart of the "Pale Blue Dot" speech, and it stems back to Protagoras, the father of relativism, who would have us believe that "man is the measure of all things" (Pl. *Prt.*). By extension, Sagan takes issue with all anthropocentric religions that profess a privileged position for humankind in the universe. Sagan's response to Protagoras is the same as Demosthenes's (*Olynthiac* 3.19): "What a man desires, he imagines to be true"—or rather, man is not the measure of all things, but he measures according to his desires.[63] For Demosthenes and Sagan, such desires are more often self-deceptions, and it is critical therefore to earnestly examine one's desires—good desires are essential to good ethics. Lauren Berlant poses a similar concept in her book *Cruel Optimism*, explaining,

> A relation of cruel optimism exists when something you desire is actually an obstacle to your flourishing. It might involve food, or a kind of love; it might be a fantasy of the good life, or a political project.[64]

We see this concept articulated in the figure of Nisus, who asks (*Aen*. 9. 184–5):

> *Dine hunc ardorem mentibus addunt,*
> *Euryale, an sua cuique deus fit dira cupido?*
>
> Do the gods not give this fire to our hearts, Euryalus,
> or does each man's dread desire become to him a god?

To Sagan, it is the latter: humans are the very gods they want to see in the world—each man's dread desire becomes to him a god. He was also well aware that by compiling the Golden Record and putting a recording of his son's voice on it, he was immortalizing himself; in a sense, Sagan's dread desire made him make himself a god, to immortalize himself through the monument. Given that "gods were disappointingly hard to find," Sagan proposes we replace religion with scientific humanism—essentially Spinozan awe at natural law and pursuit of greater knowledge of it.[65] It is time to quit clinging to the reassuring fantasy of a universe built around humans but to continue in pursuit of some dread desires, like the exploration of the awesome hugeness of a cosmos.

Dira cupido ("dread desire") comes up twice in Book 6, once in reference to Palinurus, to whom the Sibyl asks "Why, O Palinurus, have you such dread desire?" (*unde haec, o Palinure, tibi tam dira cupido*?, 6. 373) and once in reference to the mass of shades of the dead. Curiously, *dira cupido* always comes in the form of a question. Aeneas asks Anchises "why do these miserable souls have such a dread desire for life?" (*quae lucis miseris tam dira cupido*?, 6.721). Aeneas' question provides some dark insight into his psyche. For Aeneas, a refugee and survivor of outrageous misfortune, the question of rebirth into a new body is not one of merit and reward—that is, as Anchises sees it—but rather the burden of the responsibility of being alive.

At this point, halfway through the *Aeneid*, our hero has six more books of trials and tribulations ahead of him. One might see in the world-weary Aeneas a parallel to our own condition, living, as we do, halfway between crises of climate, economy, and epidemiological catastrophe, *in medio apocalypsis*, beholden to the perpetual expectation of responsibility for things that are outside our individual control but which now must necessarily be our duty. This is what it means to be Aeneas and, by extension, this is what it means to be us.

Such responsibility was on Sagan's mind as well. If we do not focus on a golden goal of some sort,

> If we continue to accumulate only power and not wisdom, we will surely destroy ourselves.... If we become even more violent, shortsighted, ignorant, and selfish than we are now, almost certainly we will have no future.[66]

Sagan here sounds remarkably like Anchises, who warns Aeneas of his fundamental responsibility as a Roman (*Aen*. 6.847–54):

> "Others will fashion quivering bronze more gracefully;
> (believe it!) others will lead faces out of marble;

Others will plead cases better; others will map out
the sky with a compass, and predict the rising stars.
But you, O Roman, remember, these will be your skills:
Rule peoples with your power, impose the custom of peace,
Have mercy on those you've vanquished, and crush the proud."

Sagan was as concerned about the possibility of total war leading to total destruction as he was about the danger of environmental catastrophe from climate change, a concern he shares with Vergil. Note that Sagan's mention of power and wisdom echoes Fulgentius's dichotomy of *scientia* (knowledge) and *doctrina* (learning).[67] His caveat: scientific discovery in the 20th century has routinely led to the creation of technologies that can wipe out humanity entirely—the *deus-ex-machina* savior of science is just as likely to create a technophilic *dies irae.* In other words, Sagan asks: "Can we human beings be trusted with civilization-threatening technologies?"[68] Or, as Vergil asks of Aeneas through Anchises, can Roman leadership be trusted to know when the ultimate power of the Empire should be wielded for war or for peace? For Sagan and Vergil, the stakes of such questions are existential.

More and more, the reason for creating an object like the Golden Record comes into focus. Sagan is providing an idea of what he thinks it means to live in a universe without a cosmic purpose defined for us by a god. If there is no god to define our meaning and purpose, no "parent to care for us, to forgive us our errors, to save us from our childish mistakes" as Aeneas has with his mother Venus, then it follows that people must become responsible to themselves and to each other; after all, "We are the custodians of life's meaning. . . . If we crave some cosmic purpose, then let us find ourselves a worthy goal."[69] What exactly is that goal? Who or what should define it? The Golden Record is his answer. In the *Aeneid*, the gods established a golden object that enables Aeneas to see the future. In reality Carl Sagan established a noble universal goal, a *raison d'etre* to define the purpose of the whole crew of the ship of Earth. Sagan's *dira cupido* did not become to him a god, but it did convince him to play the role of one.

Sagan's "worthy goal" contrasts with the *dira cupido* that afflicted Nisus and led to his demise. In place of war, humankind ought to set its sights on the lofty goal of knowing the stars. For Sagan, the purpose of humankind will ultimately be determined by what role we choose to play in the universe or what metaphor we imagine our lives as operating within. Wonderfully, or perhaps terrifyingly, we have the responsibility of choosing that metaphor for ourselves, given that there is no Anchises to reveal our fate.

Sagan recognized that a hero without a quest is no hero at all. He placed, as a god would, a divine branch for someone alien to us to retrieve. And he hid that golden branch in the shadowy forests of space, so far-flung it would long elude any but the worthiest of heroes. It would require an intelligence of tremendous genius, time, and know-how to retrieve and understand the Golden Record. The most likely such hero is humanity in the distant future, which would have to have survived storms, trials, wars, and countless unanticipated tribulations: to have endured like Aeneas and the material Golden Record itself.

Imagined as an analogue of the Golden Bough, the Golden Record reflects on humanity: to retrieve the Golden Record would be an unprecedented technological feat. It would mean the apocalypse of the Anthropocene had been delayed long enough that some level of harmonious cooperation had allowed for the development of space technology capable of leaving the solar system, finding a distant speck of satellite, a golden needle in a haystack, grasping it, diverting it from its trajectory, and returning it home. The Golden Record becomes the symbol of the human species coming of age and choosing a path of virtue. Seen from the perspective of Fulgentius, then, the retrieval of the Golden Record would mean the development of technology and knowledge balanced with wisdom to the point that humanity becomes collectively heroized, largely in virtue of not destroying ourselves. The very act of retrieving the Golden Record, just as the Golden Bough, proves the merit of the retriever. So long as it exists, the challenge of retrieving it remains an open one. And should we never retrieve it, should we foreclose our human future due to our collective *impietas*, should the storm simply sink all of our ships, should we not endure to see what comes after the Anthropocene, then perhaps some other, worthier alien-hero will come along to retrieve the Golden Record and visit our shades, hidden in space, preserved eternally in its golden grooves.

Notes

1 Though Voyager 1 and Voyager 2 were launched in reverse order, they were launched on different trajectories, such that Voyager 1 would quickly overtake Voyager 2 and justify its status as the "first" Voyager. See Pyne 2010: 78.
2 Bonestell 1972: 18.
3 Riley, Corfield, and Dolling 2015: 190. The *Voyager Workshop Manual* is the definitive source for the Voyager missions; however, there is also the JPL website (Jet Propulsion Laboratory; California Institute of Technology 2021) and Carl Sagan's *Murmurs of Earth* (Sagan, Drake, and Lomberg 1978).
4 Oxford English Dictionary 2007.
5 Analogies abound. For a number of them, see Morena 2016.
6 Space archaeology, variously dubbed "exoarchaeology" or "aerospace archeology" is a strange and relatively new field. Its interests, however, are in the present and recent past, as opposed to the far future. See Darrin and O'Leary 2009: 4–5.
7 BBC News 2021.
8 LeCouteur 2017.
9 Gilbert 1997.
10 Oliver 2013.
11 Sagan, Drake, and Lomberg 1978: 12.
12 Sagan, Drake, and Lomberg 1978: 14–5, 23.
13 For a better sense of the range of people involved in this project, see the acknowledgements in Sagan, Drake, and Lomberg 1978: 238–46.
14 Riley, Corfield, and Dolling 2015: 39.
15 The sentiment is something of a Roman trope. See *Aen.* 9. 641: *sic itur ad astra*; Sen. *Hercules* 437: *non est ad astra mollis e terris via.*
16 "The Sounds of Earth" and "The Music of Earth" in Sagan, Drake, and Lomberg 1978: 150–209.
17 National Archives and Records Adminstration 1975: 1.

18 LaFrance 2014.
19 Freudenthal 1960.
20 Sagan, Drake, and Lomberg 1978: 13.
21 Drake outlines this challenge in Ch. 2 of Sagan, Drake, and Lomberg 1978.
22 Sagan, Drake, and Lomberg 1978: 53.
23 Sagan, Drake, and Lomberg 1978: 36–7.
24 Riley, Corfield, and Dolling 2015: 156–7.
25 NASA 2003.
26 The superabundance of hydrogen in the universe does indeed make it likely, given all the other assumptions being made about these aliens, that the imagined receiver of the Golden Record might have some grasp of it. See Rigden 2003.
27 Sagan, Drake, and Lomberg 1978: 7.
28 Paglen 2013.
29 Morena 2016.
30 Mann 2018.
31 Flatow, Casani, and Massey 2007.
32 For a book-length treatment of responses to Drake's Equation, see Webb 2001.
33 Sagan, Drake, and Lomberg 1978: 51.
34 Sagan was also well aware of the efficacy of radio waves: "The primary approach quite properly is the search for radio messages transmitted in our direction by more advanced civilizations" (Sagan, Drake, and Lomberg 1978: 7).
35 Sagan 1994: 261.
36 Sagan 1990; Ehrlich et al. 1984. Another example of Sagan's love of Greek and Roman mythology: his book with Ehrlich opens with a vignette of Cassandra, the Trojan Priestess who could see the future, but no one would believe her (Ehrlich et al. 1984: 13). Cassandra is not unlike Aeneas in this respect, able to see the future but without any agency to affect it.
37 Frost 1920: 67.
38 See Dawson and Bowles 2004: ch. 1. The ICBM is also mentioned in Reynolds 2017.
39 Chaucer 1957: "The General Prologue" l. 500.
40 Puddephatt 1999: 238.
41 Morteani 1999: 40.
42 Where does gold come from? Surprisingly enough, it is alien to earth. According to Harvard astronomer Edo Berger, there is good evidence to suggest that gold is the "fireworks" of colliding neutron stars. Colliding neutron stars produced heavy metals that hurtled out into space, cooled into comets and asteroids that rained down on earth, sprinkling it with gold and precious metals some 200 million years ago. See Brown and Berger 2017.
43 Hammer and Norskov 1995.
44 Donne 2021. Illuminated manuscripts provide an example of this airy thinness: see Epstein and Frojmovic 2015: 40–6.
45 Venable 2011: 1.
46 Venable 2011: XVIII. The Apollo 1 tragedy, for example, taught NASA the importance of insulation and never skimping on materials.
47 Venable 2011: 1.
48 McLuhan coined the phrase "the medium is the message" in McLuhan 1964.
49 Eliade 2005.
50 Venable 2011: 2.
51 Brooks 1953: 276.
52 See Clark 1979: ch. 7.
53 Sergio Casali argues compellingly that when Aeneas is interrupted by the Sibyl, he in fact misses the final scene that Daedalus has carved. Vergil tells us explicitly that Daedalus does *not* carve the death of his son Icarus; Casali argues therefore that one

could infer the missing scene would be of Theseus abandoning Ariadne, a subject which "would have been too upsetting: not for its creator [Daedalus], but for the spectator [Aeneas]"—the Aeneas who had just abandoned Dido; the Aeneas who is just a few dozen lines away from meeting her again in hell; the Aeneas who would be forced to confront and reckon with his mistakes. See Casali 1995. For further discussion, see O'Neill, Chapter 8 in this volume.

54 Brooks 1953: 271.
55 Ossa-Richardson 2008.
56 Ossa-Richardson 2008: 345–6.
57 Pârvulescu 2005: 890.
58 Sagan, Drake, and Lomberg 1978: 40.
59 Quoted in Ossa-Richardson 2008: 347, 350.
60

> The strange shining bough, awaiting the hand destined to pluck it, seems a natural symbol of that visionary power granted by heaven to those whose eyes "piercing in quest" are to explore the viewless places of earth—the mysteries of life and death.'
>
> (Bodkin 1934: 133–5)

61 For a book length interpretation of this reading of the *Aeneid*, see Putnam 1998.
62 Sagan 1994: 6–7.
63 Kennedy 1852: 57.
64 Berlant 2011: 1.
65 Sagan 1994: xv.
66 Sagan 1994: 329.
67 Quoted in Ossa-Richardson 2008: 350.
68 Sagan 1994: 258.
69 Sagan 1994: 55.

References

BBC News. 2021. "What's Left Behind on the Moon?" Accessed June 24. www.bbc.co.uk/news/ampstories/moonmess/index.html.

Berlant, L.G. 2011. *Cruel Optimism*. Durham, NC: Duke University Press.

Bodkin, M. 1934. *Archetypal Patterns in Poetry: Psychological Studies of Imagination*. London: Oxford University Press.

Bonestell, C. 1972. *Beyond Jupiter: The Worlds of Tomorrow*. Boston: Little Brown.

Brooks, R.A. 1953. "Discolor Aura: Reflections on the Golden Bough." *The American Journal of Philology* 74, 3: 26–80.

Brown, D., and Berger, E. 2017. "Cosmic Alchemy: Colliding Neutron Stars Show Us How the Universe Creates Gold'." *The Conversation*, October 24. http://theconversation.com/cosmic-alchemy-colliding-neutron-stars-show-us-how-the-universe-creates-gold-86104.

Casali, S. 1995. "Aeneas and the Doors of the Temple of Apollo." *The Classical Journal* 91, 1: 1–9.

Chaucer, G. 1957. *The Works of Geoffrey Chaucer*. Edited by F.N. Robinson. Boston: Houghton Mifflin.

Clark, R.J. 1979. *Catabasis: Vergil and the Wisdom-Tradition*. Amsterdam: Grüner.

Darrin, A., and O'Leary, B.L. 2009. *Handbook of Space Engineering, Archaeology, and Heritage*. Boca Raton, FL: CRC Press.

Dawson, V.P., and Bowles, M.D. 2004. *Taming Liquid Hydrogen: The Centaur Upper Stage Rocket 1958–2002*. Nasa History Series. Washington, DC: National Aeuronautics and Space Administration.

Donne, J. 2021. "A Valediction: Forbidding Mourning." *Poetry Foundation*. www.poetryfoundation.org/poems/44131/a-valediction-forbidding-mourning.

Ehrlich, P.R., Sagan, C., Kennedy, D., and Roberts, W.O. 1984. *The Cold and the Dark: The World After Nuclear War*. New York: W.W. Norton & Company.

Eliade, M. 2005. *The Myth of the Eternal Return: Cosmos and History*. Bollingen Series. Princeton: Princeton University Press.

Epstein, M.M., and Frojmovic, E. 2015. *Skies of Parchment, Seas of Ink: Jewish Illuminated Manuscripts*. Princeton: Princeton University Press.

Flatow, I., Casani, J., and Massey, E. 2007. "Voyager Spacecraft on Never-Ending Journey." *National Public Radio*, August 24. www.npr.org/transcripts/13928794.

Freudenthal, H. 1960. *Lincos: Design of a Language for Cosmic Intercourse*. Studies in Logic and the Foundations of Mathematics. Amsterdam: North-Holland Publishing Co.

Frost, R. 1920. "Fire and Ice." *Harper's Magazine*, July.

Gilbert, J.B. 1997. *Redeeming Culture: American Religion in an Age of Science*. Chicago: University of Chicago Press.

Hammer, B., and Norskov, J.K. 1995. "Why Gold is the Noblest of All the Metals." *Nature* 376, 6537 (July): 238–40.

Jet Propulsion Laboratory; California Institute of Technology. 2021. "Voyager—Galleries." Accessed June 24. https://voyager.jpl.nasa.gov/galleries/.

Kennedy, C.R. 1852. *The Olynthiac and Other Public Orations of Demosthenes*. Bohn's Classical Library. London: Bohn.

LaFrance, A. 2014. "Humanity's Most Famous Mixtape Is Now 11 Billion Miles From Earth The Atlantic." *The Atlantic*, September 22. www.theatlantic.com/technology/archive/2014/09/humanitys-most-famous-mixtape-is-now-11-billion-miles-from-earth/380552/.

LeCouteur, C. 2017. "Adrift, A Space Junk." *The Atlantic*, October 12. www.theatlantic.com/video/index/542175/adrift-short-film-space-junk/?utm_source=atlfb.

Mann, A. 2018. "What Linguistics Can Tell Us about Talking to Aliens." *Scientific American*, October 8. www.scientificamerican.com/article/what-linguistics-can-tell-us-about-talking-to-aliens/.

McLuhan, M. 1964. *Understanding Media: The Extensions of Man*. New York: McGraw-Hill.

Morena, A.M. 2016. *The Voyager Record: A Transmission*. Brookline, MA: Rose Metal Press.

Morteani, G. 1999. "History, Economics and Geology of Gold." In H. Schmidbaur (ed.) *Gold: Progress in Chemistry, Biochemistry, and Technology*. New York: Wiley.

NASA. 2003. "NASA—Voyager Facts." www.nasa.gov/centers/goddard/news/topstory/2003/1105voyager_facts.html.

National Archives and Records Adminstration. 1975. "Video Transcript for Archival Research Catalog (ARC) Identifier 649452: Life Beyond Earth and the Mind of Man." www.archives.gov/files/social-media/transcripts/transcript-life-beyond-earth-mind-man-649452.pdf.

Oliver, K. 2013. *To Touch the Face of God: The Sacred, the Profane, and the American Space Program, 1957–1975*. New Series in NASA History. Baltimore, MD: Johns Hopkins University Press.

Ossa-Richardson, A. 2008. "From Servius to Frazer: The Golden Bough and Its Transformations." *International Journal of the Classical Tradition* 15, 3: 339–68.

Oxford English Dictionary. 2007. "Monument, n." *English*, May 7. www.oed.com/view/Entry/121852.

Paglen, T. 2013. "Friends of Space, How Are You All? Have You Eaten Yet? Or, Why Talk to Aliens Even if We Can't." *Afterall: A Journal of Art, Context and Enquiry* 32 (March): 8–19.

Pârvulescu, A. 2005. "The Golden Bough, Aeneas' Piety, and the Suppliant Branch." *Latomus* 64, 4: 882–909.

Puddephatt, R.J. 1999. "Gold Metal and Gold Alloys in Electronics and Thin Film Technology." In H. Schmidbaur (ed.) *Gold: Progress in Chemistry, Biochemistry, and Technology*. New York: Wiley.

Putnam, M.C.J. 1998. *Virgil's Epic Designs:* Ekphrasis *in the Aeneid*. New Haven: Yale University Press.

Pyne, S.J. 2010. *Voyager: Seeking Newer Worlds in the Third Great Age of Discovery (New York: Viking, 2010), p. 78.)*. New York: Viking.

Reynolds, E. 2017. *The Farthest*. Ireland: Abramorama.

Rigden, J.S. 2003. *Hydrogen: The Essential Element*. Cambridge, MA: Harvard University Press.

Riley, C., Corfield, R., and Dolling, P. 2015. *NASA Voyager 1 & 2 Owners' Workshop Manual : 1977 Onwards*. Somerset: Haynes Publishing Group.

Sagan, C. 1990. *A Path Where No Man Thought : Nuclear Winter and the End of the Arms Race*. New York: Random House.

———. 1994. *Pale Blue Dot: A Vision of the Human Future in Space*. New York: Random House.

Sagan, C., Drake, F.D., and Lomberg, J. 1978. *Murmurs of Earth: The Voyager Interstellar Record*. New York: Random House.

Venable, S.L. 2011. *Gold: A Cultural Encyclopedia*. Santa Barbara, CA: ABC-CLIO.

Webb, S. 2001. *If the Universe Is Teeming with Aliens . . . WHERE IS EVERYBODY?: Seventy-Five Solutions to the Fermi Paradox and the Problem of Extraterrestrial Life*. Cham, DEU: Springer International Publishing.

Index

Made in the USA
Las Vegas, NV
30 October 2024

cc3b3347-9b80-434b-afde-4a9d486c34e6R03